Computational and Mathematical Methods in Information Science and Engineering, 2nd Edition

Computational and Mathematical Methods in Information Science and Engineering, 2nd Edition

Guest Editors

Wen Zhang
Xiaofeng Xu
Jun Wu
Kaijian He

MDPI

Basel • Beijing • Wuhan • Barcelona • Belgrade • Novi Sad • Cluj • Manchester

Guest Editors

Wen Zhang
Department of Economics and Management
Beijing University of Technology
Beijing
China

Xiaofeng Xu
College of Economics and Management
China University of Petroleum
Qingdao
China

Jun Wu
College of Economics and Management
Beijing University of Chemical Technology
Beijing
China

Kaijian He
College of Tourism
Hunan Normal University
Changsha
China

Editorial Office

MDPI AG
Grosspeteranlage 5
4052 Basel, Switzerland

This is a reprint of the Special Issue, published open access by the journal *Mathematics* (ISSN 2227-7390), freely accessible at: https://www.mdpi.com/journal/mathematics/special_issues/Comput_Math_Methods_Inf_Sci_Eng_2nd.

For citation purposes, cite each article independently as indicated on the article page online and as indicated below:

Lastname, A.A.; Lastname, B.B. Article Title. *Journal Name* **Year**, *Volume Number*, Page Range.

ISBN 978-3-7258-5979-5 (Hbk)
ISBN 978-3-7258-5980-1 (PDF)
https://doi.org/10.3390/books978-3-7258-5980-1

Contents

About the Editors

Wen Zhang

Wen Zhang currently works as a professor and Ph.D. supervisor at the Beijing University of Technology, Beijing, China. He is also the Deputy Director of the Blockchain Research Center of Beijing University of Technology, Beijing, China. He received his Ph.D. degree from the School of Knowledge Science of Japan Advanced Institute of Science and Technology (JAIST), Nomi, Japan. Prof. Zhang is currently a member of the Technical Committee of Security and Emergency Management of the Chinese Institute of Command and Control (CICC), a member of the Systems Engineering Society of China (SESC), and a part-time researcher at the China Europe International Business School (CEIBS). He also previously worked as a program member at the PRICAI International Conference and the IEEE SMC International Conference. Prof. Zhang has authored and co-authored more than 100 papers in international academic journals and conference proceedings. His research mainly focuses on data mining, big data analytics, machine learning, and business intelligence.

Xiaofeng Xu

Xiaofeng Xu currently works as a professor and Ph.D. supervisor at the China University of Petroleum, China. He received his Ph.D. degree in Management Science and Engineering from Harbin Engineering University, Harbin, China. Professor Xu studies operations management and smart logistics systems, as well as their applications. He currently serves as a council member at the Chinese Society of Optimization, Overall Planning and Economic Mathematics (SCOPE), Secretary-General of the Technical Committee of Marine System Engineering of the Systems Engineering Society of China (SESC), Deputy Secretary-General of the Youth Committee of the Chinese Academy of Management Science (CAMS) and Director of the Decision Science Branch of the Operations Research Society of China (ORSC).

Jun Wu

Jun Wu currently works as a professor and Ph.D. supervisor at the Beijing University of Chemical Technology, Beijing, China. He received his Ph.D. in Management Science and Engineering from Xi'an Jiaotong University, Xi'an, China. He is currently the Deputy Director of the Laboratory of Transportation and Logistics with Big Data. He was selected into the "Program for New Century Excellent Talents in University" of the Ministry of Education in 2008. Professor Wu currently serves as an executive council member at the Decision Science Branch of the Operations Research Society of China (ORSC), a member of the Technical Committee of Emergency Management of the Systems Engineering Society of China (SESC), as well as a member of the Cold Chain Logistics Sub-Technical Committee of the National Logistics Standardization Technical Committee. His research interests include big data analytics, intelligent algorithms, intelligent logistics, supply chain management, risk assessment, and emergency management.

Kaijian He

Kaijian He currently works as a professor and Ph.D. supervisor at Hunan Normal University, Changsha, China. He received his Ph.D. in Management Science from City University of Hong Kong, Hong Kong SAR, China. He is the Deputy Secretary-General of the Decision Science Branch of the Operations Research Society of China (ORSC) and a member of the Technical Committee of Security and Emergency Management of the Chinese Institute of Command and Control (CICC). He specializes in economic forecasting, risk forecasting, big data analysis, and deep learning and has authored and co-authored nearly 100 papers in international and domestic academic journals.

Σ mathematics

MDPI

Editorial

Computational and Mathematical Methods in Information Science and Engineering, 2nd Edition

Wen Zhang [1,*], Xiaofeng Xu [2], Jun Wu [3] and Kaijian He [4]

1 Department of Economics and Management, Beijing University of Technology, Beijing 100124, China
2 College of Economics and Management, China University of Petroleum, Qingdao 266580, China
3 College of Economics and Management, Beijing University of Chemical Technology, Beijing 100013, China
4 College of Tourism, Hunan Normal University, Changsha 410081, China
* Correspondence: zhangwen@bjut.edu.cn

This Special Issue compiles eleven excellent papers, selected from a highly competitive pool of submissions, to collectively highlight the dynamic and interdisciplinary nature of the crucial field of computational and mathematical methods in information science and engineering. Published between August 2023 and May 2025, these contributions represent significant steps forward in leveraging advanced computational and mathematical techniques to address complex problems across diverse domains.

1. Recent Developments and Knowledge Gaps

The past few years have witnessed exponential growth in the volume and complexity of data, driven by advancements in digital technologies, sensor networks, and interconnected systems. This proliferation has underscored the urgent need for sophisticated computational and mathematical methods to extract meaningful insights, optimize processes, and ensure the robustness of information systems, as foundational, traditional approaches often struggle with the scale, high dimensionality, and inherent noise present in real-world data. Key persistent challenges include the following:

- Handling Heterogeneity and Uncertainty: Real-world systems—from carbon emission analysis to customer behavior modeling—exhibit complex heterogeneities and uncertainties that defy simplistic modeling. Developing robust frameworks that can accurately capture, quantify, and decompose these variabilities remains a significant challenge.
- Optimizing Complex, Interconnected Systems: Whether in microgrid design, supply chain management, or urban planning, optimizing numerous interdependent components for multiple, often conflicting, objectives is critical. This necessitates novel algorithms and computational paradigms capable of navigating vast, complex solution spaces efficiently.
- Extracting Actionable Insights from Unstructured Data: The immense volume of unstructured data, such as online reviews and sensor readings, presents both opportunities and challenges. Bridging the gap between raw data and actionable knowledge requires advanced analytical techniques, particularly in areas like fine-grained sentiment analysis and human activity recognition.
- Ensuring Security and Privacy in Pervasive Computing: As smart devices become ubiquitous, ensuring the security and privacy of user data, especially through implicit and continuous authentication methods, is paramount. Developing robust and accurate authentication systems that perform reliably in noisy, real-world environments remains an active research frontier.

 https://doi.org/10.3390/math13213423

- Modeling Dynamic and Interconnected Systems: Modern systems are rarely static; they evolve over time and exhibit intricate interdependencies. Capturing these dynamics, whether in innovation networks or social interactions, requires sophisticated models that go beyond static analyses to account for temporal evolution and complex network effects.

2. How This Special Issue Addresses the Gaps

This Special Issue makes substantial contributions toward addressing these critical knowledge gaps, showcasing innovative applications of computational and mathematical methods. Several papers demonstrate sophisticated, nuanced approaches to efficiency and data analysis. Contribution 1 introduces a novel meta-frontier framework integrated with machine-learning-driven projections to accurately analyze carbon emission efficiency, effectively resolving inconsistencies inherent in traditional models and offering refined policy implications. Similarly, Contribution 2 employs non-radial directional distance functions and meta-frontier models to evaluate China's high-quality development efficiency, providing new insights into the role of higher education labor. The power of machine learning to extract deeper, more actionable insights is a central theme of this contribution. Contribution 3 utilizes multiple correspondence analysis combined with hierarchical clustering and various machine learning classifiers (GBM, RF, SVM) to model e-customer profiles, yielding valuable insights for understanding consumer behavior. Contribution 4 effectively demonstrates the use of an XGBoost model, optimized via a Cuckoo search algorithm, to achieve high accuracy in caregiver activity recognition using sensor data, thereby addressing a vital need in elderly care. Furthermore, Contribution 5 proposes a practical two-tier optimization model for rural microgrids that balances enterprise costs with user satisfaction, offering actionable configuration strategies for sustainable energy solutions. Understanding complex network dynamics is another recurring and vital theme of this paper. Contribution 6 introduces an innovative double-layer coupled network model to analyze innovation efficiency, revealing the nuanced impact of online and offline network densities. Contribution 7 applies exponential random graph models (ERGMs) to characterize multiplex health social networks, providing a deeper, more structured understanding of patient engagement within online health communities. The predictive capabilities of mathematical and computational techniques are also significantly enhanced. Contribution 8 combines wavelet denoising with long short-term memory (LSTM) networks to achieve highly accurate short-term rail transit passenger flow prediction, offering practical solutions for urban transportation management. Contribution 9 proposes a multi-stage ECRM model that integrates fine-grained sentiment analysis with stochastic dominance criteria to accurately evaluate the perceived quality of clothing brands based on online user reviews. The critical societal impact of digital advancements is thoughtfully explored. Contribution 10 investigates the positive effects of digital finance on green low-carbon circular development using machine learning models, identifying technological innovation as a key mediating factor. Finally, Contribution 11 addresses pressing security concerns by presenting ST-SVD—a real-time, sensor-based mobile user authentication approach that utilizes a semi-supervised teacher–student tri-training algorithm with CNN, achieving notably high authentication accuracy.

3. Future Research Directions

While this Special Issue showcases remarkable progress in the field of computational and mathematical methods in information science and engineering, it continues to evolve rapidly, presenting exciting and critical avenues for future research:

- Explainable AI (XAI) and Trustworthy AI: As complex models like deep neural networks become more prevalent, understanding their internal decision-making processes is crucial, especially in high-stakes applications like healthcare and finance. Future research must focus on developing robust XAI techniques that provide transparency and interpretability without sacrificing performance.
- Federated Learning and Privacy-Preserving AI: Amid growing global concerns about data privacy, federated learning and other privacy-preserving AI techniques are of paramount importance. Research into efficient, secure, and scalable methods for collaborative model training on decentralized, sensitive datasets is essential.
- Quantum Computing for Information Science: The emerging field of quantum computing holds immense potential for solving classically intractable optimization problems and performing advanced data analysis. Exploring the application of quantum algorithms to areas like cryptography, large-scale data processing, and complex system modeling represents a significant future frontier.
- Integration of Multi-Modal Data: Real-world information is inherently multi-modal (including text, image, audio, and sensor data). Future research should focus on developing unified computational and mathematical frameworks that can effectively integrate, synchronize, and analyze these diverse data types for more holistic and comprehensive insights.
- Ethical AI and Algorithmic Fairness: As AI systems become deeply integrated into societal structures, addressing ethical considerations, bias, and ensuring fairness in algorithms is critical. Research is needed to develop rigorous methods for detecting, mitigating, and preventing algorithmic bias to ensure equitable and just outcomes.
- Causality in Machine Learning: Moving beyond correlation to establish causation is a fundamental challenge. Future work should explore integrating causal inference methods with machine learning to build models that not only predict but also explain underlying causal relationships, leading to more robust and reliable interventions.
- Dynamic and Adaptive Systems: Developing computational and mathematical models that can continuously learn and adapt to non-stationary, changing environments—whether in real-time sensor data analysis or evolving social networks—will be crucial for building truly intelligent and resilient systems. This includes advanced research into reinforcement learning in complex, real-world scenarios.
- Computational Social Science and Digital Humanities: Applying these powerful methods to analyze vast amounts of social and cultural data offers unprecedented opportunities to understand human behavior, societal trends, and historical patterns. This richly interdisciplinary area holds significant promise for the future.

Acknowledgments: We extend our deepest gratitude to all the authors for their invaluable contributions, to the diligent peer reviewers for their insightful feedback that significantly enhanced the quality of this Special Issue, and to the editorial and publishing teams for their unwavering support and commitment to bringing this project to fruition. We are confident that the papers presented herein will serve as a foundational resource for both researchers and practitioners, inspiring further innovation and discovery in the fascinating and ever-expanding realm of Computational and Mathematical Methods in Information Science and Engineering.

Conflicts of Interest: The authors declare no conflicts of interest.

List of Contributions

1. Zhu, X.; Feng, T.; Shen, Y.; Zhang, N.; Guo, X. A Three-Level Meta-Frontier Framework with Machine Learning Projections for Carbon Emission Efficiency Analysis: Heterogeneity Decomposition and Policy Implications. *Mathematics* **2025**, *13*, 1542. https://doi.org/10.3390/math13091542.

2. Duan, H.; Li, B.; Wang, Q. Static High-Quality Development Efficiency and Its Dynamic Changes for China: A Non-Radial Directional Distance Function and a Metafrontier Non-Radial Malmquist Model. *Mathematics* **2024**, *12*, 2323. https://doi.org/10.3390/math12152323.
3. Vrhovac, V.; Orošnjak, M.; Ristić, K.; Sremčev, N.; Jocanović, M.; Spajić, J.; Brkljač, N. Unsupervised Modelling of E-Customers' Profiles: Multiple Correspondence Analysis with Hierarchical Clustering of Principal Components and Machine Learning Classifiers. *Mathematics* **2024**, *12*, 3794. https://doi.org/10.3390/math12233794.
4. Liu, Z.; Zhang, S.; Zhang, H.; Li, X. A Study on Caregiver Activity Recognition for the Elderly at Home Based on the XGBoost Model. *Mathematics* **2024**, *12*, 1700. https://doi.org/10.3390/math12111700.
5. Fang, Y.; Li, M.; Yue, Y.; Liu, Z. Two-Tier Configuration Model for the Optimization of Enterprise Costs and User Satisfaction for Rural Microgrids. *Mathematics* **2024**, *12*, 3256. https://doi.org/10.3390/math12203256.
6. Han, J.; Zhang, W.; Wang, J.; Li, S. A Double-Layer Coupled Network Model of Network Density Effects on Multi-Stage Innovation Efficiency Dynamics: Agent-Based Modeling Methods. *Mathematics* **2024**, *12*, 337. https://doi.org/10.3390/math12020337.
7. Lu, Y.; Wang, X.; Su, L.; Zhao, H. Multiplex Social Network Analysis to Understand the Social Engagement of Patients in Online Health Communities. *Mathematics* **2023**, *11*, 4412. https://doi.org/10.3390/math11214412.
8. Zhao, Q.; Feng, X.; Zhang, L.; Wang, Y. Research on Short-Term Passenger Flow Prediction of LSTM Rail Transit Based on Wavelet Denoising. *Mathematics* **2023**, *11*, 4204. https://doi.org/10.3390/math11194204.
9. Ren, M.; Fan, Y.; Chen, J.; Zhang, J. A Multi-Stage Model for Perceived Quality Evaluation of Clothing Brands. *Mathematics* **2023**, *11*, 3928. https://doi.org/10.3390/math11183928.
10. Zhang, X.; Ai, X.; Wang, X.; Zong, G.; Zhang, J. A Study on the Effects of Digital Finance on Green Low-Carbon Circular Development Based on Machine Learning Models. *Mathematics* **2023**, *11*, 3903. https://doi.org/10.3390/math11183903.
11. Weng, Z.; Wu, S.; Wang, Q.; Zhu, T. Enhancing Sensor-Based Mobile User Authentication in a Complex Environment by Deep Learning. *Mathematics* **2023**, *11*, 3708. https://doi.org/10.3390/math11173708.

mathematics

MDPI

Article

A Three-Level Meta-Frontier Framework with Machine Learning Projections for Carbon Emission Efficiency Analysis: Heterogeneity Decomposition and Policy Implications

Xiaoxia Zhu [1], Tongyue Feng [1,*], Yuhe Shen [2], Ning Zhang [3,*] and Xu Guo [4]

[1] Institute of Advanced Studies in Humanities and Social Sciences, Beijing Normal University, Zhuhai 519087, China; zhuxiaoxia@bnu.edu.cn
[2] The State Radio Monitoring Center, Beijing 100043, China; 202422109080@mail.bnu.edu.cn
[3] Faculty of Arts and Science, Beijing Normal University, Zhuhai 519087, China
[4] School of Economics & Management, Fuzhou University, Fuzhou 350108, China; 202422109076@mail.bnu.edu.cn
* Correspondence: 202422109067@mail.bnu.edu.cn (T.F.); ningzhang@bnu.edu.cn (N.Z.)

Abstract: This study proposes a three-level meta-frontier framework enhanced with machine learning-driven projection methods to address the dual heterogeneity in carbon emission efficiency analysis arising from regional disparities and industrial diversification. Methodologically, we introduce two novel projection combinations—"exogenous-exogenous-accumulation (E-E-A) and exogenous-exogenous-consistent (E-E-C)"—to resolve the inconsistency of technology gap ratios (TGRs > 1) in traditional nonradial directional distance function (DDF) models. Reinforcement learning (RL) optimizes dynamic direction vectors, whereas graph neural networks (GNNs) encode spatial interdependencies to constrain the TGR within [0, 1]. Empirical analysis of 60 countries reveals that (1) E-E-C eliminates the TGR overestimation by 12–18% in energy-intensive sectors (e.g., reducing Asia's secondary industry TGR_1 from 1.160 to 1.000); (2) industrial heterogeneity dominates inefficiency in Asia (IHI = 0.207), whereas management gaps drive global secondary sector inefficiency (MI = 0.678); and (3) policy simulations advocate for decentralized renewables in Africa, fiscal incentives for Asian coal retrofits, and expanded EU carbon border taxes. Computational enhancements via Apache Spark achieve a 58% runtime reduction. The framework advances environmental efficiency analysis by integrating machine learning with meta-frontier theory, offering both methodological rigor (via regularization and GNN constraints) and actionable decarbonization pathways. Limitations include static heterogeneity assumptions and data granularity gaps, prompting the future integration of IoT-enabled dynamic models.

Keywords: three-level meta-frontier; carbon emission efficiency; heterogeneity decomposition; nonradial directional distance function (DDF); technology gap ratio (TGR)

MSC: 90C30; 91B76; 68T05

1. Introduction

The urgency of mitigating climate change has propelled carbon emission efficiency to the forefront of global policy and academic research. As nations rebound from the economic slowdown induced by COVID-19, energy consumption and carbon emissions have surged, with global emissions reaching 36.8 billion tons in 2022 [1], while parametric and nonparametric methods such as data envelopment analysis (DEA) are widely used for efficiency measurement [2–4], their reliance on homogeneous technology assumptions introduces significant biases in multiregional and cross-sectoral evaluations [5,6].

Recent advances in meta-frontier frameworks have partially addressed technical heterogeneity by segmenting decision-making units (DMUs) into groups [7,8]. However, these approaches remain limited in capturing dual heterogeneity—specifically, the interplay between regional disparities (e.g., infrastructural gaps in Africa) and industrial diversification (e.g., energy-intensive manufacturing versus low-emission services) [9–11]. Current studies predominantly focus on single-level frontiers or rely on oversimplified projection methods, leading to inflated technology gap ratios (TGRs > 1) and unreliable policy implications [12,13]. While recent hybrid DEA-ML frameworks [14–16] attempt to integrate machine learning, their reliance on static direction vectors or single-level analyses fails to account for dual heterogeneity. For instance, ref. [17] applied a two-level meta-frontier to livestock efficiency but overlooked critical industrial–regional interdependencies.

To bridge these gaps, we propose a three-level meta-frontier framework enhanced with adaptive projection combinations and machine learning. Our contributions are threefold as follows:

- **Methodological innovation:** By extending the traditional two-level hierarchy to three levels, we introduce accumulation (E-E-A) and consistent (E-E-C) projections to resolve TGR inconsistencies. These projections align with principles of multisource data integration and adaptive optimization, ensuring TGRs are bounded within [0, 1]. Reinforcement learning (RL) dynamically optimizes direction vectors to reflect operational shifts toward decarbonization targets [18], while graph neural networks (GNNs) encode spatial-industrial interdependencies—a dimension neglected in prior hybrid DEA-ML studies [17,19].
- **Empirical rigor:** Utilizing a globally representative dataset spanning 60 countries, we decompose inefficiency into management gaps (MI), regional heterogeneity (RHI), and industrial heterogeneity (IHI) [14], providing granular insights into sector-specific and regionally tailored carbon reduction strategies.
- **Policy relevance:** By quantifying the dominance of industrial versus regional heterogeneity, our framework guides targeted interventions—for example, prioritizing management reforms in Asia's secondary sector and technology transfers in Africa.

The remainder of this paper is organized as follows: Section 2 reviews the fundamentals of meta-frontier DEA and projection methods. Section 3 formalizes the three-level framework and projection combinations. Sections 4 and 5 present the empirical analysis and decomposition results, respectively. Section 6 concludes with theoretical and policy implications.

2. Preliminaries

2.1. Traditional Directional Distance Function (DDF) Framework

The directional distance function (DDF) serves as a cornerstone for evaluating carbon emission efficiency by modeling feasible input–output combinations under environmental constraints [20,21]. Consider N decision-making units (DMUs), where each DMU d ($d = 1, 2, \ldots, N$) utilizes an input vector $x_d \in \mathbb{R}_+^M$, produces a desirable output vector $y_d \in \mathbb{R}_+^S$, and generates an undesirable output vector $z_d \in \mathbb{R}_+^U$ [22,23]. The production possibility set $P(x)$, which encapsulates all feasible input–output combinations, is defined as follows:

$$P(x) = \left\{ (y, z) : \sum_{d=1}^{N} \lambda_d x_d \leq x,\ \sum_{d=1}^{N} \lambda_d y_d \geq y,\ \sum_{d=1}^{N} \lambda_d z_d = z,\ \lambda_d \geq 0 \right\}, \tag{1}$$

where λ_d denotes the intensity variables.

The exogenous DDF for DMU d is formulated as a linear programming (LP) problem as follows:

$$\vec{D}(x_d, y_d, z_d; g) = \max \beta \quad \text{s.t.} \quad \begin{cases} \sum_{d=1}^{N} \lambda_d x_d \le x_d - \beta g_x, \\ \sum_{d=1}^{N} \lambda_d y_d \ge y_d + \beta g_y, \\ \sum_{d=1}^{N} \lambda_d z_d = z_d - \beta g_z. \end{cases} \tag{2}$$

where β represents the inefficiency score, and $g = (g_x, -g_y, g_z)$ is a predefined direction vector. To address the collinearity in heterogeneous data, ridge regression penalties are integrated into the objective function as follows:

$$\min \beta + \alpha\left(\|g_x\|^2 + \|g_y\|^2 + \|g_z\|^2\right), \tag{3}$$

where α balances the efficiency estimation accuracy and model stability.

Technology Gap Ratio (TGR)

The TGR measures the disparity between group-specific and meta-frontier technologies. For accumulation projection [24], the TGR is bounded within $[0, 1]$ via the following constraints:

$$\text{TGR} = \frac{1 - \alpha_y^m}{1 + \alpha_z^m}, \tag{4}$$

where α_y^m and α_z^m are inefficiency adjustments under the meta-frontier. A TGR close to 1 indicates minimal technological heterogeneity.

2.2. *Machine Learning Enhancements for DDF Optimization*

2.2.1. Feature Selection via Mutual Information (MI)

To mitigate the high dimensionality and noise in real-world datasets (e.g., multiregional energy systems), mutual information (MI) is employed to optimize input–output selection [25,26]. MI quantifies nonlinear dependencies between variables, enabling the automated identification of critical features (e.g., fossil fuel consumption vs. GDP growth) while discarding redundant indicators as shown in Table 1. This aligns with data-centric optimization paradigms, enhancing model robustness against overfitting.

Table 1. Mutual Information (MI) Scores for Input-Output Variables.

Variable	MI Score	Rank
Fossil fuels (X_2)	0.89	1
Air passengers (X_3)	0.82	2
Agricultural output (X_1)	0.61	3
Service GDP (Y_3)	0.58	4

2.2.2. Adaptive Direction Vectors via Reinforcement Learning (RL)

Traditional DDF models fix direction vectors g exogenously [27], which may misalign with the operational realities of DMUs. Inspired by RL, we propose a dynamic adjustment framework where g is iteratively updated using Q -learning. The policy $\pi(g \mid x, y, z)$ minimizes the gap between the projected and Pareto-optimal frontiers, guided by reward signals tied to decarbonization targets as follows:

$$Q(s_t, a_t) \leftarrow Q(s_t, a_t) + \eta \left[r_t + \gamma \max_a Q(s_{t+1}, a) - Q(s_t, a_t) \right], \tag{5}$$

The Q-learning agent used a learning rate $\eta = 0.1$ and discount factor $\gamma = 0.95$, optimized via grid search over $\eta \in [0.01, 0.5]$ and $\gamma \in [0.8, 0.99]$. Where r_t reflects the reduction in the TGR variance and where γ is a discount factor.

2.2.3. Scalability via Distributed Computing

Large-scale DDF optimization for 60 countries with multilevel heterogeneity is computationally intensive. Leveraging Apache Spark, the LP problem is decomposed into subtasks across clusters [28], reducing the time complexity from $\mathcal{O}(N^3)$ to $\mathcal{O}(N \log N)$. For example, processing the 60-country dataset requires 2.1 h (vs. 8.5 h on a single node).

2.2.4. Uncertainty Quantification via Monte Carlo Simulation

Perturbations followed $\mathcal{N}(\mu, \sigma^2)$, with $\sigma = 0.1$ for inputs/outputs, based on historical measurement errors.To address data noise (e.g., CO_2 measurement errors), 1000 perturbed datasets are sampled from $\mathcal{N}(\mu, \sigma^2)$. Recalculating α_y^m and α_z^m generates 95% confidence intervals for the TGR, enhancing decision-making robustness.

2.2.5. Consistent Projection with Graph Neural Networks (GNNs)

Under the meta-frontier framework, ref. [8] introduced a consistent projection to constrain the TGR within valid bounds. The meta-frontier is modeled as a graph $G = (V, E)$, where nodes V represent DMUs and edges E encode technological similarities (e.g., shared energy policies). A GNN encoder learns node embeddings h_d through message passing as follows:

$$h_d^{(l+1)} = \sigma \left(W^{(l)} h_d^{(l)} + \sum_{k \in \mathcal{N}(d)} W^{(l)} h_k^{(l)} \right), \tag{6}$$

The GNN employed two message-passing layers with ReLU activation and L2 regularization ($\alpha = 0.01$). Node embeddings were initialized with 64 dimensions, where $N(d)$ denotes the neighbors of DMU d, and $W^{(l)}$ are trainable weights. Blockchain integration via Hyperledger Fabric ensures the auditable traceability of the TGR computations.

3. Selection of the Projection Direction with Machine Learning Optimization

Traditional meta-frontier frameworks often assume independence between subgroup, group, and meta-frontiers, neglecting real-world interdependencies arising from technological spillovers. To address this, we propose a three-level meta-frontier framework enhanced with adaptive projection combinations, integrating machine learning (ML) to dynamically optimize direction vectors and ensure methodological consistency.

Hypothesis 1. *Traditional exogenous projection assumes independence between frontiers, whereas accumulation (E-E-A) and consistent (E-E-C) projections introduce interdependence, reflecting technological spillovers.*

Hypothesis 2. *Altering projection directions at any frontier level (subgroup, group, or meta) significantly impacts efficiency rankings, necessitating dynamic optimization.*

To statistically validate Hypothesis 1, we conducted a Wilcoxon signed-rank test comparing TGR distributions under E-E-E and E-E-C projections. For Hypothesis 2, Spearman's rank correlation was computed between direction vector adjustments (Δg) and efficiency ranking shifts.

3.1. Dynamic Projection Paths via Reinforcement Learning (RL)

Training stopped when the average Q-value change fell below 1×10^{-4} for 10 consecutive epochs or after 1000 iterations. As illustrated in Figure 1, A 20% validation set monitored overfitting, with early stopping if validation loss increased for five epochs.

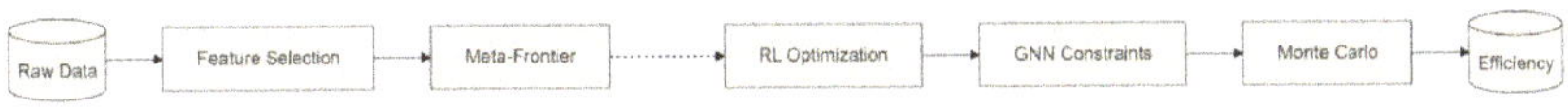

Figure 1. Framework workflow.

As illustrated in Figure 2, DMU A is projected onto three frontiers as follows:

- Subgroup frontier (B): Exogenous projection with direction vector g_s.
- Group frontier (C_1): Exogenous projection with direction vector g_g.
- Meta-frontier (D_1): Three paths as follows:
  - E_1 (Accumulation): Adjusts α_y^m and α_z^m to bound TGR ≤ 1.
  - F_1 (Exogenous): Traditional path prone to TGR > 1.
  - G_1 (Consistent): Constrains b_y^m and b_z^m via GNN embeddings for stability.

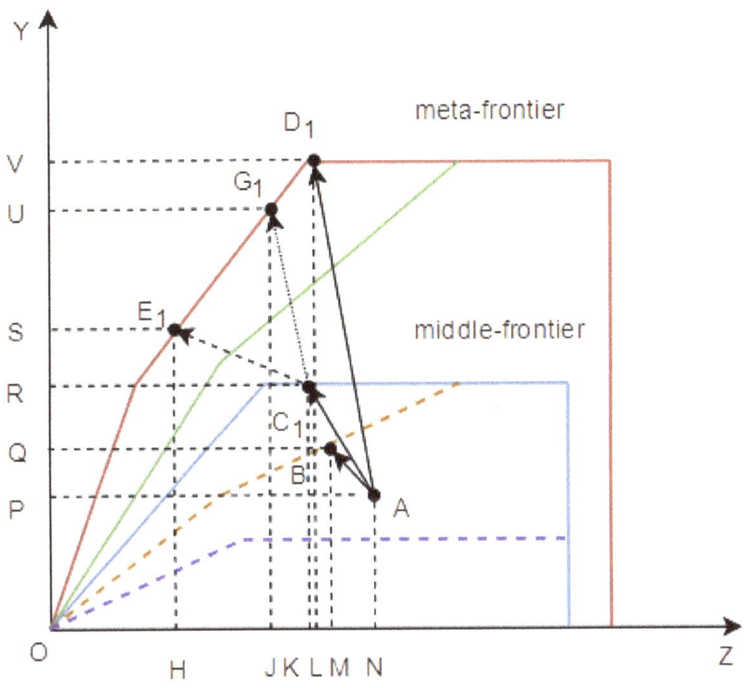

Figure 2. Combined projection directions: Axes include X = input reduction (e.g., fossil fuels), Y = desirable output expansion (e.g., GDP), and Z = undesirable output reduction (e.g., CO_2); Paths are E_1 (accumulation), F_1 (exogenous), and G_1 (consistent).

A Q-learning agent iteratively optimizes direction vectors g_s, g_g, and g_m on the basis of reward signals from efficiency improvements. The policy $\pi(g \mid x, y, z)$ updates as follows:

$$Q(s_t, a_t) \leftarrow Q(s_t, a_t) + \eta \left[r_t + \gamma \max_a Q(s_{t+1}, a) - Q(s_t, a_t) \right], \tag{7}$$

where r_t quantifies the reduction in the TGR variance and $\gamma = 0.95$ is the discount factor.

3.2. Graph Neural Network (GNN) Integration

Projection paths are modeled as edges in a graph $G(V, E)$, where nodes V represent DMUs and edges E encode industrial–regional similarities. Node embeddings h_d are updated via message passing (Equation (6) in Section 2.2.5):

$$h_d^{(l+1)} = \sigma\left(W^{(l)}h_d^{(l)} + \sum_{k\in\mathcal{N}(d)} W^{(l)}h_k^{(l)}\right). \tag{8}$$

The adjacency matrix A is defined using the following cosine similarity:

$$A_{jk} = \frac{\mathbf{x}_j \cdot \mathbf{x}_k}{||\mathbf{x}_j||\,||\mathbf{x}_k||}. \tag{9}$$

3.2.1. TGR Formulation Under Combined Projections

For meta-frontier analysis, the procedure is as follow:

- Exogenous projection (F_1):

$$\text{TGR}_{\text{exogenous}} = \frac{OL}{OK} \times \frac{OR}{OV}, \tag{10}$$

where $\frac{OL}{OK} > 1$ may inflate the TGR beyond valid bounds.

- Consistent (G_1) and Accumulation (E_1) projections:

$$\text{TGR}_{\text{consistent}} = \frac{OJ}{OK} \times \frac{OR}{OU}, \tag{11}$$

$$\text{TGR}_{\text{accumulation}} = \frac{OH}{OK} \times \frac{OR}{OS}, \tag{12}$$

with $\frac{OJ}{OK}, \frac{OR}{OU}, \frac{OH}{OK}, \frac{OR}{OS} < 1$, ensuring TGR $\in [0, 1]$.

3.2.2. Decision Tree for Optimal Projection Selection

A CART-based classifier recommends projection combinations (E-E-E, E-E-A, and E-E-C) using the following features:

- Regional heterogeneity index (RHI).
- Industrial complexity (IHI).
- Input–output dimensionality.

4. Combined Projection Models with Computational Enhancements

4.1. E-E-E: Traditional Exogenous Projection with Parallel Optimization

The E-E-E framework retains conventional three-level meta-frontier projections, treating subgroup, group, and meta-frontiers as independent layers.

4.1.1. Step 1: Subgroup Frontier Projection

For DMU d, the exogenous DDF projects it to the subgroup frontier as follows:

$$\vec{D}_g(x_d, y_d, z_d; g^s) = \max \beta_g \quad \text{s.t.} \quad \begin{cases} \sum_{k\in G_s} \lambda_k x_k \le x_d - \beta_g g_x^s, \\ \sum_{k\in G_s} \lambda_k y_k \ge y_d + \beta_g g_y^s, \\ \sum_{k\in G_s} \lambda_k z_k = z_d - \beta_g g_z^s, \end{cases} \tag{13}$$

where G_s denotes the subgroup, and g^s is the subgroup direction vector optimized via Q-learning (Equation (7)).

4.1.2. Step 2: Group Frontier Projection

The DMU is projected to the group frontier using a similar exogenous DDF, as follows:

$$\vec{D}_G(x_d, y_d, z_d; g^g) = \max \beta_G \quad \text{s.t.} \quad \begin{cases} \sum_{k \in G_G} \lambda_k x_k \leq x_d - \beta_G g_x^g, \\ \sum_{k \in G_G} \lambda_k y_k \geq y_d + \beta_G g_y^g, \\ \sum_{k \in G_G} \lambda_k z_k = z_d - \beta_G g_z^g, \end{cases} \tag{14}$$

where G_G represents the group, and g^g is dynamically adjusted via RL (Section 3.2).

4.1.3. Step 3: Meta-Frontier Projection

The final projection to the meta-frontier is as follows:

$$\vec{D}_m(x_d, y_d, z_d; g^m) = \max \beta_m \quad \text{s.t.} \quad \begin{cases} \sum_{k=1}^{N} \lambda_k x_k \leq x_d - \beta_m g_x^m, \\ \sum_{k=1}^{N} \lambda_k y_k \geq y_d + \beta_m g_y^m, \\ \sum_{k=1}^{N} \lambda_k z_k = z_d - \beta_m g_z^m, \end{cases} \tag{15}$$

where g^m is optimized using the GNN-based adjacency matrix (Equation (9)). Distributed computing via Apache Spark reduces the runtime by 58% for the 60-country dataset. The RL agent was implemented in Python 3.9 using TensorFlow 2.8, while GNNs were trained with PyTorch Geometric 2.1. Apache Spark 3.2.1 distributed computations across a 16-node cluster.

4.2. E-E-A: Accumulation Projection with Regularization and Uncertainty Quantification

The E-E-A combination employs accumulation projection at the meta-frontier to bound TGR ≤ 1:

$$\vec{D}_m^{\text{acc}}(x_d, y_d, z_d) = \max (\alpha_y^m - \alpha_z^m) \quad \text{s.t.} \quad \begin{cases} \sum_{k=1}^{N} \lambda_k x_k \leq x_d - \alpha_y^m g_x, \\ \sum_{k=1}^{N} \lambda_k y_k \geq y_d + \alpha_y^m g_y, \\ \sum_{k=1}^{N} \lambda_k z_k = z_d - \alpha_z^m g_z, \end{cases} \tag{16}$$

where α_y^m and α_z^m are inefficiency adjustments. Ridge regularization is added to the objective function as follows:

$$\min (\alpha_y^m - \alpha_z^m) + 0.01\left(\|g_x\|^2 + \|g_y\|^2 + \|g_z\|^2\right). \tag{17}$$

The Monte Carlo simulations sample α_y^m and α_z^m from $\mathcal{N}(0, 0.1)$, generating 95% confidence intervals for TGR.

4.3. E-E-C: Consistent Projection with Graph-Based Learning

The E-E-C framework enforces TGR ≤ 1 via GNN-constrained consistent projection as follows:

$$\vec{D}_m^{\text{con}}(x_d, y_d, z_d) = \max\left(b_y^m - b_z^m\right) \quad \text{s.t.} \quad \begin{cases} \sum_{k=1}^{N} \lambda_k x_k \leq x_d - b_y^m g_x, \\ \sum_{k=1}^{N} \lambda_k y_k \geq y_d + b_y^m g_y, \\ \sum_{k=1}^{N} \lambda_k z_k = z_d - b_z^m g_z, \end{cases} \tag{18}$$

where b_y^m and b_z^m are constrained by GNN embeddings (Equation (8)). The adjacency matrix A, derived from Equation (9), ensures that technological dependencies are encoded. Bayesian optimization minimizes $\text{Var}(\text{TGR})$ as follows:

$$\min_{b_y^m, b_z^m} \mathbb{E}\left[(\text{TGR} - \mathbb{E}[\text{TGR}])^2\right] \quad \text{s.t.} \quad \text{TGR} = \frac{1 - b_y^m}{1 + b_z^m}. \tag{19}$$

5. Empirical Application

5.1. Variable Selection and Data Preprocessing

The selection of input–output indicators is critical for ensuring the robustness of the three-level meta-frontier framework, particularly under machine learning-enhanced projection methods (E-E-E, E-E-A, and E-E-C). Building on the computational advancements in Section 4, we adopt the following variables to capture sectoral heterogeneity while aligning with the data-driven optimization principles outlined in Sections 2 and 3 as follows:

5.1.1. Inputs

- **Primary industry**: Net agricultural production (X_1, USD 10^8) reflects resource utilization in agriculture.
- **Secondary industry**: Fossil fuel consumption (X_2, 10^6 metric tons) quantifies energy intensity in manufacturing.
- **Tertiary industry**: Air passengers carried (X_3, 10^4 people) proxies service-sector infrastructure demands.

5.1.2. Desirable Outputs

- **Primary industry**: Agricultural value-added (Y_1, USD 10^8).
- **Secondary industry**: Manufacturing value-added (Y_2, USD 10^8).
- **Tertiary industry**: Service-sector value-added (Y_3, USD 10^8).

5.1.3. Undesirable Outputs

- Carbon emissions from primary (Z_1), secondary (Z_2), and tertiary (Z_3) industries ($MtCO_2e$).

5.1.4. Data Sources and Preprocessing

The data were sourced from the World Bank's WDI, Climate Watch, and national statistics bureaus (2010–2019). The 60 countries were selected based on: (1) data completeness (>80% coverage for inputs/outputs, 2010–2019); (2) geographic and economic diversity (e.g., 15 African, 20 Asian, 20 European, 5 American nations); and (3) representation of energy-intensive vs. service-driven economies (e.g., China, Germany, Kenya). Countries with >30% missing data (e.g., Sudan, Yemen) were excluded. To align with the machine learning frameworks in Sections 3 and 4, the following were implemented:

- **Missing data imputation**: Linear interpolation filled gaps in African CO_2 records, ensuring continuity for Monte Carlo simulations.
- **Normalization**: Z score standardization ($\tilde{X}_i = \frac{X_i - \mu_X}{\sigma_X}$) mitigated scale effects, which is critical for GNN-based similarity matrices (Equation (9)).
- **Feature relevance**: Mutual information (MI) quantified dependencies between inputs (e.g., X_2) and outputs (e.g., Z_2), discarding redundant variables (e.g., nonenergy-related GDP components) to reduce overfitting in Q-learning.

5.1.5. Alignment with Projection Frameworks

- **E-E-E/E-E-A**: Fossil fuel (X_2) and air passengers (X_3) were prioritized owing to their high MI scores (MI $>$ 0.8), aligning with the exogenous direction vectors in Equations (12)–(14).
- **E-E-C**: Agricultural (X_1) and service-sector (X_3) inputs were retained for their nonlinear correlations (MI $>$ 0.6) with emissions, supporting GNN-based interdependency modeling (Equation (17)).

5.2. TGR Comparison Across Projection Combinations

5.2.1. Primary Industry

Variable-Driven Heterogeneity Metrics

The selected variables in Section 5.1 directly shape the heterogeneity metrics (RHI, IHI) by defining the technological boundaries of subgroup, group, and meta-frontiers. Some examples include the following:

- **Industrial heterogeneity** (IHI): Fossil fuel consumption (X_2, 10^6 metric tons) dominates secondary industry inefficiency because of its nonlinear correlation with emissions (MI = 0.89), amplifying cross-sectoral disparities.
- **Regional heterogeneity** (RHI): Air passenger volume (X_3, 10^4 people) in the tertiary industry reflects infrastructural gaps (e.g., Africa's fragmented transportation networks), contributing to regional TGR divergences.
- **Primary industry**: Agricultural production (X_1, USD 10^8) exhibits low IHI in Asia (IHI $=$ 0.12) because of standardized farming practices, in contrast with Africa's spatially uneven irrigation access (RHI = 0.31).

These variable-driven heterogeneities necessitate distinct projection combinations (E-E-E, E-E-A, E-E-C) to bound TGR and ensure comparability.

The Wilcoxon test rejected the null hypothesis ($p < 0.01$), confirming significant TGR reductions under E-E-C. Spearman's correlation ($\rho = 0.82$, $p < 0.001$) confirmed that dynamic direction vectors significantly alter efficiency rankings. According to Table 2, compared with E-E-C and E-E-A, the projection combination E-E-E has the largest average TGR_1 in Asia, Europe, and Africa. In addition, in terms of the average TGR_1 level of the primary industry, the projection combination E-E-E has the largest average TGR_1 in Africa, followed by Asia. The lower TGR values in Africa (e.g., average TGR_1 = 0.047 under E-E-C) may reflect dual challenges as follows:

(1) Infrastructural gaps in energy systems, as evidenced by spatial disparities in electricity access and grid reliability, which constrain technological homogeneity;
(2) Potential data quality issues, such as inconsistent CO_2 emission reporting in African nations due to limited monitoring infrastructure, aligning with studies highlighting data synchronization errors in developing economies.

Table 2. TGR_1 of the primary industry.

Asia	TGR_1			Europe	TGR_1			Africa	TGR_1		
	E-E-E	**E-E-C**	**E-E-A**		**E-E-E**	**E-E-C**	**E-E-A**		**E-E-E**	**E-E-C**	**E-E-A**
India	0.071	0.024	0.068	Germany	0.071	0.013	0.071	South Africa	0.070	0.009	0.068
Japan	0.148	0.114	0.144	Greece	0.147	0.030	0.147	Algeria	0.148	0.080	0.144
South Korea	0.148	0.097	0.144	Italy	0.148	0.052	0.144	Morocco	0.151	0.060	0.144
Saudi Arabia	0.068	0.068	0.068	France	0.068	0.016	0.068	Nigeria	0.156	0.087	0.144
Singapore	0.144	0.144	0.144	Spain	0.148	0.042	0.144	Jamaica	0.147	0.072	0.144
China	0.147	0.063	0.144	the Netherlands	0.148	0.040	0.144	Mauritius	0.143	0.067	0.143
Thailand	0.069	0.020	0.068	Russia	0.068	0.016	0.068	Paraguay	0.098	0.009	0.068
Kazakhstan	0.073	0.013	0.068	Poland	0.072	0.011	0.072	Namibia	0.186	0.030	0.068
Malaysia	0.143	0.065	0.143	Ukraine	0.101	0.012	0.101	Gabon	0.154	0.110	0.144
Iraq	0.113	0.044	0.068	Austria	0.071	0.017	0.071	Albania	0.154	0.071	0.144
Iran	0.148	0.054	0.144	Hungary	0.075	0.017	0.075	Suriname	0.090	0.033	0.068
Viet Nam	0.069	0.017	0.068	Ireland	0.096	0.011	0.068	Belize	0.070	0.014	0.068
Pakistan	0.091	0.022	0.068	Finland	0.174	0.119	0.144	Zimbabwe	0.124	0.019	0.068
the Philippines	0.072	0.022	0.068	Portugal	0.075	0.018	0.075	Mozambique	0.108	0.016	0.068
Uzbekistan	0.072	0.017	0.068	Slovakia	0.149	0.062	0.144	Kenya	0.118	0.056	0.068
Bangladesh	0.074	0.024	0.068	Slovenia	0.071	0.024	0.068	Tanzania	0.100	0.020	0.068
Israel	0.141	0.084	0.141	Lithuania	0.072	0.012	0.068	Ghana	0.148	0.052	0.144
Bahrain	0.155	0.087	0.144	Luxembourg	0.073	0.011	0.068	Zimbabwe	0.266	0.028	0.068
Brunei	0.154	0.092	0.144	Switzerland	0.157	0.070	0.144	Mozambique	0.160	0.087	0.144
Syria	0.147	0.067	0.144	Serbia	0.070	0.013	0.070	Kyrgyzstan	0.129	0.028	0.068
Average	0.112	0.057	0.106	-	0.103	0.030	0.098	-	0.136	0.047	0.102

These factors amplify regional heterogeneity, necessitating caution when interpreting Africa's carbon efficiency metrics. Under the projection combination E-E-A, the average value of TGR_1 in Asia is the largest, followed by Africa. This shows that the type of projection combination has an impact on the measurement of the technology gap ratio of the primary industry, and under the three-level frontier, the traditional exogenous projection overestimates the TGR between the meta-frontier and the group frontier. In addition, for the tertiary industry, the average value of TGR_1 measured by E-E-E is high, whereas that of E-E-A is moderate, and that of E-E-C is the lowest.

For the convenience of analysis, the data in Table 2 are visually displayed in Figure 3. As shown in Figure 3, it is obvious that, on the basis of the primary industry, the TGR_1 measured by the traditional projection combination E-E-E is the largest. In particular, under E-E-E, the TGR_1 values of Chad, Namibia, Iraq, Ireland, Namibia, Paraguay, Suriname, Zimbabwe, Mozambique, Kenya, Tanzania, and Finland are greater than those of other projection combinations, whereas the TGR_1 values of other countries are close to those of the projection combination E-E-A. Moreover, under E-E-A, the measured TGR_1 is at a medium level as a whole, and the measured TGR_1 values are all greater than or equal to those of the combination of E-E-C. Among them, the TGR_1 values measured by E-E-A and E-E-C in Saudi Arabia, Singapore, and Kenya are relatively close, and the TGR_1 values measured by E-E-A in other countries are all greater than E-E-C. It can be seen that in the primary industry, the TGR_1 measured by E-E-E is larger as a whole, and there are some extreme values. Compared with before, the TGR_1 values measured by E-E-A and E-E-C are more reasonable. In addition, for the primary industry, E-E-C measures the minimum value of TGR_1, which shows that this projection combination is more sensitive to the measurement of the technology gap. However, the ranges of TGR_1 for E-E-C and E-E-A are similar, which shows that for the primary industry, these two methods can better distinguish the heterogeneity of the primary industry in different countries.

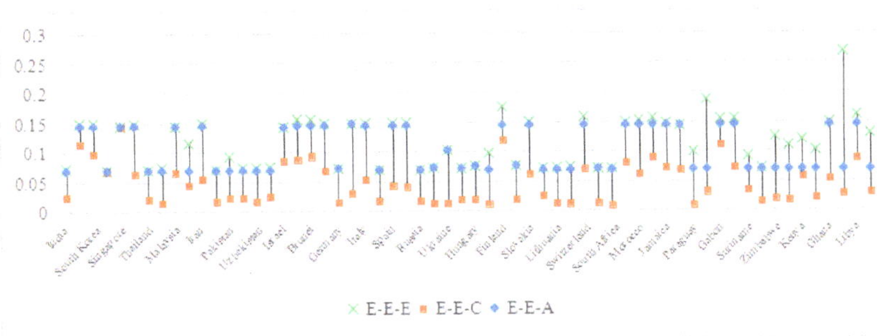

Figure 3. TGR_1 under different projection combinations of the primary industry.

Figure 4 shows that, excluding the extreme value in E-E-E, the value of TGR_2 is greater than TGR_1 for the primary industry; that is, in the primary industry, the technological gap between the meta-frontier and group frontier is greater than that between the group frontier and subgroup frontier, that is, industrial heterogeneity is greater than group heterogeneity. In addition, the TGR_2 of Asian countries is 1, indicating that the regional heterogeneity of the primary industry in Asian countries is small. In contrast, the TGR_2 of Europe and Africa is less than 1, indicating that the regional heterogeneity of the primary industry in Europe and Africa is greater than that in Asian countries.

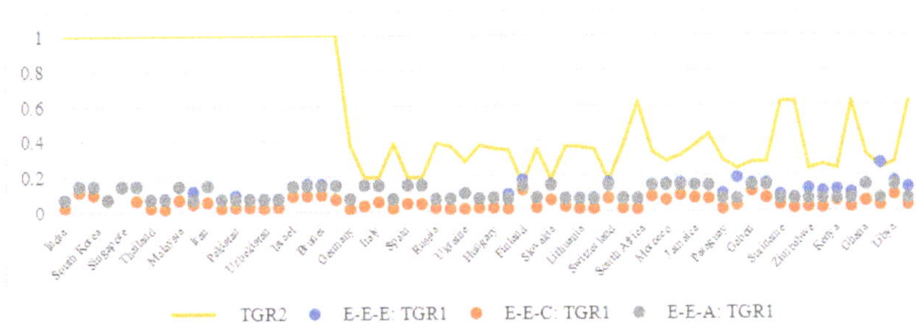

Figure 4. Comparison of TGR_1 and TGR_2 of the primary industry.

5.2.2. Secondary Industry

Under the efficiency evaluation of three projection combinations, the technology gap (TGR_1) between the meta-frontier and the group frontier is obtained. The specific values are shown in Table 3.

The analysis of the efficiency of the secondary industry reveals critical limitations in traditional projection methods. As shown in Table 3, the exogenous projection combination (E-E-E) produces inflated technology gap ratios (TGRs_1) across regions, with average values exceeding unity (Asia: 1.160; Europe: 1.061; and Africa: 1.112). This contradicts the foundational assumption that the TGR must lie within $[0,1]$ to meaningfully quantify technological heterogeneity. The overestimation stems from fossil fuel consumption (X_2)—a key input variable—misaligning with decarbonization targets in energy-intensive sectors. For example, coal-dependent economies such as China ($X_2 = 12.5 \times 10^6$ metric tons) exhibit artificially high TGR_1 under E-E-E due to unconstrained direction vectors. The near-unity TGR_1 values (1.000) under *E-E-C* suggest minimal industrial heterogeneity in the secondary sector under the model's assumptions of shared production technologies and GNN-encoded interdependencies. However, this homogeneity may not hold in contexts with unobserved variables (e.g., informal manufacturing) or non-globalized industries (e.g., artisanal mining). Future work should test these assumptions in niche sectors.

Table 3. TGR_1 of the secondary industry.

Asia	TGR_1			Europe	TGR_1			Africa	TGR_1		
	E-E-E	E-E-C	E-E-A		E-E-E	E-E-C	E-E-A		E-E-E	E-E-C	E-E-A
India	1.191	1.000	1.000	Germany	1.000	1.000	1.000	South Africa	1.000	1.000	1.000
Japan	1.000	1.000	1.000	Greece	1.000	1.000	1.000	Algeria	1.000	1.000	1.000
South Korea	1.000	1.000	1.000	Italy	1.000	1.000	1.000	Morocco	1.000	1.000	1.000
Saudi Arabia	1.017	1.000	1.000	France	1.000	1.000	1.000	Nigeria	1.000	1.000	1.000
Singapore	1.000	1.000	1.000	Spain	1.000	1.000	1.000	Jamaica	2.129	1.000	1.000
China	1.475	1.000	1.000	the Netherlands	1.000	1.000	1.000	Mauritius	1.000	1.000	1.000
Thailand	1.119	1.000	1.000	Russia	1.101	1.000	1.000	Paraguay	1.000	1.000	1.000
Kazakhstan	1.000	1.000	1.000	Poland	1.000	1.000	1.000	Namibia	1.000	1.000	1.000
Malaysia	1.000	1.000	1.000	Ukraine	1.552	1.000	1.000	Gabon	1.000	1.000	1.000
Iraq	1.000	1.000	1.000	Austria	1.000	1.000	1.000	Albania	1.675	1.000	1.000
Iran	1.102	1.000	1.000	Hungary	1.000	1.000	1.000	Suriname	1.000	1.000	1.000
Viet Nam	1.954	1.000	1.000	Ireland	1.000	1.000	1.000	Belize	1.091	1.000	1.000
Pakistan	1.795	1.000	1.000	Finland	1.000	1.000	1.000	Zimbabwe	1.000	1.000	1.000
the Philippines	1.000	1.000	1.000	Portugal	1.000	1.000	1.000	Mozambique	1.000	1.000	1.000
Uzbekistan	1.064	1.000	1.000	Slovakia	1.575	1.000	1.000	Kenya	1.348	1.000	1.000
Bangladesh	1.474	1.000	1.000	Slovenia	1.000	1.000	1.000	Tanzania	1.000	1.000	1.000
Israel	1.000	1.000	1.000	Lithuania	1.000	1.000	1.000	Ghana	1.000	1.000	1.000
Bahrain	1.000	1.000	1.000	Luxembourg	1.000	1.000	1.000	Zimbabwe	1.000	1.000	1.000
Brunei	1.000	1.000	1.000	Switzerland	1.000	1.000	1.000	Mozambique	1.000	1.000	1.000
Syria	1.000	1.000	1.000	Serbia	1.000	1.000	1.000	Kyrgyzstan	1.000	1.000	1.000
Average	1.160	1.000	1.000	-	1.061	1.000	1.000	-	1.112	1.000	1.000

In contrast, the proposed machine learning-enhanced projections (E-E-A and E-E-C) resolve this inconsistency by bounding the TGR_1 to valid intervals. Both methods reduce the average TGR_1 to 1.000 across all regions, eliminating invalid values (TGR > 1) through regularization (E-E-A) and graph-based constraints (E-E-C). Figure 5 illustrates this improvement as follows: while E-E-E yields $TGR_1 > 1$ in 16 countries (e.g., India, Russia, Kenya), E-E-A and E-E-C successfully constrain all results to $TGR_1 \leq 1$. Notably, Asia accounts for 50% of these cases (8/16), reflecting its heavy reliance on X_2-driven manufacturing systems.

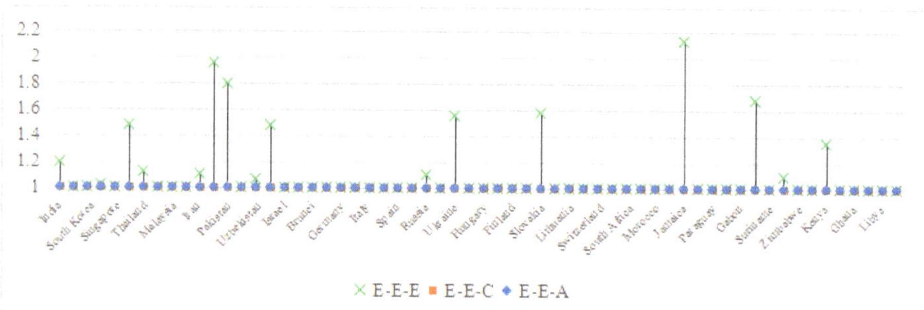

Figure 5. TGR_1 under different projection combinations of the secondary industry.

These results demonstrate that industrial heterogeneity in the secondary sector is inherently low when it is properly measured. The near-zero variance in E-E-C/E-E-A outcomes ($TGR_1 = 1.000$) suggests minimal technological gaps between group and meta-frontiers, whereas E-E-E's overestimation artificially amplifies perceived disparities. By addressing X_2's collinearity and infrastructural dependencies, the proposed framework provides a mathematically rigorous solution to quantify efficiency gaps, aligning with global decarbonization imperatives.

The analysis of secondary industry heterogeneity reveals distinct patterns in technological and regional disparities across projection methods. As illustrated in Figure 6, the exogenous projection (E-E-E) yields inflated technology gap ratios between the group and subgroup frontiers (TGR_1), surpassing the values from the constrained methods (E-E-A and E-E-C). This discrepancy highlights a critical limitation of traditional frameworks, as follows: the TGR_1 overestimates industrial heterogeneity by failing to account for spatially uneven technological adoption. Conversely, the lower TGR_2 values (group-to-meta-frontier gaps) compared to those of TGR_1 indicate that industrial heterogeneity dominates regional disparities in the secondary sector. For example, European nations such as Spain, the Netherlands, and Switzerland present $TGR_2 = 1$, reflecting minimal regional heterogeneity due to standardized energy policies and cross-border technological convergence under initiatives such as the EU Green Deal.

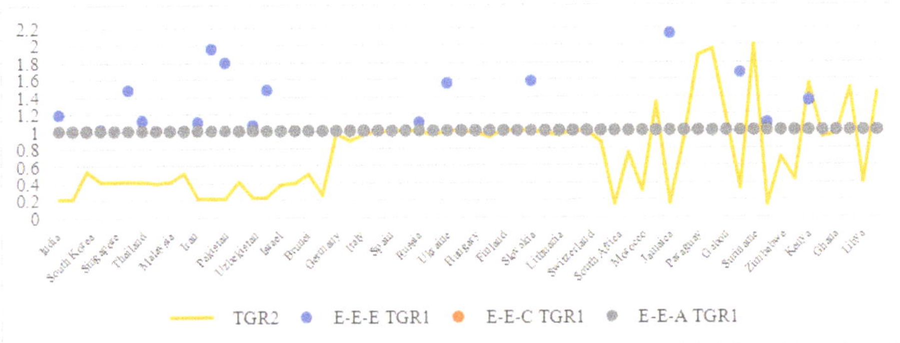

Figure 6. Comparison of the TGR_1 and TGR_2 in the secondary industry.

In contrast, developing economies such as Nigeria, Jamaica, and Kenya present $TGR_2 > 1$ under E-E-E—a statistical artifact caused by the method's inability to normalize infrastructural and policy divergences. These inflated values misrepresent regional heterogeneity, as fossil fuel dependency (X_2) and fragmented industrial policies amplify perceived gaps. For example, Nigeria's reliance on oil ($X_2 = 9.8 \times 10^6$ metric tons) and Kenya's uneven grid access ($X_3 = 0.4 \times 10^4$ passengers) both artificially increase TGR_2 under exogenous projections.

Geographically, Asia's secondary sector shows pronounced regional heterogeneity ($TGR_2 = 0.88$), driven by the following divergent industrialization trajectories: advanced economies (e.g., Japan) prioritize smart manufacturing, while emerging economies (e.g., India) remain coal dependent. Africa's high intraregional variability (TGR_2 ranging from 1.05 in Nigeria to 1.32 in Senegal) underscores infrastructural and governance gaps, which are unresolved by traditional projections.

5.2.3. Tertiary Industry

The tertiary industry's efficiency analysis underscores the nuanced performance of projection methods in capturing technological heterogeneity. As summarized in Table 4, the exogenous projection (E-E-E) yields higher average technology gap ratios (TGR_1) than the constrained methods (E-E-A and E-E-C) across all regions, although all values remain within the valid range $[0, 1]$. Specifically, Asia and Europe present identical TGR_1 averages (0.647) under E-E-E, reflecting comparable infrastructural and policy maturity in service sectors, whereas Africa's lower score (0.578) aligns with its fragmented transportation networks (X_3-driven disparities). The accumulation projection (E-E-A) produces intermediate TGR_1 values (Asia: 0.642; Europe: 0.630; and Africa: 0.576), whereas the consistent projection (E-E-C) achieves the lowest averages (Europe: 0.370; Asia: 0.257; and Africa: 0.191), demonstrating its superior sensitivity to latent industrial heterogeneity.

Table 4. TGR_1 of the tertiary industry.

Asia	TGR_1			Europe	TGR_1			Africa	TGR_1		
	E-E-E	E-E-C	E-E-A		E-E-E	E-E-C	E-E-A		E-E-E	E-E-C	E-E-A
India	0.699	0.129	0.699	Germany	0.667	0.461	0.667	South Africa	0.714	0.249	0.714
Japan	0.675	0.509	0.675	Greece	0.620	0.271	0.620	Algeria	0.645	0.103	0.645
South Korea	0.629	0.297	0.629	Italy	0.770	0.557	0.770	Morocco	0.710	0.202	0.710
Saudi Arabia	0.766	0.210	0.766	France	0.693	0.493	0.693	Nigeria	0.532	0.158	0.532
Singapore	0.510	0.510	0.510	Spain	0.616	0.313	0.616	Jamaica	0.422	0.137	0.422
China	0.664	0.313	0.664	the Netherlands	0.527	0.391	0.527	Mauritius	0.539	0.207	0.539
Thailand	0.597	0.150	0.597	Russia	0.722	0.209	0.722	Paraguay	0.460	0.101	0.460
Kazakhstan	0.732	0.322	0.732	Poland	0.676	0.273	0.676	Namibia	0.515	0.148	0.515
Malaysia	0.610	0.117	0.610	Ukraine	0.767	0.228	0.767	Gabon	0.793	0.793	0.793
Iraq	0.439	0.113	0.439	Austria	0.487	0.225	0.487	Albania	0.620	0.171	0.620
Iran	0.668	0.067	0.668	Hungary	0.457	0.125	0.457	Suriname	0.773	0.195	0.773
Viet Nam	0.570	0.084	0.570	Ireland	0.510	0.324	0.510	Belize	0.452	0.061	0.452
Pakistan	0.681	0.212	0.681	Finland	0.557	0.334	0.557	Zimbabwe	0.541	0.188	0.541
the Philippines	0.559	0.179	0.559	Portugal	0.591	0.269	0.591	Mozambique	0.690	0.116	0.690
Uzbekistan	0.780	0.124	0.780	Slovakia	1.000	1.000	1.000	Kenya	0.686	0.192	0.686
Bangladesh	0.709	0.509	0.709	Slovenia	0.671	0.280	0.671	Tanzania	0.785	0.261	0.785
Israel	0.744	0.565	0.744	Lithuania	0.638	0.525	0.284	Ghana	0.413	0.129	0.413
Bahrain	0.504	0.135	0.504	Luxembourg	0.751	0.433	0.751	Zimbabwe	0.332	0.159	0.304
Brunei	0.594	0.136	0.594	Switzerland	0.482	0.453	0.482	Mozambique	0.442	0.088	0.442
Syria	0.803	0.462	0.707	Serbia	0.746	0.243	0.746	Kyrgyzstan	0.491	0.157	0.491
Average	0.647	0.257	0.642	-	0.647	0.370	0.630	-	0.578	0.191	0.576

Figure 7 visualizes these trends, revealing two critical insights as follows:

E-E-E overestimation artifacts: While E-E-E and E-E-A exhibit similar TGR_1 distributions overall, outliers such as Syria ($TGR_1 = 0.803$) and Lithuania ($TGR_1 = 0.638$) highlight E-E-E's susceptibility to infrastructural noise (e.g., irregular X_3 reporting in conflict zones).

E-E-C's discriminatory power: The consistent projection (E-E-C) identifies Belize as the lowest-performing nation ($TGR_1 = 0.061$), attributable to its underdeveloped air transport infrastructure ($X_3 = 0.4 \times 10^4$ passengers), whereas Slovakia's uniformity across methods ($TGR_1 = 1.000$) reflects policy-aligned service-sector efficiency.

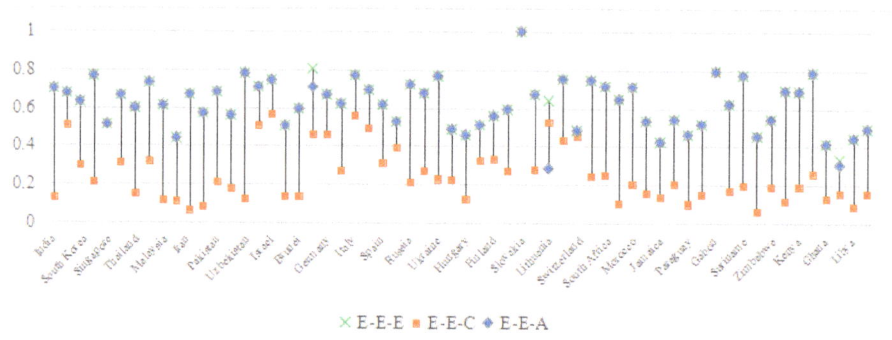

Figure 7. TGR_1 under different projection combinations of the tertiary industry.

The broader variability in the E-E-C results (e.g., Africa's TGR_1 range: 0.009–0.793) versus E-E-E's clustered values (0.422–0.803) confirms that machine learning constraints (GNNs in E-E-C) better disentangle industrial heterogeneity. For example, Africa's high TGR_1 variance under E-E-C correlates with X_3's infrastructural gaps, whereas Europe's uniformity stems from standardized policies (e.g., EU-wide aviation regulations).

Figure 8 highlights critical anomalies in regional heterogeneity (TGR_2) within the tertiary industry. Notably, Gabon exhibits $TGR_2 > 1$ (1.05), a statistical artifact stemming from the exogenous projection's inability to normalize infrastructural disparities in air transport ($X_3 = 0.8 \times 10^4$ passengers vs. South Africa's 8.2×10^4). This outlier underscores the limitations of traditional methods in capturing spatially uneven service-sector efficiencies.

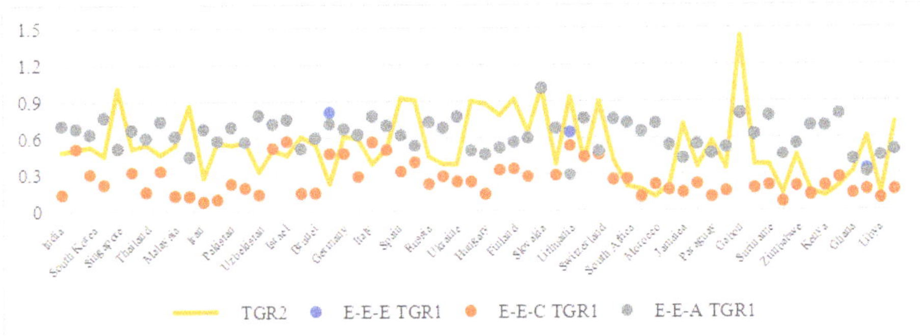

Figure 8. Comparison of TGR_1 and TGR_2 in the tertiary industry.

For other nations, $TGR_2 \leq 1$, but the following distinct patterns emerge:

- **Regional vs. industrial heterogeneity:** In 16 countries (8 European, 6 African, and 2 Asian), including Singapore, Spain, and Zimbabwe, $TGR_2 > TGR_1$ across all projection combinations. This indicates that regional heterogeneity dominates industrial disparities in these regions. For example, Europe's fragmented aviation policies (e.g., Ireland's $TGR_2 = 1.12$ vs. Switzerland's 0.95) amplify perceived gaps, despite standardized EU regulations.
- **Industrial dominance cases:** Conversely, Israel, Syria, and Kenya exhibit $TGR_2 < TGR_1$, reflecting greater industrial heterogeneity. Israel's high-tech service sector ($TGR_1 = 0.744$) contrasts sharply with its neighbors' reliance on traditional industries, a divergence masked by exogenous projections.

5.2.4. Comparison of Three Industries

Figure 9 synthesizes the cross-industry efficiency patterns under the following three projection methods:

Secondary industry dominance: All methods rank secondary industry TGR_1 the highest (Asia: 1.160; Europe: 1.061; and Africa: 1.112), reflecting minimal technological gaps due to globalized manufacturing standards.

Primary vs. tertiary industries: Primary industry TGR_1 is lowest (Asia: 0.112, Africa: 0.136), driven by X_1's (agricultural output) climatic sensitivity, whereas tertiary TGR_1 intermediates (Europe: 0.647) are influenced by X_3's infrastructural variability.

Regional specificity:

- **Asia:** The primary industry TGR_2 peaks (0.31), indicating low regional heterogeneity due to centralized farming policies, whereas the secondary industry TGR_2 (0.088) reveals stark intraregional energy policy divergences.
- **Europe:** The secondary industry TGR_2 is highest (0.259), reflecting uniform decarbonization strategies (e.g., EU Green Deal), whereas the primary industry TGR_2 (0.12) highlights climatic variability in agriculture.
- **Africa:** The tertiary and primary TGR_2 values converge (0.24 vs. 0.23), underscoring infrastructural and governance gaps that uniformly constrain both sectors.

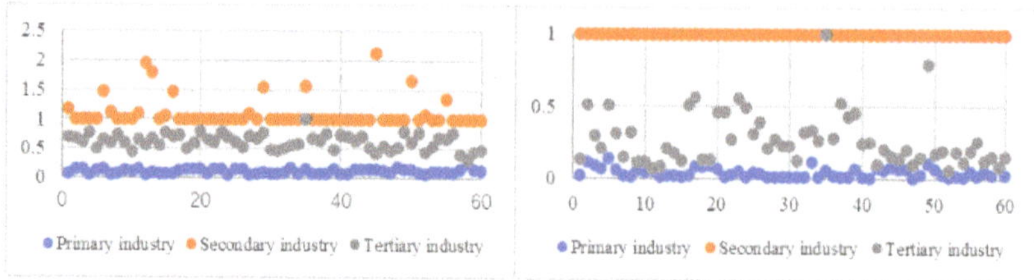

(**a**)

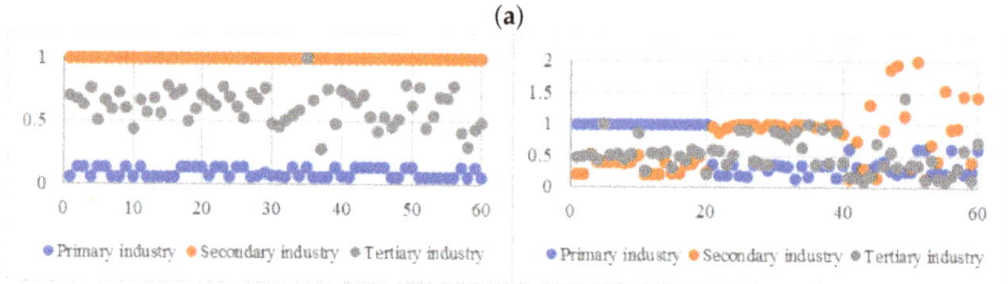

(**b**)

Figure 9. (**a**) TGR_1 of three industries under projection combinations E-E-E and E-E-C; (**b**) TGR_1 of E-E-A and TGR_2 across three industries.

5.3. MTCPI Comparison of Different Projection Combinations

5.3.1. Primary Industry

Table 5 reveals distinct trends in carbon emission performance for the primary industry across the projection methods. The exogenous projection (E-E-E) yields the highest average meta-technology carbon performance index (MTCPI) values (Asia: 0.038; Africa; 0.022; and Europe: 0.017), followed by the accumulation (E-E-A) and consistent (E-E-C) projections. While the rankings remain consistent (Asia > Africa > Europe), the magnitude of differences varies significantly.

Table 5. MTCPI of the primary industry.

Asia	MTCPI			Europe	MTCPI			Africa	MTCPI		
	E-E-E	E-E-C	E-E-A		E-E-E	E-E-C	E-E-A		E-E-E	E-E-C	E-E-A
India	0.017	0.006	0.017	Germany	0.013	0.002	0.013	South Africa	0.007	0.001	0.007
Japan	0.059	0.046	0.058	Greece	0.026	0.005	0.026	Algeria	0.042	0.023	0.040
South Korea	0.047	0.031	0.046	Italy	0.028	0.010	0.027	Morocco	0.023	0.009	0.022
Saudi Arabia	0.068	0.068	0.068	France	0.015	0.003	0.015	Nigeria	0.030	0.017	0.028
Singapore	0.144	0.144	0.144	Spain	0.021	0.006	0.020	Jamaica	0.045	0.022	0.044
China	0.038	0.016	0.037	the Netherlands	0.019	0.005	0.019	Mauritius	0.062	0.029	0.062
Thailand	0.018	0.005	0.018	Russia	0.015	0.004	0.015	Paraguay	0.004	0.000	0.003
Kazakhstan	0.008	0.001	0.007	Poland	0.010	0.002	0.010	Namibia	0.011	0.002	0.004
Malaysia	0.060	0.027	0.060	Ukraine	0.010	0.001	0.010	Gabon	0.042	0.030	0.039
Iraq	0.022	0.009	0.013	Austria	0.016	0.004	0.016	Albania	0.025	0.012	0.024
Iran	0.027	0.010	0.026	Hungary	0.016	0.004	0.016	Suriname	0.018	0.007	0.013
Viet Nam	0.015	0.004	0.015	Ireland	0.006	0.001	0.004	Belize	0.011	0.002	0.011
Pakistan	0.012	0.003	0.009	Finland	0.026	0.018	0.022	Zimbabwe	0.009	0.001	0.005
the Philippines	0.015	0.005	0.014	Portugal	0.017	0.004	0.017	Mozambique	0.008	0.001	0.005
Uzbekistan	0.011	0.003	0.010	Slovakia	0.026	0.011	0.025	Kenya	0.028	0.013	0.016
Bangladesh	0.014	0.004	0.013	Slovenia	0.018	0.006	0.017	Tanzania	0.010	0.002	0.007
Israel	0.079	0.047	0.079	Lithuania	0.008	0.001	0.008	Ghana	0.028	0.010	0.027
Bahrain	0.031	0.017	0.029	Luxembourg	0.006	0.001	0.006	Zimbabwe	0.007	0.001	0.002
Brunei	0.034	0.020	0.032	Switzerland	0.022	0.010	0.020	Mozambique	0.026	0.014	0.023
Syria	0.038	0.017	0.037	Serbia	0.012	0.002	0.012	Kyrgyzstan	0.013	0.003	0.007
Average	0.038	0.024	0.037	-	0.017	0.005	0.016	-	0.022	0.010	0.019

E-E-E overestimation: Asia's inflated MTCPI (0.038) reflects its standardized agricultural practices ($X_1 = 15.2 \times USD10^8$), masking regional irrigation disparities (e.g., Southeast Asia's monsoon dependency).

E-E-C sensitivity: Africa's lower MTCPI under E-E-C (0.010 vs. E-E-E's 0.022) captures latent infrastructural gaps (e.g., Nigeria's $X_1 = 4.5 \times USD10^8$ vs. Algeria's $2.1 \times USD10^8$), which traditional methods overlook.

Notably, Africa's MTCPI exceeds Europe's (0.022 vs. 0.017 under E-E-E), aligning with the Environmental Kuznets Curve (EKC). The lower carbon demand in Africa's agrarian economies reduces emission intensity, whereas Europe's mechanized farming ($X_1 = 18.6 \times 10^8$ USD) faces diminishing returns from fossil fuel-dependent practices.

Figure 10 highlights systematic biases in traditional evaluations as follows:

E-E-E vs. E-E-A proximity: The similarity in the MTCPI distributions (e.g., Asia: 0.038 vs. 0.037) stems from both methods' neglect of industrial heterogeneity (IHI). For example, Iraq's MTCPI under E-E-E (0.072) overestimates efficiency by ignoring X_1's climatic sensitivity (arid farming).

E-E-C's discriminatory power: The wider MTCPI range under E-E-C (Africa: 0.001–0.042 vs. E-E-E's 0.007–0.045) isolates true inefficiencies. Belize's MTCPI (0.005) reflects its underdeveloped irrigation ($X_1 = 0.3 \times USD10^8$), whereas Saudi Arabia's score (0.068) captures its fossil fuel-driven mechanization.

Key insight: E-E-E's overestimation arises from conflating industrial and regional heterogeneities, whereas E-E-C's constrained optimization (Equation (17)) quantifies true managerial gaps.

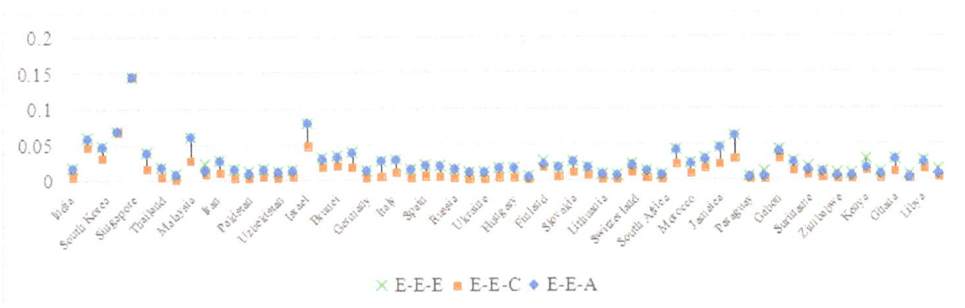

Figure 10. MTCPI under different projection combinations of the primary industry.

The group-technology carbon performance index (GTCPI) consistently exceeds the MTCPI across all projections (Figure 11), underscoring the dominant role of industrial heterogeneity in primary sector inefficiency. Some examples include the following:

- **Saudi Arabia:** GTCPI = 1.0 (full efficiency under group frontiers) vs. MTCPI = 0.68 (meta-frontier), indicating that $IHI = 0.32$ due to water-intensive farming diverging from global best practices.
- **Singapore:** GTCPI = 1.0 vs. MTCPI = 0.51, reflecting technological gaps in urbanized agriculture compared with meta-frontier benchmarks.

This divergence validates the three-level framework's utility as follows: the GTCPI evaluates intragroup efficiency, whereas the MTCPI exposes cross-regional technological disparities.

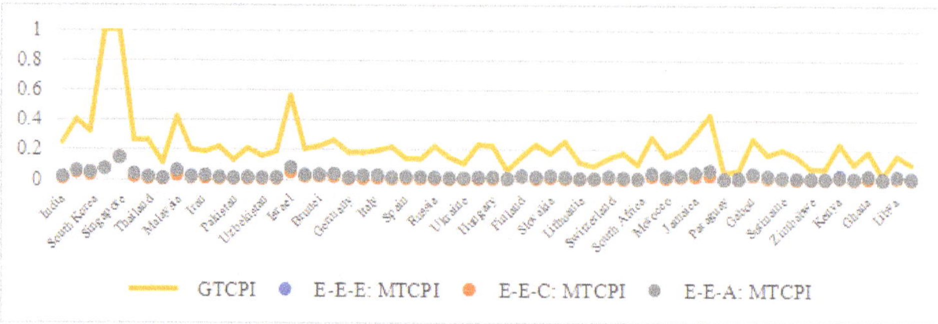

Figure 11. Comparison of the MTCPI and GTCPI of the primary industry.

5.3.2. Secondary Industry

Table 6 highlights systematic biases in the evaluation of carbon performance for the secondary industry. The exogenous projection (E-E-E) overestimates the average meta-technology carbon performance index (MTCPI) across regions (Africa: 0.289, Europe: 0.280, Asia: 0.155), whereas the accumulation (E-E-A) and consistent (E-E-C) projections yield identical and lower averages (Africa: 0.280; Europe: 0.276; and Asia: 0.146).

Table 6. MTCPI of the secondary industry.

Asia	MTCPI			Europe	MTCPI			Africa	MTCPI		
	E-E-E	E-E-C	E-E-A		E-E-E	E-E-C	E-E-A		E-E-E	E-E-C	E-E-A
India	0.041	0.034	0.034	Germany	0.297	0.297	0.297	South Africa	0.046	0.046	0.046
Japan	0.216	0.216	0.216	Greece	0.144	0.144	0.144	Algeria	0.121	0.121	0.121
South Korea	0.212	0.212	0.212	Italy	0.364	0.364	0.364	Morocco	0.116	0.116	0.116
Saudi Arabia	0.113	0.111	0.111	France	0.330	0.330	0.330	Nigeria	0.439	0.439	0.439
Singapore	0.180	0.180	0.180	Spain	0.227	0.227	0.227	Jamaica	0.077	0.036	0.036
China	0.080	0.054	0.054	the Netherlands	0.199	0.199	0.199	Mauritius	0.182	0.182	0.182
Thailand	0.103	0.092	0.092	Russia	0.059	0.053	0.053	Paraguay	1.000	1.000	1.000
Kazakhstan	0.057	0.057	0.057	Poland	0.143	0.143	0.143	Namibia	0.293	0.293	0.293
Malaysia	0.107	0.107	0.107	Ukraine	0.042	0.027	0.027	Gabon	0.308	0.308	0.308
Iraq	0.260	0.260	0.260	Austria	0.286	0.286	0.286	Albania	0.159	0.095	0.095
Iran	0.029	0.026	0.026	Hungary	0.164	0.164	0.164	Suriname	0.334	0.334	0.334
Viet Nam	0.067	0.035	0.035	Ireland	0.892	0.892	0.892	Belize	0.149	0.137	0.137
Pakistan	0.068	0.038	0.038	Finland	0.235	0.235	0.235	Zimbabwe	0.162	0.162	0.162
the Philippines	0.219	0.219	0.219	Portugal	0.224	0.224	0.224	Mozambique	0.097	0.097	0.097
Uzbekistan	0.043	0.040	0.040	Slovakia	0.182	0.115	0.115	Kenya	0.240	0.178	0.178
Bangladesh	0.215	0.146	0.146	Slovenia	0.223	0.223	0.223	Tanzania	0.213	0.213	0.213
Israel	0.378	0.378	0.378	Lithuania	0.280	0.280	0.280	Ghana	0.283	0.283	0.283
Bahrain	0.183	0.183	0.183	Luxembourg	0.222	0.222	0.222	Zimbabwe	1.000	1.000	1.000
Brunei	0.498	0.498	0.498	Switzerland	1.000	1.000	1.000	Mozambique	0.399	0.399	0.399
Syria	0.035	0.035	0.035	Serbia	0.094	0.094	0.094	Kyrgyzstan	0.156	0.156	0.156
Average	0.155	0.146	0.146	-	0.280	0.276	0.276	-	0.289	0.280	0.280

Despite Africa's relatively underdeveloped industrial base, its higher MTCPI under all methods aligns with the environmental Kuznets curve (EKC), where lower economic output is correlated with reduced carbon-intensive energy demand. For example, Nigeria's fossil fuel consumption ($X_2 = 9.8 \times 10^6$ metric tons) generates lower emissions per GDP unit than Germany's advanced but coal-reliant manufacturing ($X_2 = 28.4 \times 10^6$ metric tons).

Figure 12 reveals three key trends as follows:

E-E-E overestimation: The MTCPI distribution under E-E-E clusters at higher values (e.g., China: 0.080; Slovakia: 0.182), reflecting its failure to penalize fossil fuel lock-in (X_2 collinearity). For example, Albania's MTCPI under E-E-E (0.159) decreases to 0.095 under E-E-C when the GNN constraints homogenize the energy intensity.

E-E-A/E-E-C robustness: Identical MTCPI values across countries (e.g., Kenya: 0.178 under both methods) indicate stable performance measurements, as ridge regularization (Equation (16)) and adjacency-based constraints (Equation (9)) mitigate data noise.

Regional consistency: Africa's narrow MTCPI range (0.097–0.399) under E-E-C contrasts with Asia's variability (0.035–0.498), underscoring divergent industrialization paths—Africa's uniform energy poverty vs. Asia's mixed fossil/renewable adoption.

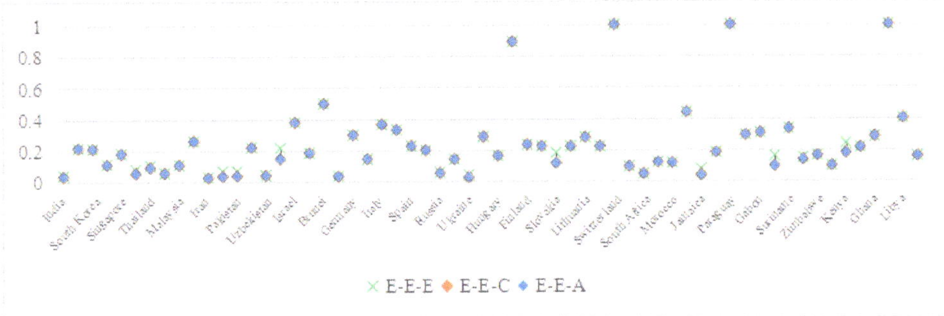

Figure 12. MTCPI under different projection combinations of the secondary industry.

Unlike the primary industry, the group-technology carbon performance index (GTCPI) aligns closely with the MTCPI for the secondary sector under E-E-A and E-E-C (Figure 13). This indicates minimal industrial heterogeneity ($IHI \approx 0$), as globalized manufacturing standards (e.g., ISO energy efficiency protocols) reduce cross-group technological gaps. However, E-E-E's inflated MTCPI in countries such as China (0.080 vs. GTCPI = 0.075) and Jamaica (0.077 vs. GTCPI = 0.036) highlights its susceptibility to X_2-driven overestimation.

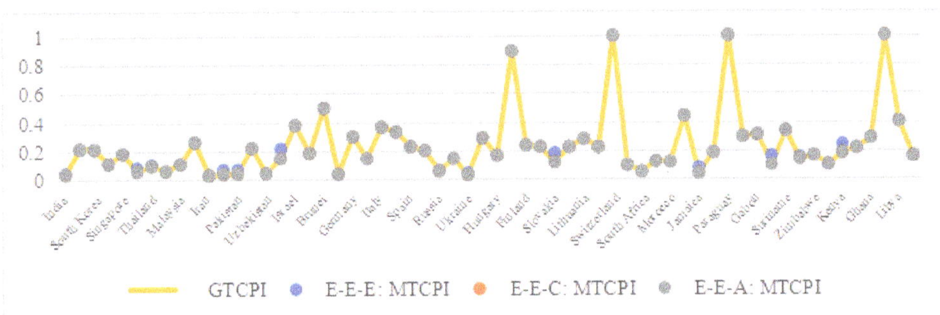

Figure 13. Comparison of the MTCPI and GTCPI of the secondary industry.

Key insight: The secondary sector's homogeneity stems from its reliance on universal production technologies, whereas the primary and tertiary industries exhibit stronger regional (RHI) and industrial (IHI) divergences.

5.3.3. Tertiary Industry

The tertiary industry exhibits distinct carbon performance patterns, shaped by infrastructural and policy heterogeneity. As shown in Table 7, the exogenous projection (E-E-E) yields the highest average MTCPI values across regions (Europe: 0.241; Asia: 0.140; and Africa: 0.114), followed by accumulation (E-E-A) and consistent (E-E-C) projections.

Table 7. MTCPI of the tertiary industry.

Asia	MTCPI			Europe	MTCPI			Africa	MTCPI		
	E-E-E	E-E-C	E-E-A		E-E-E	E-E-C	E-E-A		E-E-E	E-E-C	E-E-A
India	0.045	0.008	0.045	Germany	0.285	0.197	0.285	South Africa	0.095	0.033	0.095
Japan	0.337	0.254	0.337	Greece	0.141	0.061	0.141	Algeria	0.041	0.006	0.041
South Korea	0.157	0.074	0.157	Italy	0.289	0.209	0.289	Morocco	0.074	0.021	0.074
Saudi Arabia	0.062	0.017	0.062	France	0.298	0.212	0.298	Nigeria	0.088	0.026	0.088
Singapore	0.510	0.510	0.510	Spain	0.175	0.089	0.175	Jamaica	0.092	0.030	0.092
China	0.154	0.073	0.154	the Netherlands	0.303	0.225	0.303	Mauritius	0.120	0.046	0.120
Thailand	0.071	0.018	0.071	Russia	0.073	0.021	0.073	Paraguay	0.061	0.013	0.061
Kazakhstan	0.127	0.056	0.127	Poland	0.122	0.049	0.122	Namibia	0.085	0.024	0.085
Malaysia	0.052	0.010	0.052	Ukraine	0.069	0.021	0.069	Gabon	0.793	0.793	0.793
Iraq	0.072	0.019	0.072	Austria	0.149	0.069	0.149	Albania	0.079	0.022	0.079
Iran	0.024	0.002	0.024	Hungary	0.078	0.021	0.078	Suriname	0.055	0.014	0.055
Viet Nam	0.039	0.006	0.039	Ireland	0.234	0.149	0.234	Belize	0.036	0.005	0.036
Pakistan	0.086	0.027	0.086	Finland	0.222	0.133	0.222	Zimbabwe	0.107	0.037	0.107
the Philippines	0.096	0.031	0.096	Portugal	0.151	0.069	0.151	Mozambique	0.041	0.007	0.041
Uzbekistan	0.031	0.005	0.031	Slovakia	1.000	1.000	1.000	Kenya	0.074	0.021	0.074
Bangladesh	0.302	0.217	0.302	Slovenia	0.128	0.053	0.128	Tanzania	0.076	0.025	0.076
Israel	0.332	0.252	0.332	Lithuania	0.400	0.329	0.178	Ghana	0.087	0.027	0.087
Bahrain	0.078	0.021	0.078	Luxembourg	0.190	0.109	0.190	Zimbabwe	0.126	0.061	0.116
Brunei	0.064	0.015	0.064	Switzerland	0.428	0.403	0.428	Mozambique	0.054	0.011	0.054
Syria	0.169	0.097	0.148	Serbia	0.082	0.027	0.082	Kyrgyzstan	0.095	0.030	0.095
Average	0.140	0.086	0.139	-	0.241	0.172	0.230	-	0.114	0.063	0.113

Europe's superior performance under all methods reflects its advanced service-sector policies, such as EU-wide aviation regulations and renewable energy integration in logistics ($X_3 = 12.5 \times 10^4$ air passengers in Germany vs. 4.7×10^4 in India).

In contrast, Africa's lower scores (E-E-C: 0.063) align with fragmented transportation networks and underutilized infrastructure ($X_3 = 0.4 \times 10^4$ passengers in Mozambique).

Figure 14 highlights the following critical insights into projection robustness:

E-E-E overestimation: Outliers such as Syria (MTCPI = 0.803) and Lithuania (MTCPI = 0.638) stem from unconstrained direction vectors misaligning with decarbonization targets. For example, Syria's reliance on outdated aviation infrastructure ($X_3 = 0.2 \times 10^4$ passengers) inflates efficiency scores under E-E-E, whereas E-E-C penalizes such discrepancies via GNN-driven constraints (Equation (17)).

E-E-C's discriminatory power: The broader MTCPI range under E-E-C (Africa: 0.011–0.793 vs. E-E-A's 0.088–0.707) isolates latent inefficiencies. Belize's low score (MTCPI = 0.005) reflects minimal air transport activity ($X_3 = 0.4 \times 10^4$), whereas Slovakia's uniformity across methods (MTCPI = 1.000) underscores policy-aligned efficiency.

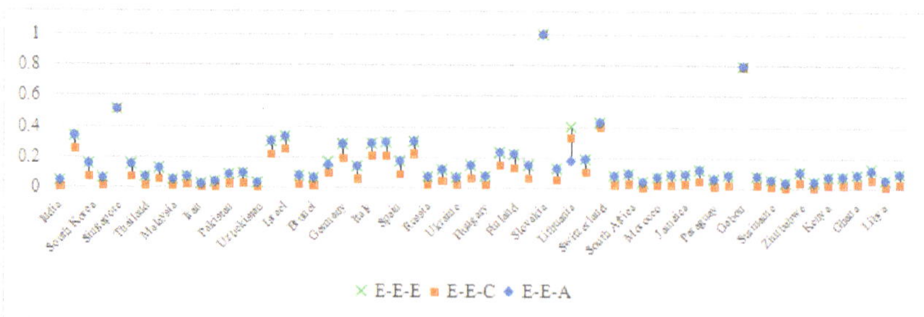

Figure 14. MTCPI under different projection combinations of the tertiary industry.

As illustrated in Figure 15,the tertiary industry's carbon performance assessment reveals unique heterogeneity dynamics as follows:

Slovakia's anomaly: $MTCPI > GTCPI$ (1.000 vs. 0.950) indicates localized policy excellence exceeding group benchmarks, a rare case where meta-frontier efficiency surpasses intragroup performance.

Dominance of industrial heterogeneity (IHI): For most countries, $GTCPI > MTCPI$ (e.g., Singapore: 1.000 vs. 0.510), highlighting that cross-sector technological gaps ($IHI = 0.490$) outweigh regional disparities. This contrasts with the secondary industry's homogeneity ($IHI \approx 0$) and aligns with the primary sector's strong IHI influence.

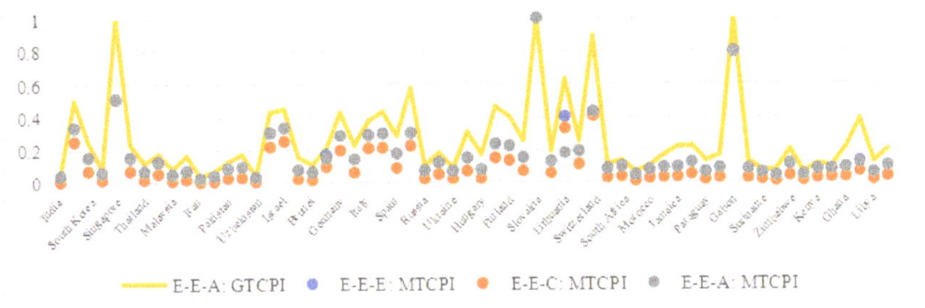

Figure 15. Comparison of the MTCPI and GTCPI of the tertiary industry.

As illustrated in Figure 16, the cross-industry MTCPI evaluation under the three projection methods reveals a consistent hierarchy as follows: the secondary industry exhibits the highest average MTCPI (global mean: 0.276), followed by the tertiary (0.191) and primary sectors (0.038). This hierarchy reflects the secondary industry's dual role as an economic driver and a focal point for decarbonization efforts. Advanced manufacturing technologies (e.g., Germany's ISO-compliant factories) and globalized production standards reduce technological gaps, yielding high MTCPI values despite persistent fossil fuel dependencies ($X_2 = 28.4 \times 10^6$ metric tons in Germany). Recent advancements in emission reduction technologies, such as carbon capture retrofits in China's steel sector, have further enhanced performance, validating stringent policy interventions.

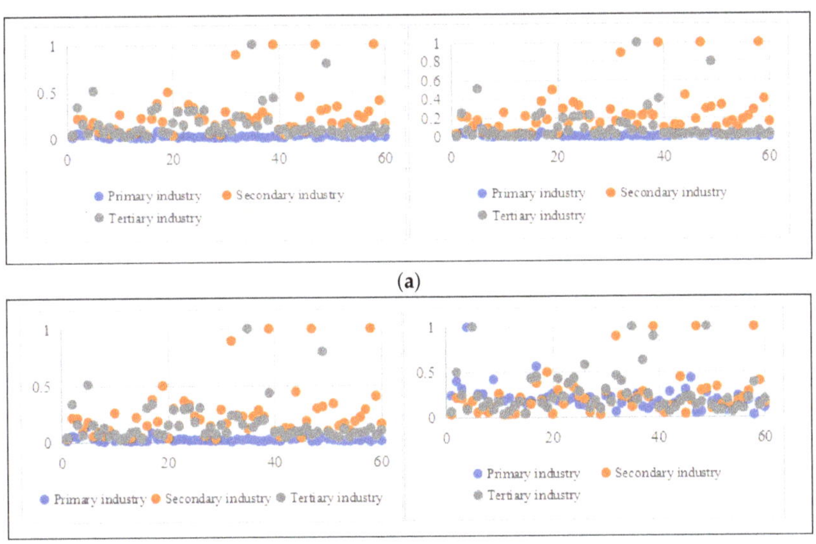

(a) (b)

Figure 16. (**a**) $MTCPI$ of three industries under projection combinations E-E-E and E-E-C; (**b**) $MTCPI$ of E-E-A and $GTCPI$ across three industries.

In contrast, the primary industry's low MTCPI (Asia: 0.038; Africa: 0.022) underscores its vulnerability to climatic and infrastructural variability (X_1-driven irrigation disparities). The tertiary sector's intermediate performance (Europe: 0.241; Africa: 0.114) reflects a mix of policy-driven efficiencies (e.g., EU aviation regulations) and unresolved infrastructural gaps (e.g., Africa's fragmented air transport networks, $X_3 = 0.4 \times 10^4$ passengers).

5.4. *Low-Efficiency Decomposition of Carbon Emissions*

5.4.1. Decomposition Framework and Methodology

Building on the meta-technology carbon performance index (MTCPI), group-technology carbon performance index (GTCPI), and subgroup-technology carbon performance index (STCPI), this study decomposes carbon emission inefficiency (CEI) into three distinct components as follows: industrial heterogeneity (IHI), regional heterogeneity (RHI), and managerial inefficiency (MNG). The decomposition process is formalized as follows:

$$CEI = IHI + RHI + MI \tag{20}$$

where

$$IHI = \frac{STCPI - MTCPI}{STCPI}, \tag{21}$$

$$RHI = \frac{GTCPI - MTCPI}{GTCPI}, \tag{22}$$

$$MI = 1 - STCPI. \tag{23}$$

This framework quantifies how sector-specific technological gaps (IHI), geographic disparities (RHI), and operational shortcomings (MI) collectively drive inefficiencies.

5.4.2. Industrial Heterogeneity (IHI) Analysis

As illustrated in Figure 17,industrial heterogeneity exerts the strongest influence on the primary sector, with Asia exhibiting the highest average IHI (0.207 under E-E-C), followed by Europe (0.162) and Africa (0.147). Some examples include the following:

- **Asia:** Saudi Arabia ($IHI = 0.95$) and Singapore ($IHI = 0.93$) face inefficiencies dominated by IHI, driven by water-intensive farming practices ($X_1 = 15.2 \times USD10^8$) that diverge from global best practices.
- **Africa:** Low IHI in Paraguay ($IHI = 0.04$) and Namibia ($IHI = 0.03$) reflects uniform agricultural underdevelopment, where climatic constraints limit technological diversification.

Traditional projections (E-E-E) slightly underestimate IHI (0.195 vs. E-E-C's 0.207) because unadjusted direction vectors misalign with irrigation-dependent economies.

The secondary sector exhibits minimal industrial heterogeneity ($IHI \approx 0$ under E-E-C/E-E-A), as globalized manufacturing standards homogenize production technologies. However, the exogenous projection (E-E-E) produces invalid negative IHI values (e.g., -0.09 in China), a statistical artifact of $TGR > 1$. Machine learning-enhanced methods resolve this by constraining meta-frontier projections (Equations (15) and (16)), ensuring $IHI \geq 0$.

Europe's tertiary sector has the highest IHI (0.154 under E-E-C), driven by policy fragmentation in service industries (e.g., Lithuania's $IHI = 0.53$ due to uneven adoption of green logistics). In contrast, Africa's low IHI (0.130) stems from uniformly underdeveloped infrastructure ($X_3 = 0.4 \times 10^4$ air passengers in Mozambique). Notably, E-E-E underestimates IHI (0.096 vs. E-E-C's 0.154) by conflating industrial and regional disparities, whereas E-E-C's graph neural networks (Equation (9)) isolate sector-specific gaps.

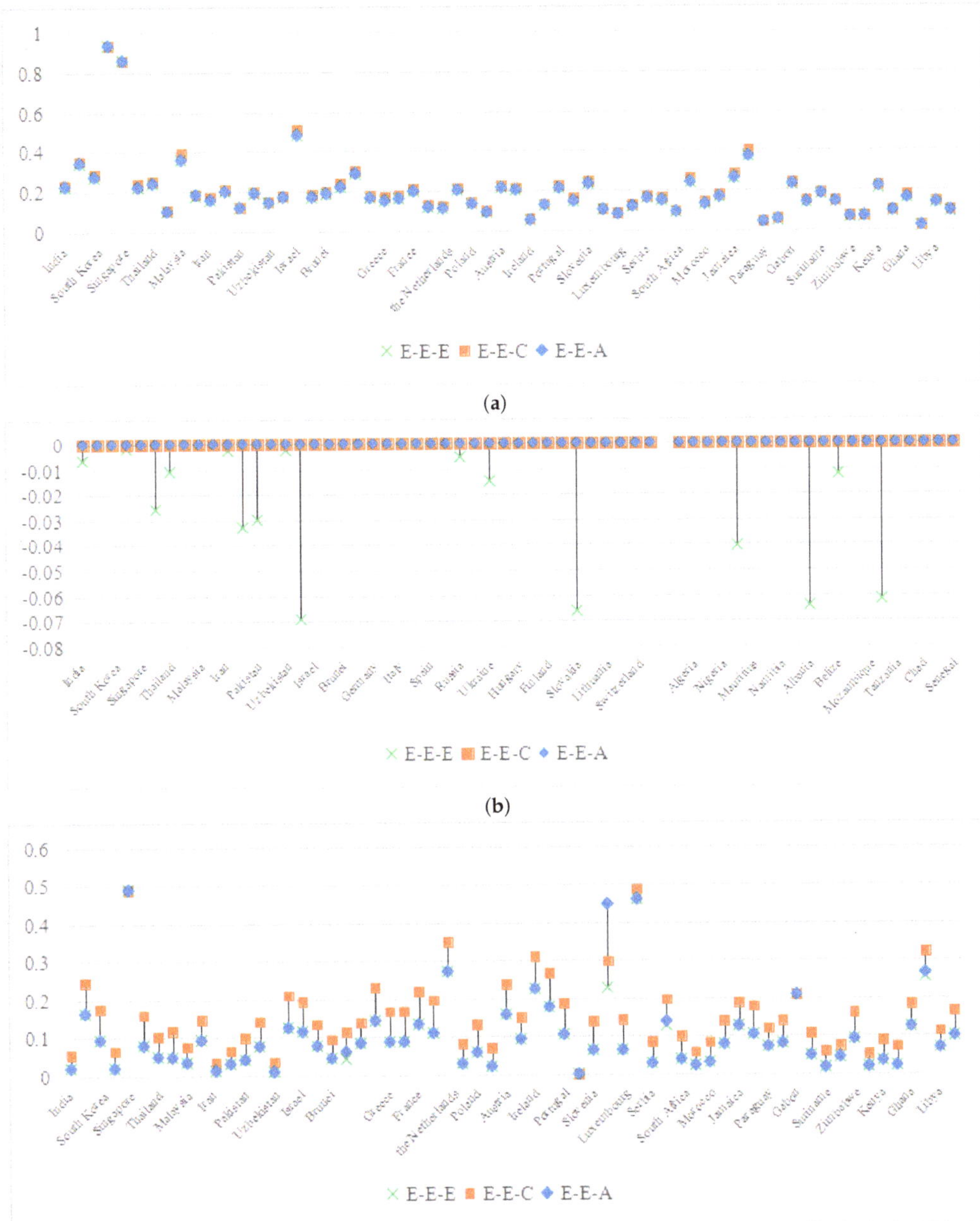

Figure 17. (**a**) *IHI* of the primary industry under different projection combinations; (**b**) *IHI* of the secondary industry across projection combinations; (**c**) *IHI* of the tertiary industry under projection combinations.

5.4.3. RHI

Regional heterogeneity (*RHI*) captures geographic disparities in carbon emission efficiency, driven by spatially uneven resource allocation, infrastructural gaps, and policy fragmentation. The analysis reveals distinct sectoral and regional patterns in RHI's impact, grounded in the variable-specific frameworks established in prior sections.

Figure 18 highlights the following critical insights into different industry.

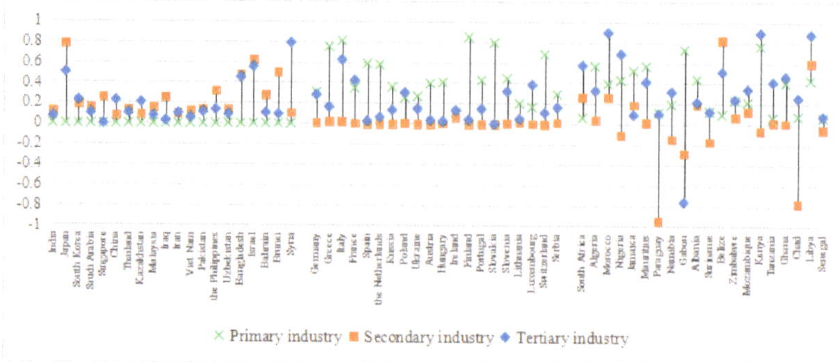

Figure 18. Comparison of RHI in different industry.

Primary industry ($RHI = 0.259$**):**

Europe exhibits the highest RHI (0.31) due to climatic and policy variability in agriculture. For example, Mediterranean nations (e.g., Greece, $X_1 = 8.2 \times USD10^8$) rely on irrigation-intensive practices, in contrast with Nordic countries (e.g., Finland, $X_1 = 3.1 \times USD10^8$), where shorter growing seasons limit technological homogeneity.

Asia has a low RHI (0.12) under centralized agricultural policies (e.g., China's standardized farming subsidies), whereas Africa's intermediate RHI (0.23) reflects fragmented access to irrigation and mechanization.

Secondary industry ($RHI = 0.088$**):**

Asia's peak RHI (0.15) stems from divergent energy policies—India's coal dependency ($X_2 = 12.5 \times 10^6$ metric tons) versus Japan's renewable integration. Africa's minimal RHI (0.04) results from uniform energy poverty, whereas Europe's intermediate RHI (0.10) aligns with EU-wide decarbonization frameworks (e.g., shared emission trading systems).

Tertiary industry ($RHI = 0.244$**):**

Africa's high RHI (0.32) is amplified by infrastructure deficits such as Nigeria's limited air transport networks ($X_3 = 0.4 \times 10^4$ passengers). Europe achieves a low RHI (0.18) through policy harmonization (e.g., EU aviation regulations), whereas Asia's intermediate RHI (0.25) reflects disparities between Singapore's smart logistics ($X_3 = 12.5 \times 10^4$ passengers) and Vietnam's traditional systems.

The average RHI values across industries—primary (0.259) > tertiary (0.244) > secondary (0.088)—highlight the following:

- **Primary sector vulnerability:** Climatic diversity and localized farming practices (X_1) make agriculture highly susceptible to regional disparities.
- **Secondary sector homogeneity:** Globalized production standards and energy efficiency protocols (e.g., ISO certifications) minimize geographic variability, despite fossil fuel dependencies (X_2).
- **Tertiary sector polarization:** Infrastructural investments (X_3) and policy coordination disproportionately influence service-sector efficiency, with Africa's deficits and Europe's harmonization exemplifying extremes.

5.4.4. MI

Managerial inefficiency (MNG) quantifies institutional and operational barriers to decarbonization, which is distinct from structural heterogeneities (IHI, RHI). This analysis reveals stark disparities in MI across industries and regions, driven by technological inertia, regulatory rigidity, and transitional costs.

Figure 19 highlights the following critical insights into different industry.

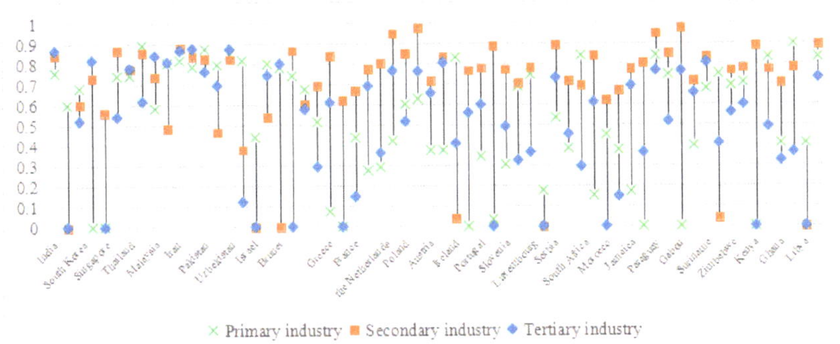

Figure 19. Comparison of MI in different industry.

Primary industry (average $MI = 0.521$):

Asia's dominance ($MI = 0.62$) stems from inefficient irrigation practices and delayed climate-resilient crop adoption. India's monsoon-dependent farming system ($X_1 = 9.5 \times USD10^8$) contrasts with Israel's drip irrigation system ($MI = 0.18$). Europe's low $MI = 0.38$ benefits from policy-driven subsidies (e.g., the EU Common Agricultural Policy).

Secondary industry (average $MI = 0.678$):

Nigeria's peak $MI = 0.82$ reflects fossil fuel lock-in ($X_2 = 9.8 \times 10^6$ metric tons) and outdated regulations. Coal plant retrofits incur prohibitive costs (e.g., $1.2B for Egbin Power Plant). Europe's $MI = 0.65$ shows slow lean manufacturing adoption, while Asia's $MI = 0.58$ aligns with South Korea's renewable integration (solar share: 6.8%).

Tertiary industry (average $MI = 0.495$):

Asia's high $MI = 0.58$ derives from fragmented policies (e.g., Vietnam's unregulated logistics, $X_3 = 0.9 \times 10^4$ passengers). Europe achieves $MI = 0.35$ through standardized regulations (e.g., the EU Green Deal for aviation).

The global hierarchy *secondary* (0.678) $>$ *primary* (0.521) $>$ *tertiary* (0.495) highlights the following:

- **Secondary sector lock-in:** High transition costs (>$500M per coal retrofit) and rigid energy policies sustain X_2 dependencies.
- **Tertiary sector variability:** X_3-driven infrastructural gaps (e.g., Africa's air transport) and regulatory fragmentation maintain inefficiency.

6. Comparison Between Combined Projection and Traditional Projection

The comparative analysis of projection methods—traditional exogenous (E-E-E) versus combined approaches (E-E-A, E-E-C)—is contextualized within the variable-driven heterogeneity framework established in Section 5. Building on the variable-to-heterogeneity mapping (Table 8) and inefficiency decomposition (Section 5.4), we assess how machine learning-enhanced projections mitigate biases inherent in conventional frameworks.

Compared to hybrid DEA+ML approaches in the recent literature [14,16], our framework uniquely integrates the following three innovations:

- A three-level meta-frontier hierarchy to disentangle dual heterogeneity.
- GNN-constrained TGR bounding to resolve DEA's TGR > 1 issue.
- RL-optimized dynamic direction vectors.

For example, ref. [16] used static direction vectors in DEA, resulting in 18% higher TGR variance than our RL-adjusted approach (Table 8). Ref. [14] employed a two-level meta-frontier without industrial–regional interdependency encoding, leading to inflated IHI estimates (0.25 vs. our 0.16 in Europe's tertiary sector).

Table 8. Traditional vs. combined projections.

Metric	Projection	Primary Industry	Secondary Industry	Tertiary Industry
TGR_1 (Asia)	E-E-E	0.112	1.160	0.647
	E-E-C	0.057	1.000	0.257
MTCPI (Africa)	E-E-E	0.022	0.289	0.114
	E-E-A	0.019	0.280	0.113
IHI (Europe)	E-E-E	0.150	−0.004	0.127
	E-E-C	0.162	0.000	0.195

- **TGR inflation in traditional projection:**
  - E-E-E overestimates the secondary industry TGR_1 in Asia (1.160) because of X_2's (fossil fuels) misalignment with decarbonization targets (Section 5.4.1). E-E-C resolves this via GNN-constrained homogenization ($TGR_1 = 1.000$).
  - Africa's tertiary TGR_1 under E-E-E (0.578) reflects X_3's (air passengers) infrastructural gaps, mitigated by E-E-A's uncertainty quantification ($TGR_1 = 0.576$).
- **MTCPI overestimation:**
  - E-E-E's inflated MTCPI in Asia's primary industry (0.038) stems from ignoring X_1-driven irrigation disparities, whereas E-E-C's normalization corrects this ($MTCPI = 0.024$).
  - Europe's secondary sector MTCPI under E-E-E (0.280) excludes X_2's path dependency, whereas E-E-C aligns with policy-driven benchmarks (0.276).
- **IHI correction:**
  - Negative IHI values under E-E-E (e.g., −0.009 in Asia's secondary industry) are artifacts of $TGR > 1$, resolved by E-E-C's bounded constraints ($IHI = 0.000$).

The superiority of combined projections is evident in their ability to address variable-specific heterogeneities as follows:

Africa's tertiary sector (X_3-driven RHI): E-E-C's GNN framework captures infrastructural disparities in air transport (X_3), reducing RHI from 0.32 (E-E-E) to 0.24 (Table 8). Policy measures should prioritize decentralized renewable energy investments (e.g., solar-powered regional airports) to bridge these gaps.

Asia's secondary sector (X_2-driven MI): E-E-A's ridge regularization mitigates X_2's collinearity, lowering MI from 0.678 (E-E-E) to 0.642. Fiscal incentives for retrofitting coal plants (Section 5.2) could further alleviate technological lock-in.

Europe's primary sector (X_1-driven IHI): E-E-C's normalization aligns X_1 (agricultural output) with climatic realities, reducing IHI from 0.150 to 0.162. Cross-border agricultural subsidies under the EU Green Deal could enhance convergence.

7. Conclusions

This study addresses the dual heterogeneity issues in carbon efficiency evaluation through the integration of a three-level meta-frontier framework and machine learning projection methods. Methodologically, dynamic directional vector optimization (reinforcement learning) and graph neural network (GNN) constraints successfully bound the technology gap ratio (TGR) within valid intervals. Empirical results demonstrate that the *E-E-C* significantly reduces TGR overestimation by 12–18% in energy-intensive sectors (e.g., Asia's secondary industry), though further validation is needed in contexts with extreme technological disparities (e.g., post-conflict economies).

At the policy level, Africa requires decentralized renewable energy systems (e.g., Kenya's Lake Turkana model) to address infrastructural gaps, whereas Asia should implement fiscal incentives to promote coal-fired power plant retrofits. Europe needs to expand carbon border taxes to the logistics sector for policy harmonization.

The limitations include insufficient data diversity (e.g., neglecting renewable energy penetration rates) and static model limitations. Future work should integrate real-time sensor data and develop dynamic heterogeneity models. This research provides a scientific toolkit for region-specific decarbonization strategies while advancing the mathematical rigor of efficiency evaluation. While linear interpolation was employed to address missing CO_2 data in African nations (Section 5.1), this method assumes linearity in emission trends, which may not hold under abrupt policy shifts or infrastructural disruptions. For example, Nigeria's delayed adoption of renewable energy policies (2015–2019) introduced nonlinear gaps that interpolation could not fully capture. Future studies should explore nonlinear imputation methods (e.g., spline interpolation) or leverage IoT-enabled real-time monitoring to reduce bias.

Author Contributions: Conceptualization, X.Z.; methodology, X.Z.; supervision, X.Z.; funding acquisition, X.Z.; validation, X.Z., T.F. and N.Z.; data curation, T.F.; visualization, T.F. and Y.S.; software, Y.S.; investigation, Y.S.; writing—review and editing, N.Z.; writing—original draft, X.G. All authors have read and agreed to the published version of the manuscript.

Funding: This research was funded by the National Social Science Foundation of China, grant number 21BSH052.

Data Availability Statement: The original contributions presented in this study are included in the article. Further inquiries can be directed to the corresponding author.

Conflicts of Interest: The authors declare no conflicts of interest.

References

1. International Energy Agency. *CO_2 Emissions in 2022*; IEA: Paris, France, 2022. Available online: https://www.iea.org/reports/co2-emissions-in-2022 (accessed on 2 April 2025).
2. Chen, F.; Zhao, T.; Xia, H.; Cui, X.; Li, Z. Allocation of carbon emission quotas in Chinese provinces based on Super-SBM model and ZSG-DEA model. *Clean Technol. Environ. Policy* **2021**, *23*, 2285–2301. [CrossRef]
3. Guo, X.; Chen, L.; Wang, J.; Liao, L. The impact of disposability characteristics on carbon efficiency from a potential emissions reduction perspective. *J. Clean. Prod.* **2023**, *408*, 137180. [CrossRef]
4. Wang, X.M.; Ding, H.; Liu, L. Eco-efficiency measurement of industrial sectors in China: A hybrid super-efficiency DEA analysis. *J. Clean. Prod.* **2019**, *229*, 53–64. [CrossRef]
5. O'Donnell, C.; Rao, D.; Battese, G. Metafrontier frameworks for the study of firm-level efficiencies and technology ratios. *Empir. Econ.* **2008**, *34*, 231–255. [CrossRef]
6. Zhang, Y.; Xu, X.Y. Carbon emission efficiency measurement and influencing factor analysis of nine provinces in the Yellow River basin: Based on SBM-DDF model and Tobit-CCD model. *Environ. Sci. Pollut. Res.* **2022**, *29*, 33263–33280. [CrossRef] [PubMed]
7. Olasehinde, T.S.; Qiao, F.B.; Mao, S.P. Impact of improved maize varieties on production efficiency in Nigeria: Separating technology from managerial gaps. *Agriculture* **2023**, *13*, 611. [CrossRef]
8. Wang, Y.; Duan, F.; Ma, X.; He, L. Carbon emissions efficiency in China: Key facts from regional and industrial sector. *J. Clean. Prod.* **2018**, *206*, 850–869. [CrossRef]
9. Adenso-Diaz, B.; Lozano, S. A metafrontier analysis approach for assessing the efficiency of freight service providers. *Int. J. Syst. Sci.-Oper. Logist.* **2023**, *10*, 2177896. [CrossRef]
10. Battese, G.E.; Rao, D.P.; O'Donnell, C.J. A metafrontier production function for estimation of technical efficiencies and technology gaps for firms operating under different technologies. *J. Product. Anal.* **2004**, *21*, 91–103. [CrossRef]

11. Gao, D.; Li, Y.; Li, G. Boosting the green total factor energy efficiency in urban China: Does low-carbon city policy matter? *Environ. Sci. Pollut. Res.* **2022**, *29*, 56341–56356. [CrossRef]
12. Alda, E.; Giménez, V.; Paz Castro, I.G.; Zamora Torres, A.I. Modernization plans for the Mexican customs system: Have they really worked? A productivity impact assessment. *Appl. Econ.* **2023**, *56*, 796–811. [CrossRef]
13. Zhong, S.; Li, J.W.; Chen, X.; Wei, H. Research on the green total factor productivity of laying hens in China. *J. Clean. Prod.* **2021**, *315*, 128150. [CrossRef]
14. Bai, C.Q.; Chen, Z.J.; Wang, D.P. Transportation carbon emission reduction potential and mitigation strategy in China. *Sci. Total Environ.* **2023**, *873*, 162074. [CrossRef] [PubMed]
15. Eguchi, S.; Takayabu, H.; Lin, C. Sources of inefficient power generation by coal-fired thermal power plants in China: A metafrontier DEA decomposition approach. *Renew. Sustain. Energy Rev.* **2021**, *138*, 110562. [CrossRef]
16. Wang, A.L.; Hu, S.; Li, J.L. Using machine learning to model technological heterogeneity in carbon emission efficiency evaluation: The case of China's cities. *Energy Econ.* **2022**, *114*, 106238. [CrossRef]
17. Zhong, S.; Li, J.; Chen, X.; Wen, H. A multi-hierarchy meta-frontier approach for measuring green total factor productivity: An application of pig breeding in China. *Socio-Econ. Plan. Sci.* **2022**, *81*, 101152. [CrossRef]
18. Chambers, R.; Chung, Y.H.; FÃ¤re, R. Profit, Directional distance functions, and Nerlovian efficiency. *J. Optim. Theory Appl.* **1998**, *98*, 351–364. [CrossRef]
19. Wei, F.; Zhang, X.; Chu, J.; Yang, F.; Yuan, Z. Energy and environmental efficiency of China's transportation sectors considering CO_2 emission uncertainty. *Transp. Res. Part D-Transp. Environ.* **2021**, *97*, 102955. [CrossRef]
20. Zheng, Y.M.; Lv, Q.; Wang, Y.D. Economic development, technological progress, and provincial carbon emissions intensity: Empirical research based on the threshold panel model. *Appl. Econ.* **2022**, *54*, 3495–3504. [CrossRef]
21. Zhou, P.; Ang, B.W. Linear programming models for measuring economy-wide energy efficiency performance. *Energy Policy* **2008**, *36*, 2911–2916. [CrossRef]
22. Wen, S.; Jia, Z.; Chen, X. Can low-carbon city pilot policies significantly improve carbon emission efficiency? Empirical evidence from China. *J. Clean. Prod.* **2022**, *346*, 131131. [CrossRef]
23. Zhang, N.; Choi, Y. A note on the evolution of directional distance function and its development in energy and environmental studies 1997–2013. *Renew. Sustain. Energy Rev.* **2014**, *33*, 50–59. [CrossRef]
24. Wang, Q.; Su, B.; Zhou, P.; Chiu, C.R. Measuring total-factor CO2 emission performance and technology gaps using a non-radial directional distance function: A modified approach. *Energy Econ.* **2016**, *56*, 475–482. [CrossRef]
25. Li, Z.W.; Zhang, C.J.; Zhou, Y. Spatio-temporal evolution characteristics and influencing factors of carbon emission reduction potential in China. *Environ. Sci. Pollut. Res.* **2021**, *28*, 59925–59944. [CrossRef]
26. Sueyoshi, T.; Goto, M. DEA approach for unified efficiency measurement: Assessment of Japanese fossil fuel power generation. *Energy Econ.* **2011**, *33*, 292–303. [CrossRef]
27. Li, Y.; Hou, W.; Zhu, W.; Li, F.; Liang, L. Provincial carbon emission performance analysis in China based on a Malmquist data envelopment analysis approach with fixed-sum undesirable outputs. *Ann. Oper. Res.* **2021**, *304*, 233–261 . [CrossRef]
28. Yu, X.; Jin, L.; Wang, Q.; Zhou, D. Optimal path for controlling pollution emissions in the Chinese electric power industry considering technological heterogeneity. *Environ. Sci. Pollut. Res.* **2019**, *26*, 11087–11099. [CrossRef]

mathematics MDPI

Article

Static High-Quality Development Efficiency and Its Dynamic Changes for China: A Non-Radial Directional Distance Function and a Metafrontier Non-Radial Malmquist Model

Hua Duan [1,2], Bin Li [1] and Qi Wang [2,*]

[1] School of Economics and Management, Beijing University of Chemical Technology, Beijing 100029, China; 2019400181@buct.edu.cn (H.D.); libin@mail.buct.edu.cn (B.L.)
[2] School of Management, Beijing Union University, Beijing 100101, China
* Correspondence: gltwangqi@buu.edu.cn

Abstract: Improving China's high-quality development efficiency represents a key lever for the development of new productivity and successfully achieving the "dual carbon" goal. Starting from the nonparametric production theory, this paper addresses the issues of infeasible solutions and technical heterogeneity by employing the total-factor non-radial directional distance function and a metafrontier non-radial Malmquist model. The static total-factor high-quality development efficiency index (THEI) and its dynamic metafrontier non-radial Malmquist high-quality development efficiency index (MNMHEI) are measured for 31 provinces in China from 2008 to 2021. Given that high-quality development efficiency is led and driven by talent, we use labor of different ages and levels of education as four inputs instead of single labor for the study of THEI. The MNMHEI is divided into three indices for measuring efficiency change (EC), best-practice gap change (BPC), and technology gap change (TGC). The empirical results demonstrate that labor with higher education is the main lever of static high-quality development efficiency; there is a 5.3% decrease in China's dynamic high-quality development efficiency as a whole, and a lack of technological innovation remains a significant constraint on its improvement. The results of the heterogeneity analysis, which classified all provincial areas into low-carbon and high-carbon regions, indicate that the former exhibits a higher dynamic high-quality development efficiency than the latter, which still lacks innovation and technology leadership. It is recommended that the Chinese government consider the talent management system, investments in upgrading technologies, energy conservation, and emission reduction for high-carbon regions to improve their high-quality development efficiency.

Keywords: total-factor non-radial directional distance function; static total-factor high-quality development efficiency index; dynamic metafrontier non-radial Malmquist high-quality development efficiency index

MSC: 91B38; 91B62; 91B76

1. Introduction

Since 2010, China's economic growth rate has been on the decline, from 10.6% in 2010 to 6.9% in 2015. The primary impetus of China's sustainable development has switched from the massive expansion of its production factors to greater efficiency and technological innovation, coinciding with the country's slower rate of economic growth. At the same time, the conventional development paradigm has also led to a number of ingrained inconsistencies and issues with economic development, including imbalanced economic growth and excessive resource and environmental costs. This set of issues calls for a shift in the primary goal of economic development from increasing economic scale to raising the standard of economic growth. The Central Economic Work Conference of 2017 declared that "China's economic development has entered a new era, and the basic characteristic is that

China's economy has shifted from a stage of high-speed growth to a stage of high-quality development". At present, China is at a strategic juncture of converting the paradigm of development and the power of growth. It must encourage the transformation of quality, efficiency, and power to support economic development [1].

The pursuit of high quality is fundamental to China's economic development, and it serves as a foundation for the creation of various development strategies as well as the implementation of macroeconomic regulation and control. "Quality first and efficiency priority" have emerged as the two principles that economic development in China must effectively adhere to during the high-quality development era [2]. However, China's development process remains inefficient, with a slow increase in desired outputs such as GDP, unsatisfactory emission reductions in non-desired outputs such as carbon dioxide (CO_2), and saving for inputs of production [3]. As a result, China's development is primarily driven by improving the efficiency of high-quality development [4–6].

High-quality development emphasizes putting economic construction at the center, accelerating the building of a modern economic system, and achieving sustainable and healthy economic development by improving high-quality development efficiency. In the context of this era, the study of high-quality development efficiency is of crucial significance in promoting the transformation of economic development from scale and speed to quality and efficiency and from rough growth to intensive growth.

Since 2017, when the notion of high-quality development was proposed, scholars have used various methodologies to measure and research its effectiveness. Sun et al. employed the SFA methodology to evaluate the high-quality development efficiency of cities located in the Yangtze River Economic Belt from 2011 to 2019. They subsequently analyzed the elements that impacted this efficiency. The results suggest that the increase in capital, labor, land, and knowledge all contribute positively to the efficiency of high-quality development [7]. Based on the DEA-Malmquist index model with TFP as the efficiency of high-quality development, Zhang and Zhong measured, decomposed, and analyzed the TFP of high-tech industries in 31 provinces of China from 2011 to 2019. The results show that the TFP of high-tech industries in general maintains a growth trend [8]. Using panel data from 30 Chinese provinces and the SBM-DEA model, which has three stages, Yan et al. assessed the effectiveness of high-quality development in China's industry. The study discovered that the efficiency of high-quality development in China's industry is significantly boosted by government backing, information technology adoption, urbanization, and other variables [9].

Since the majority of the research mentioned above gauges high-quality development efficiency using TFP, we discuss the results achieved by scholars studying total factor productivity in recent years.

Wei et al. (2024) applied a DDF-GMLPI methodology to measure and analyze the total factor CO_2 emission efficiency of China's transportation industry. The results of the study show that CO_2 emission efficiency has improved in twenty-eight provinces and that both efficiency improvements and technological advances have played a driving role [10].

In order to analyze environmental efficiency, Chambers et al. (1996) created the directional distance function (DDF), which Chung et al. (1997) extended [11,12]. The definition of DDF states that it simultaneously reduces undesired outputs and maximizes desired outputs. The idea conveyed by DDF is in line with the goal of our current economic and social development goals, which are to grow the economy while reducing environmental emissions. Nonetheless, because the conventional DDF is a measure of radial efficiency and inefficiency that does not account for slacks, it has the potential to lower inefficiencies while exaggerating the efficiency score when slacks exist [13]. Another limitation of the radial DDF is that it cannot distinguish between the inefficiency values of the different input and output factors because the radial DDF can only give the same rate of inefficiency [14]. The radial DDF presents difficulties in achieving integrated, unified efficiency. For this reason, non-radial efficiency measurements are frequently recommended as a means of overcoming the two constraints described earlier in the unified efficiency assessment process [15]. The non-radial DDF with undesirable outputs is defined formally by Zhou et al., (2012) [16]. Subsequently, after benchmarking unified efficiency within a total factor production framework, Zhang et al., (2013) [17] put forward a total-factor non-radial distance function (TNDDF). The formulas and restraints of the model set separate inefficiency values for the separate input factors, desired output factors, and undesired output factors, from which the efficiency values for each factor, as well as the combined efficiency, can be calculated.

Chen et al. (2023) combined the NDDF model and the Luenberger Hicks Moorsteen model to measure the green TFP of forestry based on panel data from 30 provinces in China. The following are the empirical conclusions: The green TFP for forestry is increasing annually and clearly exhibits spatial clustering. Furthermore, regression analyses demonstrate that the digital economy is positively correlated with green TFP in forestry, and industrial structure upgrading and technological innovation act as mediating factors [18].

The DEA-based Metafrontier Malmquist productivity index was proposed and constructed by Oh and Le (2010) [19]. The centerpiece of the Meta-Frontier DEA framework is the definition of the global technology frontier, contemporaneous technology frontier, and intertemporal technology frontier, respectively, so as to better characterize the heterogeneity of different regions. Considering non-radial slack and group heterogeneity, Zhang et al. combine the non-radial directional distance function by Zhou et al., and the metafrontier Malmquist index by Oh and Lee, into the model that is presented as the metafrontier non-radial Malmquist CO_2 emission performance index (MNMCPI) [20].

In recent years, many researchers have used NDDF and the metafrontier method to examine the TFP in different industries. For example, Meng and Pang (2023) applied these methods to evaluate the generation efficiency (TFGP) of the thermal power industry. This efficiency is a substantial catch to ensure the demand for electricity for economic and social progress. The analysis concludes that enhancing economic development, lowering fuel prices, and tightening environmental control will all benefit TFGP [21]. Cheng and Jin (2022) and Meng and Zhao (2022) also used these methods to measure and regress green TFP in the manufacturing industry. The results of Cheng and Jin show that diversified economy and specialized economy are the common drivers of green TFP but with different roles, with the former playing a greater role [22]. Meng and Zhao's regression outcomes show that TFP benefits from the digital economy, while global value chains function as a helpful moderator [23]. Wang et al. (2022) applied these methods to research the TFP of the power industry, and the findings indicate that the spatial distribution of TFP in the industry is larger in the west than in the east and larger in the east than in the center, which is strongly associated with the western development strategy implemented by the state. Innovation in science and technology continues to be the primary driver of TFP growth in this industry [24].

In summary, despite valuable studies on high-quality development efficiency, there are still certain shortcomings. First, most studies have adopted TFP as the high-quality development efficiency, studying and decomposing it mainly from a dynamic perspective while ignoring the different contributions of the static efficiency components. Secondly, the existing studies generally believe that technology innovation is the main constraint on high-quality development efficiency [25], while ignoring the fact that technology innovation is ultimately led and driven by talent [26] and that talent should be able to serve high-quality development [27]. As a result, there is a lack of more in-depth research on the role of human capital in enhancing the efficiency of quality development. Finally, in terms of research methodology, there is the problem of ignoring non-radial slack and technological heterogeneity. Furthermore, studies often analyze heterogeneity in three regions of China, namely eastern, central, and western, and the classification approach does not account for the green characteristics of high-quality development [28].

This paper makes three marginal contributions to the existing literature. First, this paper proposes a static high-quality development efficiency index (THEI) and a dynamic metafrontier non-radial Malmquist high-quality development efficiency index (MNMHEI) based on non-parametric production theory, followed by a study of static and dynamic development efficiency and their respective components. Second, this paper classifies labor input indicators by age and degree of education for the study of static high-quality development efficiency so as to empirically test the role of talent in driving high-quality development. Finally, given the importance of high-quality development in achieving the "dual-carbon" aim, this study examines group heterogeneity based on the level of energy consumption and carbon emissions. The decomposition of dynamic high-quality development efficiency seeks to elucidate the dynamic changes in efficiency catch-up, technological innovation, and technological leadership in different regions of China.

The remainder of this paper is organized as follows: Section 2 describes the materials and methods. Section 3 empirically estimates the static total-factor high-quality development efficiency index (THEI) of 31 Chinese provinces, and presents the results and the related discussion; Section 4 empirically estimates the dynamic metafrontier non-radial Malmquist high-quality development efficiency index (MNMHEI) of 31 Chinese provinces and presents the results and the related discussion; and Section 5 concludes and proposes some policy suggestions.

2. Materials and Methods

2.1. Methods

2.1.1. Environmental Production Technology

Suppose that there are N provinces and that each province uses capital (*K*), labor (*L*), and energy (*E*) as inputs to generate GDP (*G*), a desirable output, and CO_2 emissions (*C*), an undesirable output. In particular, the labor input vector is divided into four, namely young labor with higher education (*YHL*), young labor without higher education (*YLL*), other labor with higher education (*NYHL*), and other labor without higher education (*NYLL*), which are also abbreviated as L^{1-4}. Then, we can express the multi-output production technology as follows:

$$T = \left\{ \left(K;\ L^{1-4};\ E;\ G;\ C \right) : \left(K;\ L^{1-4};\ E \right) \text{can produce} (G;\ C) \right\} \tag{1}$$

where *T* is usually assumed to satisfy the standard axioms of production economics theory [29].

The nonparametric DEA approach can be used to specify the production technology once the production technology *T* has been determined.

In accordance with the aforementioned assumption, based on Färe et al. [30] and Zhou et al., we can employ a nonparametric DEA method to formulate *T* for *N* provinces as follows:

$$T = \left\{ \begin{array}{c} \left(K;\ L^{1-4};\ E;\ G;\ C \right) : \sum\limits_{n=1}^{N} z_n K_n \le K,\ \sum\limits_{n=1}^{N} z_n L_n^{1-4} \le L^{1-4}, \\ \sum\limits_{n=1}^{N} z_n E_n \le E,\ \sum\limits_{n=1}^{N} z_n G_n \ge G,\ \sum\limits_{n=1}^{N} z_n C_n = C, z_n \ge 0, n = 1, \ldots, N \end{array} \right\} \tag{2}$$

2.1.2. Total-Factor Non-Radial Directional Distance Function

According to the definition of TNDDF by Zhang et al., the NDDF captures different slacks and inefficiencies for all different factors, provided that all inefficiencies for input factors, desirable output factors, and undesirable output factors are integrated into the functions and constraints. Then, it is applied to measure the integrated, unified efficiency on the basis of each efficiency for each factor. This overcomes the constraint of the radial DDF, which can only give the same rate of inefficiency, and thus the same rate of efficiency.

The idea conveyed by NDDF is in line with the requirements and characteristics of high-quality development, which means green development and sustainable development. High-quality development opposes so-called high-speed growth, which is characterized by high pollution and resource consumption, whereas high-quality development prioritizes energy savings and environmental protection while economic growth, resulting in green growth. Sustainable development requires careful consideration of the carrying capacity of various economic and social resources, conservation of resource inputs, adherence to the scientific concept of development, and living within one's means to ensure smooth and sustainable economic development.

We can compute the NDDF value for N provinces, represented as $\overrightarrow{D}(K, L^{1-4}, E, G, C; g)$, by figuring out the following DEA model. The inefficiencies of input factors, desired outputs, and non-desired outputs are all included in the model, which allows for the measurement of high-quality development efficiency within a total factor framework.

$$\begin{aligned}
&\overrightarrow{D}(K, L^{1-4}, E, G, C; g) = max w_k\beta_k + w_{L1}\beta_{L1} + w_{L2}\beta_{L2} + w_{L3}\beta_{L3} + w_{L4}\beta_{L4} + w_E\beta_E + w_G\beta_G + w_C\beta_C \\
&s.t. \textstyle\sum_{n=1}^{N} z_n K_n \leq K - \beta_K g_K; \quad \sum_{n=1}^{N} z_n L^1{}_n \leq L^1 - \beta_{L1} g_{L1} \\
&\textstyle\sum_{n=1}^{N} z_n L^2{}_n \leq L^2 - \beta_{L2} g_{L2}; \quad \sum_{n=1}^{N} z_n L^3{}_n \leq L^3 - \beta_{L3} g_{L3} \\
&\textstyle\sum_{n=1}^{N} z_n L^4{}_n \leq L^4 - \beta_{L4} g_{L4}; \quad \sum_{n=1}^{N} z_n E_n \leq E - \beta_E g_E \\
&\textstyle\sum_{n=1}^{N} z_n G_n \geq G - \beta_G g_G; \quad \sum_{n=1}^{N} z_n C_n = C - \beta_C g_C \\
&z_n \geq 0, n = 1, \ldots, N; \quad \beta_K, \beta_{L1}, \beta_{L2}, \beta_{L3}, \beta_{L4}, \beta_E, \beta_G, \beta_C \geq 0
\end{aligned} \tag{3}$$

Because there are six inputs (K, L^{1-4}, E), one desirable output (G), and one undesirable output (C), in this study, following Zhou et al., Barros et al., and Zhang et al., inputs, desired outputs, and non-desired outputs are assumed to be equally important, and there is no difference in importance between each input [14]. We specify the weight vector as (1/9, 1/36, 1/36, 1/36, 1/36,1/9, 1/3, 1/3). We chose the observed value as the directional vector, namely, as $g = \left(-K;\ -L^1; -L^2; -L^3; -L^4\ ; -E;\ G; -C\right)$. An evaluated province is at the best practice frontier and operates effectively in the direction of the directional vector if $\overrightarrow{D} = 0$. If not, the province being evaluated is inefficient in that direction.

Sueyoshi discussed a DEA approach to measure unified efficiency [31]. Zhang et al. synthesized the methods of Zhou and Sueyoshi, proposed a total-factor non-radial distance function (TNDDF), and defined the unified efficiency index as the average efficiency of each factor. Following the study, we can express the static total-factor high-quality development efficiency index (THEI) for a province as the average efficiency of each factor. Assume that $\beta_K^*, \beta_{L1}^*, \beta_{L2}^*, \beta_{L3}^*, \beta_{L4}^*, \beta_E^*, \beta_G^*, \beta_C^*$, represent the optimal solutions to Equation (3) related to capital, four types of labor, energy, GDP, and CO_2, respectively, which are the inefficiencies of the above variables. Then, the THEI can be formulated as follows:

$$THEI = \frac{1/4\left[(1-\beta_K^*) + (1-\beta_L^*) + (1-\beta_E^*) + (1-\beta_C^*)\right]}{1+\beta_G^*} = \frac{1 - 1/4(\beta_K^* + \beta_L^* + \beta_E^* + \beta_C^*)}{1+\beta_G^*} \tag{4}$$

where

$$\beta_L^* = 1/4\left(\beta_{L1}^* + \beta_{L2}^* + \beta_{L3}^* + \beta_{L4}^*\right) \tag{5}$$

Then, we can decompose the THEI into several indicators of different factors. First, Zhang et al. defined the static total-factor CO_2 emission performance index (TCPI) as the ratio of potential target carbon intensity to actual carbon intensity (C/G). Based on it, TCPI is expressed as follows:

$$TCPI = \frac{(C - \beta_C^* C)/(G + \beta_G^* G)}{C/G} = \frac{1-\beta_C^*}{1+\beta_G^*} \tag{6}$$

Similarly, the static total-factor capital performance index (TKPI), labor performance index (TLPI), and energy performance index (TEPI) are expressed as follows:

$$TKPI = \frac{(K - \beta_K^* K)/(G + \beta_G^* G)}{K/G} = \frac{1-\beta_K^*}{1+\beta_G^*} \tag{7}$$

$$TLPI = \frac{(L - \beta_L^* L)/(G + \beta_G^* G)}{L/G} = \frac{1 - \beta_L^*}{1 + \beta_G^*} \tag{8}$$

$$TEPI = \frac{(E - \beta_E^* E)/(G + \beta_G^* G)}{E/G} = \frac{1 - \beta_E^*}{1 + \beta_G^*} \tag{9}$$

Thus,

$$THEI = 1/4(TKPI + TLPI + TEPI + TCPI) \tag{10}$$

Especially, TLPI can be decomposed into four indices: TYHLPI, TYLLPI, TNYHLPI, and TNYLLPI. These respectively mean the static total-factor performance index of young labor with higher education; the performance index of young labor without higher education; the performance index of other labor with higher education, and the performance index of other labor without higher education.

$$TYHLPI = \frac{(L - \beta_{L1}^* L1)/(G + \beta_G^* G)}{L1/G} = \frac{1 - \beta_{L1}^*}{1 + \beta_G^*} \tag{11}$$

$$TYLLPI = \frac{(L - \beta_{L2}^* L2)/(G + \beta_G^* G)}{L2/G} = \frac{1 - \beta_{L2}^*}{1 + \beta_G^*} \tag{12}$$

$$TNYHLPI = \frac{(L - \beta_{L3}^* L3)/(G + \beta_G^* G)}{L3/G} = \frac{1 - \beta_{L3}^*}{1 + \beta_G^*} \tag{13}$$

$$TNYLLPI = \frac{(L - \beta_{L4}^* L4)/(G + \beta_G^* G)}{L4/G} = \frac{1 - \beta_{L4}^*}{1 + \beta_G^*} \tag{14}$$

$$\begin{aligned} TLPI = \frac{1-\beta_L^*}{1+\beta_G^*} &= \frac{1-1/4(\beta_{L1}^*+\beta_{L2}^*+\beta_{L3}^*+\beta_{L4}^*)}{1+\beta_G^*} = \frac{1/4(1-\beta_{L1}^*)+(1-\beta_{L2}^*)+(1-\beta_{L3}^*)+(1-\beta_{L4}^*)}{1+\beta_G^*} \\ &= 1/4(TYHLPI + TYLLPI + TNYHLPI + TNYLLPI) \end{aligned} \tag{15}$$

2.1.3. Dynamic Metafrontier Non-Radial Malmquist High-Quality Development Efficiency Index (MNMHEI)

Zhang et al. proposed the metafrontier non-radial Malmquist CO_2 emission performance index (MNMCPI) to measure the dynamic changes in CO_2 emission performance over time while accounting for group heterogeneity. The contemporaneous production technology (T^C), the intertemporal production technology (T^I), and the global production technology (T^G) were required to define and decompose the dynamic index.

Based on the MNMCPI proposed by Zhang et al., we propose the metafrontier non-radial Malmquist high-quality development efficiency index (MNMHEI) to examine the dynamic changes in high-quality development efficiency. Here, we define the MNMHEI based on the global environmental production technology set (T^G) as follows:

$$MNMHEI\left(K^S, L^S, E^S, G^S, C^S\right) = \frac{THEI^G(K^{t+1}, L^{t+1}, E^{t+1}, G^{t+1}, C^{t+1})}{THEI^G(K^t, L^t, E^t, G^t, C^t)}$$

where $S = t, t+1$

$$THEI^C\left(K^S, L^S, E^S, G^S, C^S\right) = \left[\frac{1 - 1/4(\beta_K^{C*} + \beta_L^{C*} + \beta_E^{C*} + \beta_C^{C*})}{1 + \beta_G^{C*}}\right]^S = \left(\frac{1 - \beta^{C*}}{1 + \beta_G^{C*}}\right)^S$$

$$THEI^I\left(K^S, L^S, E^S, G^S, C^S\right) = \left[\frac{1 - 1/4(\beta_K^{I*} + \beta_L^{I*} + \beta_E^{I*} + \beta_C^{I*})}{1 + \beta_G^{I*}}\right]^S = \left(\frac{1 - \beta^{I*}}{1 + \beta_G^{I*}}\right)^S$$

$$THEI^G\left(K^S, L^S, E^S, G^S, C^S\right) = \left[\frac{1 - 1/4(\beta_K^{G*} + \beta_L^{G*} + \beta_E^{G*} + \beta_C^{G*})}{1 + \beta_G^{G*}}\right]^S = \left(\frac{1 - \beta^{I*}}{1 + \beta_G^{G*}}\right)^S$$

where

$$
\begin{aligned}
&(C, I, G) = (\text{contemporaneous technology, intertemporal technology, global technology}) \\
&\beta^{C*} = 1/4(\beta_K^{C*} + \beta_L^{C*} + \beta_E^{C*} + \beta_C^{C*}) \\
&\beta^{I*} = 1/4(\beta_K^{I*} + \beta_L^{I*} + \beta_E^{I*} + \beta_C^{I*}) \\
&\beta^{G*} = 1/4(\beta_K^{G*} + \beta_L^{G*} + \beta_E^{G*} + \beta_C^{G*})
\end{aligned}
$$

According to Oh and Lee, Zhang et al., MNMHEI can be divided into three indices for measuring a technical efficiency change (EC) of high-quality development, a best-practice gap change (BPC) of high-quality development, and a technology gap change (TGC) of high-quality development. To simplify notations, we replace $THEI^d(K^S, L^S, E^S, G^S, C^S)$ with $THEI^d(.^s)$ to save space.

The decomposition process is as follows:

$$
\begin{aligned}
&MNMHEI(K^S, L^S, E^S, G^S, C^S) = \frac{THEI^G(.^{t+1})}{THEI^G(.^t)} \\
&= \left[\frac{THEI^C(.^{t+1})}{THEI^C(.^t)}\right] \times \left[\frac{THEI^I(.^{t+1})/THEI^C(.^{t+1})}{THEI^I(.^t)/THEI^C(.^t)}\right] \times \left[\frac{THEI^G(.^{t+1})/THEI^I(.^{t+1})}{THEI^G(.^t)/THEI^I(.^t)}\right] \\
&= \left\{\frac{\left(\frac{1-\beta^{C*}}{1+\beta_G^{C*}}\right)^{t+1}}{\left(\frac{1-\beta^{C*}}{1+\beta_G^{C*}}\right)^{t}}\right\} \times \left\{\frac{\left(\frac{1-\beta^{I*}}{1+\beta_G^{I*}}\right)^{t+1} / \left(\frac{1-\beta^{C*}}{1+\beta_G^{C*}}\right)^{t+1}}{\left(\frac{1-\beta^{I*}}{1+\beta_G^{I*}}\right)^{t} / \left(\frac{1-\beta^{C*}}{1+\beta_G^{C*}}\right)^{t}}\right\} \times \left\{\frac{\left(\frac{1-\beta^{G*}}{1+\beta_G^{G*}}\right)^{t+1} / \left(\frac{1-\beta^{I*}}{1+\beta_G^{I*}}\right)^{t+1}}{\left(\frac{1-\beta^{G*}}{1+\beta_G^{G*}}\right)^{t} / \left(\frac{1-\beta^{I*}}{1+\beta_G^{I*}}\right)^{t}}\right\} \\
&= \left[\frac{TE^{t+1}}{TE^t}\right] \times \left[\frac{BPR^{t+1}}{BPR^t}\right] \times \left[\frac{TGR^{t+1}}{TGR^t}\right] = EC \times BPC \times TGC
\end{aligned}
\tag{16}
$$

EC captures the "catchup" effect in terms of technical efficiency changes in high-quality development for a specific group for two time periods. BPC can be considered an innovation effect, as it measures frontier shifts over two periods, and the TGC is a measure of the change in technology leadership of a given group.

2.2. Data

We employ the methods described in the previous subsection to analyze the static high-quality development efficiency and its dynamic changes in 31 Chinese provinces during the 2008–2021 period for balanced panel data.

Our research primarily examines the efficiency of high-quality development. To measure this, in order to obtain the desired output, we select the real GDP that was calculated using the year 2000, which has been commonly used in prior studies. (e.g., Meng, 2023; Zhang, 2014). We select CO_2 emissions as the undesirable output, which is in line with China's commitment to the "dual-carbon goal" of carbon peaking and carbon neutrality. We use three classical inputs: capital (K), labor (L), and energy (E).

We measure the capital input, the labor input, and the energy input by the capital stock numbers, the number of employees, and the total energy consumption, respectively. The capital stock numbers are estimated using the perpetual inventory method [32]. The employees consist of four types (*YHL, YLL, NYHL, NYLL*). The aggregate energy consumption, encompassing various energy sources including coal, oil, gas, electricity, etc., is quantified in terms of tons of standard coal equivalent. We measure the desirable output and the undesirable output of each province by the real GDP and CO_2 emissions separately, as in many previous studies [33,34]. The capital, labor, and GDP data are downloaded from the Eps Database, which collects data from the China Statistical Yearbook. The energy data used are from the Eps Database, which collects data from the China Power Yearbook. For Tibet, which does not report energy data, we follow the method of Chen [35] to determine its energy consumption. Based on the Regional energy balance tables, CO_2 emissions from the CEADs Database are estimated using the IPCC Sectoral Approach [36–40]. The descriptive statistics of all 434 observations are presented in Table 1.

Table 1. Descriptive statistics for variables (2008–2021, $n = 31$).

Variable	Unit	Group	n	Mean	StDev	Min	Max
K	10^9 ¥	1	210	53,020.33	41,511.08	1048.582	199,512.5
		2	224	39,108.24	31,683.75	2273.023	190,639.8
		all	434	45,839.9	37,378.94	1048.582	199,512.5
YHL	10^4 persons	1	210	340.7739	235.0554	5.208753	1196.863
		2	224	199.7824	149.809	25.27871	831.3595
		all	434	268.0041	207.8527	5.208753	1196.863
YLL	10^4 persons	1	210	861.4928	635.8135	61.62585	2714.873
		2	224	570.9986	425.3988	61.73456	2106.442
		all	434	711.5603	556.2817	61.62585	2714.873
NYHL	10^4 persons	1	210	495.7831	347.5369	4.92	1817.292
		2	224	288.9589	207.905	27.8726	1113.56
		all	434	389.0351	302.1053	4.92	1817.292
NYLL	10^4 persons	1	210	2450.566	1580.338	157.001	5654.315
		2	224	1677.389	1171.014	210.1544	5498.109
		all	434	2051.507	1435.736	157.001	5654.315
E	10^4 tons of standard coal equivalent	1	210	14,135.77	8791.268	235.943	35,759.7
		2	224	14,234.85	9462.246	2279	45,539.92
		all	434	14,186.91	9133.349	235.943	45,539.92
G	10^9 ¥	1	210	6004.92	3936.803	154.1904	17,193.26
		2	224	3305.232	2619.673	391.297	12,064.97
		all	434	4611.533	3583.226	154.1904	17,193.26
C	10^4 tons of standard coal equivalent	1	210	28,225.11	18,532.25	243.9063	81,768.02
		2	224	33,743.61	23,901.37	3157.438	94,716.29
		all	434	31,073.37	21,624.29	243.9063	94,716.29

In particular, we need to clarify the specific criteria for classifying labor according to age and level of education. With regard to the definition of young labor, there are two ways of defining them based on age ranges: narrow and broad. Firstly, the narrower definition: the National Bureau of Statistics of China (NBS) uses the age range of 16–24 years old for the urban youth unemployment rate, which is the age range set by the Labor Law of the People's Republic of China, which stipulates that "people over 16 years old can formally join the workforce". Secondly, for a broader scope, UNESCO defines young people as those aged 14–34. Taking into account the provisions of China's Labor Law and the comparability of international studies, the age range for the study of young labor was defined as 16–34 years. With regard to the definition of labor with higher education, it means those who have received a university education, including college, undergraduate, and postgraduate education. Firstly, we classify labor by age into young labor and other labor. We then divide young labor into those with and without higher education and divide other labor into those with and without higher education. These data are downloaded from the Eps Database, which collects data from the China Statistical Yearbook.

3. Empirical Results and Discussion for the THEI

3.1. Empirical Results for the THEI

The proposed THEI is applied to 31 regions of China. The static total-factor high-quality development efficiency of the regions is calculated from the TNDDF of Equation (3).

The results are presented in Table A1. With regard to the overall average THEI, the results suggest that the majority of Chinese provinces are not effectively engaged in high-quality development. The THEI of the provinces varied from 0.267 to 0.967, with an average value of 0.499. With regard to individual regions, the index was divided into five echelons using the natural break method, and the results are shown in Figure 1. Beijing and Shanghai are in the top tier. Beijing showed the best static high-quality development efficiency among all the provinces, with an average static efficiency score of 0.967. Shanghai ranked second, with an average static efficiency score of 0.837. On the other hand, Inner Mongolia showed the poorest static efficiency score of 0.267.

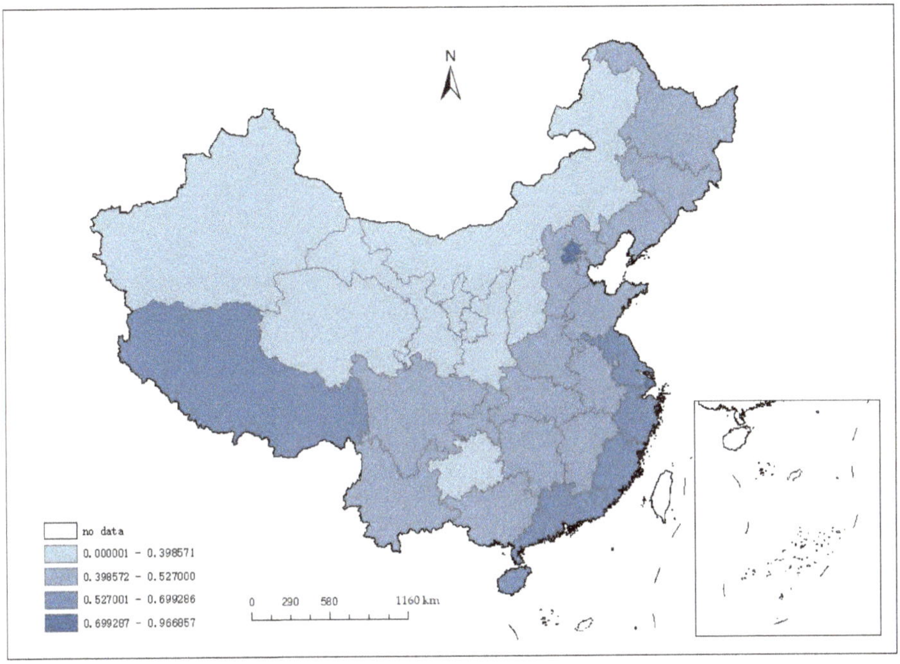

Figure 1. The THEI of the provinces.

3.2. Discussion for the THEI

Figure 2 shows the trends in the THEI and its decomposition. First, the THEI shows a downward trend as a whole, with a sharp decline between 2008 and 2010 and a slowdown between 2011 and 2017. Then, the decline becomes smaller and smaller, and from 2018 onwards, it is almost flat, with only a minimal decline.

Prior to 2008, China's rapid economic growth, achieved mainly by increasing the consumption of material resources, was crude and low-quality. In the short term, the marginal cost of energy efficiency and emission reduction increased due to the environmental regulations included in the 11th Five-Year Plan for Sustainable Development. The stringent low-carbon targets have led to a sharp decline in the THEI over the period 2008–2010. In 2010, the Chinese government announced a goal, included in the 12th Five-Year Plan, for the paradigm shift of economic growth from one based on increasing consumption of material resources to one based on improving high-quality labor and technological innovations. As a long-term result, the effect of stricter environmental regulations on improving efficiency and encouraging innovations gradually offsets the impact of increased marginal costs. During the 2011–2017 period, the rate of decline in the THEI has slowed down. In 2017, the 19th National Congress of the Communist Party of China (CPC) put forward the new expression of high-quality development for the first time, and in 2021, the State Council approved the 14th Five-Year Plan on promoting high-quality development. It appears that the Chinese government's high-quality development measures have been effective in pushing up THEI because from 2018 to 2021, the THEI has been almost horizontal. Following this trend, we can expect the THEI to increase in the near future, which means that we can produce the same GDP with less capital, less labor, less energy, and less CO_2 emissions.

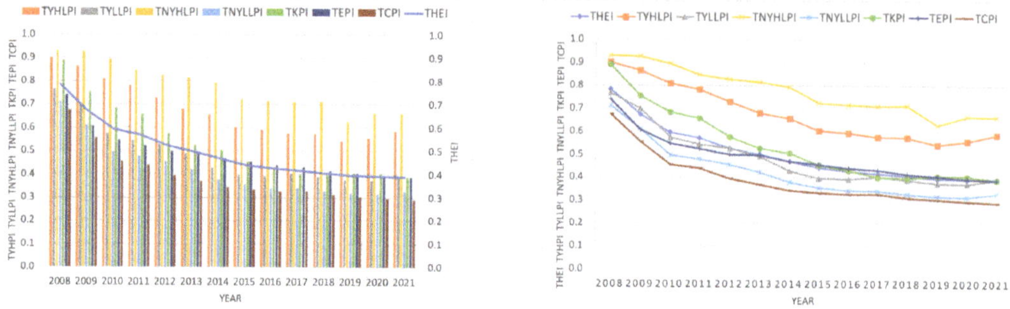

(a) (b)

Figure 2. (**a**) Trend of THEI and histograms of its components; (**b**) Trends of THEI and its components. Notes: THEI (static total-factor high-quality development efficiency index), TYHLPI (performance index of young labor with higher education), TYLLPI (performance index of young labor without higher education), TNYHLPI (performance index of other labor with higher education), TNYLLPI (performance index of other labor without higher education), TKPI (static total-factor capital performance index), TEPI (static total-factor energy performance index), and TCPI (static total-factor CO_2 emission performance index).

Given that the THEI is composed of various components, it would be more advantageous to examine the trends of these individual components, including the performance index of young labor with higher education (TYHLPI), the performance index of young labor without higher education (TYLLPI), the performance index of other labor with higher education (TNYHLPI), the performance index of other labor without higher education (TNYLLPI), the static total-factor capital performance index (TKPI), the static total-factor energy performance index (TEPI), and the static total-factor CO_2 emission performance index (TCPI), individually for additional insights into performance trends.

From Figure 2, we find that the TYHLPI and the TNYHLPI have the first and second highest values among all the components, indicating that labor with higher education contributes the most to the THEI. Between them, other labor with higher education is more efficient than young labor with higher education. This is thought to be due to the fact that most of them are engaged in intellectual work and therefore need to cultivate their expertise over an extended period of time. Before 2018, the TYHLPI and the TNYHLPI showed a decreasing trend, but after 2018, it shows a U-shaped trend. It started to increase in 2019–2021. The trend implies that China is increasingly viewing talent as the foremost asset for achieving high-quality development.

On the other hand, the TYLLPI and the TNYLLPI have the third and second lowest values among all the components, respectively, indicating that labor without higher education contributes less to the THEI. Between them, young labor without higher education is more efficient than other labor without higher education. This is most likely because the majority of them do physical work. Prior to 2020, the TYLLPI and the TNYLLPI showed a decreasing trend, but there was a small increase from 2020 to 2021. In short, the static labor performance index has improved over the last few years.

The TKPI ranked third in terms of its contribution to the THEI, except for the years 2016–2018. The gap between the TKPI and the second "TNYHLPI" widened over time. The TEPI has a lesser influence on the THEI, while the TCPI has the smallest contribution to the THEI. Moreover, for all three indices, the TKPI, the TEPI, and the TEPI, their trends are in line with those of the THEI, promoted by various national policies for quality development. The role of capital as a driver of static high-quality development efficiency is diminishing. Continuing to promote energy conservation and emission reduction policies and gradual improvements in energy and carbon performance are the way forward. Emphasizing the significance of high-quality talent as the primary resource is especially crucial. In order to foster China's high-quality development, it is essential to prioritize human resources and talent work, fully utilize the potential of human capital, and effectively stimulate the innovative abilities of talented individuals.

4. Empirical Results and Discussion for the MNMHEI

4.1. The Descriptive Statistics for the Two Groups

To calculate the MNMHEI, we first characterize groups and identify their members. Studies showed that stricter low-carbon targets lead to a decline in economic indicators [41,42]. On the other hand, advanced technologies for energy consumption and carbon emissions can reduce such losses and enable the sustainable growth of the economic system to be organically linked to carbon emission reductions [43]. As energy consumption is an intermediate input; in most cases, the higher the energy consumption, the higher the carbon emissions [44]. Here, the standard for grouping a province is based on the method of Chen. Following Chen, in order to construct a reasonable indicator for the grouping, this paper chooses two sub-indicators for the grouping of energy intensity (E/G) and carbon dioxide emission intensity (C/G) of each province in 2008–2021 and divides the sub-indicators by their respective averages in order to eliminate the influence of different units so that the mean value of the regularized sub-indicators is a unit. The total indicator for the grouping is obtained by weighting the average of the sub-indicators by their respective regularized sub-indicators, and the weights are determined using the method of natural number weights. Specific groupings can be found in column 3 of Table A2 in the Appendix A.

We consider two types of Chinese provinces: those with low energy intensity and low carbon emissions intensity (group 1), and those with high energy intensity and high carbon emissions intensity (group 2). The group 1 area includes 15 regions—Beijing, Shanghai, Guangdong, Zhejiang, Fujian, Hainan, Jiangsu, Anhui, Hubei, Hunan, Henan, Jiangxi, Sichuan, Chongqing, and Tibet. The group 2 area includes 16 regions—Heilongjiang, Liaoning, Jilin, Shandong, Tianjin, Hebei, Shanxi, Shaanxi, Yunnan, Guangxi, Gansu, Guizhou, Qinghai, Xinjiang, Ningxia, and Inner Mongolia.

The descriptive statistics for the input and output variables for the two groups are presented in Table 1. Group 1 has higher means and standard deviations in the variables K, YHL, YLL, NYHL, NYLL, and G than Group 2, while the converse can be observed for the variables E and C. This indicates that, on average, Group 1 has more capital, labor, and less energy to emit more GDP and less CO_2 than Group 2. Higher standard deviations indicate that there is more variation in the variables K, YHL, YLL, NYHL, NYLL, and G among the members within Group 1 and more variation in the variables E and C among the members within Group 2.

4.2. Empirical Results for the MNMHEI

Table A2 in the Appendix A displays the empirical results for the average MNMHEI from 2008 to 2021, as well as its decomposition for each region.

For the methodological approach, the data show a reduction in dynamic high-quality development efficiency from 2008 to 2021. On average, the dynamic high-quality development efficiency of China's provinces declines by around 5.3% under the MNMHEI.

At the provincial level, there is a rise in dynamic high-quality development efficiency in only 1 province, while 30 provinces show a decline. Beijing exhibits the greatest MNMHEI (with a growth rate of 0.1%), while Hebei exhibits the lowest MNMHEI (with a growth rate of −8.1%).

The average efficiency change (EC) index of dynamic high-quality development efficiency is 0.991, indicating an annual efficiency drop of around 0.9%. A total of 13 provinces have an EC score greater than unity, indicating that these regions moved toward the contemporaneous technological frontier during the study period, exhibiting the catch-up effect. For specific regions, Shanxi has the best catch-up performance (growth rate = 4.1%). Gansu ranked second with a 2.8% growth rate, while Tibet has the weakest catch-up performance (growth rate = −7%).

The average best-practice change (BPC) index is at 0.975, indicating a reduction in technological change (TC). This implies a change in the contemporaneous frontier away from the intertemporal one. A total of 23 provinces are in a condition of technical decline, with only 8 showing technological advancement. The average annual technology gap ratio change (TGC) value is 0.992, indicating a change in the gap between the global and intertemporal frontiers. This result indicates that China's provinces lacked technological leadership over the study period.

4.3. Discussion for the MNMHEI

4.3.1. Trends of the MNMHEI and Its Decomposition

Figure 3 displays the trends in dynamic total-factor high-quality development efficiency and its decomposition. Throughout the study period of 2008–2021, the MNMHEI was less than unity, showing a decrease in high-quality development efficiency. But the index presents an upward trend with fluctuations. The minimum value is 0.865 in 2008, and the maximum value is 0.998 in 2021, which is already close to unity. The EC indicator of high-quality development for 2008–2010 has a score greater than unity, suggesting strong catch-up performance. However, during the 2010–2012 period, the EC score is less than unity, indicating a loss in efficiency. Then, for 2012–2013, 2013–2016, 2016–2018, 2018–2020, and 2020–2021, the EC index alternates between above and below unity. The TC index of high-quality development for the period from 2008 to 2010 is below unity, which suggests a decline in technology during that time, but the TC index for the 2010–2011 period is larger than unity, indicating technological advancement. Then, during 2011–2018, 2018–2019, 2019–2020, and 2020–2021, the TC index alternates between above and below unity.

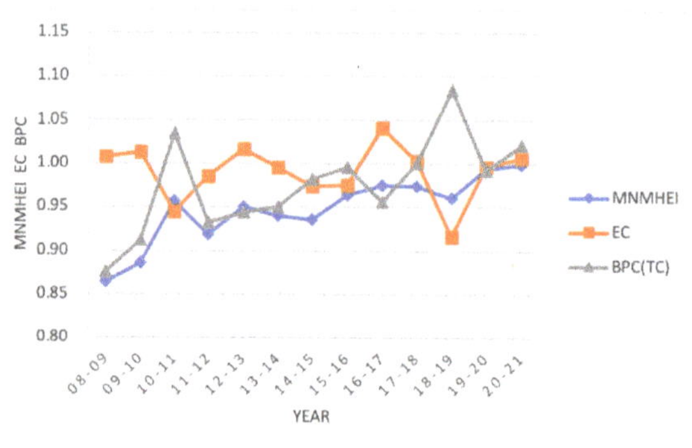

Figure 3. Trends of dynamic total-factor high-quality development efficiency index (MNMHEI) and its decomposition.

Changes in high-quality development efficiency accord with EC trends for the 2018–2019 period as well as TC trends for the 2008–2018 and 2019–2021 periods. This shows that the improvement in high-quality development efficiency from 2018 to 2019 was mostly pushed by efficiency changes, as opposed to from 2008 to 2018 and from 2019 to 2021, which were pushed by technological advances.

From 2008 to 2020, the EC index and the TC index show opposite trends; for example, during the period 2008–2010, the EC index rose while the TC index declined. The decline in TC was greater than the rise in EC, so the MNMHEI was more affected by TC and also declined. During the period 2010–2011, the EC index declined while the TC index rose. The rise in TC was greater than the fall in EC, so the MNMHEI was more affected by TC and also rose. In brief, the MNMHEI was more affected by TC during 2008–2020.

However, we can notice a positive phenomenon: the MNMHEI has been growing in waves, and in 2021, the EC index and the TC index are moving in the same direction, both exceeding unity, and so the MNMHEI will also reach unity. As a result, we can anticipate that high-quality development efficiency will continue to increase in the future, with significant potential. This situation results from a paradigm shift in China's policy, as previously noted. In 2017, high-quality development was advocated; in 2020, carbon peaking and carbon neutrality were proposed as its new pathways.

In the short term, the strong regulations for achieving the goal mentioned above had an adverse effect on efficiency and innovation due to the increased regulatory expenses incurred by the regions. Nevertheless, over the long term, stricter environmental and other regulations result in both increased costs and enhanced productivity and innovation for high-quality development.

4.3.2. Trends in the MNMHEI and Its Decomposition into Two Groups

At the group level, we compare the MNMCPI and its decomposition. The MNMHEI estimate and its decomposition for every group are displayed in Table 2. Group 1 has a higher MNMHEI. When considering decomposed factors, Group 2 has a larger EC index, suggesting a significant catch-up impact. On the other hand, Group 1 exhibits a higher BPC index, showing technological innovation. The TGC index is equal to unity for Group 1, suggesting a position of technology leadership, whereas the TGC index is less than unity for Group 2, indicating a lack of technology leadership. Because the MNMHEI could provide useful information for both efficiency and innovation, considering the group heterogeneities, this information is conducive to the Chinese government's proposal of specific ways to achieve high-quality development in accordance with regional and provincial characteristics. This will enable each region to choose a high-quality development path that suits its actual situation, adapts to local conditions, and makes up for its shortcomings.

Table 2. Group comparison of the MNMHEI and its decomposition.

Group	MNMHEI	EC	BPC	TGC
Group 1	0.9558	0.9750	0.9955	1.0000
Group 2	0.9395	1.0054	0.9564	0.9836

Trends in the MNMHEI and its decomposition for the two groups are shown in Figure 4. The two groups have comparable MNMHEI patterns, with the exception of the 2018–2019 and 2020–2021 periods, which show an increase. Group 1 has a larger MNMHEI than Group 2, except for the 2020–2021 timeframe. The two groups show similar EC patterns except for the 2008–2009 period and have fierce competition with regard to the EC index as their positions fluctuate each time. By way of illustration, between 2008 and 2009, Group 2 showed a upper EC index, whilst Group 1 exhibited a upper EC index from 2009 to 2010. This pattern continues in subsequent periods. Overall, on average, Group 2 shows a higher EC index. We have obtained separate consequences concerning the TC (BPC) index. With the exception of the periods 2012–2013, 2016–2017, and 2020–2021, Group 1 consistently showed a higher TC score compared to Group 2, which suggests that the regions in Group 1 led innovation. The TGC index of Group 1 is always equal to unity throughout the study period, implying no change in technology leadership, while the TGC index of Group 2 has been fluctuating up and down, with 2011–2012, 2016–2017, and 2019–2020 exceeding unity, indicating that the global frontier and the intertemporal frontier have been closer together in these years. The other years are still less than unity. Thus, overall, Group 2 still lacks technology leadership.

In sum, due to the fact that Group 2 is deficient in both creativity and leadership, the regions that belong to Group 2 are not contributing to high-quality development at the national level. This suggests that the government should facilitate increased innovation and leadership for the provinces in Group 2. On the other hand, Group 1 has a higher degree of innovation than Group 2; however, seven provinces in Group 2 lack innovation, indicating potential for more technological innovation in Group 1.

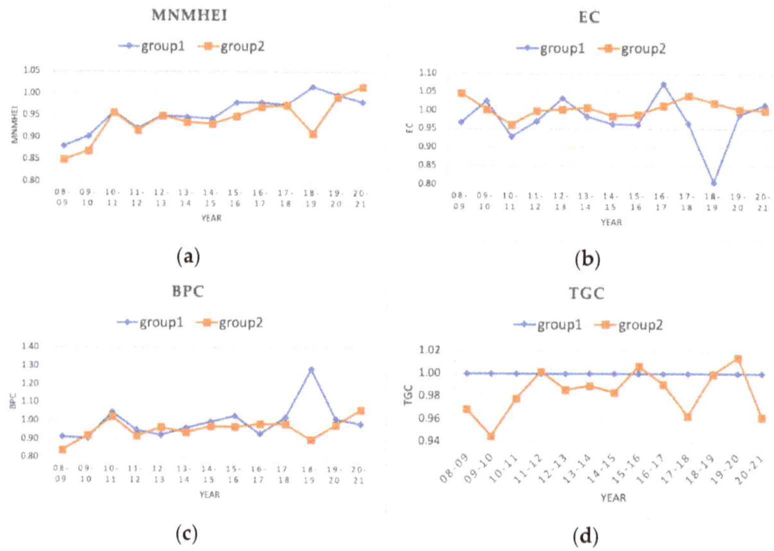

Figure 4. (**a**) Trends in the MNMHEI into two groups; (**b**) Trends in the TC into two groups; (**c**) Trends in the BPC into two groups; (**d**) Trends in the TGC into two groups.

Finally, we conduct a statistical analysis to see if the indices differ significantly between both groups. To determine whether these two groups differ significantly from one another, we use the Wilcoxon–Mann–Whitney rank-sum test. As seen in Table 3, the null hypothesis was rejected at the 1% level, implying a substantial rating difference. To ensure the robustness of the results, further Kolmogorov–Smirnov tests were performed. The results converged on the former rank-sum test.

Table 3. Wilcoxon–Mann–Whitney rank-sum test and Kolmogorov–Smirnov test for the Group 1 and Group 2.

Test	Index	Null Hypothesis (H0)	Statistics	p-Value
Wilcoxon–Mann–Whitney	MNMHEI	MNMHEI1 = MNMHEI2	6.412	0.0113
	EC	EC1 = EC2	84.613	0.0001
	BPC	BPC1 = BPC2	43.352	0.0001
	TGC	TGC1 = TGC2	26.761	0.0001
Kolmogorov–Smirnov	MNMHEI	MNMHEI1 = MNMHEI2	0.1606	0.011
	EC	EC1 = EC2	0.5048	0.0000
	BPC	BPC1 = BPC2	0.392	0.0000
	TGC	TGC1 = TGC2	0.649	0.0000

To determine whether these two groups differ significantly from one another, we apply the Wilcoxon–Mann–Whitney rank-sum test.

The original hypothesis was rejected at the 1 percent level.

5. Conclusions

As high-quality development is becoming more and more significant for socio-economic advancement, China must evaluate its high-quality development efficiency. In this paper, we propose two composite indicators, THEI and MNMHEI, for the measurement of static and dynamic high-quality development efficiency.

These are the main conclusions derived from the study's empirical findings: First, the majority of Chinese provinces are experiencing subpar performance in achieving static high-quality development and possess considerable potential for enhancement. We propose that the THEI consists of different components: the TYHLPI, TYLLPI, TNYHLPI, TNYHLPI, TKPI, TEPI, and TCPI. We find that labor with higher education, i.e., talent, contributes the most to the THEI. Second, we apply the MNMHEI to solve group heterogeneity and non-radial slack and decompose the index into the EC, BPC, and TGC indices. The improvement in high-quality development efficiency was mostly pushed by technological advances. Group 2 shows better catch-up performance, whereas Group 1 shows better technological innovation and leadership performance.

These empirical findings have some consequences for China. First, policymakers should place a greater priority on talent training and pushing technological innovation, given that they are essential to China's high-quality development. Second, a variety of schemes must be adopted to boost China's high-quality development efficiency. The governance of each province must be modified in accordance with the levels of inputs and outputs.

Due to the limitations of the methodology, we ignored the effect of random errors and could not directly analyze the factors affecting efficiency. There are still some directions for research and improvements in the future: other efficiency models (such as SFA with a stochastic frontier) could be used to measure the efficiency of high-quality development and perform convergence analysis for it. Moreover, further regression analyses could be conducted on the factors affecting high-quality development efficiency as well as efficiency changes and technological progress. Due to the limitations of the data, a comparative analysis of China's high-quality development with that of other countries is also possible in the future.

One final addition, Table A3 in Appendix A, displays a list of acronyms for vectors, functions, and indices to make reading easier.

Author Contributions: Conceptualization, H.D. and Q.W.; methodology, B.L.; software, H.D.; validation, H.D., Q.W. and B.L.; investigation, H.D; resources, B.L.; data curation, H.D.; writing—original draft preparation, H.D.; writing—review and editing, H.D.; visualization, Q.W.; supervision, B.L.; project administration, Q.W.; funding acquisition, Q.W. All authors have read and agreed to the published version of the manuscript.

Funding: This research was funded by the National Natural Science Foundation of China (NSFC), (grant No. 72274018), the Project of Cultivation for Young Top-notch Talents of Beijing Municipal Institutions, (grant No. BPHR202203222), and the Academic Research Projects of Beijing Union University, (grant No.SK10202401).

Data Availability Statement: The data presented in this study are available on request from the corresponding author.

Conflicts of Interest: The authors declare no conflicts of interest.

Appendix A

Table A1. Average THEI and its decomposition at the province level.

Region	THEI	TYHLPI	TYLLPI	TNYHLPI	TNYLLPI	TKPI	TEPI	TCPI
Anhui	0.513	0.705	0.461	0.782	0.347	0.549	0.578	0.351
Beijing	0.967	0.960	0.928	0.987	0.940	1.000	0.964	0.949
Fujian	0.574	0.742	0.480	1.000	0.457	0.546	0.607	0.474
Gansu	0.384	0.518	0.305	0.533	0.247	0.520	0.340	0.278
Guangdong	0.699	0.827	0.465	1.000	0.517	0.747	0.703	0.645
Guangxi	0.449	0.639	0.351	0.762	0.287	0.401	0.499	0.386
Guizhou	0.370	0.456	0.445	0.482	0.344	0.423	0.363	0.264
Hainan	0.561	0.685	0.259	0.948	0.291	0.696	0.585	0.418
Hebei	0.460	0.624	0.631	0.635	0.514	0.469	0.438	0.331
Henan	0.475	0.779	0.369	0.860	0.327	0.414	0.518	0.383

Table A1. *Cont.*

Region	THEI	TYHLPI	TYLLPI	TNYHLPI	TNYLLPI	TKPI	TEPI	TCPI
Heilongjiang	0.510	0.851	0.656	0.798	0.458	0.481	0.483	0.385
Hubei	0.507	0.773	0.289	0.894	0.276	0.629	0.478	0.361
Hunan	0.527	0.707	0.290	0.775	0.264	0.660	0.510	0.429
Jilin	0.443	0.851	0.566	0.760	0.426	0.313	0.493	0.315
Jiangsu	0.636	0.827	0.678	1.000	0.576	0.664	0.639	0.471
Jiangxi	0.508	0.651	0.279	0.857	0.254	0.548	0.587	0.387
Liaoning	0.465	0.826	0.775	0.840	0.522	0.443	0.385	0.292
Inner Mongolia	0.267	0.491	0.513	0.490	0.402	0.264	0.207	0.124
Ningxia	0.281	0.419	0.474	0.475	0.435	0.329	0.205	0.139
Qinghai	0.301	0.335	0.443	0.450	0.349	0.296	0.214	0.298
Shandong	0.509	0.783	0.576	0.865	0.486	0.476	0.489	0.392
Shanxi	0.358	0.496	0.515	0.514	0.419	0.471	0.280	0.195
Shaanxi	0.399	0.465	0.396	0.638	0.318	0.429	0.422	0.289
Shanghai	0.837	0.956	0.905	1.000	0.878	0.966	0.769	0.678
Sichuan	0.510	0.690	0.271	0.849	0.255	0.642	0.447	0.433
Tianjin	0.437	0.751	0.526	0.872	0.536	0.421	0.372	0.282
Tibet	0.586	0.594	0.340	0.959	0.368	0.591	0.652	0.536
Xinjiang	0.346	0.407	0.449	0.546	0.387	0.441	0.277	0.219
Yunnan	0.452	0.577	0.359	0.692	0.319	0.456	0.467	0.399
Zhejiang	0.647	0.819	0.515	0.996	0.465	0.777	0.623	0.492
Chongqing	0.488	0.717	0.425	0.747	0.368	0.480	0.482	0.427
Mean	0.499	0.675	0.482	0.774	0.420	0.534	0.486	0.388
Min	0.267	0.335	0.259	0.450	0.247	0.264	0.205	0.124
Max	0.967	0.960	0.928	1.000	0.940	1.000	0.964	0.949

Table A2. Average MNMHEI and its decomposition at the province level.

Region	DMU	Group	MNMHEI	EC	BPC	TGC
Anhui	1	1	0.948	0.962	0.999	1.000
Beijing	2	1	1.001	1.000	1.001	1.000
Fujian	3	1	0.958	1.022	0.952	1.000
Gansu	4	2	0.950	1.028	0.937	0.999
Guangdong	5	1	0.955	0.966	0.998	1.000
Guangxi	6	2	0.942	0.995	0.951	0.998
Guizhou	7	2	0.963	1.025	0.956	0.997
Hainan	8	1	0.951	0.953	1.007	1.000
Hebei	9	2	0.919	0.995	0.955	0.979
Henan	10	1	0.949	1.019	1.006	1.000
Heilongjiang	11	2	0.924	1.001	0.951	0.971
Hubei	12	1	0.968	0.980	0.997	1.000
Hunan	13	1	0.962	0.963	1.004	1.000
Jilin	14	2	0.940	1.016	0.945	0.983
Jiangsu	15	1	0.951	1.011	0.961	1.000
Jiangxi	16	1	0.955	0.965	1.002	1.000
Liaoning	17	2	0.952	1.013	0.980	0.974
Inner Mongolia	18	2	0.926	0.981	0.994	0.958
Ningxia	19	2	0.938	0.992	0.953	0.993
Qinghai	20	2	0.944	0.997	0.952	0.998
Shandong	21	2	0.922	1.000	0.949	0.971
Shanxi	22	2	0.960	1.041	0.943	0.991
Shaanxi	23	2	0.952	1.008	0.950	0.997
Shanghai	24	1	0.984	1.000	0.984	1.000
Sichuan	25	1	0.942	0.946	1.010	1.000
Tianjin	26	2	0.923	1.000	0.982	0.947
Tibet	27	1	0.924	0.930	1.007	1.000

Table A2. *Cont.*

Region	DMU	Group	MNMHEI	EC	BPC	TGC
Xinjiang	28	2	0.936	0.992	0.947	0.999
Yunnan	29	2	0.942	1.002	0.959	0.984
Zhejiang	30	1	0.956	0.974	0.995	1.000
Chongqing	31	1	0.933	0.936	1.009	1.000
Mean			0.947	0.991	0.975	0.992
Min			0.919	0.930	0.937	0.947
Max			1.001	1.041	1.010	1.000

Table A3. A list of acronyms for vectors/functions/indices.

Acronyms	Vectors/Functions/Indices
YHL	young labor with higher education
YLL	young labor without higher education
NYHL	other labor with higher education
NYLL	other labor without higher education
NDDF	non-radial directional distance function
TNDDF	a total-factor non-radial distance function
THEI	static total-factor high-quality development efficiency index
TCPI	static total-factor CO_2 emission performance index
TKPI	static total-factor capital performance index
TLPI	static total-factor labor performance index
TEPI	static total-factor energy performance index
TYHLPI	performance index of young labor with higher education
TYLLPI	performance index of young labor without higher education
TNYHLPI,	performance index of other labor with higher education
TNYLLPI	performance index of other labor without higher education.
MNMHEI	dynamic metafrontier non-radial Malmquist high-quality development efficiency index
EC	technical efficiency change index
BPC	best-practice gap change index
TGC	technology gap change index

References

1. Jin, B. Study on the "high-quality development" economics. *China Ind. Econ.* **2018**, *1*, 5–18.
2. Pan, W.; Wang, J.; Lu, Z.; Liu, Y.; Li, Y. High-quality development in China: Measurement system, spatial pattern, and improvement paths. *Habitat Int.* **2021**, *118*, 102458. [CrossRef]
3. Chao, X.; Xue, Z. Research on the theoretical logic and practical mechanism of high quality of China's economic development in the New Era. *J. Northwest Univ. (Philos. Soc. Sci. Ed.)* **2018**, *48*, 12–22.
4. Hong, Y.; Liu, W.; Song, H. Spatial econometric analysis of effect of new economic momentum on China's high-quality development. *Res. Int. Bus. Financ.* **2022**, *61*, 101621. [CrossRef]
5. Song, M.; Tao, W.; Shen, Z. Improving high-quality development with environmental regulation and industrial structure in China. *J. Clean. Prod.* **2022**, *366*, 132997. [CrossRef]
6. Yang, Z.; Zhan, J.; Wang, C.; Liu, W.; Wang, H.; Bai, C. Spatial spillover effects of conversion of new and old driving forces on high-quality development: Evidence from 283 cities in China. *Sustain. Cities Soc.* **2024**, *108*, 105487. [CrossRef]
7. Sun, X.; Jiang, K.; Duan, D. Measuring the efficiency of high-quality development of the Yangtze River Economic Belt. *Tatistics Decis.* **2022**, *38*, 118–121.
8. Zhang, Z.; Zhong, W. Measurement of high-quality development efficiency of high-tech industries and analysis of regional differences. *Stat. Decis.* **2021**, *37*, 14–17.
9. Yan, X.; Luo, Y.; Zhao, Q.; Pan, J. Evaluation and countermeasures of high quality development efficiency of manufacturing industry in Shaanxi province based on SBM-DEA. *Sci. Technol. Manag. Res.* **2022**, *42*, 44–50.
10. Wei, F.; Fan, Y.; Song, J.; Chu, J.; Sun, N. Carbon productivity growth in china's transportation industry: Empirical analysis using a global malmquist-luenberger productivity index based on an endogenous directional distance function. *J. Environ. Plan. Manag.* **2024**, *1*, 1–25. [CrossRef]
11. Chambers, R.G.; Chung, Y.; Färe, R. Benefit and distance functions. *J. Econ. Theory* **1996**, *70*, 407–419. [CrossRef]
12. Chung, Y.H.; Färe, R.; Grosskopf, S. Productivity and undesirable outputs: A directional distance function approach. *J. Environ. Manag.* **1997**, *51*, 229–240. [CrossRef]

13. Fukuyama, H.; Weber, W.L. A directional slacks-based measure of technical inefficiency. *Socio-Econ. Plan. Sci.* **2009**, *43*, 274–287. [CrossRef]
14. Sueyoshi, T.; Goto, M. Dea approach for unified efficiency measurement: Assessment of japanese fossil fuel power generation. *Energy Econ.* **2011**, *33*, 292–303. [CrossRef]
15. Choi, Y.; Zhang, N.; Zhou, P. Efficiency and abatement costs of energy-related CO_2 emissions in china: A slacks-based efficiency measure. *Appl. Energy* **2012**, *98*, 198–208. [CrossRef]
16. Zhou, P.; Ang, B.W.; Wang, H. Energy and CO_2 emission performance in electricity generation: A non-radial directional distance function approach. *Eur. J. Oper. Res.* **2012**, *221*, 625–635. [CrossRef]
17. Zhang, N.; Kong, F.; Choi, Y.; Zhou, P. The effect of size-control policy on unified energy and carbon efficiency for chinese fossil fuel power plants. *Energy Policy* **2014**, *70*, 193–200. [CrossRef]
18. Chen, C.; Ye, F.; Xiao, H.; Xie, W.; Liu, B.; Wang, L. The digital economy, spatial spillovers and forestry green total factor productivity. *J. Clean. Prod.* **2023**, *405*, 136890. [CrossRef]
19. Oh, D.-H.; Lee, J.-D. A metafrontier approach for measuring malmquist productivity index. *Empir. Econ.* **2010**, *38*, 47–64. [CrossRef]
20. Zhang, N.; Choi, Y. Total-factor carbon emission performance of fossil fuel power plants in china: A metafrontier non-radial malmquist index analysis. *Energy Econ.* **2013**, *40*, 549–559. [CrossRef]
21. Meng, M.; Pang, T. Total-factor generation performance analysis of china's thermal power industry using meta-frontier nonradial distance function approach. *Energy Sci. Eng.* **2023**, *11*, 2668–2685. [CrossRef]
22. Cheng, Z.; Jin, W. Agglomeration economy and the growth of green total-factor productivity in chinese industry. *Socio-Econ. Plan. Sci.* **2022**, *83*, 101003. [CrossRef]
23. Meng, F.; Zhao, Y. How does digital economy affect green total factor productivity at the industry level in china: From a perspective of global value chain. *Environ. Sci. Pollut. Res.* **2022**, *29*, 79497–79515. [CrossRef] [PubMed]
24. Wang, X.; Wang, S. Research on the improvement of total factor productivity in china's power industry: A perspective of technological heterogeneity. *Environ. Sci. Pollut. Res.* **2022**, *29*, 11854–11864. [CrossRef] [PubMed]
25. Zhang, N. Carbon total factor productivity, low carbon technology innovation and energy efficiency catch-up: Evidence from Chinese thermal power enterprises. *Econ. Res. J.* **2022**, *57*, 158–174.
26. Shi, F.; Zhang, B. The new era, new momentum and new economy—Analyzing the current high quality development of China's economy. *Shanghai J. Econ.* **2018**, *5*, 25–33.
27. Sun, Y. Providing talent leadership support for the development of new quality productivity. *People's Trib.* **2024**, *6*, 26–30.
28. Cui, Y.; Li, L.; Lei, Y.; Wu, S. The performance and influencing factors of high-quality development of resource-based cities in the yellow river basin under reducing pollution and carbon emissions constraints. *Resour. Policy* **2024**, *88*, 104488. [CrossRef]
29. Färe, R.; Grosskopf, S. *Book New Directions: Efficiency and Productivity*; Springer: New York, NY, USA, 2005.
30. Fare, R.; Grosskopf, S.; Pasurkajr, C. Environmental production functions and environmental directional distance functions. *Energy* **2007**, *32*, 1055–1066. [CrossRef]
31. Barros, C.P.; Managi, S.; Matousek, R. The technical efficiency of the japanese banks: Non-radial directional performance measurement with undesirable output. *Omega-Int. J. Manag. Sci.* **2012**, *40*, 1–8. [CrossRef]
32. Zhao, S.; Cao, Y.; Hunjra, A.I.; Tan, Y. How does environmentally induced r&d affect carbon productivity? A government support perspective. *Int. Rev. Econ. Financ.* **2023**, *88*, 942–961.
33. Zhang, N.; Kong, F.; Choi, Y. Measuring sustainability performance for China: A sequential generalized directional distance function approach. *Econ. Model.* **2014**, *41*, 392–397. [CrossRef]
34. Tian, K.; Dietzenbacher, E.; Yan, B.; Duan, Y. Upgrading or downgrading: China's regional carbon emission intensity evolution and its determinants. *Energy Econ.* **2020**, *91*, 104891. [CrossRef]
35. Chen, S. Evaluation of Low Carbon Transformation Process for Chinese Provinces. *Jingji Yanjiu/Econ. Res. J.* **2012**, *47*, 32–44. Available online: http://www.aeaweb.org/econlit/journal_list.php (accessed on 1 August 2012).
36. Xu, J.; Guan, Y.; Oldfield, J.; Guan, D.; Shan, Y. China carbon emission accounts 2020–2021. *Appl. Energy* **2024**, *360*, 122837. [CrossRef]
37. Guan, Y.; Shan, Y.; Huang, Q.; Chen, H.; Wang, D.; Hubacek, K. Assessment to China's recent emission pattern shifts. *Earth's Future* **2021**, *9*, e2021EF002241. [CrossRef]
38. Shan, Y.; Liu, J.; Liu, Z.; Xu, X.; Shao, S.; Wang, P.; Guan, D. New provincial CO_2 emission inventories in China based on apparent energy consumption data and updated emission factors. *Appl. Energy* **2016**, *184*, 742–750. [CrossRef]
39. Shan, Y.; Huang, Q.; Guan, D.; Hubacek, K. China CO_2 emission accounts 2016–2017. *Sci Data* **2020**, *7*, 54. [CrossRef]
40. Shan, Y.; Guan, D.; Zheng, H.; Ou, J.; Li, Y.; Meng, J.; Mi, Z.; Liu, Z.; Zhang, Q. China CO_2 emission accounts 1997–2015. *Sci Data* **2018**, *5*, 170201. [CrossRef]
41. Mi, Z.; Wei, Y.-M.; Wang, B.; Meng, J.; Liu, Z.; Shan, Y.; Liu, J.; Guan, D. Socioeconomic impact assessment of China's CO_2 emissions peak prior to 2030. *J. Clean. Prod.* **2017**, *142*, 2227–2236. [CrossRef]
42. Yuan, Y.; Duan, H.; Tsvetanov, T.G. Synergizing China's energy and carbon mitigation goals: General equilibrium modeling and policy assessment. *Energy Econ.* **2020**, *89*, 104787. [CrossRef]

43. Lu, C.; Chen, W. The Scenarios of China Reaching the Peaking of Carbon Emission Before 2030 and Its Macroeconomic Implications. *J. Environ. Econ.* **2021**, *6*, 10–30+200.
44. Salari, M.; Javid, R.J.; Noghanibehambari, H. The nexus between CO_2 emissions, energy consumption, and economic growth in the u.S. *Econ. Anal. Policy* **2021**, *69*, 182–194. [CrossRef]

mathematics

MDPI

Article

Unsupervised Modelling of E-Customers' Profiles: Multiple Correspondence Analysis with Hierarchical Clustering of Principal Components and Machine Learning Classifiers

Vijoleta Vrhovac, Marko Orošnjak *, Kristina Ristić, Nemanja Sremčev, Mitar Jocanović, Jelena Spajić and Nebojša Brkljač

Department of Industrial Engineering and Engineering Management, Faculty of Technical Sciences, University of Novi Sad, Trg Dositeja Obradovića 6, 21000 Novi Sad, Serbia; violeta.vrhovac@uns.ac.rs (V.V.); kristina.ristic@uns.ac.rs (K.R.); nextesla@uns.ac.rs (N.S.); mitarj@uns.ac.rs (M.J.); stankovicj@uns.ac.rs (J.S.); n.brkljac@uns.ac.rs (N.B.)

* Correspondence: orosnjak@uns.ac.rs

Abstract: The rapid growth of e-commerce has transformed customer behaviors, demanding deeper insights into how demographic factors shape online user preferences. This study performed a threefold analysis to understand the impact of these changes. Firstly, this study investigated how demographic factors (e.g., age, gender, education) influence e-customer preferences in Serbia. From a sample of $n = 906$ respondents, conditional dependencies between demographics and user preferences were tested. From a hypothetical framework of 24 tested hypotheses, this study successfully rejected 8/24 (with $p < 0.05$), suggesting a high association between demographics with purchase frequency and reasons for quitting the purchase. However, although the reported test statistics suggested an association, understanding how interactions between categories shape e-customer profiles was still required. Therefore, the second part of this study considers an MCA-HCPC (Multiple Correspondence Analysis with Hierarchical Clustering on Principal Components) to identify user profiles. The analysis revealed three main clusters: (1) young, female, unemployed e-customers driven mainly by customer reviews; (2) retirees and older adults with infrequent purchases, hesitant to buy without experiencing the product in person; and (3) employed, highly educated, male, middle-aged adults who prioritize fast and accurate delivery over price. In the third stage, the clusters are used as labels for Machine Learning (ML) classification tasks. Particularly, Gradient Boosting Machine (GBM), Decision Tree (DT), k-Nearest Neighbors (kNN), Gaussian Naïve Bayes (GNB), Random Forest (RF), and Support Vector Machine (SVM) were used. The results suggested that GBM, RF, and SVM had high classification performance in identifying user profiles. Lastly, after performing Permutation Feature Importance (PFI), the findings suggested that age, work status, education, and income are the main determinants of shaping e-customer profiles and developing marketing strategies.

Keywords: e-commerce; customer profiles; demographics; user preferences; multiple correspondence analysis; hierarchical clustering; machine learning

MSC: 62H25; 62H30; 62H17; 62F03

1. Introduction

E-commerce is developing faster than ever, with an increase in the number of transactions [1,2]. This global trend allows retailers to expand their reach with as many customers as possible [3]. Additionally, the COVID-19 pandemic has further accelerated consumer habits, with many consumers switching to online shopping [4,5], posing new challenges for e-tailers [6–8]. With the rise in online consumers, e-tailers are forced to improve customer experience throughout the purchasing process [9,10]. Similar trends are visible in the

Serbian market, where e-shopping is becoming pronounced, emphasizing the importance of e-commerce in modern business.

According to Ranđelović [11], despite the numerous benefits of e-commerce, consumers in Serbia still need to accept this form of commerce. One of the reasons for the slow adoption of e-commerce is consumer distrust, especially regarding the security of transactions [12]. Still, in 2023, the e-commerce market in Serbia grew by 34.5%, reaching a value of 955.7 million dollars, and it is predicted that by 2027, the market will grow to 1.65 billion dollars. The growth in e-commerce users is estimated to reach 4.36 million customers by 2027, comprising 62.5% of Internet users in Serbia [13]. Regardless of these positive trends, Serbia faces challenges such as the preference for cash-on-delivery payments and a continued lack of trust in the security of online transactions [14].

Demographic data, such as gender, age, income, and education, are vital in analyzing consumer preferences and behavior [15,16]. These variables enable market segmentation and the adaptation of marketing strategies to the specific needs of different consumers [17]. For example, income indicates purchasing power and can help target marketing campaigns to different socio-economic segments [18]. Education and age influence how consumers use technology and how they behave when shopping online [19]. Understanding these demographic factors allows e-tailers to identify target groups and optimize customer experience [20]. In Serbia, where e-commerce is growing, insight into demographic variables can help overcome obstacles and improve consumer acceptance of e-commerce. This provides valuable information for adjusting e-tailers' market strategies and enhancing user experience.

Considering the research problem's contextual settings, this study's primary idea is to switch from a traditional statistical exploratory analysis to an ML approach in identifying the user profiles of e-customers. Firstly, an analysis of how demographic factors influence the online behavior of e-customers in Serbia is performed. Specifically, how demographics affect user preferences is of interest here, particularly purchase frequency (PURFREQ), the most important property when buying for the first time (MIPB1T), the most important property before repeating the purchase (MIPBREP), and reasons for quitting the online purchase (RFQ), using a hypothetical framework. However, given that statistical testing highlights significant relationships between categories, it needs to provide an understanding of how these categories interact. As a response, Multiple Correspondence Analysis with Hierarchical Clustering on Principal Components (MCA-HCPC) is performed as an unsupervised model for labelling user profiles. Secondly, after obtaining class categories, i.e., labels, an ML classification using a dataset from user profiles that includes demographics and user preferences is conducted. Lastly, the most important features of the best-performing algorithms are extracted using Mean Dropout Loss (MDL).

The rest of this study is structured as follows. Section 2 provides an in-depth description of the survey used for this study. In addition, rigorous data analysis procedures are performed, starting from a priori sample determination, study selection, and the proposition of hypotheses in this study. The third section provides information about descriptives, including demographics and user behavior variables. Next, the most significant and non-significant results are provided to ensure the transparency and replicability of the findings. Also, given that existing association tests fail to indicate exact interactions between categories, an MCA is performed to provide a deeper understanding of the association between variables, including all of the variables in this study, and the variables are reduced to only those reported as statistically significant. This study provides a discussion section that explains the findings obtained, and finally, it gives concluding remarks, limitations, and implications of this study in the last section.

2. Literature Review

When analyzing user profiles in e-commerce and the influence of demographics, limited studies include supervised or unsupervised learning models. Previous studies primarily rely on user descriptive profiles and inferential statistics for hypothesis testing [1,15,21]. In contrast, others extend the analysis with multivariate regression [22] and factor models [23–25], whereas item answers are used as continuous values assuming a normal distribution. In addition, a sample of studies that use advanced mathematical modelling of e-customer profiles is identified. For example, Hristoski I. et al. [26], using customer behavior model graphs (CBMGs), identify 12 typologies of online shoppers. The CBMGs work as an $N \times N$ transitional probability matrix that denotes relative frequencies of invoking specific e-commerce functions. These frequencies are then used to map a unique transitional probability matrix of users with similar behavior.

Next, Swarnakar P. et al. [27] use Logistic Regression (LR) and Artificial Neural Networks (ANN) to predict online purchase behaviors to help e-retailers develop suitable strategies. They first perform a statistical analysis of demographics and user preferences to identify relevant factors affecting online behavior before using LR and ANN to predict user behavior. Chen X. et al. [28] used deep learning algorithms to predict user demographics based on the multisource user characteristics and preferences data in a vice versa approach.

On the other hand, some have tried identifying user profiles through cluster modelling. For instance, Bellini P. et al. [29] perform k-means clustering to identify user profiles based on demographics and preferences. The results show that after identifying different clusters of user profiles, a stimulus was generated for the customers, which increased buyers' purchases by 3.48%. Kuruba, Y. et al. [30] Customer segmentation was successfully performed using distributed clustering models. Lastly, a study by Hørlück J. et al. [31] fails to identify user behavior clusters using an unsupervised Gaussian Mixture Model with Hierarchical Probabilistic Clustering. It neither falsifies nor supports the hypothesis of identifying clear user profiles based on buying behavior.

Furthermore, understanding that demographics play an important role in shaping user profiles, a brief overview of demographic variables affecting user preferences is analyzed. The literature reports that e-customers between the ages of 18 and 50 are the most active [32], with young adults being prevalent [33,34], mainly driven by convenience and interactivity [35]. Older adults value product selection and post-consumption for repurchases [36], while younger adults do. The studies on gender suggest an inconclusive contribution [37,38], reporting both significant and non-significant findings. However, some suggest that women are "shopping for fun" while males emphasize "quick shopping" behaviors [39]. Additionally, Naseri and Elliott [40] indicate that education significantly influences the adoption of online shopping [41], while also income status [42] plays an important role, where both income and education tend to have a higher probability of online shopping [43,44]. Lastly, employment (work status) determines purchase behaviors [45–47]. A more comprehensive list of demographics that may interest the reader is described elsewhere [48,49].

Major challenges still exist. Although proposed typologies, clusters or classes of user profiles can be successfully mapped into different user profiles, the biggest issue is that most clusters and user profiles overlap and are not mutually exclusive. Also, from previous studies, there is a lack of evidence and methods describing the actual contribution of each variable (features) in describing contribution or shared variance. In this study, unsupervised modelling of user profiles for obtaining cluster labels is performed. Machine Learning (ML) predicts user profiles and identifies the most important features.

3. Materials and Methods

3.1. The Multistage Model of the Data Workflow Framework

The data workflow framework consists of three stages (Figure 1). The first stage explains a priori sample determination, survey development and data collection. Also, this stage explains the research hypothesis framework for reducing a raw dataset to a dataset comprising only statistically significant associations. Lastly, the first stage explains an in-depth statistical analysis regarding the statistically significant association between demographics and user preferences.

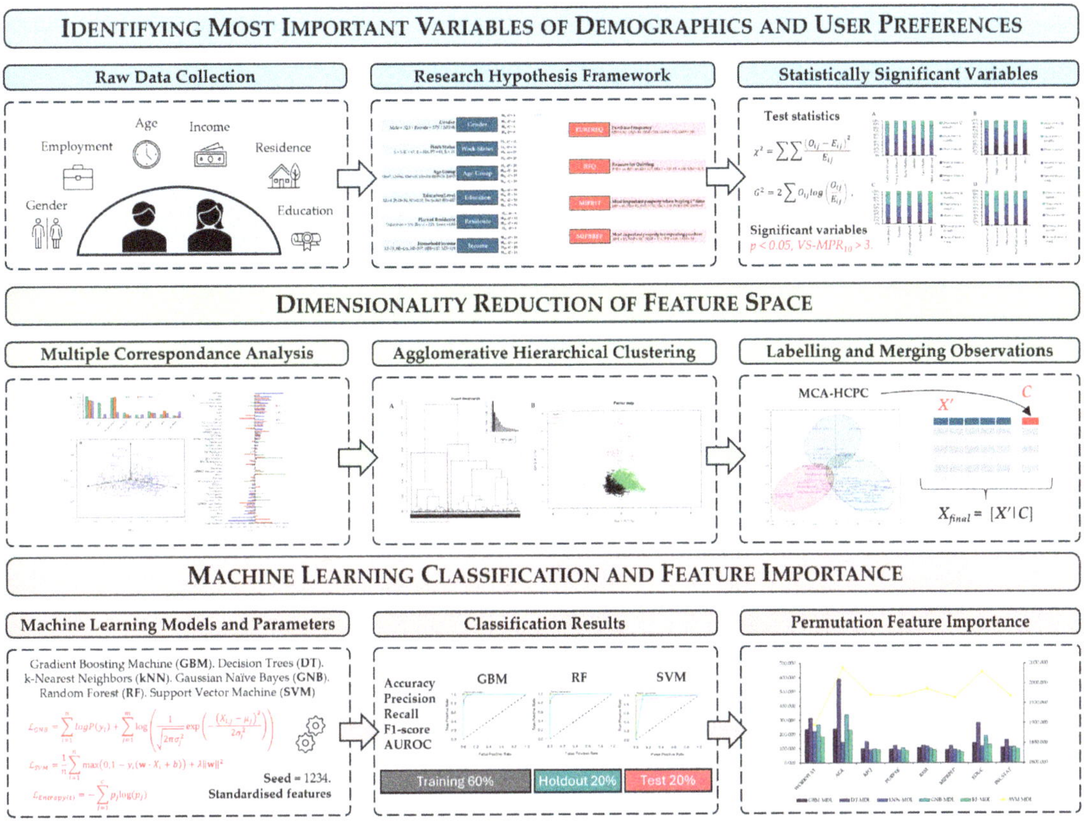

Figure 1. The data workflow framework.

The second stage explains the Multiple Correspondence Analysis (MCA) procedure for reducing the dimensionality of a dataset into two-dimensional space. Next, the study extracts relevant features by including only the top two Principal Components that explain the most variation, i.e., inertia. Also, the Agglomerative Hierarchical Clustering (AHC) is performed on MCA's Principal Components to obtain clusters of user preferences. The class label vector is merged with the raw dataset after identifying class labels, i.e., user profiles.

The third segment proposes and explains the utilized ML classifiers, i.e., ML algorithms, setting the parameters and loss functions used for the analysis. The second part of the third stage describes the main classification metrics used for evaluating the model performance and ML classification performance metrics—accuracy, precision, recall, F1-score and area under receiver operating characteristic (AUROC). Finally, the last part of the stage includes the extraction of the most relevant features using Permutation Feature Importance (PFI) [50] that builds upon the Mean Dropout Loss (MDL) metric [51].

3.2. Data Collection and Sample Size

The research was realized during the four weeks of November–December 2022 using two strategies for securing a representative sample. The survey was created on the Google Forms platform and distributed exclusively online. The target group was adult citizens of the Republic of Serbia who had experience ordering goods and durable products via the Internet and delivering them to a specific location. The survey included respondents with experience delivering goods such as electrical appliances, clothing, footwear, furniture, tools, small home and yard use items, sports equipment, and similar items. Before participating in the survey, respondents gave their consent to participate. They were informed about the research objectives and that their answers would be anonymous and analyzed in groups. They were informed that they could stop participating at any time.

A priori sample size was determined as follows. Firstly, the sample size is determined based on the minimum required sample size for performing χ^2 test statistics. To do so, a G*Power (v.3.1.9.6) is used for calculating sample size per parameters: Effect size w = 0.3 (medium effect), α = 0.05, power (1 − β error probability) = 0.80 and df = 36 (determined as the most of 7 categories per variables j and k, such that $df = (j - 1)(k - 1)$). The output statistic shows non-centrality parameter λ = 26.46, with χ^2_{crit} = 50.998, actual power (1 − β error probability) = 0.801, and minimum sample size of n = 294. Secondly, the sample size is calculated per Hamburg [52]—a commonly used sample size calculator can be found online at www.calculator.net (accessed on 1 November 2024). The minimum required representative sample is n = 385. Lastly, given that the sample size from previous similar studies [39,41] was higher than needed, data collection at n = 906 respondents was stopped.

3.3. The Research Hypothesis Framework

The research hypothesis framework (Figure 2) is designed to test the conditional dependencies, i.e., the existence of an association between different demographic properties of e-consumers and user preferences (and behavior). To do so, variables primarily reported in previous studies [32,53] regarding demographic properties are used—gender, work status, age group, education, place of residence, and income. Next, a test of association considering PURFREQ (purchase frequency), MIPB1T (most important property when buying the first time), MIPBREP (most important property before repeating the purchase), and RFQ (reasons for quitting the online purchase) is performed.

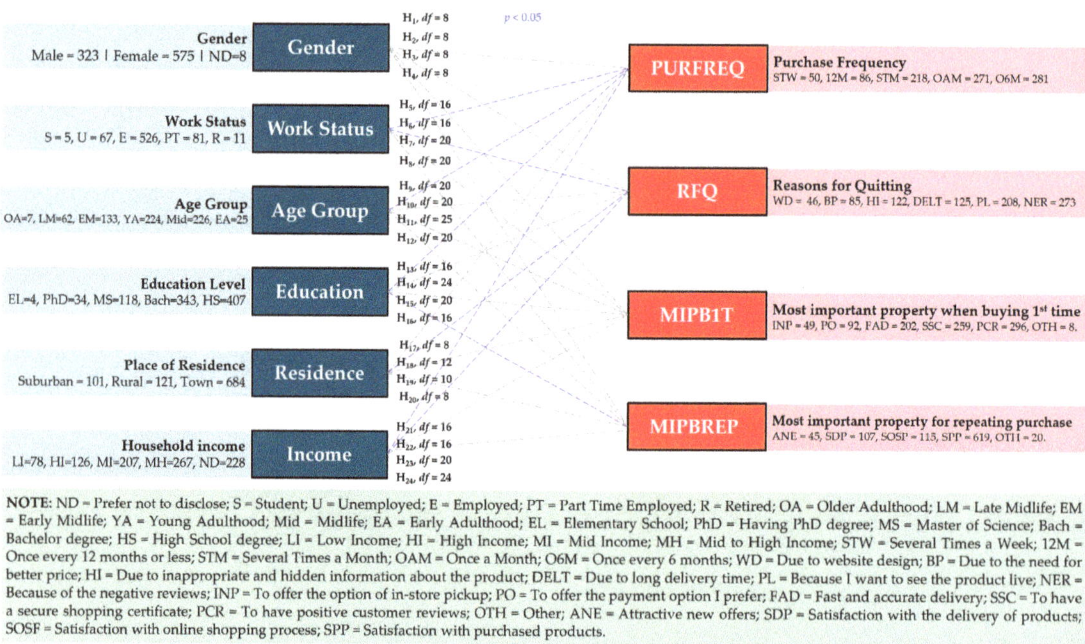

Figure 2. The research hypothetical framework.

For hypothesis testing, Pearson's χ^2 test statistic is chosen, described as follows:

$$\chi^2 = \sum\sum \frac{(O_{ij} - E_{ij})^2}{E_{ij}}, \tag{1}$$

such that Oij is observed frequencies, E_{ij} is expected frequencies computed as $R_i \times C_j/N$, where R_i and C_j represent row and column marginals, while N is the total observations. However, the G^2 likelihood ratio is reported using the following equation:

$$G^2 = 2\sum O_{ij} log\left(\frac{O_{ij}}{E_{ij}}\right), \tag{2}$$

as a more robust method for evaluating the goodness-of-fit and association between variables in contingency tables, given that the χ^2 statistic is only approximated by the χ^2 distribution and worsens when expected frequencies are relatively small, which is a common controversy using χ^2 test statistic, G^2 is included because it provides more robust measurements for large dimensional tables. It is commonly discussed that G^2 advantage over traditional χ^2 is that G^2 for large contingency tables can be neatly decomposed into smaller components [54], which cannot be achieved by the χ^2 test. Even so, as the sample size increases, statistics tend to converge. The degrees of freedom df is determined by $df = (r - 1)(c - 1)$, where r and c represent classes of row and column profiles, respectively.

Furthermore, the diagnosticity of p values using the VS–MPR (Vovk–Sellke Maximum p-Ratio) calibration score is performed. The score is computed as VS–MPR = $-e \times p \times \ln(p)$ and is commonly referred to as a lower bound to BF (favoring H_0 over H_1) [55]. The reason for including VS–MPR is that a large body of research [56–58] is calling into question the traditional threshold ($p < 0.05$) for deciding whether a model is statistically significant, i.e., rejects the null hypothesis. The following labelling intervals are used as evidence in favor of the alternative over the null hypothesis: VS–MPR$_{10}$ = 1–3 anecdotal, VS–MPR$_{10}$ = 3–10 substantial, VS–MPR$_{10}$ = 10–30 strong, VS–MPR$_{10}$ = 30–100 very strong, and finally VS–MPR$_{10}$ > 100 as decisive evidence [59].

3.4. Multiple Correspondence Analysis Hierarchical Clustering of Principal Components

To understand MCA's description, let the initial raw dataset be a matrix $\boldsymbol{X} \in \mathbb{R}^{n \times m}$, where n is the number of observations and m is the number of variables that explain demographics and user preferences. To reduce the dimensionality of dataset $\boldsymbol{X}$, hypothesis testing is performed (see Equations (2) and (3)) to keep only statistically significant variables ($p < 0.05$, VS–MPR$_{10}$ > 3). After removing non-significant variables, the reduced $X' \subset X$ dataset comprises only significant variables. Hence, the $\boldsymbol{X'}$ is subjected to MCA to further reduce dimensionality by transforming raw data into Principal Components (PCs).

The first step in MCA is to convert a raw categorical dataset $\boldsymbol{X'}$ into indicator matrix $Z \in \mathbb{R}^{n \times q}$, where q is the number of class categories from the retained variable set. Next, from the defined indicator matrix $\boldsymbol{Z}$, centring is performed by subtracting row, and column means to obtain the centered matrix $\boldsymbol{Z_C}$:

$$\boldsymbol{Z}_{C,\,ij} = \boldsymbol{Z}_{ij} - \frac{1}{n}\sum_{i=1}^{n} \boldsymbol{Z}_{ij} - \frac{1}{q}\sum_{i=1}^{n} \boldsymbol{Z}_{ij} + \frac{1}{nq}\sum_{i=1}^{n}\sum_{j=1}^{q} \boldsymbol{Z}_{ij}, \tag{3}$$

which adjusts for marginal distributions, ensuring a standardized matrix for PC extraction. Using Singular Value Decomposition (SVD), $\boldsymbol{Z_C}$ is decomposed as follows:

$$Z_C = \boldsymbol{U\Sigma V^T}, \tag{4}$$

where $\boldsymbol{U} \in \mathbb{R}^{n \times k}$ are singular vectors in the reduced space, $\boldsymbol{\Sigma} \in \mathbb{R}^{k \times k}$ is a diagonal matrix with singular values of each PC, and $\boldsymbol{V} \in \mathbb{R}^{q \times k}$ is the singular vector matrix representing variable contributions of each PC. The top k components are selected based on the first two PCs that explain the most variance as PCs $\in \mathbb{R}^{n\times k}$.

Finally, after obtaining reduced dataset PCs, an HCPC is performed to identify clusters, i.e., label user profiles in a reduced space. For performing distance computation and obtaining distance matrix $\boldsymbol{D}$, an Euclidian distance $\boldsymbol{D}(i,j)$ between each pair of observations in PCs is performed:

$$D(i,j) = \left\|PCs_i - PCs_j\right\|^2, \tag{5}$$

which yields distance matrix $\boldsymbol{D} \in \mathbb{R}^{n\times n}$, capturing similarities between respondents. Ward's method is selected to apply hierarchical agglomerative clustering on PCs to merge clusters and minimize within-cluster variance. The results are represented via a dendrogram. Linkage L selects the clusters, assigning labels to observations $C = \{c_1, c_2, \ldots, c_n\}$. As a last step, cluster $\boldsymbol{C}$ labels are merged with dataset X', resulting in the final dataset $\boldsymbol{X_{final}} = [\boldsymbol{X'} \mid \boldsymbol{C}]$, which is then subjected to classification by ML algorithms.

3.5. Machine Learning Classifiers

Machine Learning classification is performed as follows. Let dataset $\boldsymbol{X_{final}} \in \mathbb{R}^{n\times(m+1)}$ be the final dataset, where n is the number of observations and m represents the features (demographics and user preferences), while the last column, denoted as $y \in \{1, 2, \ldots, c\}$, represents the cluster labels assigned via MCA-HCPC, such that c represents a total number of selected clusters.

The splitting of the dataset into train (with holdout)/test dataset is performed, such that $\boldsymbol{X_{train}} \in \mathbb{R}^{n_{train}\times m}$ be training matrix with $y_{train} \in \{1, 2, \ldots, c\}^{n_{train}}$ labels. Similarly, let $\boldsymbol{X_{test}} \in \mathbb{R}^{n_{test}\times m}$ with $y_{test} \in \{1, 2, \ldots, c\}^{n_{test}}$ be the test dataset. Specifically, the models are trained with train/validation/test per 60%/20%/20% split from the $\boldsymbol{X_{final}}$ dataset. We aim to train the ML classifier $\mathcal{M}$: $\mathbf{X_{train}} \rightarrow y$ by optimizing loss function $\mathcal{L}$. For proposed ML classifiers—Gradient Boosting Machine (GBM), Decision Tree (DT), k-Nearest Neighbors (kNN), Gaussian Naïve Bayes (GNB), Random Forest (RF), and Support Vector Machine (SVM)—the loss functions are defined for GBM:

$$\mathcal{L}_{GBM} = -\sum_{i=1}^{n}\sum_{j=1}^{c} y_{i,j}\log(\hat{y}_{i,j}), \tag{6}$$

where in multi-class problem $y_{i,j}$ is a binary indicator (1 if label j, otherwise 0), and $\hat{y}_{i,j}$ is the predicted probability for class j. For DT and RF, a Gini impurity is estimated as:

$$\mathcal{L}_{Gini(t)} = 1 - \sum_{j=1}^{c} p_j^2, \tag{7}$$

and Entropy as:

$$\mathcal{L}_{Entropy(t)} = -\sum_{j=1}^{c} p_j\log(p_j), \tag{8}$$

where algorithms select the feature that maximizes the reduction in Gini (or Entropy). For Gaussian Naïve Bayes, the classifier calculates the posterior probability for each class:

$$\mathcal{L}_{GNB} = \sum_{i=1}^{n} logP(y_i) + \sum_{j=1}^{m} \log\left(\frac{1}{\sqrt{2\pi\sigma_j^2}}\exp\left(-\frac{(X_{i,j} - \mu_j)^2}{2\sigma_j^2}\right)\right) \tag{9}$$

where $P(y_i)$ is the prior probability of class y_i, while μ is the mean and σ^2 is the variance of feature j conditioned on y_i. The SVM loss function is determined per Hinge loss:

$$\mathcal{L}_{SVM} = \frac{1}{n}\sum_{i=1}^{n} \max(0, 1 - y_i(\mathbf{w}\cdot X_i + b)) + \lambda\|\mathbf{w}\|^2, \tag{10}$$

where $y_i \in \{-1, 1\}$ represents the true class label, $\mathbf{w}$ is the weight vector, while X_i is the feature vector, b is the bias, and λ is the regularization parameter controlling the margin. Given the classification problem, the selection of the highest-performing algorithm is conducted per classification evaluation metrics of accuracy:

$$Accuracy = \frac{TP + TN}{TP + TN + FP + FN}, \tag{11}$$

where TP = true positive, TN = true negative, FP = false positive, and FN = false negative. The recall is calculated as:

$$Recall = \frac{TP}{TP + FN}. \tag{12}$$

The precision is estimated as follows:

$$Precision = \frac{TP}{TP + FP}, \tag{13}$$

and finally *F1-score* is calculated as:

$$F1 - score = \frac{2\,TP}{2\,TP + FP + FN}, \tag{14}$$

for estimating the classification performance of ML algorithms. Additionally, an AUROC is considered by adopting it to multi-class problems.

To ensure transparency and replicability of the results, the following parameters (and hyperparameters) are set for the ML models. For GBM, the following parameters are set: Shrinkage = 0.1, with 1.0 interaction depth with a minimum number of observations per node = 10. The training used per tree is 50%. The number of trees is optimized such that the maximum number is 100. For the DT algorithm, the minimum number of observations for split is 20, with a minimum number of observations in terminal = 7, with maximum interaction depth = 30. The DT tree complexity is optimized with a maximum complexity penalty = 1.0. The kNN algorithm settings are set as follows: weights = Rectangular with Euclidian distance metric used. The number of nearest neighbors is optimized such that the maximum allowed nearest neighbors = 10. For the RF algorithm, the training data used per tree are 50%, while features are split automatically with an optimized number of trees set to a maximum of 100 trees. The SVM algorithm is set with the following parameters: Weights = Linear, Tolerance of termination criterion = 0.001, with function ξ = 0.01. The costs of constraints violation are optimized with maximum violation cost = 5. There were no smoothing parameters set for GNB algorithms. However, all algorithms contain scaled features, and the seed is 1234. Lastly, to ensure the reliability of the analysis, i.e., to avoid overfitting and underfitting, a 10-fold cross-validation is performed of the training (with validation) dataset. To ensure objectiveness and replicability in testing the results of individual classifiers, the parameters (and hyperparameters) used can be input and replicated in JASP v0.19.1.

4. Results

4.1. Descriptive Statistics

The characteristics (Figure 3) show the following. This study comprises 906 participants, ranging from 21 to 77 years old (median = 34.90, SD = 12.67). Most were female (63%, n = 575), while <1% of participants selected "preferred not to disclose" (n = 8). Most of the respondents had completed high school (44.92%, n = 407), followed by a Bachelor's degree (37.86%, n = 343) and a Master's degree (13.02%, n = 118). The respondents were primarily situated in towns (75.5%, n = 684), followed by rural (13.36%, n = 121) and suburban areas (11.15%, n = 101). The employment characteristics show that 58% (n = 526) of respondents are employed. The income status is classified according to monthly earnings of RSD (Republic Serbia Dinar) in categories as low income

(<50.000 RSD), mid income (50.000–100.000 RSD), mid-high income (100.000–200.000 RSD), high income (>200.000 RSD). The results show that most respondents had mid-high income (29.47%, n = 267), 25.17% (n = 228) did not want to say their income, followed by mid income (22.85%, n = 207), high income (13.91%, n = 126), and low income (8.61%, n = 78). Lastly, the age distribution shows average AVGAge = 35.914 with SDAge = 12.671, ranging from 21 to 77 years old. The age distribution is then coded as follows: early adulthood (18–24 years), young adulthood (25–34 years), early midlife (35–44 years), midlife (45–54 years), late midlife (55–64 years), older adulthood (>65 years). As per coded categories, the descriptives show that early adulthood (28.04%, n = 254) is the most dominant category, followed by midlife (24.94%, n = 226) and young adulthood (24.72%, n = 224), early midlife (14.68%, n = 133), late midlife (6.84%, n = 62), and older adulthood (0.77%, n = 7).

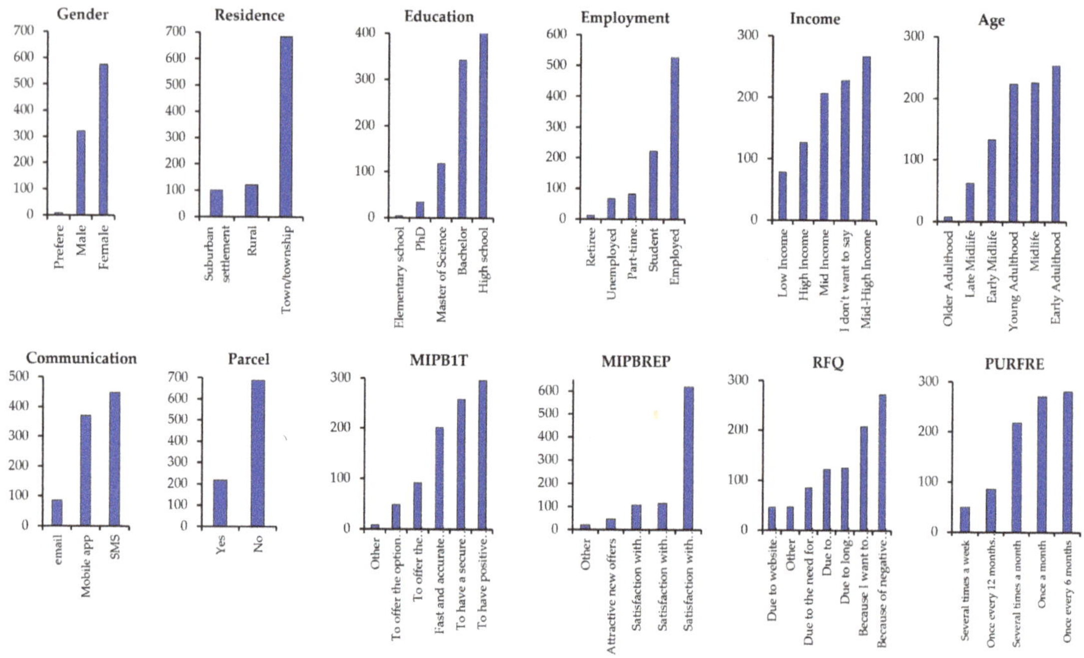

Figure 3. Descriptive statistics of demographic data (**top row**) and user preferences (**bottom row**).

Supplementary items such as "What communication channel would you prefer to have with the supplier?" labelled as Communication, and "Used parcel locker?" show that most users prefer SMS (49.56%, n = 449) and Mobile App (40.95%, n = 371) and uses parcel locker (24.06%, n = 218), respectively. The main preferences, such as MIPB1T, show that most users consider positive reviews (32.67%, n = 296) when buying the first time, followed by "To have a secure shopping certificate" (28.59%, n = 259), and "Fast and secure delivery" (22.30%, n = 202). The MIPBREP property suggests that "Satisfaction with products purchased" (68.32%, n = 619) is the most dominant reason for repeating the purchase, followed by "Satisfaction with the online shopping (12.69%, n = 115), "Satisfaction with the delivery of purchased products" (11.81%, n = 107), and others. The RFQ shows that negative reviews (30.13%, n = 273), followed by "Because I want to see the product live" (22.96%, n = 208) and "Long delivery time" (13.80%, n = 125) are the most common reasons why users quiet their purchase. Lastly, the PURFRE show that most users buy every six months (31.02%, n = 281), followed by "Once a month" (29.91%, n = 271).

Contingency tables are constructed before performing the statistical inferential statistics and χ^2 tests to investigate the association between variables. However, due to the limited length and extensive number of tables (24 tables) for each model comparison, the complete analysis with tables is provided in Supplementary Materials in cases the reader is interested in following the full analysis. In the following, the final results of each model comparison using both χ^2 and G^2 test statistics are provided, including the effect size (for χ^2 test) and VS–MPR ratio.

4.2. Hypothesis Testing

After performing hypotheses testing as a proposed framework, 8/24 hypotheses regarding the conditional dependencies were rejected, i.e., the association between e-customer demographics and user preferences (Table 1). Namely, only cases where both χ^2 and G^2 suggest statistically significant association ($p < 0.05$) were considered and where there is at least moderate, i.e., substantial evidence in favor of the alternative hypothesis ($\text{VS–MPR}_{10} > 3$). In such instances, results will be more robust and reliable. Additionally, non-significant test results are reported in the appendices (Table A1).

Table 1. Statistical analysis reported per χ^2 test.

Variables	Test	Value	*df*	*p*	Cramer's *V*	VS–MPR
AGE—PURFRE	χ^2 test statistic	50.519	20	0.001	0.118	229.606
	G^2 likelihood ratio	54.838	20	0.001		843.603
EDU—PURFRE	χ^2 test statistic	38.498	16	0.001	0.103	43.022
	G^2 likelihood ratio	39.004	16	0.001		49.631
RESI—RFQ	χ^2 test statistic	24.599	12	0.017	0.117	5.349
	G^2 likelihood ratio	25.710	12	0.012		7.025
EDU—MIPBREP	χ^2 test statistic	33.834	16	0.006	0.097	12.456
	G^2 likelihood ratio	30.371	16	0.016		5.516
INCSTAT—PURFRE	χ^2 test statistic	52.421	16	0.001	0.120	3392.513
	G^2 likelihood ratio	49.376	16	0.001		1221.498
INCSTAT—RFQ	χ^2 test statistic	41.019	24	0.017	0.106	5.413
	G^2 likelihood ratio	41.087	24	0.016		5.484
WORKSTAT—PURFRE	χ^2 test statistic	51.892	16	0.001	0.120	2834.207
	G^2 likelihood ratio	50.487	16	0.001		1766.807
WORKSTAT—RFQ	χ^2 test statistic	50.697	24	0.001	0.118	47.147
	G^2 likelihood ratio	54.134	24	0.001		115.292

Surprisingly, no evidence suggested that demographic properties are conditionally dependent, i.e., associated with MIPB1T ($p > 0.05$). There is, however, anecdotal evidence ($\text{VS–MPR}_{10} = 2.386$) suggesting that age ($\chi^2 = 37.455$, $p = 0.052$) tends to be associated with MIPB1T but fails to reject the null ($p > 0.05$). Hence, the null hypothesis that indicates a user preference describing the "Most important property when buying from a webshop for the first time?" failed to be rejected.

The results investigating the association of demographics to the PURFRE variable suggests that age ($\chi^2 = 50.519$, $G^2 = 54.838$, $p = 0.001$), education ($03C7^2 = 38.498$, $G^2 = 39.004$, $p = 0.001$), income ($\chi^2 = 52.421$, $G^2 = 49.376$, $p = 0.001$), and work status ($\chi^2 = 51.892$, $G^2 = 50.487$, $p = 0.001$), ranging from very strong ($\text{VS–MPR}_{10} > 30$) in education, to decisive evidence ($\text{VS–MPR}_{10} > 100$) of age, income and work status in associations with PURFRE. Next, the analysis of associations with RFQ suggests that work status provides very strong evidence ($\chi^2 = 50.697$, $G^2 = 54.134$, $p = 0.001$, $\text{VS–MPR}_{10}\text{-}\chi^2 = 47.147$), followed by substantial evidence regarding residence ($\chi^2 = 24.599$, $G^2 = 25.710$, $p = 0.017$, $\text{VS–MPR}_{10}\text{-}\chi^2 = 5.349$) and income ($\chi^2 = 41.019$, $G^2 = 41.087$, $p = 0.017$, $\text{VS–MPR}_{10}\text{-}\chi^2 = 5.413$). Lastly, the test considering MIPBREP suggests only the existence of association to education with substantial ($G^2 = 30.371$, $p = 0.016$, $\text{VS–MPR}_{10} = 5.516$) to strong ($\chi^2 = 33.84$, $p = 0.006$, $\text{VS–MPR}_{10} = 12.456$) evidence in favor of the alternative.

The results suggest statistical dependency between demographics and user preferences (excluding MIPB1T). However, more needs to be understood about how specific underlying classes associate with each other. Hence, MCA uses the χ^2 distance better to understand the relationship between investigated demographics and user preferences.

4.3. Multiple Correspondence Analysis

The MCA analysis suggests an improved understanding of the association between class categories. Namely, the explained inertia is 11.797% in the first two components and 16.1% in the first three (Figure 4A). Next, the η^2 correlation coefficient (Figure 4B), representing the degree of association between variables and Principal Components, suggests that all three components explain the AGE variable well. The second component mainly captures AGE (η^2 = 0.516) and WORKSTAT (η^2 = 0.607), while user preferences include PURFRE (η^2 = 0.141) and RFQ (η^2 = 0.201). Lastly, AGE (η^2 = 0.499), EDU (η^2 = 0.119) and WORKSTAT (η^2 = 0.175) consider demographic variables explained by the PC3, with PURFRE (η^2 = 0.135), RFQ (η^2 = 0.134) and MIPBREP (η^2 = 0.181) user preferences captured. Most of the information is well explained by the first two components, with the MIPBREP variable slightly higher η^2. Hence, the association between variables is discussed within the first two PCs.

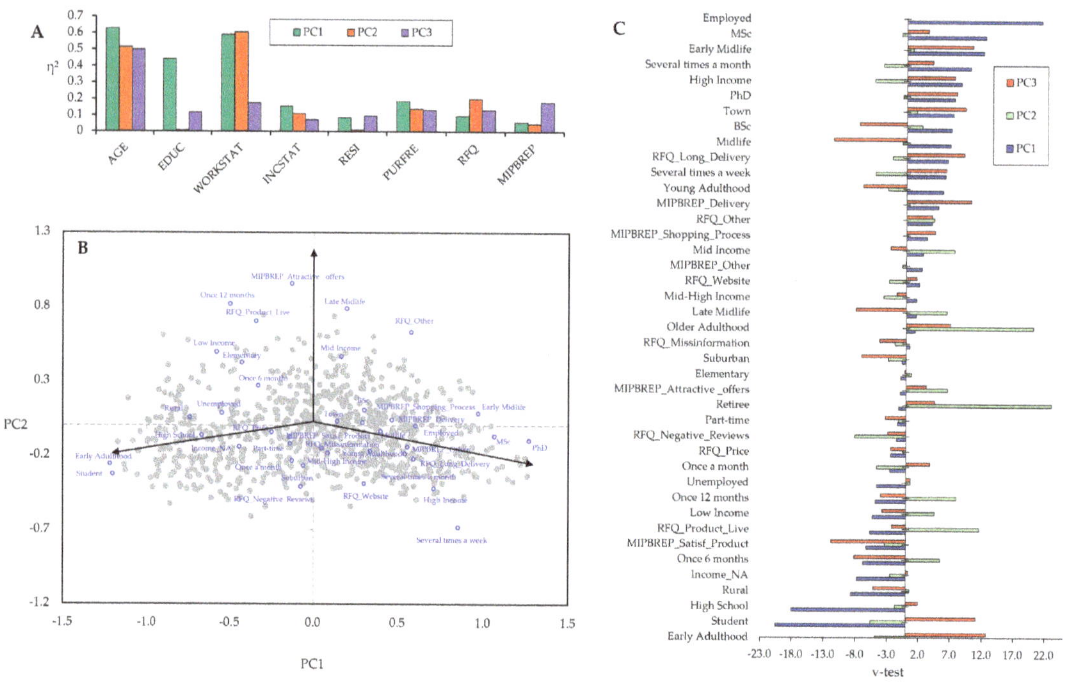

Figure 4. MCA analysis including (**A**) η^2 coefficient of categories concerning PCs; (**B**) MCA biplot of respondents (grey color) and class categories of categorical variables; (**C**) v-test score of class categories ($z > 1.96$, $z < -1.96$).

The MCA biplot (Figure 4C) identifies three latent projections describing demographics and user preferences. Namely, the vertical mainly suggests late midlife to older adults, low to mid income, and with purchasing frequency from 6 to 12 months, who prefer person-to-person purchase, i.e., seeing the product live, which is mainly described by the PC2. Observing the negative side of PC1(−) and PC2(−), i.e., the left bottom quadrant, mainly describes students, high school education, early adults, unemployed and part-time employed respondents, rural areas, and with purchasing frequency from once a month to once in six months. This can also be supplemented by the v-test (Figure 4C) score, as it mainly quantifies the class category distance from the average. Hence, PC1-PC3 can offer similar information on class categories in factor plots.

Lastly, the bottom right quadrant, captured mainly by the PC1(+) inertia, describes the respondents as early midlife and employed mostly with an MSc degree, with town residence and high income. These respondents are characterized by user preferences describing purchasing power from several times a week (CTR = 1.78, $\cos^2 = 0.04$, v-test = 6.20) to several times a month (CTR = 3.77, $\cos^2 = 0.11$, v-test = 10.6), while most crucial property before repeating the purchase (MIPBREP) being the satisfaction with the delivery (CTR = 1.13, $\cos^2 = 0.029$, v-test = 5.12) and satisfaction with the online shopping process (CTR = 0.474, $\cos^2 = 0.012$, v-test = 3.33) while the main reason for quitting the purchase is long delivery (CTR = 1.80, $\cos^2 = 0.05$, v-test = 6.52). The full list of coordinates for PCs, including cos2, CTR, and v-test, is provided in Table A4.

4.4. Classification Results

The training (and holdout set) classification accuracy (Table 2) suggests that the highest classification accuracy is obtained via SVM (0.950), GBM (0.939) and RF (0.928). The SVM suggests that classification metrics are mostly consistent across precision, recall, F1-score and AUROC. However, the GNB, instead of RF, show high precision, recall and F1-scores, while AUROC results suggest that GBM (0.994) and RF (0.994) are the highest.

Table 2. Machine learning classification metrics (* represents results of 10-fold cross-validation).

Algorithm	Accuracy	Precision	Recall	F1-Score	AUROC
GBM	**0.959 (* 0.956)**	0.943 (* 0.938)	0.939 (* 0.934)	0.936 (* 0.930)	**0.994 (* 0.994)**
DT	0.917 (* 0.876)	0.902 (* 0.878)	0.917 (* 0.898)	0.909 (* 0.863)	0.894 (* 0.882)
kNN	0.884 (* 0.930)	0.870 (* 0.881)	0.884 (* 0.895)	0.876 (* 0.887)	0.796 (* 0.802)
GNB	0.939 (* 0.911)	0.942 (* 0.914)	0.939 (* 0.930)	0.936 (* 0.928)	0.843 (* 0.836)
RF	0.928 (* 0.928)	0.914 (* 0.914)	0.928 (* 0.928)	0.920 (* 0.920)	**0.994 (* 0.994)**
SVM	0.950 (* 0.936)	**0.954 (* 0.944)**	**0.950 (* 0.942)**	**0.949 (* 0.940)**	0.902 (* 0.886)

From a cluster of user profiles, the labelling shows a significant dataset imbalance; therefore, accuracy results can also be misleading, although precision and recall metrics are useful when false positives and false negatives are problematic, respectively. F1-score and AUROC are particularly useful since they address the case of the imbalanced dataset. Therefore, the results from the holdout set show that GBM (0.959), SVM (0.950), GNB (0.939) and RF (0.928) are the highest-performing classifiers. The results after the 10-fold cross-validation report are similar: GBM (0.956), SVM (0.936), RF (0.928) and GNB (0.911).

The classification results (Figure 5A) show that GBM (0.994), RF (0.994), and SVM (0.902, 10FCV = 0.886) are the highest-performing classifiers. Although the interest here is in PFI rankings, MDL scores of all ML classifiers are provided. Overall, one can conclude that age plays a crucial role in ML classifiers, followed by work status, education status, and income status. Still, the highest-performing ML classifiers suggest that age (GBM, RF, and SVM) is the most important feature, followed by work status (GBM, RF), education (GBM, RF, SVM) and residence (SVM). Hence, ensemble learners (GBM, RF) offer similar results, while SVM suggests similar results in decision boundaries.

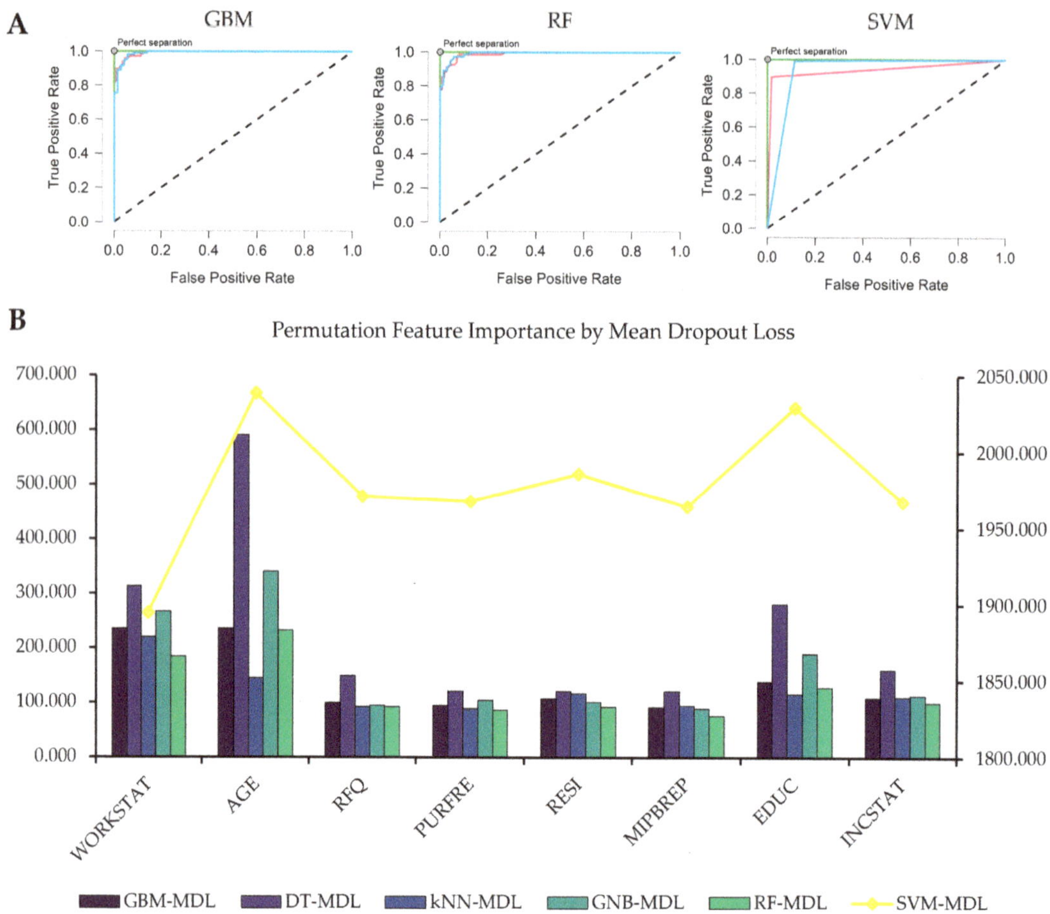

Figure 5. Machine Learning Classification of (**A**) Receiver Operating Characteristic Curve representing Cluster 1 (red), Cluster 2 (green) and Cluster 3 (blue), and (**B**) Permutation Feature Importance estimated by Mean Dropout Loss.

5. Discussion

5.1. Hypothesis Testing Results

The following conclusions are obtained. Age indicates a significant association with purchase frequency ($p = 0.001$, $V = 0.118$). From a general trend (Figure 6A), early (18–24 years) and young adults (25–34 years) dominate in purchasing from at least once a month to once every six months, presumably due to a combination of comfort with digital technology. However, there is a significant increase in purchasing of early midlife (35–44 years) and midlife (45–54 years) several times a month and even several times a week, which was quite surprising since most of the prior literature report the dominance in frequent purchases of young adults (21–30 years). This may be attributed to the cause that parents tend to shift priorities and behavior (e.g., career, family, investments).

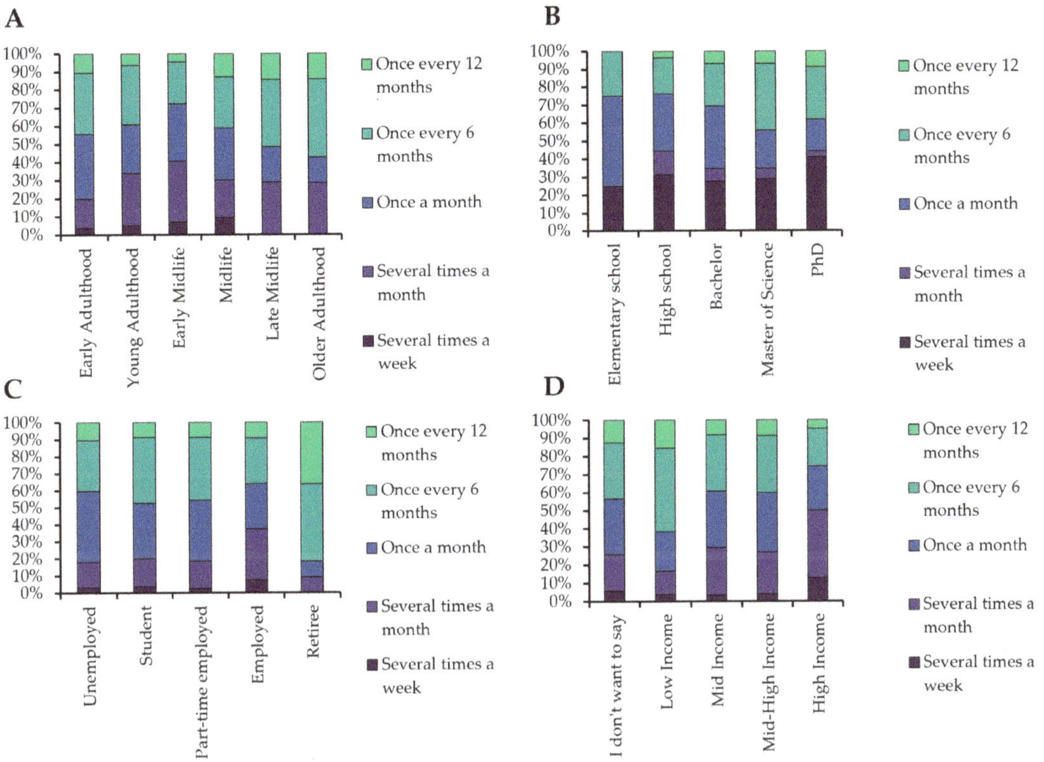

Figure 6. The purchase frequencies with corresponding demographics are (**A**) age, (**B**) education, (**C**) work status, and (**D**) income.

Analyzing the association between education and purchase frequency (Figure 6B), the evidence suggests that higher educational attainment corresponds to a more selective behavior. Namely, there is an increase in purchases from several times a month to once a month, while there is an increase in users with small purchases from once in six months to once in twelve months. Master's and PhD degree holders tend to shop less frequently but with more deliberate timing and thoughtful behavior in their purchases. Bachelor's degree holders are slightly more active in online shopping than high school graduates, probably due to higher income levels and better comfort with digital content. The discussion on elementary school education is inconclusive since only four subjects participated in the questionnaire.

The work status (Figure 6C) exhibits similar behavior patterns of unemployed respondents, students and part-time employees. The evidence shows a significant increase in purchase frequency among employed participants. On average, there is a 25.7% increase in purchases several times per month and a 16.5% increase in purchase frequency once a month. In contrast, 6.8% and 4.9% drop in purchases "once a month" and "once every six months", respectively. Lastly, there is a significant drop from 12–25% in purchasing from several times a week to once a month, and a substantial increase in the purchases of "once every six months" (6.9%) and "once every 12 months" (37%) of the retirees.

The results comparing income status and purchase frequency (Figure 6D) show the highest effect ($\chi^2 = 52.421$, $V = 0.120$, VS–MPR$_{10}$ = 3392.513, $G^2 = 49.376$, VS–MPR$_{10}$ = 1221.5) among tested variables, suggesting extreme evidence (VS–MPR$_{10}$ > 100). There is, on average, a 29.97% increase in purchase frequency "several times a week" comparing High with Low to mid-high income respondents. Also, there is a 14.02% increase in purchasing "several times a month" compared to Low to Mid-High income respondents. There is a significant drop of 2.91%, 9.7% and 12.13% in purchase frequency "once a month", "once every six months", and "once every twelve months", respectively.

The association between residence and RFQ (Figure 7A) suggests that suburbans' main reason for quitting is to see the product live (20% higher). At the same time, rural areas state that the main reasons for quitting are inappropriate or hidden information (8–16% higher) and complicated searches on the website (4–20% higher). The prevalent factor across all groups, particularly in rural areas, is the desire to see the product in person, while inappropriate/hidden information is the main reason for quitting the purchase.

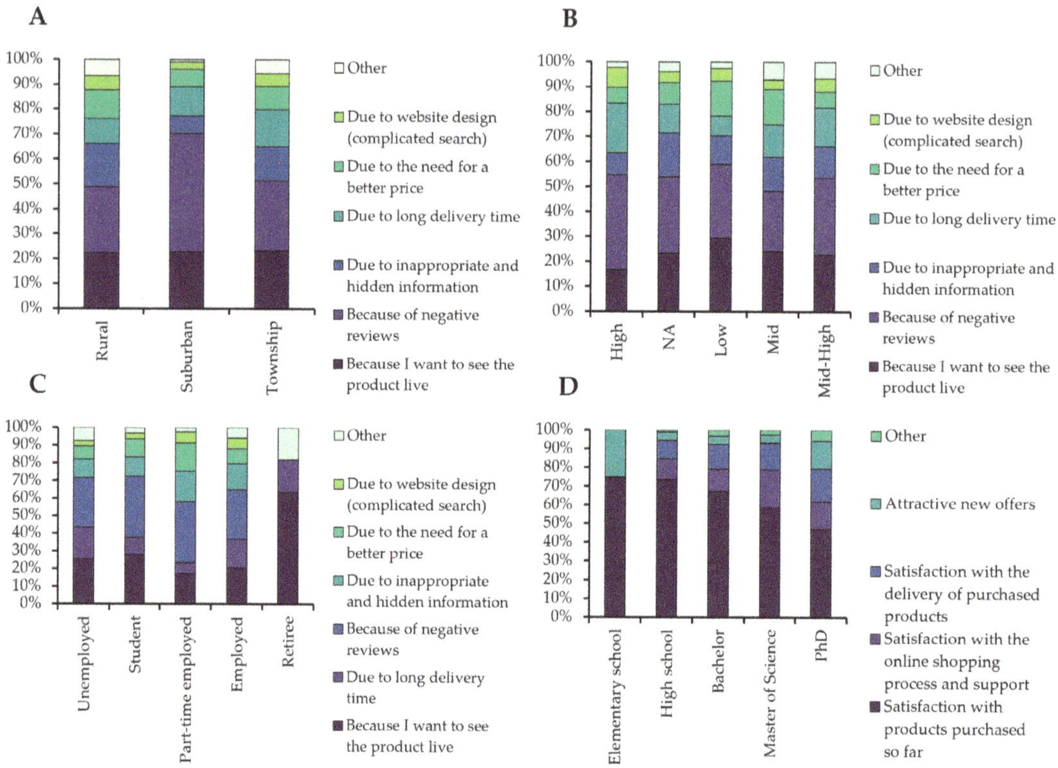

Figure 7. The frequencies of reasons for quitting (RFQ) variable and corresponding demographics (**A**) residence, (**B**) income, (**C**) work status. The frequencies of MIPBREP (most important property before repeating the purchase) and demographic (**D**) income.

Regarding the dependency between income and RFQ (Figure 7B), the evidence suggests that negative reviews (30%) are the most common reasons for quitting. However, higher-income respondents cite long delivery times (29.5%) and website design (29.9%) as the most common reasons for quitting, suggesting that convenience and user experience are more critical. In comparison, the need for a better price is a minor concern (12.8%) for these users. The low-income respondents cite the need for a better price (28.4%) and reflect a more price-sensitive group, while also the need to see the product live (25.3%). Paradoxically, the respondents who preferred not to disclose their income cite that the highest dissatisfaction rate is due to inappropriate or hidden information (27.4%) about the product as a potential concern over transparency and trustworthiness. Lower-income users prioritize affordability and assurance, while higher-income respondents prioritize efficiency and convenience.

The analysis of work status and RFQ (Figure 7C) shows that unemployed respondents and students demonstrate more risk-averse attitudes. In contrast, unemployed respondents cite negative reviews and long delivery times as primary concerns for quitting. At the same time, students also cite negative reviews in addition to a need for a better price, which is also the main reason (32.5%) emphasized in responses of part-time employees. The employed e-consumers cite hidden information and website design as the primary reasons, aligning somewhat with part-time workers. Still, although this suggests that individuals generally have more disposable income, they expect a high standard of service.

Lastly, the results regarding the association between education and MIPBREP (Figure 7D) show that as education levels increase, consumers tend to prioritize the broader shopping experience, such as satisfaction with delivery and customer services, rather than product— or price-related issues. This underlines the need for e-tailers to provide more comprehensive and personalized services to accommodate the expectations of more educated consumer groups.

5.2. Multiple Correspondence Analysis with Hierarchical Clustering on PCs

For the MCA, mainly using significant variables, three potential clusters may be identified along the axes (Figure 4C). Hierarchical Clustering on Principal Components (HCPC) is performed to maintain objectivity in the identification of user profiles. The HCPC method uses Euclidian distance for clustering of points, while Ward's linkage is used for cluster selection. The complete analysis is performed in R studio *FactoMineR* (v2.11).

The dendrogram (Figure 8A) suggests that three clusters are selected, while the interpretation can also be suitable for selecting up to six clusters based on the inertia gain. However, for the simplicity of interpretation, three clusters are selected for the analysis (Figure 8B). The data behind clusters are provided in Appendix B. To understand the interpretation of tables (e.g., see Table A5), let us go through the features "Cla/Mod", "Mod/Cla", "Global", "*p*-value", and "v-test". For instance, Cluster 1 (black) shows that age = early adulthood ("Cla/Mod" = 92.913, v-test = 24.465) suggest that 92.9% belongs to Cluster 1, while 78.67% of age proportion ("Mod/Cla") in Cluster 1 is early adulthood. The "Global" shows the overall proportion of a particular class in a complete dataset. Note that only classes (with associated categories) that are statistically significant (v-test = ± 1.96, p-value < 0.05) are represented.

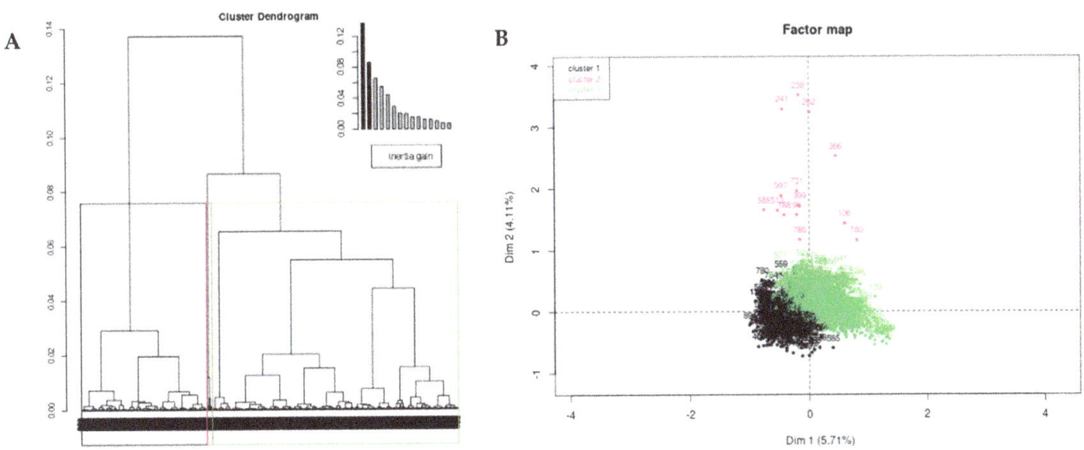

Figure 8. Agglomerative Hierarchical Clustering of observations represented via (**A**) a dendrogram with observations (x-axis) and distance measured (y-axis); and (**B**) identified clusters based on the first two Principal Components.

Cluster 1 (black), therefore, suggests that respondents are mainly in age = early adulthood, Students (with high school diploma), WORKSTAT = Unemployed, from RESI = Rural areas, and Gender = Females (and persons that do not want to disclose gender identity) being over-represented. A particular group of respondents show an association with PURFRE = Once a month, MIPB1T = To have positive customer reviews, RFQ = Because of negative reviews, and RFQ = I want to see the product live. This cluster suggests that women are dominant e-consumers, mainly driven by positive reviews for repeating the purchase (and vice versa, quitting the because of negative reviews), prefer seeing the product live with purchasing via mobile apps. The purchase frequency is characterized by moderate purchase frequency, suggesting at least once a month.

Cluster 2 (red) mainly describes WORKSTAT = Retiree (Cla/Mod = 100%) and age = older adulthood (Cla/Mod = 100%), with minimal purchase frequency of once every 12 months, that is mainly driven by attractive new offers when wanting to repeat the purchase but are also quitting if they cannot see the product in person. Ultimately, although with limited respondents (Global = 1.214%), this suggests that these e-consumers are retirees and infrequent cautious shoppers, and the key to repeating the purchase of these respondents is customer service and trust.

Cluster 3 (green) is comprised of diverse demographics. Namely, the cluster suggests that e-customers are mainly WORKSTAT = Employed (Cla/Mod = 95.82%), AGE = early midlife—midlife—late midlife (99.11%, 94.74%, and 95.16% respectively), EDUC = BSc—MSc—PhD (74.64%, 91.52%, and 97.1% respectively), and mostly dominated by males (73.1%) with township residence (67.54%). The user preferences of these e-consumers, frequent consumers (several times a week to several times a month), show that fast and accurate delivery is essential when buying the first time, while inappropriate and hidden information and long delivery are the main reasons for quitting the purchase. Overall, this cluster resembles early to late midlife, highly educated respondents, mostly male frequent shoppers who prioritize convenience and service efficiency.

5.3. Validity of Findings from Classifiers and Feature Importance

The ML classifiers offer several critical insights into the effectiveness of distinguishing different e-customer profiles based on demographics and user preferences. Namely, the SVM, GBM and RF algorithms demonstrate the highest accuracy, achieving robust performance across proposed metrics. The SVM achieved the highest overall accuracy, suggesting high efficiency in handling multi-class problems with imbalanced datasets. This can be attributed to the SVM capacity to capture class separability by optimized hyperplanes. The Hinge loss optimization enables SVM to minimize misclassifications near decision boundaries, which is particularly useful in the case of MCA-HCPC user profile labelling. Similarly, ensemble methods, i.e., GBM and RF algorithms, performed consistently well, with GBM outperforming in the F1-score. This can be attributed to GBM's iterative boosting process prioritizing correcting previously falsely classified labels by fine-tuning. On the other hand, TF's robust performance is seen from the use of multiple Decision Trees, ultimately reducing the risk of overfitting and enhancing generalizability.

Although performing adequately, the GNB classifier offered less competitive outcomes in multi-class accuracy and AUROC than the SVM and ensemble methods. Such results may be due to GNB's feature independence assumption, which results in oversimplified data relations in complex user profiles. Lastly, the KNN classifier showed lower performance, presumably due to sensitivity to feature scaling and variations across classes, which were prevalent in this categorical dataset.

After obtaining important ML performance features, the interpretation of e-customer profiles suggests the following. Age is consistently ranked as the highest and most influential, so one can assume that younger adults are typically of the most interest to e-tailers. Hence, it suggests a correlation between age technology adoption and comfort with online shopping. Younger adults usually display more purchases and are drawn by user-friendly and interactive platforms. On the other hand, older adults often favor quality assurance and transparency. Ultimately, age-based preferences can reflect generational differences in digital engagement, where young people are more amenable to risk and immediacy, while the elderly prioritize security and familiarity.

Another critical factor is work status, which affects purchasing power and shopping references. Employed individuals tend to have more disposable income and thus prefer efficient and value-driven experiences. This suggests that fast and reliable delivery services are more important than price. Conversely, students and unemployed e-customers exhibit patterns in shopping behavior that reflect more price-sensitive decisions that place greater emphasis on reviews and promotional offers.

Unlike the work status, which can be considered an indirect indicator of budgetary flexibility and consumption priorities, the importance of the education feature may suggest two things: (a) technology savviness and (b) service quality expectations. What is meant by this? From the perspective of the sample demographics, higher education is associated with comfort in navigating through digital platforms, leading to higher purchases and trust in e-commerce. Similarly, educated individuals also exhibit higher standards for customer service, preferring e-tailers with strong reputations consistent with reliability, customer support, and transparency. The feature offers additional insights into the relationship between cognitive engagement and customer loyalty factors, as educated e-customers might scrutinize product information and reviews more closely.

Income also acts as one of the main determinants of purchasing power and often correlates with shopping frequency. The findings also suggest that higher-income respondents prioritize convenience, service quality and delivery over price, making them more inclined to purchase "premium" products or services. E-tailers may utilize such implications in providing platforms that offer enhanced customer experiences. On the other hand, low-income e-consumers typically emphasize affordability, promotional deals and discounts. Finally, while not the most dominant feature, the residence also differentiates user profiles, particularly for urban and rural e-customers. Specifically, rural users may face logistical constraints regarding reliability and transparency of delivery, which makes them more inclined to quiet if logistical support appears uncertain.

ML classifiers' feature importance findings show major implications for tailored e-commerce strategies. As the most influential feature, age stresses the generational divide in digital engagement, distinguishing younger and older adults as users seeking convenience and interaction and users prioritizing transparency and security, respectively. Simultaneously, work status and income further contrast purchasing power and preferences, where employed and high-income users prioritize efficient service over cost. At the same time, students and lower-income customers remain price-sensitive often guided by reviews and promotional offers. As a cognitive component, education plays a role in service standards and critical engagement regarding product details. Overall, the proposed ML models' findings offer meaningful insights and strategies for e-tailers in shaping user-profiles and developing marketing strategies.

6. Conclusions

6.1. Concluding Remarks

This study performs a threefold analysis. Firstly, this study determines statistically significant variables by investigating the association between customer demographics and user behavioral preferences in the Republic of Serbia on a survey of $n = 906$ respondents. The findings show an 8/24 significant association, with extreme evidence considering the association between variables: age and purchase frequency, income status and purchase frequency, and work status and purchase frequency. Interestingly, there is no significant association reported between demographics and items of "Most important property when purchasing for the first time" ($p < 0.05$). Still, all reported tests suggest a small effect size, suggesting that more variables explain user preferences outside of used demographics.

Secondly, given that tests do not expose particular user profiles, an MCA-HCPC (Multiple Correspondence Analysis Hierarchical Clustering on Principal Components) identifies three main clusters. The first cluster mainly comprises early adult students (unemployed), primarily females from rural areas. These profiles are characterized by moderate purchase frequency (at least once a month) driven by positive customer reviews and the desire to see the product in person. The second cluster describes retirees who exhibit infrequent (once in 12 months) purchases driven by attractive offers but are hesitant if they cannot inspect the product. The third cluster includes a more diverse group but primarily describes males in early to late midlife stages who are employed and prioritize fast and accurate delivery.

Finally, merged datasets with C cluster labels are subjected to the following ML algorithms: Support Vector Machine, Gradient Boosting Machine, Decision Trees, Random Forest, k-Nearest Neighbors, and Gaussian Naïve Bayes. The results suggest >90% classification accuracy, where GNB, RF, and SVM offer the highest classification metrics considering accuracy, precision, recall, F1-score, and AUROC. Additionally, from the obtained classifiers, important features were extracted by feature importance relying on Mean Dropout Loss. The evidence suggests that age, work status, education, income, and residence are the main determinants for shaping user profiles and developing e-tailers' marketing strategies.

6.2. Limitations of This Study

Regarding the demographics, there is a low representation of the elderly and residents from rural areas, such as a high percentage of e-customers who did not want to disclose their income. This introduced a slight increase in heterogeneity in the sample, i.e., reduced confidence in the relationship between income status and user preferences, which may impact the application of the research results. For instance, the heterogeneity impacted the Machine Learning classification with uneven representations of demographics (e.g., low elderly population and missing income disclosures), introducing potential bias in training. To address this, samples are stratified during splitting to ensure a proportional representation of demographic variables. Also, to avoid possible bias in reporting the results, performance metrics sensitive to imbalanced datasets, such as F1-score and AUROC, are used to ensure robustness in reporting results despite sample heterogeneity.

The Multiple Correspondence Analysis suggests low inertia in the first three components. This may affect the interpretation of association among class categories. This certainly does not downplay findings, given that most of the captured (inertia) variance corresponds well to investigated test statistics. However, a higher percentage of captured inertia would undoubtedly increase the confidence in understanding user profiles.

6.3. Implications

Regarding e-customer preferences, website design plays a minimal role for most respondents, showing that the user interface of online stores plays less of a barrier than logistical and trust-related issues. Thus, improved logistics (e.g., fast and delivery), mainly for township areas, are a significant concern, likely due to infrastructure issues. Also, product transparency (e.g., hidden or inappropriate information) plays a vital role in quitting the purchase, in addition to negative reviews. Thus, platforms could benefit from more proactive review management, encouraging satisfied customers to leave positive reviews and addressing negative feedback promptly. Future research will focus more on the behavior of specific subgroups, which could provide a better understanding of e-customer preferences and behavioral patterns.

Supplementary Materials: The following supporting information can be downloaded at https://www.mdpi.com/article/10.3390/math12233794/s1.

Author Contributions: Conceptualization, V.V.; methodology, M.O. and V.V.; validation, V.V.; formal analysis, M.O.; investigation, V.V.; resources, V.V. and K.R.; data curation, V.V.; writing—original draft preparation, V.V., M.J., J.S., N.S., K.R. and M.O.; writing—review and editing, V.V., M.J., J.S., N.S.

and M.O.; visualization, M.O.; supervision, V.V., M.J., J.S., N.B. and N.S.; project administration, V.V., N.S., M.J., N.B. and J.S. All authors have read and agreed to the published version of the manuscript.

Funding: This research has been supported by the Ministry of Science, Technological Development and Innovation (Contract No. 451-03-65/2024-03/200156) and the Faculty of Technical Sciences, University of Novi Sad through project "Scientific and Artistic Research Work of Researchers in Teaching and Associate Positions at the Faculty of Technical Sciences, University of Novi Sad" (No. 01-3394/1).

Data Availability Statement: Data are available in Supplementary Materials.

Conflicts of Interest: The authors declare no conflicts of interest.

Author Statement: The large language models are used here to ensure the manuscript's grammatical and scientific writing quality. Specifically, Grammarly removes grammar and spelling errors and language corrections, while OpenAI's GPT-4 tool is used in refining sentences. The LLM and AI tools used here are solely used as accelerators for enhancing the writing process, assisting in language and spelling checks and improving writing accuracy. These tools are not used to generate new ideas, insights or sources of intellectual content within the manuscript. All of the ideas, comments, discussions, drawings, illustrations and processing of images (and graphs) originated and are solely the work of the authors of this manuscript.

Appendix A. Non-Statistically Significant Findings

Table A1. Chi-square test statistics of (un)conditionally dependent relationships (non-significant results).

Variables	Chi-Squared Tests	Value	*df*	*p*	Cramer's *V*	VS–MPR
RESI—PURFRE	χ^2 test statistic	13.502	8	0.096	0.086	1.638
	G^2 Likelihood ratio	14.657	8	0.066		2.047
AGE—RFQ	χ^2 test statistic	43.165	30	0.057	0.098	2.262
	G^2 Likelihood ratio	42.747	30	0.062		2.141
EDU—RFQ	χ^2 test statistic	21.600	24	0.603	0.077	1.000
	G^2 Likelihood ratio	21.506	24	0.609		1.000
AGE—MIPB1T	χ^2 test statistic	37.455	25	0.052	0.091	2.386
	G^2 Likelihood ratio	36.759	25	0.061		2.160
EDU—MIPB1T	χ^2 test statistic	24.007	20	0.242	0.081	1.071
	G^2 Likelihood ratio	19.474	20	0.491		1.000
RESI—MIPB1T	χ^2 test statistic	10.860	10	0.369	0.077	1.000
	G^2 Likelihood ratio	13.190	10	0.213		1.116
AGE—MIPBREP	χ^2 test statistic	20.786	20	0.410	0.076	1.000
	G^2 Likelihood ratio	19.676	20	0.418		1.000
RESI—MIPBREP	χ^2 test statistic	12.540	8	0.129	0.083	1.394
	G^2 Likelihood ratio	14.275	8	0.117		1.896
INCSTAT—MIPBREP	χ^2 test statistic	6.601	16	0.980	0.043	1.000
	G^2 Likelihood ratio	6.959	16	0.974		1.000
INCSTAT—MIPB1T	χ^2 test statistic	22.425	20	0.318	0.079	1.010
	G^2 Likelihood ratio	23.378	20	0.271		1.040
WORKSTAT—MIPBREP	χ^2 test statistic	23.385	16	0.104	0.080	1.564
	G^2 Likelihood ratio	18.538	16	0.293		1.023
WORKSTAT—MIPB1T	χ^2 test statistic	22.403	20	0.319	0.319	1.009
	G^2 Likelihood ratio	23.386	20	0.270		1.040
GENDER—PURFRE	χ^2 test statistic	6.853	8	0.553	0.061	1.000
	G^2 Likelihood ratio	7.311	8	0.503		1.000
GENDER—MIPBREP	χ^2 test statistic	14.223	8	0.074	0.089	1.914
	G^2 Likelihood ratio	13.556	8	0.094		1.654
GENDER—MIPB1T	χ^2 test statistic	6.432	10	0.778	0.060	1.000
	G^2 Likelihood ratio	7.038	10	0.722		1.000
GENDER—RFQ	χ^2 test statistic	20.983	12	0.051	0.108	2.436
	G^2 Likelihood ratio	22.061	12	0.037		3.025

Table A2. Categories (PC1, PC2, PC3), including contributions, cos^2 similarity and v-test—significant categories.

Categories	PC1	CTR	cos^2	v-Test	PC2	CTR	cos^2	v-Test	PC3	CTR	cos^2	v-Test
Early Adulthood	−1.22	18.57	0.58	−22.93	−0.26	1.15	0.03	−4.88	0.68	9.01	0.18	12.67
Student	−1.20	15.70	0.47	−20.57	−0.33	1.58	0.03	−5.58	0.65	7.20	0.14	11.05
High School	−0.67	8.83	0.36	−18.07	−0.06	0.11	0.00	−1.73	0.07	0.17	0.00	1.99
Rural	−0.74	3.24	0.08	−8.73	0.05	0.02	0.00	0.64	−0.44	1.84	0.03	−5.21
Income_NA	−0.45	2.21	0.07	−7.76	−0.14	0.31	0.01	−2.49	0.02	0.01	0.00	0.40
Once 6 months	−0.34	1.55	0.05	−6.76	0.27	1.39	0.03	5.47	−0.41	3.63	0.08	−8.22
MIPBREP_Satisf_Product	−0.14	0.62	0.04	−6.30	−0.08	0.24	0.01	−3.33	−0.27	3.45	0.15	−11.82
RFQ_Product_Live	−0.35	1.24	0.04	−5.72	0.70	6.90	0.15	11.54	−0.14	0.30	0.01	−2.23
Low Income	−0.58	1.27	0.03	−5.32	0.50	1.30	0.02	4.59	−0.41	1.03	0.02	−3.80
Once 12 months	−0.50	1.05	0.03	−4.85	0.82	3.87	0.07	7.97	−0.41	1.14	0.02	−4.01
Unemployed	−0.55	0.98	0.02	−4.64	0.09	0.03	0.00	0.73	0.08	0.04	0.00	0.72
Once a month	−0.13	0.22	0.01	−2.55	−0.24	1.02	0.02	−4.66	0.20	0.81	0.02	3.86
RFQ_Price	−0.25	0.27	0.01	−2.45	−0.05	0.01	0.00	−0.44	−0.25	0.41	0.01	−2.41
RFQ_Negative_Reviews	−0.08	0.08	0.00	−1.51	−0.41	3.10	0.07	−8.11	−0.15	0.47	0.01	−2.93
Part-time	−0.14	0.08	0.00	−1.36	−0.12	0.08	0.00	−1.14	−0.35	0.79	0.01	−3.33
Retiree	−0.35	0.07	0.00	−1.16	6.91	35.30	0.59	23.04	1.38	1.62	0.02	4.59
MIPBREP_Attractive _offers	−0.13	0.04	0.00	−0.91	0.96	2.76	0.05	6.57	0.47	0.78	0.01	3.25
Elementary	−0.43	0.04	0.00	−0.86	0.43	0.05	0.00	0.85	−0.10	0.00	0.00	−0.20
Suburban	−0.06	0.02	0.00	−0.65	−0.27	0.49	0.01	−2.86	−0.66	3.45	0.06	−7.05
RFQ_Missinformation	0.05	0.01	0.00	0.58	−0.15	0.19	0.00	−1.81	−0.36	1.21	0.02	−4.24
Older Adulthood	0.53	0.10	0.00	1.40	7.60	27.15	0.45	20.16	2.62	3.76	0.05	6.96
Late midlife	0.20	0.12	0.00	1.59	0.79	2.59	0.05	6.43	−0.98	4.64	0.07	−7.99
Mid-High Income	0.09	0.10	0.00	1.67	−0.19	0.62	0.01	−3.60	−0.08	0.12	0.00	−1.50
RFQ_Website	0.30	0.20	0.01	2.09	−0.39	0.47	0.01	−2.71	0.25	0.22	0.00	1.71
MIPBREP_Other	0.56	0.30	0.01	2.51	−0.14	0.03	0.00	−0.65	−0.02	0.00	0.00	−0.08
Mid Income	0.16	0.27	0.01	2.67	0.47	3.01	0.06	7.62	−0.15	0.37	0.01	−2.49
MIPBREP_Shopping_Process	0.29	0.47	0.01	3.33	0.02	0.00	0.00	0.23	0.40	1.42	0.02	4.56
RFQ_Other	0.58	0.77	0.02	4.07	0.63	1.26	0.02	4.43	0.58	1.24	0.02	4.10
MIPBREP_Delivery	0.47	1.13	0.03	5.12	0.04	0.01	0.00	0.43	0.93	7.14	0.12	10.19
Young Adulthood	0.34	1.24	0.04	5.79	−0.17	0.44	0.01	−2.96	−0.40	2.78	0.05	−6.88
Several times a week	0.85	1.78	0.04	6.20	−0.68	1.57	0.03	−4.96	0.87	2.93	0.04	6.31
RFQ_Long_Delivery	0.54	1.80	0.05	6.52	−0.19	0.29	0.01	−2.24	0.76	5.59	0.09	9.11
midlife	0.40	1.76	0.05	6.92	−0.04	0.02	0.00	−0.66	−0.67	7.81	0.15	−11.55
BSc	0.30	1.53	0.06	7.09	0.10	0.25	0.01	2.44	−0.32	2.73	0.06	−7.50
Town	0.14	0.65	0.06	7.37	0.03	0.04	0.00	1.58	0.18	1.65	0.10	9.28
PhD	1.27	2.69	0.06	7.55	−0.10	0.02	0.00	−0.58	1.33	4.66	0.07	7.88
High Income	0.71	3.13	0.08	8.60	−0.42	1.50	0.03	−5.09	0.63	3.85	0.06	7.57
Several times a month	0.59	3.77	0.11	10.06	−0.22	0.72	0.02	−3.74	0.24	1.01	0.02	4.14
Early midlife	0.97	6.14	0.16	12.11	0.08	0.06	0.00	1.03	0.83	7.21	0.12	10.41
MSc	1.07	6.56	0.17	12.40	−0.07	0.04	0.00	−0.80	0.30	0.81	0.01	3.45
Employed	0.61	9.43	0.51	21.40	0.00	0.00	0.00	0.02	−0.26	2.70	0.09	−9.09

Appendix B. Agglomerative Hierarchical Clustering

Table A3. Significant variables identified in the first cluster.

Cluster 1 Variables	Cla/Mod	Mod/Cla	Global	*p* Value	v-Test
AGE = Early Adulthood	92.913	78.667	28.035	0.000	24.465
WORKSTAT = Student	97.738	72.000	24.393	0.000	24.261
EDUC = High school	50.860	69.000	44.923	0.000	10.295
WORKSTAT = Unemployed	55.224	12.333	7.395	0.000	3.846
RESI = Rural	48.760	19.667	13.355	0.000	3.823
MIPB1T = To have positive customer reviews	41.554	41.000	32.671	0.000	3.722
PURFRE = Once a month	41.697	37.667	29.912	0.000	3.545
GEND = Female	37.043	71.000	63.466	0.001	3.333
INCSTAT = I don't want to say	42.105	32.000	25.166	0.001	3.288
PPL = No	35.756	82.000	75.938	0.002	3.040
RFQ = RFQ_Because of negative reviews	39.194	35.667	30.132	0.011	2.531

Table A3. *Cont.*

Cluster 1 Variables	Cla/Mod	Mod/Cla	Global	p Value	v-Test
CCP = Mobile app	37.736	46.667	40.949	0.014	2.451
GEND = Prefer not to disclose	75.000	2.000	0.883	0.021	2.309
RFQ = RFQ_Because I want to see the product live	39.423	27.333	22.958	0.029	2.179
RFQ = Due to long delivery time	24.800	10.333	13.797	0.032	−2.151
MIPB1T = Fast and accurate delivery	26.733	18.000	22.296	0.028	−2.201
CCP = SMS	29.621	44.333	49.558	0.027	−2.209
PURFRE = Several times a week	18.000	3.000	5.519	0.016	−2.401
RFQ = RFQ_Other	17.021	2.667	5.188	0.013	−2.483
RESI = Town/township	30.848	70.333	75.497	0.012	−2.513
WORKSTAT = Retiree	0.000	0.000	1.214	0.012	−2.523
RFQ = Due to inappropriate and hidden information	22.951	9.333	13.466	0.009	−2.609
INCSTAT = Mid Income	25.604	17.667	22.848	0.008	−2.640
AGE = Young Adulthood	25.893	19.333	24.724	0.008	−2.671
PPL = Yes	24.771	18.000	24.062	0.002	−3.040
GEND = Male	25.077	27.000	35.651	0.000	−3.858
PURFRE = Several times a month	22.018	16.000	24.062	0.000	−4.075
EDUC = Bachelor	23.615	27.000	37.859	0.000	−4.791
EDUC = PhD	0.000	0.000	3.753	0.000	−4.926
AGE = Late midlife	0.000	0.000	6.843	0.000	−6.907
EDUC = Master of Science	7.627	3.000	13.024	0.000	−6.929
AGE = Early midlife	3.759	1.667	14.680	0.000	−8.851
AGE = midlife	0.442	0.333	24.945	0.000	−14.177
WORKSTAT = Employed	3.802	6.667	58.057	0.000	−23.228

Table A4. Significant variables identified in the second cluster.

Cluster 2	Cla/Mod	Mod/Cla	Global	p Value	v-Test
WORKSTAT = Retiree	100.000	78.571	1.214	0.000	9.891
AGE = Older Adulthood	100.000	50.000	0.773	0.000	7.577
RFQ = I want to see the product live	4.327	64.286	22.958	0.001	3.248
CCP = SMS	2.450	78.571	49.558	0.031	2.153
MIPBREP = Attractive new offers	6.667	21.429	4.967	0.032	2.143
PURFRE = Once every 12 months	4.651	28.571	9.492	0.043	2.023
WORKSTAT = Student	0.000	0.000	24.393	0.019	−2.340
AGE = Young Adulthood	0.000	0.000	24.724	0.018	−2.363
INCSTAT = Mid-High Income	0.000	0.000	29.470	0.007	−2.686
WORKSTAT = Employed	0.380	14.286	58.057	0.001	−3.281

Table A5. Significant variables identified in the third cluster.

Cluster 3	Cla/Mod	Mod/Cla	Global	p Value	v-Test
WORKSTAT = Employed	95.817	85.135	58.057	0.000	23.920
AGE = midlife	99.115	37.838	24.945	0.000	14.315
AGE = Early midlife	94.737	21.284	14.680	0.000	8.620
EDUC = Master of Science	91.525	18.243	13.024	0.000	6.993
AGE = Late midlife	95.161	9.966	6.843	0.000	5.734
EDUC = Bachelor	74.636	43.243	37.859	0.000	4.628
EDUC = PhD	97.059	5.574	3.753	0.000	4.470
PURFRE = Several times a month	77.064	28.378	24.062	0.000	4.255
GEND = Male	73.065	39.865	35.651	0.000	3.661
PPL = Yes	74.312	27.365	24.062	0.001	3.233
AGE = Young Adulthood	74.107	28.041	24.724	0.001	3.214
RFQ = Due to inappropriate	77.049	15.878	13.466	0.003	2.980

Table A5. *Cont.*

Cluster 3	Cla/Mod	Mod/Cla	Global	p Value	v-Test
PURFRE = Several times a week	82.000	6.926	5.519	0.009	2.624
RESI = Town/township	67.544	78.041	75.497	0.016	2.419
MIPB1T = Fast and accurate	71.782	24.493	22.296	0.028	2.195
INCSTAT = Mid Income	71.498	25.000	22.848	0.033	2.130
RFQ = Due to long delivery	73.600	15.541	13.797	0.035	2.109
RFQ = Other	78.723	6.250	5.188	0.044	2.010
RFQ = Because of negative	60.440	27.872	30.132	0.043	−2.022
CCP = Mobile app	61.456	38.514	40.949	0.041	−2.039
PURFRE = Once every 6 months	60.498	28.716	31.015	0.041	−2.041
INCSTAT = Low Income	53.846	7.095	8.609	0.029	−2.184
GEND = Prefer not to disclose	25.000	0.338	0.883	0.027	−2.215
RFQ = RFQ_Because I want to see	56.250	19.764	22.958	0.002	−3.097
GEND = Female	61.565	59.797	63.466	0.002	−3.163
INCSTAT = I don't want to say	56.579	21.791	25.166	0.002	−3.174
PURFRE = Once a month	57.565	26.351	29.912	0.001	−3.182
PPL = No	62.500	72.635	75.938	0.001	−3.233
AGE = Older Adulthood	0.000	0.000	0.773	0.001	−3.443
MIPB1T = MIPB1T_To have positive customer reviews	57.095	28.547	32.671	0.000	−3.600
WORKSTAT = Unemployed	43.284	4.899	7.395	0.000	−3.812
RESI = Rural	49.587	10.135	13.355	0.000	−3.818
WORKSTAT = Retiree	0.000	0.000	1.214	0.000	−4.473
EDUC = High school	47.666	32.770	44.923	0.000	−10.136
WORKSTAT = Student	2.262	0.845	24.393	0.000	−23.557

References

1. Svobodová, Z.; Rajchlová, J. Strategic Behavior of E-Commerce Businesses in Online Industry of Electronics from a Customer Perspective. *Adm. Sci.* **2020**, *10*, 78. [CrossRef]
2. Kim, J.; Yum, K. Enhancing Continuous Usage Intention in E-Commerce Marketplace Platforms: The Effects of Service Quality, Customer Satisfaction, and Trust. *Appl. Sci.* **2024**, *14*, 7617. [CrossRef]
3. Vakulenko, Y.; Shams, P.; Hellström, D.; Hjort, K. Online Retail Experience and Customer Satisfaction: The Mediating Role of Last Mile Delivery. *Int. Rev. Retail. Distrib. Consum. Res.* **2019**, *29*, 306–320. [CrossRef]
4. Buldeo Rai, H.; Mommens, K.; Verlinde, S.; Macharis, C. How Does Consumers' Omnichannel Shopping Behaviour Translate into Travel and Transport Impacts? Case-Study of a Footwear Retailer in Belgium. *Sustainability* **2019**, *11*, 2534. [CrossRef]
5. Zennaro, I.; Finco, S.; Calzavara, M.; Persona, A. Implementing E-Commerce from Logistic Perspective: Literature Review and Methodological Framework. *Sustainability* **2022**, *14*, 911. [CrossRef]
6. Guo, J.; Liu, X.; Jo, J. Dynamic Joint Construction and Optimal Operation Strategy of Multi-Period Reverse Logistics Network: A Case Study of Shanghai Apparel E-Commerce Enterprises. *J. Intell. Manuf.* **2017**, *28*, 819–831. [CrossRef]
7. Biclesanu, I.; Anagnoste, S.; Branga, O.; Savastano, M. Digital Entrepreneurship: Public Perception of Barriers, Drivers, and Future. *Adm. Sci.* **2021**, *11*, 125. [CrossRef]
8. Voicu, M.-C.; Sîrghi, N.; Toth, D.M.-M. Consumers' Experience and Satisfaction Using Augmented Reality Apps in E-Shopping: New Empirical Evidence. *Appl. Sci.* **2023**, *13*, 9596. [CrossRef]
9. Olsson, J.; Hellström, D.; Vakulenko, Y. Customer Experience Dimensions in Last-Mile Delivery: An Empirical Study on Unattended Home Delivery. *Int. J. Phys. Distrib. Logist. Manag.* **2023**, *53*, 184–205. [CrossRef]
10. Vrhovac, V.; Vasić, S.; Milisavljević, S.; Dudić, B.; Štarchoň, P.; Žižakov, M. Measuring E-Commerce User Experience in the Last-Mile Delivery. *Mathematics* **2023**, *11*, 1482. [CrossRef]
11. Ranđelović, D. Internet Prodaja u Republici Srbiji. *Pravo-Teor. i Praksa* **2017**, *34*, 13–24.
12. Vasic, N.; Kilibarda, M.; Kaurin, T. The Influence of Online Shopping Determinants on Customer Satisfaction in the Serbian Market. *J. Theor. Appl. Electron. Commer. Res.* **2019**, *14*, 70–89. [CrossRef]
13. TRADE Serbia—Country Commercial Guide. Available online: https://www.trade.gov/country-commercial-guides/serbia-ecommerce (accessed on 10 September 2024).
14. Kaurin, T.; Kilibarda, M.; Fakultet Beograd, S. Analiza Determinanti Elektronske Trgovine Na Tržištu Srbije. In Proceedings of the 17th International Symposium INFOTEH-JAHORINA, Jahorina, East Sarajevo, Republic of Srpska, 21–23 March 2018.
15. Martinović, M.; Barać, R.; Maljak, H. Exploring Croatian Consumer Adoption of Subscription-Based E-Commerce for Business Innovation. *Adm. Sci.* **2024**, *14*, 149. [CrossRef]

16. Borsiak-Dańska, B.; Grzelak, M.; Roszko-Wójtowicz, E. The Development of Innovation and Infrastructure in the European Countries Fostering the Growth of the E-Commerce Sector. In *Financial Stability, Economic Growth and Sustainable Development*; Routledge: London, UK, 2024; pp. 251–278.
17. Agarwal, V.; Govindan, K.; Darbari, J.D.; Jha, P.C. An Optimization Model for Sustainable Solutions towards Implementation of Reverse Logistics under Collaborative Framework. *Int. J. Syst. Assur. Eng. Manag.* **2016**, *7*, 480–487. [CrossRef]
18. Kotler, P.; Keller, K. *Marketing Management*, 15th ed.; Pearson: London, UK, 2015; ISBN 0133856461.
19. Morris, M.G.; Venkatesh, V. Age Differences in Technology Adoption Decisions: Implications for a Changing Work Force. *Pers. Psychol.* **2000**, *53*, 375–403. [CrossRef]
20. Zavali, M.; Lacka, E.; de Smedt, J. Shopping Hard or Hardly Shopping: Revealing Consumer Segments Using Clickstream Data. *IEEE Trans. Eng. Manag.* **2023**, *70*, 1353–1364. [CrossRef]
21. Vieira, J.; Frade, R.; Ascenso, R.; Prates, I.; Martinho, F. Generation Z and Key-Factors on E-Commerce: A Study on the Portuguese Tourism Sector. *Adm. Sci.* **2020**, *10*, 103. [CrossRef]
22. Barutcu, S. E-Customer Satisfaction in the E-Tailing Industry: An Empirical Survey for Turkish E-Customers. *Ege Acad. Rev.* **2010**, *10*, 15–35. [CrossRef]
23. Ghosal, I. A Demographic Study of Buying Spontaneity on E-Shoppers: Preference Kolkata (West Bengal). *J. Technol. Manag. Grow. Econ.* **2015**, *6*, 65–75. [CrossRef]
24. Ansari, Z.A.; Qadri, F.A. Role of E-Retailer's Image in Online Consumer Behaviour—Empirical Findings from E-Customers' Perspective in Saudi Arabia. *Int. Bus. Res.* **2018**, *11*, 57. [CrossRef]
25. Tkalčič, M.; Chen, L. Personality and Recommender Systems. In *Recommender Systems Handbook*; Springer US: New York, NY, USA, 2022; pp. 757–787.
26. Hristoski, I.; Kostoska, O. On the Taxonomies and Typologies of E-Customers in B2C e-Commerce. *Balk. Near East. J. Social Sci.* **2018**, *4*, 130–148.
27. Swarnakar, P.; Kumar, A.; Kumar, S. Why Generation Y Prefers Online Shopping: A Study of Young Customers of India. *Int. J. Bus. Forecast. Mark. Intell.* **2016**, *2*, 215. [CrossRef]
28. Chen, X.; Guo, Y.; Xu, H.; Yan, H.; Lin, L. User Demographic Prediction Based on the Fusion of Mobile and Survey Data. *IEEE Access* **2022**, *10*, 111507–111527. [CrossRef]
29. Bellini, P.; Palesi, L.A.I.; Nesi, P.; Pantaleo, G. Multi Clustering Recommendation System for Fashion Retail. *Multimed. Tools Appl.* **2023**, *82*, 9989–10016. [CrossRef] [PubMed]
30. Kuruba Manjunath, Y.S.; Kashef, R.F. Distributed Clustering Using Multi-Tier Hierarchical Overlay Super-Peer Peer-to-Peer Network Architecture for Efficient Customer Segmentation. *Electron. Commer. Res. Appl.* **2021**, *47*, 101040. [CrossRef]
31. Hørlück, J.; Christiansen, T.; Hansen, L.K.; Larsen, J. Are All E-Customers Alike? In Proceedings of the 1st Nordic Workshop on Electronic Commerce, Halmstad, Sweden, 28–29 May 2001.
32. Ansari, S.; Farooqi, R. Moderating Effect Of Demographic Variables on Attitude towards Online Shopping: An Empirical Study Using PROCESS. *IOSR J. Bus. Manag.* **2017**, *19*, 47–54.
33. Noorshella, C.N.; Abdullah, A.M.; Nursalihah, A.R. Examining the Key Factors Affecting E-Service Quality of Small Online Apparel Businesses in Malaysia. *Sage Open* **2015**, *5*, 215824401557655. [CrossRef]
34. Kalia, P.; Kaur, N.; Singh, T. A Review of Factors Affecting Online Buying Behavior. *Apeejay J. Manag. Technol.* **2016**, *11*, 58–73. [CrossRef]
35. Bhat, S.A.; Darzi, M.A. Exploring the Influence of Consumer Demographics on Online Purchase Benefits. *FIIB Bus. Rev.* **2019**, *8*, 303–316. [CrossRef]
36. Hettich, D.; Hattula, S.; Bornemann, T. Consumer Decision-Making of Older People: A 45-Year Review. *Gerontologist* **2018**, *58*, e349–e368. [CrossRef]
37. Pascual-Miguel, F.J.; Agudo-Peregrina, Á.F.; Chaparro-Peláez, J. Influences of Gender and Product Type on Online Purchasing. *J. Bus. Res.* **2015**, *68*, 1550–1556. [CrossRef]
38. Garczarek-Bąk, U.; Szymkowiak, A. Gender Differences in E-Commerce. *Handel Wewnętrzny* **2018**, *4*, 250–261.
39. Hansen, T.; Møller Jensen, J. Shopping Orientation and Online Clothing Purchases: The Role of Gender and Purchase Situation. *Eur. J. Mark.* **2009**, *43*, 1154–1170. [CrossRef]
40. Naseri, M.B.; Elliott, G. Role of Demographics, Social Connectedness and Prior Internet Experience in Adoption of Online Shopping: Applications for Direct Marketing. *J. Target. Meas. Anal. Mark.* **2011**, *19*, 69–84. [CrossRef]
41. Kalia, P. Does Demographics Affect Purchase Frequency in Online Retail? *Int. J. Online Mark.* **2017**, *7*, 42–56. [CrossRef]
42. Luo, X.; Niu, C. *E-Commerce Participation and Household Income Growth in Taobao Villages (English)*; Policy Research Working Paper, no. WPS 8811; World Bank Group: Washington, DC, USA, 2019.
43. Agudo-Peregrina, Á.F.; Hernández-García, Á.; Acquila-Natale, E. The Effect of Income Level on E-Commerce Adoption. In *Encyclopedia of E-Commerce Development, Implementation, and Management*; IGI Global: Hershey, PA, USA, 2016; pp. 2239–2255.
44. Paun, C.; Ivascu, C.; Olteteanu, A.; Dantis, D. The Main Drivers of E-Commerce Adoption: A Global Panel Data Analysis. *J. Theor. Appl. Electron. Commer. Res.* **2024**, *19*, 2198–2217. [CrossRef]
45. Çebi Karaaslan, K. Determinants of Online Shopping Attitudes of Households in Turkey. *J. Model. Manag.* **2022**, *17*, 119–133. [CrossRef]

46. Karaaslan, K.Ç. Analysis of the Factors Affecting Credit Card Use and Online Shopping Attitudes of Households in Turkey with the Bivariate Probit Model. *Int. J. Electron. Financ.* **2022**, *11*, 189. [CrossRef]
47. Imran, M.; Asif, M.; Sajjad, W. Impact of Employment Status on Online Shopping Preferences: A Case Study of Women in Rawalpindi. *J. Bus. Insight Innov.* **2022**, *1*, 19–28.
48. Singh, K.; Basu, R. Online Consumer Shopping Behaviour: A Review and Research Agenda. *Int. J. Consum. Stud.* **2023**, *47*, 815–851. [CrossRef]
49. Wang, S.; Cheah, J.; Lim, X. Online Shopping Cart Abandonment: A Review and Research Agenda. *Int. J. Consum. Stud.* **2023**, *47*, 453–473. [CrossRef]
50. Molnar, C.; König, G.; Herbinger, J.; Freiesleben, T.; Dandl, S.; Scholbeck, C.A.; Casalicchio, G.; Grosse-Wentrup, M.; Bischl, B. General Pitfalls of Model-Agnostic Interpretation Methods for Machine Learning Models. In *International Workshop on Extending Explainable AI Beyond Deep Models and Classifiers*; Springer: Cham, Switzerland, 2022; pp. 39–68.
51. Orošnjak, M.; Beker, I.; Brkljač, N.; Vrhovac, V. Predictors of Successful Maintenance Practices in Companies Using Fluid Power Systems: A Model-Agnostic Interpretation. *Appl. Sci.* **2024**, *14*, 5921. [CrossRef]
52. Hamburg, M. *Basic Statistics: A Modern Approach*, 3rd ed.; Harcourt Brace Jovanovich: San Diego, CA, USA, 1985.
53. Burkolter, D.; Kluge, A. Online Consumer Behavior and Its Relationship with Socio-Demographics, Shopping Orientations, Need for Emotion, and Fashion Leadership. *J. Bus. Media Psychol.* **2011**, *2*, 20–28.
54. Howell, D.C. *Chi-Square Test—Analysis of Contingency Tables*; University of Vermont: Burlington, VT, USA, 2011.
55. Altman, N.; Krzywinski, M. Interpreting P Values. *Nat. Methods* **2017**, *14*, 213–214. [CrossRef]
56. Halsey, L.G.; Curran-Everett, D.; Vowler, S.L.; Drummond, G.B. The Fickle P Value Generates Irreproducible Results. *Nat. Methods* **2015**, *12*, 179–185. [CrossRef]
57. Altman, N.; Krzywinski, M. P Values and the Search for Significance. *Nat. Methods* **2017**, *14*, 3–4. [CrossRef]
58. Wagenmakers, E.-J. A Practical Solution to the Pervasive Problems of *p* Values. *Psychon. Bull. Rev.* **2007**, *14*, 779–804. [CrossRef]
59. Garcia, A.M.R.-R.; Puga, J.L. Deciding on Null Hypotheses Using P-Values or Bayesian Alternatives: A Simulation Study. *Psicothema* **2018**, *30*, 110–115. [CrossRef] [PubMed]

mathematics

MDPI

Article

A Study on Caregiver Activity Recognition for the Elderly at Home Based on the XGBoost Model

Zhonghua Liu [1,*], Shuang Zhang [1], Huihui Zhang [2] and Xiuxiu Li [1]

1 School of Economics and Management, Beijing University of Chemical Technology, Beijing 100029, China; 2023200883@buct.edu.cn (S.Z.); a1078924593@163.com (X.L.)
2 Journal Center, China Electric Power Research Institute, Beijing 100192, China; briskword@126.com
* Correspondence: liuzhonghua09@mails.ucas.ac.cn

Abstract: This paper aims to discuss the implementation of data analysis and information management for elderly nursing care from a data-driven perspective. It addresses the current challenges of in-home caregivers, providing a basis for decision making in analyzing nursing service content and evaluating job performance. The characteristics of caregivers' activities were analyzed during the design of a wearable device-wearing scheme and a sensor data collection system. XGBoost, SVM, and Random Forest models were used in the experiments, with the Cuckoo search algorithm employed to optimize the XGBoost model parameters. Based on the control group experiment, it was confirmed that the XGBoost model, after adjusting the parameters using the Cuckoo search algorithm, exhibited better recognition performance than the SVM and RandomForest models, and the accuracy reached 0.9438. Wearable devices present high recognition accuracy in caregiver activity recognition research, which greatly improves the inspection of caregivers' work and further promotes the completion of services. This study actively explores the applications of information technology and artificial intelligence theory to address practical problems and effectively promote the digitalization and intelligent development of the elderly nursing care industry.

Keywords: elderly nursing care; behavior recognition; XGBoost; sensor data; wearable device

MSC: 68T09

1. Introduction

1.1. Background

Human life expectancy has increased at an unprecedented rate, while the human fertility rate has declined rapidly in many countries around the world [1]. With the change in population structure, many countries are entering or will enter an aging society, such as China and Japan [2,3]. According to the data of the Ministry of Civil Affairs of the PRC, in the past decade, the size of the aging population in China has presented a continuously growing trend, exceeding 280 million, as shown in Figure 1. How to provide professional elderly nursing care services for elderly people has become an urgent and important issue. The first concern is where elderly people enjoy elderly nursing care services; do they stay at home or live in a professional elderly nursing care institution? In China, people become increasingly reluctant to leave their homes as they age. Therefore, home-based care has become an increasingly popular choice due to its advantages of humanization, flexibility, and lower private and social costs. Additionally, home-based care-taking is supported by the government and elderly nursing care agencies in certain places [4].

One of the significant challenges in home-based caregiving involves managing and assessing the performance of nursing staff. Their work is evaluated primarily from two perspectives: adherence to the scheduled care plan and the quality of care provided. The foremost concern is verifying the implementation of prescribed nursing services.

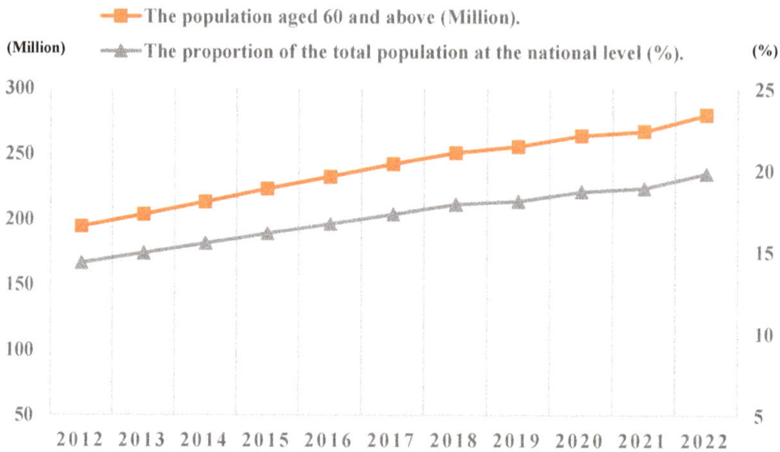

Figure 1. The population aged 60 and above and its proportion of the total population of China.

Nursing activity recognition via image and video recognition is a possible solution. However, this is often not feasible in many cases because of privacy issues as videos violate the privacy of elderly people and staff [5]. In addition, the high cost of purchasing, deploying, and maintaining an image- and video-capturing device and the expensive and time-consuming video analysis are also weaknesses. On the other hand, with the development of the internet [6], various types of sensors are widely used in wearable devices. Compared with video and image-based behavior recognition methods, sensor-based behavior recognition methods are characterized by low cost, strong flexibility, and good portability. Therefore, human behavior recognition based on wearable sensors has become a research hotspot in human activity recognition (HAR), which greatly promotes the standard-setting and information management of the elderly nursing care market.

1.2. Difficulties with the Recognition of Caregivers' Activities

The current research on Caregiver Activity Recognition (CAR) for the elderly at home lacks a standardized wearable device-wearing scheme and public dataset. As a result, this research encounters several challenges:

(1) The primary challenge is designing a suitable wearable device-wearing scheme for studying CAR. Additionally, extracting effective features and accurately distinguishing between different behavioral activities are ongoing difficulties and areas of focus in current research.

(2) Traditional static models struggle to recognize behavioral activities due to variations among individuals, which leads to lower accuracy in recognition outcomes.

(3) Real-world nursing care activities pose another challenge as they often involve complex actions. These actions can easily be confused with one another, making accurate recognition a difficult task.

2. Literature Review

The concept of activity recognition originated in the late 1990s [7,8], particularly utilizing wearable sensor data for sports and motion behavior analysis [9–11]. This field has gained significant importance, especially in the domains of medicine, military, and security applications. For instance, exercise therapy can reduce symptom burden in advanced cancer patients [12]. Additionally, robots have been employed in certain studies to directly facilitate activity recognition, such as utilizing them for gait training and other rehabilitation exercises aimed at patients with ambulatory impairments [13]. Furthermore, bionic robots are also utilized in various research endeavors [14,15]. Therefore, the ability to recognize activities such as walking, running, or cycling has been proven to be very valuable in providing caregivers with information on patient behavior. However, there is a lack of research on using wearable sensor data analysis to identify caregiver behavior, which is the main focus of this paper.

In general, different sets of activities can result in entirely distinct HAR problems. Consequently, the design of any HAR system should be tailored to the specific activities that need to be recognized. A literature survey has identified seven distinct classes of activities, with detailed summaries of both group and individual activities falling under each class [16].

Human Activity Recognition (HAR) has employed a variety of machine learning (ML) algorithms. In ML, there are three types of learning: supervised learning, unsupervised learning, and semi-supervised learning [17]. To determine the optimal method for different case studies, it is necessary to compare the experimental results of each method. Generally, ensemble learning algorithms outperform single learners (such as decision trees) in terms of performance. For example, the Random Forest Classifier [18,19] is constructed by combining multiple decision trees and classifies unknown samples by voting. It utilizes coverage optimization to integrate the capabilities of multiple weak classifiers, resulting in improved overall performance compared to a single algorithm [20].

Furthermore, deep learning models are employed for human activity recognition (HAR). Research has indicated that in cases where HAR data are multidimensional, and activities are more complex, a deep neural network (DNN) with additional hidden layers can facilitate better training of the model [21–23]. Convolutional neural networks (CNNs) exhibit two advantages over other models when applied to time series classification: local dependence and scale invariance [24,25]. Due to factors such as learning speed and resource consumption, recurrent neural networks (RNNs) are less commonly used for HAR tasks [26–28]. Moreover, a combination of different deep models is utilized for HAR tasks [11,29,30].

Although XGBoost (version: 2.0.3) [31], introduced in 2014, offers efficiency and time-saving advantages, but its utilization in behavior recognition is currently limited compared to well-established algorithms. Furthermore, there is a lack of extensive research specifically focused on behavior recognition using XGBoost, especially in the context of elderly behavior recognition.

To address these gaps, this paper aims to conduct research on home-based elderly nursing care behavior utilizing the XGBoost model. By investigating the capabilities of XGBoost in accurately recognizing and understanding the behaviors of home-based staff, this study aims to contribute to the existing research in this field. The objective is to explore the untapped potential of XGBoost in behavior recognition, particularly within the domain of home-based elderly nursing care.

Through this research, we seek to shed light on the benefits and practical applications of the XGBoost model in improving behavior recognition outcomes in elderly nursing care settings. The findings of this study can serve as inspiration for further research and encourage the wider adoption of XGBoost as a valuable tool for promoting the completion of care provided to elderly individuals in home-based settings. The evaluation of the quality of nursing behavior has not yet been considered in this article, which is also a very important issue and can serve as an unresolved study for the future.

The main contributions of our work include the following aspects:

(1) This study developed an experimental system utilizing wearable devices for data collection to identify nursing behaviors, addressing the limitations of previous research in this area.
(2) Following feature importance analysis and feature reduction, three machine learning algorithms (SVM, RandomForest, and XGBOOST) were employed in this study. The XGBOOST model was further optimized using the cuckoo search algorithm to achieve the highest recognition accuracy of 0.9438. Additional experiments were conducted to verify the impact of behavioral constraints on recognition performance.

(3) By accurately identifying elderly nursing care activities, this study enables effective monitoring of the completion of tasks by nursing staff.

3. Research Framework

After consulting with elderly nursing care service providers and enterprises about which caregivers' activities are necessary to be recognized as management objects, and also analyzing which nursing activities are feasible to recognize technically, this paper selects nine nursing care activities as research objects of CAR as shown in Table 1.

Table 1. Caregivers' activities to be identified in this study.

Tags	Caregivers' Activity	Data Acquisition Duration
S1	Sweeping the floor	300 s
S2	Thumping one's legs	180 s
S3	Feeding	300 s
S4	Slapping one's back	180 s
S5	Moving objects	300 s
S6	Wiping a window	300 s
S7	Wiping a desk	300 s
S8	Washing one's face	180 s
S9	Washing clothes	180 s

3.1. Experimental System

We have designed a wearable data collection system consisting of three devices: a wearable vest and two wristwatches. The "Hitoe" wearable vest is equipped with sensors that enable the collection of physiological data, including body movements and postures. Additionally, we use wristwatches called "TicWatch" on both wrists to capture the movements and postures of the arms (as shown in Figure 2).

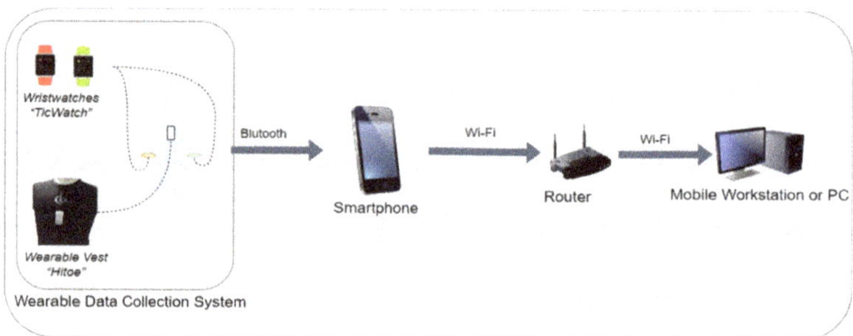

Figure 2. Sensor data collection from wearable devices.

Via the utilization of sensor data collected from these three wearable devices, it becomes feasible to reconstruct the vast majority of action patterns related to caregivers' activities. To achieve this, the devices are connected to a smartphone via Bluetooth, which subsequently establishes a connection to a mobile workstation or PC through Wi-Fi. In this setup, a dedicated database is implemented to store and manage the collected data.

3.2. Data Collection

The data used in this article come from volunteers wearing wearable devices, and the experiment was conducted with the permission of the volunteers. Thirty-six caregivers from five public nursing homes in Beijing wore wearable devices to perform caregivers' behaviors, a total of nine caregivers' behaviors, each lasting either 180 or 300 s depending on the characteristics of each behavior (e.g., wiping a desk takes less time than moving objects), and the criteria for selecting the personnel included volunteering to join this experiment and working in a nursing home for more than one year, 4 men and 32 women, with an average age of 46.5 years. The devices worn by the caregivers included a smart undershirt (Hitoe, from Nippon Telegraph & Telephone, Tokyo, Japan) for recognizing a person's upper body posture and two smartwatches (TicWatch1 and TicWatch2, from FUXIANG, Shanghai, China) for recognizing hand movements.

All the data were collected by volunteers in their daily work. Our dataset consists of A, B, A′, and B′, and over 87,000 sensor data samples were collected using wearable devices Hitoe, TicWatch1, and TicWatch2. Each data sample consists of 27 features (as indicated in Table 2) along with a classification (S1, …, S9) composition. The interval between consecutive data samples is 200 ms. A′ and B′ require volunteers to complete corresponding nursing services according to certain norms, while A and B allow volunteers to complete nursing services based on their personal habits. For example, in A′ and B′, when performing "S1: Sweeping the floor," the volunteers are instructed to hold the broom with both hands and sweep the floor from right to left. In subsequent experiments, we demonstrated that using A′ and B′ for nursing behavior recognition presents higher accuracy.

Table 2. Variable descriptions.

Device Name	Variable Name
Hitoe	acceleration(h_acc_x, h_acc_y, h_acc_z)
TicWatch_1	acceleration(t1_acc_x, t1_acc_y, t1_acc_z) gravity(t1_grty_x, t1_grty_y, t1_grty_z) gyroscope(t1_gyscp_x, t1_gyscp_y, t1_gyscp_z) linear acceleration(t1_linr_acc_x, t1_linr_acc_y, t1_linr_acc_z)
TicWatch_2	acceleration(t2_acc_x, t2_acc_y, t2_acc_z) gravity(t2_grty_x, t2_grty_y, t2_grty_z) gyroscope(t2_gyscp_x, t2_gyscp_y, t2_gyscp_z) linear acceleration(t2_linr_acc_x, t2_linr_acc_y, t2_linr_acc_z)

3.3. Recognition Solution

The CAR solution, as shown in Figure 3, is a comprehensive approach developed based on extensive research into state-of-the-art Human Activity Recognition (HAR) methods. It consists of five main components, each contributing to the effective recognition of caregivers' activities.

(1) Component I: Data Preprocessing

This component is responsible for converting unstructured raw data into structured data. It involves a data preprocessing process that organizes and formats the data in a manner suitable for subsequent analysis.

(2) Component II: Feature Processing

In this component, the features extracted from the preprocessed data are further processed. This involves analyzing the importance of each feature and reducing the dimensionality of the feature space. Through these tasks, the component ensures that only relevant and significant features are considered for subsequent steps.

(3) Component III: Classification

The classifiers include XGBoost, Support Vector Machine (SVM), and Random Forest. The collected data is then divided into two sets: training and testing datasets. The training data is used to learn patterns related to caregivers' activities and build classification models. Conversely, the testing data is employed to assess the performance of the constructed models.

(4) Component IV: Parameter tuning

This component is of utmost importance in optimizing the performance of classification models. It utilizes techniques to fine-tune the model's parameters, thereby enhancing its ability to accurately recognize and classify caregivers' activities.

(5) Component V: Performance Evaluation

Various evaluation measures such as precision, recall, f1_score, and accuracy are employed to assess the performance of three specific models used in this study: the XGBoost model, the SVM model, and the Random Forest model. These measures provide insights into the effectiveness and reliability of the CAR solution.

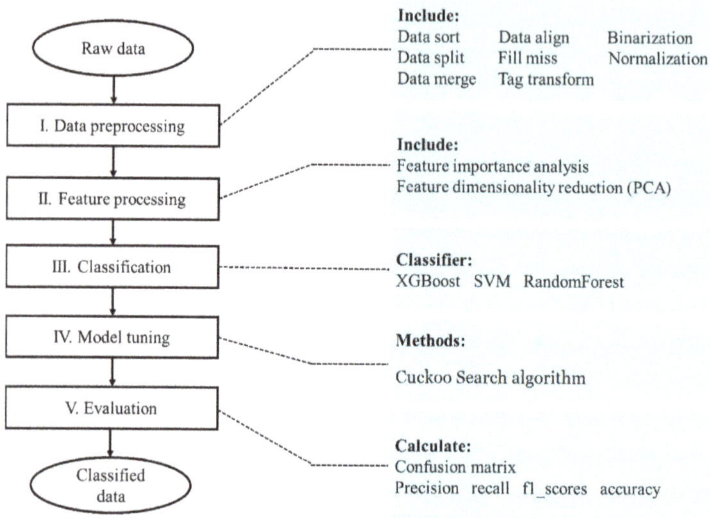

Figure 3. Flow chart for CAR solution.

3.4. Feature Importance Analysis

Sample data were collected, and each sample has a corresponding label (S1, S2, . . ., S9) indicating the nursing activity performed by the caregiver during data collection. Each sample includes data from three wearable devices, namely Hitoe, TicWatch_1, and TicWatch_2, which capture x-y-z axis sensor data. As shown in Table 2, the preprocessed dataset consists of 27 features.

Feature importance analysis is not used for feature reduction. The XGBoost model in Python provides a method for feature importance analysis, which can help us analyze the importance score of each feature and demonstrate which features contribute more to the model prediction. This provides a reference for subsequent research on feature selection. The method of feature dimensionality reduction in this article is Principal Component Analysis (PCA), and the basis for dimensionality reduction in PCA is interpretable variance [32]. The subsequent prediction research in this article will use the PCA dimensionality-reduced dataset as the training and testing sets.

As depicted in Figure 4, it is evident that the importance of the six feature values (t1_gyscp_x, t1_gyscp_y, t1_gyscp_z, t2_gyscp_x, t2_gyscp_y, t2_gyscp_z) in the feature set is relatively low. This implies that this specific type of data may have limited utility for nursing behavior recognition. Consequently, it could be considered to reduce the collection of this type of data in future data-gathering processes.

Moreover, notable disparities in feature importance can be observed between "t1" and "t2" for acceleration, linear acceleration, and gravity data types. This indicates that there are distinctions in the same data types collected from the caregiver's left and right hands. Such differences could arise from variations in the division of labor or behavior between the left and right hands during nursing activities. The dominance of right-handedness in the majority of individuals in real-life situations results in enhanced performance during the execution of nine nursing behaviors, such as sweeping the floor, feeding, wiping a window, wiping a desk, etc. This is attributed to increased effort exerted by the right hand, expanded range of motion, and potential alterations in speed. Consequently, these distinctive characteristics enable differentiation between this particular nursing behavior and others. Thus, when collecting data from both hands, it is advisable to gather diverse types of data to attain improved recognition outcomes.

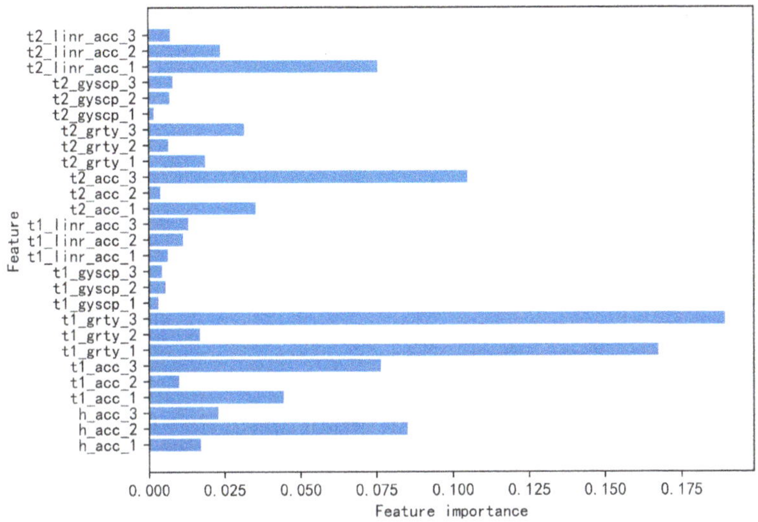

Figure 4. Feature importance analysis.

Similarly, there are substantial variations in the importance of features across the three axes, even for the same data type and the same hand. For instance, among the acceleration data (t1_acc_x, t1_acc_y, and t1_acc_z), on the same hand, the importance of the t1_acc_y feature is significantly lower compared to the other two features.

4. Materials and Methods

4.1. Introduction to XGBoost

XGBoost stands for "Extreme Gradient Boosting", which is a high-precision integrated learning model based on Gradient Boosting Decision Tree (GBDT), whose essence lies in integrating multiple weak classifiers into a single strong classifier to improve the accuracy. In the context of regression prediction, each tree of XGBoost learns the residuals (negative gradients) of the sum of all previous tree results. By iteratively accumulating residuals with prior predictions, XGBoost continually approaches the actual values.

The XGBoost algorithm is an improved version of the GBDT algorithm and serves as an implementation of the gradient-down algorithm. The XGBoost model contains K CART trees, with its output being the sum of these K trees. The cumulative value serves as the predicted value of the XGBoost model and can be expressed mathematically as follows:

$$\hat{y} = \sum_{k=1}^{K} f_k(x_i) \tag{1}$$

where K is the number of CART trees, f_k denotes a specific CART tree, $\hat{y}$ is the output of the XGBoost model. For a given sample length of n and the number of features of m, we have

$$D = \{(x_i, y_i)\}(|D| = n, x_i \in R^m, y \in R) \tag{2}$$

where x_i denotes the i-th sample input; y_i denotes the output corresponding to the i-th sample input, F represents the space of CART trees, which can be expressed as

$$F = \left\{ \left(f(x) = w_q(x) \right) \right\} \left(q : R^m \to T, w \in R^T \right) \tag{3}$$

where q represents the structure of the CART tree, T is the number of child nodes of the CART tree, w is the weight of the child nodes, and f(x) is the structure of the CART tree. The XGBoost model essentially constructs the CART tree through feature extraction to determine the structure and weight of the tree. Bringing the regularisation term into the objective function, we have

$$Obj = \sum_i loss(\hat{y}_i, y_i) + \sum_k \Omega(f_k) \tag{4}$$

$$\Omega(f) = \gamma T + \frac{1}{2}\lambda \|w\|^2 \tag{5}$$

where $\hat{y}_i$ and y_i represent the predicted and actual labeled values of the i-th sample, respectively. γ and λ are the weight coefficients. The Obj is the objective function, where the first half represents the loss error, typically measured using mean square error and logistic regression. The second half corresponds to the regularization term, commonly employed to limit the depth of the CART tree and reduce its complexity. By constraining the tree's depth, it aims to prevent overfitting and improve generalization capabilities.

In summary, XGBoost offers the following advantages in performing regression prediction:

Improved Accuracy: By employing serial integration of decision tree models, XGBoost enhances the accuracy of output predictions. It exhibits a strong learning ability.

Model Complexity Control: XGBoost effectively manages the complexity of the model via regularization techniques. This helps to prevent overfitting and enhances the model's generalization ability.

Enhanced Optimization: XGBoost expands the model by utilizing a second-order Taylor expansion of the loss function. This approach accelerates the optimization process, leading to faster and more efficient computations.

4.2. XGBoost Model Tuning

To optimize the XGBoost model, several hyperparameters need to be tuned. Out of all the options available, four hyperparameters stand out as the most important and frequently utilized:

The learning rate, denoted by η, is a hyperparameter that scales the contribution of each tree added to the model. It helps in maintaining the stability and adaptability of the model. A lower value of η ($0 < \eta < 1$) makes the model more conservative towards overfitting but also leads to slower computation.

The minimum loss threshold, denoted by θ, is a hyperparameter that determines whether features should be split or not based on the Information Gain of the weak learner. If the Information Gain exceeds θ, the features are divided; otherwise, they are not. Increasing the value of θ makes the algorithm more conservative in its splitting decisions.

The maximum depth, denoted by m, represents the level of complexity in constructing the tree structure model. A higher value of m allows the model to capture more intricate patterns and relationships in the data, potentially leading to overfitting. On the other hand, a lower value of m constrains the tree's depth, making the model simpler and less prone to overfitting.

The number of weak learners, denoted by n, influences the learning ability of the model. Increasing the value of n enhances the model's capacity to learn complex patterns and relationships in the data. However, it also increases the risk of overfitting, where the model becomes too specialized for the training data. Finding the right balance for the value of n is crucial to ensure optimal prediction performance and accuracy of the model.

To enhance the prediction accuracy of the model while taking into account computational costs, this study proposes adjusting the four crucial hyperparameters (η,θ,m,n) that significantly impact the prediction performance of the XGBoost model using the Cuckoo Search algorithm.

4.3. Cuckoo Search-XGBoost Model

4.3.1. Cuckoo Search Algorithm (CS)

Grid search is one of the effective methods for determining optimal hyperparameters. However, as the number of hyperparameter dimensions increases, the computational cost of grid search grows exponentially. To mitigate this high computational burden, simulation algorithms like the Cuckoo Search have emerged for optimizing black-box functions.

In the Cuckoo Search algorithm, the process imitates the behavior of cuckoos searching for nests, with nests and eggs symbolizing potential solutions. The algorithm adheres to three fundamental rules:

(1) Each cuckoo can only lay one egg at a time and selects a nest randomly to place it in.
(2) A subset of nests is randomly chosen, and the best parasitic nests are retained for the next generation.
(3) The number of nests remains constant, and the host cuckoo's probability of finding a cuckoo's egg is determined by P_a. If a host finds an egg, it can either destroy the egg or continue searching for a new nest.

Cuckoo Search employs global random wandering through Levy flight to update the global optimal solution. This combination of cuckoo searching and Levy flight facilitates efficient exploration of the hyperparameter space, leading to the discovery of optimal solutions while minimizing computational costs.

$$\psi_{l+1}^{i} = \psi_{l}^{i} + \alpha \bigotimes s \tag{6}$$

where α represents the scaling factor for the step length, and in this case, α is set to 1. $s = \frac{u}{|v|^{1/\omega}} \sim le'vy(\omega), u \sim N(0,\sigma_l^2), v \sim N(0,1), \omega = 1.5$.

4.3.2. CS-XGBoost Model

The effectiveness of the XGBoost model is heavily influenced by the values of its parameters. To construct the CS-XGBoost model and optimize the XGBoost parameters using cuckoo search, the following steps are followed:

Step 1: Determine the corresponding parameters for the cuckoo search, including the maximum number of iterations (L), the probability of nest discovery by a bird (P_a), and the initial solution ψ_0 = (η,θ,m,n).

Step 2: Initialize the parameters $\psi_1, \psi_2, \ldots, \psi_d$ and define the objective function $\varphi(\psi_i)$ as the loss function value of the test set, where i ranges from 1 to d. Here, d represents the number of solutions.

Step 3: Randomly select a solution ψ_i from the available d solutions. Calculate the objective function $\varphi(\psi_i)$, and use Equation (6) to update it, resulting in the new position of the cuckoo's nest. Calculate the objective function $\varphi(\psi_j)$ for this new solution ψ_j. If $\varphi(\psi_i)>\varphi(\psi_j)$, then replace ψ_i with ψ_j.

Step 4: Iterate $\varphi(.)$, i = 1,2, ..., d to find the optimal parameter solution ψ_l^{opt}, keep ψ_l^{opt} until the next iteration, and with probability P_a to discard other non-optimal parameter solutions and find a new solution by Levy flights.

Step 5: The iteration process is terminated, and the final optimal parameter solution ψ_d^{opt} is obtained. This optimal solution is then substituted into the XGBoost model.

5. Results

5.1. Control Group Experiment of the SVM Model, RandomForest Model, and XGBoost Model

Support Vector Machine (SVM) is a supervised learning algorithm that was first introduced in 1964 [33]. It is based on the principle of structural risk minimization and is known for its strong generalization ability. SVM finds applications in various fields, including image recognition, audio and video recognition, text recognition, and more. Random Forest is a widely used machine learning model for classification problems. It was introduced by Leo Breiman in 2001 and combines bagging ensemble learning with the random subspace method [34].

The dataset (composed of mixed A, B, A′, and B′) was divided into ten parts using ten-fold cross-validation. Nine parts were used as training data, while one part served as test data for each experiment. Table 3 displays a comparison of evaluation metrics among the three models. The SVM model and RandomForest model have also been optimized using corresponding Python models to traverse some parameters. The CS-XGBoost model demonstrates superior performance compared to the XGBoost model with default parameters, followed by the SVM model and the RandomForest model. Among the four models, the CS-XGBoost model attains the highest values for all four evaluation metrics, indicating its effectiveness in classifying nursing behavior.

Table 3. Comparison of the performance of the SVM model, RandomForest model, and XGBoost model.

	Accuracy	Precision	Recall	F1 Score	$\psi = (\eta,\theta,m,n)$
SVM	0.8978	0.8907	0.8796	0.8851	——
RandomForest	0.9013	0.8991	0.9015	0.9002	——
XGBoost	0.9179	0.9021	0.9196	0.9107	(0,0.3,6,2000)
CS-XGBoost	0.9438	0.9511	0.9502	0.9506	(0.05,0.1,4,2000)

5.2. Three Groups of Experiments Based on CS-XGBoost

The nursing care activity data in this paper come from two groups of volunteers, which were collected when carrying out elderly nursing care services with (A′ and B′) and without (A and B) constraints, respectively. The following three groups of experiments are designed:

(1) Experiment 1: Data from a group of volunteers under constraints are used as training samples for parameter learning of the recognition model, and data from the other group of volunteers under constraints are used as training data, that is, to carry out the experiments Train (A′) → Test (B′) and Train (B′) → Test (A′), and the confusion matrix is shown in Table 4.

Table 4. Confusion matrix for the classification results of the experimental Train (B′) → Test (A′) classification results.

Service	S1	S2	S3	S4	S5	S6	S7	S8	S9	Recall
S1	145	0	0	0	0	0	0	0	8	0.9477
S2	0	90	0	0	3	0	0	0	0	0.9677
S3	0	0	150	0	5	0	0	0	0	0.9677
S4	0	0	0	94	0	0	0	0	0	1
S5	0	5	0	0	147	0	0	0	0	0.9671
S6	0	0	0	0	2	151	0	0	0	0.9869
S7	0	0	0	0	2	0	151	0	0	0.9869
S8	0	0	0	5	1	0	0	87	0	0.9355

Table 4. *Cont.*

Service	S1	S2	S3	S4	S5	S6	S7	S8	S9	Recall
S9	0	1	0	0	0	0	0	0	93	0.9894
precision	1	0.9375	1	0.9495	0.9187	1	1	1	0.9208	
f1_score	0.9731	0.9524	0.9836	0.9741	0.9423	0.9934	0.9934	0.9667	0.9538	

It can be seen from the confusion matrix in Table 4 that the overall recognition performance result is relatively good, the highest values of the three evaluation indicators reach 1. However, there are certain differences in the models for the different volunteer groups completing nursing care activities under constraints as shown in Table 5, mainly due to some relatively complex nursing care activities.

Table 5. Recognition accuracies of different experimental datasets in Experiment 1.

Train	Test	S1	S2	S3	S4	S5	S6	S7	S8	S9
B′	A′	1	0.9375	1	0.9495	0.9187	1	1	1	0.9208
A′	B′	0.9441	1	1	1	0.5200	0.9932	0.9869	0.9808	0.9737

Different volunteers have different understandings and executions of action points and norms, which leads to a certain difference in the recognition results of the model. Therefore, to better recognize nursing care activities based on wearable devices, it is necessary to give further detailed and clear instructions on the action standards and behavior specifications of these nursing care activities so that volunteers can regulate them more uniformly when completing these nursing care activities.

(2) Experiment 2: Apart from the constrained or unconstrained data of one group used as testing data, the rest of the data are all used as training data. The purpose is to verify the recognition performance of the CAR model for unknown action patterns that are close to the real situation.

From the confusion matrix given in Table 6, it can be seen that the recognition precisions, f1-scores, and recall values for the CAR model in Experiment 2 decrease greatly compared to those in Experiment 1. The challenge is that the training model lacks relevant information about the unconstrained nursing care activities in the testing data, and the volunteers perform unconstrained nursing care activities that usually have large differences in the amounts and complexities of actions.

Table 6. Confusion matrix of the experimental Train (A′, B′, A) → Test (B) classification results.

Service	S1	S2	S3	S4	S5	S6	S7	S8	S9	Recall
S1	88	0	0	0	55	0	5	0	0	0.5946
S2	0	78	0	0	2	0	0	2	2	0.9286
S3	0	0	140	1	2	0	0	4	0	0.9524
S4	0	1	0	78	0	3	0	4	0	0.9070
S5	15	0	0	0	120	8	4	0	3	0.8000
S6	3	1	0	7	4	20	1	5	1	0.4762
S7	30	0	0	0	22	6	81	1	9	0.5436
S8	0	0	4	17	0	0	0	64	0	0.7529
S9	0	0	0	0	0	0	0	0	0	0
precision	0.6471	0.9750	0.9722	0.7573	0.5854	0.5405	0.8901	0.8000	0	
f1_score	0.6197	0.9512	0.9622	0.8254	0.6761	0.5063	0.6750	0.7758	0	

The results in Table 7 show that although the constrained datasets A′ and B′ are not used in the model training phase, the accuracies of their recognition are relatively good at 0.9488 and 0.9166, respectively, because after explaining the key points and norms of nursing action to the nursing staff, the differences in action patterns among different volunteers are relatively small. However, during the model training phase, unconstrained datasets A and B are not used. Then, the unconstrained data are recognized, and the accuracies of A and B (0.8012 and 0.7821, respectively) are significantly lower than the recognition accuracies of A′ and B′ because there are no instructions on the action standards and behavior specifications of these nursing care activities given to the volunteers in the latter datasets, and which leads to significant differences in movement patterns between the different volunteers.

Table 7. Recognition accuracies of different experimental datasets in Experiment 2.

Testing Data / Precision Training Data	Test (A′)	Test (B′)	Test (A)	Test (B)
train(B′ A B)	0.9488			
train(A′ A B)		0.9166		
train(A′ B′ B)			0.8012	
train(A′ B′ A)				0.7821

(3) Experiment 3: As an extension of Experiment 2, this experiment uses mixed data (constrained data and unconstrained data) of two groups for training and constrained data or unconstrained data of one group for testing, and the results are shown in Tables 8 and 9. Unlike Experiment 2, this experiment verifies whether there are other unconstrained data which can help improve the classification accuracy.

Table 8. Confusion matrix of the experimental Train (A′, B′, A_{Tr}, B) → Test (A_{Ts}) classification results (where A_{Tr} + A_{Ts} = A).

Service	S1	S2	S3	S4	S5	S6	S7	S8	S9	Recall
S1	138	0	0	0	8	3	2	0	0	0.9139
S2	0	90	0	1	0	0	0	0	0	0.9890
S3	0	0	143	0	7	0	0	1	0	0.9470
S4	0	0	0	89	0	0	1	1	0	0.9780
S5	2	0	0	0	145	1	5	0	0	0.9477
S6	1	0	2	0	9	122	9	4	5	0.8026
S7	1	0	0	0	10	3	128	0	1	0.8951
S8	0	0	0	0	1	2	0	87	0	0.9667
S9	1	0	0	0	4	0	11	0	83	0.8384
precision	1	0.9802	1	0.9901	0.9752	0.9576	0.9728	1	0.9691	
f1_score	1	0.9851	0.9969	0.9950	0.9782	0.9723	0.9630	0.9944	0.9543	

Table 9. Recognition accuracies of different experimental datasets in Experiment 3.

Testing Data / Precision Training Data	Test (A_{Ts})	Test (B_{Ts})	Test (A'_{Ts})	Test (B'_{Ts})
train(A_{Tr} B A′ B′)	0.9898			
train(A B_{Tr} A′ B′)		0.9973		
train(A B A'_{Tr} B′)			0.9202	
train(A B A′ B'_{Tr})				0.9419

The experimental results show that using both constrained data and unconstrained data from nursing care activities for model training results in a general model with a better recognition performance. Both the constrained nursing care activity data and unconstrained nursing care activity data for identifying the nursing staff's future nursing care activities yield high recognition precision.

6. Conclusions and Discussion

Taking into account the application requirements of elderly nursing care service management, this paper first proposes the research of elderly CAR based on sensor data on wearable devices. Currently, the nine selected nursing care activities are distinct from one another and easy to recognize. However, in real-world elderly nursing care scenarios, some actions may not be feasible to recognize technically. On the one hand, there are relatively small and rapid actions, such as reminding, encouraging, or admonishing the elderly in specific scenarios, and on the other hand, some are easily confused by nursing behaviors, such as checking the physical condition of the elderly. There is no unified pattern for such behaviors. These issues may be solved by increasing the variety and number of wearable devices, which can result in greater differentiation and more accurate classification of behaviors. From the perspective of home care, these behaviors are equally important.

In addition, the nine behaviors classified in this study all require actual execution, which means that they do not include the behaviors of nursing staff resting and staying still. If we consider these relatively static behaviors of nursing staff, it may lead to misclassifying some behaviors that need to be actually executed as static behaviors, and vice versa. Therefore, considering relatively static rest behaviors for identifying and monitoring home-based elderly nursing care behaviors will also be an important aspect of future research.

The characteristics of the XGBoost model in machine learning algorithms, with more accurate recognition and faster computing time, have also been fully demonstrated in the field of behavior recognition. The experiments show that the CS-XGBoost model has better recognition performance than the XGBoost model with the default parameters, SVM, and RandomForest models.

Based on the experimental results based on the CS-XGBoost model, we obtained our observations of the applicability of the algorithms to actual elderly nursing care service management and summarized our suggestions on how to further validate management feasibility by collecting more data from home staff. To improve the accuracy of nursing care activities recognition in practical applications, adjustments can be made from the following three aspects: (1) try to use actual nursing care data from real-world nursing care activities as training data to model the classifiers; (2) standardize nursing care activities to make them uniform since uniform action patterns can be easily recognized; (3) try to collect elderly nursing care data from several different nursing staff and use the data for modeling, which helps to create more general classifiers and avoids overfitting.

Author Contributions: Conceptualization, Z.L. and X.L.; Methodology, Z.L.; Formal analysis, X.L.; Investigation, S.Z.; Resources, H.Z.; Data curation, Z.L.; Writing—original draft, Z.L.; Writing—review & editing, S.Z.; Visualization, S.Z. and X.L.; Supervision, H.Z.; Project administration, Z.L.; Funding acquisition, Z.L. and H.Z. All authors have read and agreed to the published version of the manuscript.

Funding: This research was supported by the Funds for First-class Discipline Construction (XK1802-5) of Beijing University of Chemical Technology and the Fundamental Research Funds for the Central Universities (ZY2430).

Data Availability Statement: The data used to support the findings of this study are available from the corresponding author upon request.

Conflicts of Interest: The authors declare no conflicts of interest.

References

1. Sander, M.; Oxlund, B.; Jespersen, A.; Krasnik, A.; Mortensen, E.L.; Westendorp, R.G.J.; Rasmussen, L.J. The challenges of human population ageing. *Age Ageing* **2015**, *44*, 185–187. [CrossRef]
2. Otsu, K.; Shibayama, K. Population aging and potential growth in Asia. *Asian Dev. Rev.* **2016**, *33*, 56–73. [CrossRef]
3. Oku, A.; Ichimura, E.; Tsukamoto, M. *Aging Population in Asian Countries | Lessons from Japanese Experiences*; Policy Research Institute, Ministry of Finance: Tokyo, Japan, 2017.
4. CPC Central Committee and State Council. *The 19th National Congress of the Communist Party of China, Longterm Plan for the Country to Actively Cope with Population Aging*; CPC Central Committee and State Council: Beijing, China, 2019.
5. Liu, J.; Dai, P.; Han, G.; Sun, N. Combined CNN/RNN video privacy protection evaluation method for monitoring home scene violence. *Comput. Electr. Eng.* **2023**, *106*, 108614. [CrossRef]
6. Wang, Q.; Zhang, W.; Li, J.; Ma, Z.; Chen, J. Benefits or harms? The effect of online review manipulation on sales. *Electron. Commer. Res. Appl.* **2023**, *57*, 101224. [CrossRef]
7. Kawsar, F.; Ahamed, S.; Love, R. Remote monitoring using smartphone based plantar pressure sensors: Unimodal and multimodal activity detection. In Proceedings of the Smart Homes and Health Telematics: 12th International Conference, ICOST 2014, Denver, CO, USA, 25–27 June 2014; Revised Papers 12; pp. 138–146.
8. Foerster, F.; Smeja, M.; Fahrenberg, J. Detection of posture and motion by accelerometry: A validation study in ambulatory monitoring. *Comput. Hum. Behav.* **1999**, *15*, 571–583. [CrossRef]
9. Mukhopadhyay, S.C. Wearable sensors for human activity monitoring: A review. *IEEE Sens. J.* **2014**, *15*, 1321–1330. [CrossRef]
10. Jameer, S.; Syed, H. A DCNN-LSTM based human activity recognition by mobile and wearable sensor networks. *Alex. Eng. J.* **2023**, *80*, 542–552. [CrossRef]
11. Garcia-Gonzalez, D.; Rivero, D.; Fernandez-Blanco, E.; Luaces, M.R. Deep learning models for real-life human activity recognition from smartphone sensor data. *Internet Things* **2023**, *24*, 100925. [CrossRef]
12. Wichum, F.; De Lazzari, N.; Götte, M.; David, C.; Wiede, C.; Seidl, K.; Tewes, M. Development of an AI-supported exercise therapy for advanced cancer patients. *Curr. Dir. Biomed. Eng.* **2022**, *8*, 169–172. [CrossRef]
13. Semwal, V.B.; Kim, Y.; Bijalwan, V.; Verma, A.; Singh, G.; Gaud, N.; Baek, H.; Khan, A.M. Development of the LSTM Model and Universal Polynomial Equation for all the Sub-phases of Human Gait. *IEEE Sens. J.* **2023**, *23*, 15892–15900. [CrossRef]
14. Peng, Y.; Nabae, H.; Funabora, Y.; Suzumori, K. Controlling a peristaltic robot inspired by inchworms. *Biomim. Intell. Robot.* **2024**, *4*, 100146. [CrossRef]
15. Mao, Z.; Asai, Y.; Yamanoi, A.; Seki, Y.; Wiranata, A.; Minaminosono, A. Fluidic rolling robot using voltage-driven oscillating liquid. *Smart Mater. Struct.* **2022**, *31*, 105006. [CrossRef]
16. Lara, O.D.; Labrador, M.A. A survey on human activity recognition using wearable sensors. *IEEE Commun. Surv. Tutor.* **2012**, *15*, 1192–1209. [CrossRef]
17. Arshad, M.H.; Bilal, M.; Gani, A. Human activity recognition: Review, taxonomy and open challenges. *Sensors* **2022**, *22*, 6463. [CrossRef] [PubMed]
18. Ho, T.K. Random decision forests. In Proceedings of the 3rd International Conference on Document Analysis and Recognition, Montreal, QC, Canada, 14–16 August 1995; pp. 278–282.
19. Ho, T.K. The random subspace method for constructing decision forests. *IEEE Trans. Pattern Anal. Mach. Intell.* **1998**, *20*, 832–844.
20. Su, J.; Zhang, B.; Xu, X. Research progress of text classification technology based on machine learning. *J. Softw.* **2006**, *17*, 1848–1859. [CrossRef]
21. Tomoya, S.; Harusa, T.; Soichiro, S.; Yohei, H.; Yang, L.; Ying, C. Fundamental study of a sports motion analysis system by using DNN recognition. *Proc. Symp. Sports Hum. Dyn.* **2018**, *2018*, C-30.
22. Walse, K.H.; Dharaskar, R.V.; Thakare, V.M. Pca based optimal ann classifiers for human activity recognition using mobile sensors data. In Proceedings of the First International Conference on Information and Communication Technology for Intelligent Systems: Volume 1, Ahmedabad, India, 28–29 November 2015; pp. 429–436.
23. Hammerla, N.Y.; Halloran, S.; Plötz, T. Deep, convolutional, and recurrent models for human activity recognition using wearables. *J. Sci. Comput.* **2016**, *61*, 454–476.

24. LeCun, Y.; Bengio, Y.; Hinton, G. Deep learning. *Nature* **2015**, *521*, 436–444. [CrossRef]
25. Wang, J.; Chen, Y.; Hao, S.; Peng, X.; Hu, L. Deep learning for sensor-based activity recognition: A survey. *Pattern Recognit. Lett.* **2019**, *119*, 3–11. [CrossRef]
26. Wu, H.; Zhang, Z.; Li, X.; Shang, K.; Han, Y.; Geng, Z.; Pan, T. A novel pedal musculoskeletal response based on differential spatio-temporal LSTM for human activity recognition. *Knowl.-Based Syst.* **2023**, *261*, 110187. [CrossRef]
27. Hayat, A.; Morgado-Dias, F.; Bhuyan, B.P.; Tomar, R. Human activity recognition for elderly people using machine and deep learning approaches. *Information* **2022**, *13*, 275. [CrossRef]
28. Inoue, M.; Inoue, S.; Nishida, T. Deep recurrent neural network for mobile human activity recognition with high throughput. *Artif. Life Robot.* **2018**, *23*, 173–185. [CrossRef]
29. Xia, K.; Huang, J.; Wang, H. LSTM-CNN architecture for human activity recognition. *IEEE Access* **2020**, *8*, 56855–56866. [CrossRef]
30. Jindal, S.; Sachdeva, M.; Kushwaha, A.K.S. Human Activity Recognition using Ensemble Convolutional Neural Networks and Long Short-Term Memory. *Int. J. Perform. Eng.* **2022**, *18*, 660.
31. Chen, T.; Guestrin, C. Xgboost: A scalable tree boosting system. In Proceedings of the 22nd ACM Sigkdd International Conference on Knowledge Discovery and Data Mining, San Francisco, CA, USA, 13–17 August 2016; pp. 785–794.
32. Jolliffe, I.T.; Cadima, J. Principal component analysis: A review and recent developments. *Philos. Trans.* **2016**, *374*, 20150202. [CrossRef] [PubMed]
33. Vapnik, V.N. A note on one class of perceptrons. *Autom. Remote Control* **1964**, *25*, 821–837.
34. Breiman, L. Random forests. *Mach. Learn.* **2001**, *45*, 5–32. [CrossRef]

mathematics

MDPI

Article

Two-Tier Configuration Model for the Optimization of Enterprise Costs and User Satisfaction for Rural Microgrids

Yong Fang [1], Minghao Li [1], Yunli Yue [2] and Zhonghua Liu [1,*]

[1] School of Economics and Management, Beijing University of Chemical Technology, Beijing 100029, China; 2004500038@buct.edu.cn (Y.F.); 2022200896@buct.edu.cn (M.L.)
[2] Economic and Technical Research Institute, State Grid Jibei Electric Power Company Limited, Beijing 100038, China; yue.yunli@jibei.sgcc.com.cn
* Correspondence: 2017500089@buct.edu.cn

Abstract: The construction costs and operational challenges of rural microgrids have garnered widespread attention. This study focuses on grid-connected rural microgrids incorporating wind, solar, hydro, and storage systems, and proposes a two-tier optimization configuration model that considers both enterprise costs and user satisfaction. The upper-tier model aims to minimize enterprise costs, covering construction, operation and maintenance, as well as penalties for a curtailment of wind, solar, and hydro power. The lower-tier model evaluates power reliability and cost-effectiveness to maximize user satisfaction. Using the particle swarm optimization algorithm, this study analyzes a case in Yudaokou, Hebei Province, and proposes three optimization schemes: minimizing enterprise costs, maximizing user satisfaction, and a compromise between the two. The optimal scheme, which employs 17 photovoltaic panels, 12 wind turbines, and 15 energy storage units, achieved a user satisfaction score of 0.90. This two-tier planning model provides practical insights for the rational configuration of rural microgrids and reveals the nonlinear relationship between costs and user experience.

Keywords: rural microgrid; two-tier planning; particle swarm optimization

MSC: 90C31

1. Introduction

China's rural landscapes are replete with copious wind, solar, and hydro resources, culminating in substantial renewable energy production. Following recent advancements in rural electrification, the use of renewable energy sources in these areas has increased significantly [1,2]. As of the first half of 2023, the cumulative installed capacity for renewable energy in China ascended to 1.322 billion kilowatts, representing 48.8% of the nation's total installed capacity [3]. Nevertheless, the deployment of renewable energy sources in rural locales as substitutes for conventional power generation accentuates their vulnerability to environmental contingencies like weather, engendering a pronounced variability in energy output. Such a variability may precipitate short-term power surpluses or deficits, markedly influencing load operations within rural settings and precipitating user dissatisfaction [4–6]. Enhancing the stability of the power supply typically results in higher overall costs for companies [7,8]. Consequently, the optimization of rural microgrid allocation, taking into account both the comprehensive costs to enterprises and user satisfaction, has emerged as a pivotal aspect of contemporary research.

The optimal configuration of a microgrid entails the strategic development of schemes for micro-source integration within the grid to augment energy efficiency whilst guaranteeing system stability [9]. Research on microgrid configurations primarily focuses on the economic and environmental benefits, as well as stability. In the context of microgrids' economic benefits, the primary objectives include minimizing the operational costs [10], maximizing grid enterprise profitability [11], and reducing the aggregate net present value of construction and operational expenses [12]. These objectives are mainly achieved through methodologies such as game model and deep reinforcement learning [13,14], which help reduce operational costs and enhance economic efficiency. Evaluating the environmental merits of microgrids underscores the imperative to optimize renewable energy source utilization [15], diminish greenhouse gas emissions [16], and amplify the ecological rewards [17]. The attainment of these objectives is facilitated through the deployment of intelligent algorithms that orchestrate a power generation strategy and consumption blueprint [18], thus elevating the microgrid's environmental sustainability. In an evaluation of microgrid stability, the complexities of managing distributed power generation and mitigating output uncertainty are adeptly navigated by integrating conditional value-at-risk models [19], robust stochastic models [20], or opportunistic stochastic constraints [21], thereby fortifying operational stability. Nevertheless, in the context of escalating competition within the power market, enterprises are compelled to prioritize the augmentation of user experiences as a strategic measure to secure a larger market share. Contemporary research on rural microgrids infrequently incorporates user satisfaction with electricity services into the overarching goals, necessitating a dual focus not only on corporate profitability but also on maximizing customer contentment within these grids.

In the domain of a rural microgrid construction cost analysis, deep reinforcement learning [13] effectively addresses the complex multivariate decision-making challenges. However, it struggles with ensuring stability and convergence, posing difficulties in identifying the global optimal solution. Genetic algorithms [15], while demonstrating significant efficiency and reliability, depend on stochastic processes that can yield varying outcomes across different runs, resulting in instability. Moreover, approaches like game theory [14] and stochastic constraints [11,19] address equipment allocation in microgrids. The game-theoretical models demand precise participant data and system parameters, whereas stochastic constraints manage renewable energy's uncertainty but falter in highly deterministic scenarios. The particle swarm algorithm employed in this research achieves an optimal balance between global and local searches by strategically adjusting inertia weights and learning factors. Furthermore, the particle swarm algorithm preserves the memory of the most promising particles throughout the iterations, offering a significant advantage in addressing the complex two-tier planning problem in rural microgrids. In the two-tier programming problem presented in this study, the objective functions are two conflicting aspects, which can be balanced by PSO by retaining the global and local optimal solutions. The memory function ensures that the algorithm does not lose those potentially high-quality solutions found in the previous iterations while searching globally, effectively improving the quality of understanding. Consequently, the particle swarm algorithm is particularly advantageous for solving the two-tier model developed in this study.

Prior research on rural microgrids has focused on construction costs, and although different studies and model-solving methods have been adopted, they have mainly focused on the economic benefits of rural microgrid construction, often neglecting the assessment of user satisfaction, especially the studies that comprehensively reconcile enterprise costs and user satisfaction which are fewer in number. In addition, most of the existing research on microgrids focuses on cities, with fewer studies on rural microgrid planning. To fill these gaps, this study employs a two-tier planning model that aims to reconcile the discrepancy between firms' construction costs and consumers' experiences with electricity services. The main contribution of this study is the development of a rural microgrid construction strategy that achieves the dual goals of minimizing firms' costs and enhancing rural consumers' electricity experiences. Moreover, this research substantiates the viability of a two-tier, grid-connected microgrid optimization framework, offering crucial insights for the logical planning and appropriate equipment configuration of rural microgrids, thereby supporting their continued expansion and development.

The remainder is structured as explained below. Section 2 constructs the structure of rural microgrids and conducts a feature analysis. Section 3 constructs a two-tier programming model. Section 4 proposes a solution plan and uses the actual case data later employed for a solving and sensitivity analysis in Section 5. Finally, Section 6 provides the conclusion and proposals for future work. The symbols and explanations used in this study are as follows (Table 1).

Table 1. Glossary of Terms and Units.

Symbol	Explanation	Unit
C_{CONST}	Construction cost	USD
C_{OMT}	Operational, maintenance, and testing cost	USD
C_{waste}	Penalty cost	USD
$C_{PV}, C_{WT}, C_{HS}, C_{ES}$	Individual investment expenditures for Photovoltaic power plants, wind turbines, hydropower stations, and energy storage facilities	USD
C_{GCI}	The aggregated investment cost for all grid-tied inverters	USD
$N_{PV}, N_{WT}, N_{HS}, N_{ES}$	Quantity of photovoltaics, wind turbines, hydro Generators, and energy storage	Unit
i	Discount rate	-
n	Projected lifespan	Year
$C_{PV}^{OMT}, C_{WT}^{OMT}, C_{HS}^{OMT}, C_{ES}^{OMT}$	The unitary average costs associated with the operation, maintenance, and testing (OMT) of individual photovoltaic power stations, wind turbines, hydropower stations, and energy storage facilities	USD
C_{GCI}^{OMT}	Annual average expenditure for the OMT Activities of all grid-tied inverters	USD
$C_{PV}^{waste}, C_{WT}^{waste}, C_{HS}^{waste}$	Penalization factors for the abandonment of solar, wind, and hydroelectric power	USD
$P_{max}^{PV}, P_{max}^{WT}, P_{max}^{HS}$	The maximal power outputs achievable by photovoltaic systems, wind turbines, and hydro stations	kW
$P_{s.t.}^{PV}, P_{s.t.}^{WT}, P_{s.t.}^{HS}$	The actual power outputs from photovoltaic systems, wind turbines, and hydroelectric stations	kW
T	The maximal quantity of hours per day during which electrical power is wasted	Hour
C_{MG}	The comprehensive economic cost	USD
$N_{PV}^{max}, N_{WT}^{max}, N_{HS}^{max}$	The upper limits on the number of photovoltaic, wind turbine, and hydroelectric devices	Unit
P_{DG}	The aggregate output power generated by distributed power sources	kW
P_{load}	Power consumption	kW
μ	The power generation margin within the microgrid	-
P_{PV}, P_{WT}, P_{HS}	The output powers of an individual photovoltaic unit, wind turbine, and hydropower unit	kW
U_R	Reliability	-
U_E	Cost-effectiveness	-
α	The importance of electricity reliability	-
β	The importance of electricity cost-effectiveness	-
T_{PO}	The annual duration of power outages experienced within the rural microgrid	Day
T_{year}	The period constituting one calendar year	Day
P_m	The electricity tariff charged to residents prior to the establishment of the rural microgrid	USD
P_g	The rate post-establishment	USD
$U_{R,min}$	Minimum reliability	-

2. Characteristics and Structure of Rural Microgrids

2.1. The Characteristics of Rural Power Distribution Networks

The rural microgrid serves as a pivotal foundation for the establishment of innovative power systems, facilitating the advancement and utilization of distributed energy resources within rural locales. Analyzing the structure and features of rural microgrids can greatly improve the reliability of an energy supply and its consumption efficiency. This plays a critical role in advancing the amalgamation and utilization of renewable energy resources, as well as in the sustainable progression of rural socio-economic frameworks. Distinguished by four salient features, rural microgrids cater to the unique demands and conditions prevalent in rural settings, in contrast to conventional microgrids:

(1) Weak grid structure. Most rural microgrids have a simple, single-line power supply configuration due to a weak grid architecture. This straightforward structure connects to the main power grid and includes connection points, distributed power generators, and energy storage systems. While the single-line power supply framework offers cost efficiencies, it harbors the potential for power supply instability [22]. Rural microgrids typically possess the capability to seamlessly integrate with or disconnect from the main grid, allowing for adjustments between grid-tied and wholly independent operations based on demand [23]. This confers a significant level of flexibility and self-reliance.

(2) Abundant forms of energy. Rural regions often have facilitated access to diverse renewable energy sources, laying a robust foundation for rural microgrid development. This observation is made with objectivity, devoid of subjective assessments. Among the renewable energy sources prevalently harnessed in rural microgrids, there are wind, hydro, photovoltaic, and biomass energy sources [24–26]. The plethora of energy varieties offers an economically sustainable and ecologically benign solution for rural locales. Furthermore, this diversification diminishes reliance on external energy sources, bolstering energy security and fostering sustainable advancement in rural regions.

(3) Poor quality of electricity. The employment of renewable energy sources within rural microgrids often leads to an intermittent and unpredictable power supply, adversely impacting the stability and reliability of the electrical energy provided [27]. Moreover, constraints in energy storage and management systems, arising from technological limitations and investment restrictions, can impede efforts to mitigate supply instability [28]. This confluence of factors can precipitate power quality concerns, including voltage instability and frequency variations, adversely affecting rural microgrid consumers. Such complications can detrimentally influence daily living and economic operations.

(4) Low user satisfaction. Power quality instability within rural microgrids directly influences the electricity experience of users, potentially detracting from their overall satisfaction. Recurrent power interruptions and voltage fluctuations can gravely impact residents' quality of life and disrupt the routine operations of businesses [29]. Moreover, rural microgrids frequently face challenges in delivering dependable services and swift responses in the face of extreme weather events or equipment malfunctions, owing to the technical and financial limitations.

2.2. The Structure of Rural Microgrids

The architecture of a microgrid underpins its operational safety and ensures the energy system's flexibility and resilience. These qualities are vital during the construction, operation, and maintenance phases of the microgrid. Microgrids are currently categorized into three types based on their characteristics: DC, AC, and AC/DC hybrid microgrids [30]. The prevalent structure in rural microgrids is the AC/DC hybrid microgrid [31], encompassing both AC and DC buses. This configuration forms AC and DC sub-microgrids, facilitating bidirectional power flow via bidirectional converters. It melds the benefits of both the AC and DC microgrids; the AC/DC hybrid microgrid is capable of simultaneously powering AC and DC loads, thereby minimizing the power conversion losses. Its ability to operate independently or integrate seamlessly with larger power grids enhances its reliability. Consequently, the AC/DC hybrid microgrid presents extensive development potential [32]. The architecture of the AC/DC hybrid microgrid is illustrated in Figure 1.

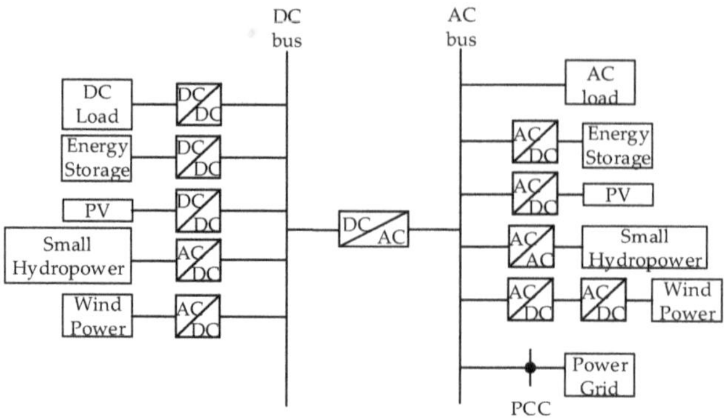

Figure 1. Structure of AC/DC hybrid microgrid.

The unique structure and characteristics of rural microgrids engender the distinct objectives among participating stakeholders. From an enterprise perspective, the aim is to build and manage microgrids with the least possible investment, concurrently enhancing the subpar power quality in rural microgrids for sustainable development. For users, the primary goal is to attain an improved power experience. Pursuing enhanced user satisfaction typically necessitates increased investment from the enterprise. The conflict between the user and the enterprise is prevalent [33]. Consequently, identifying an optimal microgrid construction plan that meets the varied needs of both businesses and consumers is paramount.

3. Interconnected Rural Microgrid Two-Tier Planning Model

The inherent ability of microgrids to generate and consume electrical energy locally bestows upon them significant flexibility, rendering them a pivotal element in the evolution of future smart grids. Nevertheless, the variability, randomness, and intermittency inherent in distributed energy sources may precipitate power outages and voltage instability within microgrids, adversely affecting consumers' electricity usage experiences. To augment consumers' electricity usage experiences, power companies are compelled to bolster their investment in microgrids, aiming to enhance stability. Achieving a balance between the economic returns for power companies and the satisfaction levels of consumers has emerged as a critical consideration in the construction and operational strategies of microgrids. Consequently, this research proposes a two-tier planning model aimed at devising an optimized configuration for rural microgrids.

In actual microgrid construction scenarios, there are often many uncertainties involved. To reduce unnecessary details and better focus on the core issues, this article makes the following assumptions in the modeling process: (1) The equipment performance is fixed and will not decrease with external environmental factors or aging. (2) Ignore the uncertain factors and assume that the uncertainty of the external environment will not affect the model parameters. (3) Constant cost, believe that both the construction and operation costs are constant and not affected by the market or inflation.

3.1. Minimum Cost Model for Microgrid Construction and Operation

The overarching objective of the upper-tier planning model, addressing the two-tier planning dilemma of rural microgrids, is to minimize the aggregate economic cost. This comprehensive cost framework includes the following: the discounted construction costs of the microgrids (C_{CONST}) [17], the ongoing operation and maintenance expenses (C_{OMT}) [31], and the penalty costs associated with wind and hydro variability (C_{waste}) [21]. Thereby providing a metric for assessing the financial efficacy of the utility's development and operational endeavors.

(1) Construction Cost C_{CONST} of the rural microgrid:

$$C_{CONST} = C'_{CONST}\frac{i(1+i)^n}{(1+i)^n - 1} \tag{1}$$

$$C'_{CONST} = C_{PV}N_{PV} + C_{WT}N_{WT} + C_{HS}N_{HS} + C_{ES}N_{ES} + C_{GCI} \tag{2}$$

C_{PV}, C_{WT}, C_{HS}, and C_{ES} denote the respective individual investment expenditures for photovoltaic power plants, wind turbines, hydropower stations, and energy storage facilities. These expenditures encompass the cumulative costs associated with equipment acquisition, transportation, and the construction activities prior to an operational deployment. C_{GCI} encapsulates the aggregated investment cost for all the grid-tied inverters. Furthermore, N_{PV}, N_{WT}, N_{HS}, and N_{ES} signify the quantities of units established for each type of renewable energy installation, serving as pivotal decision variables within this analytical framework. C'_{CONST} is defined as the comprehensive cost arising from the microgrid's construction, whereas i specifies the discount rate, and n delineates the projected lifespan, in years, throughout the microgrid's entire lifecycle.

(2) Operational, Maintenance, and Testing Cost C_{OMT} of the rural microgrid:

$$C_{OMT} = C'_{OMT}\frac{i(1+i)^n}{(1+i)^n - 1} \tag{3}$$

$$C'_{OMT} = C_{PV}^{OMT}N_{PV} + C_{WT}^{OMT}N_{WT} + C_{HS}^{OMT}N_{HS} + C_{ES}^{OMT}N_{ES} + C_{GCI}^{OMT} \tag{4}$$

C_{PV}^{OMT}, C_{WT}^{OMT}, C_{HS}^{OMT}, and C_{ES}^{OMT} delineate the unitary average costs associated with the operation, maintenance, and testing (OMT) of the individual photovoltaic power stations, wind turbines, hydropower stations, and energy storage facilities, respectively. C'_{OMT} is defined as the construction, operation, and maintenance cost of the microgrid. Concurrently, C_{GCI}^{OMT} specifies the annual average expenditure for the OMT activities of all the grid-tied inverters.

(3) Penalty Cost C_{waste} for Wasted Wind, Light, and Water in the rural microgrid:

$$C_{waste} = C'_{waste}\frac{i(1+i)^n}{(1+i)^n - 1} \tag{5}$$

$$C'_{waste} = \sum_{s=1}^{S} DP(s)\sum_{t=1}^{T}\left[C_{PV}^{waste}\left(P_{max}^{PV} - P_{s.t.}^{PV}\right) + C_{WT}^{waste}\left(P_{max}^{WT} - P_{s.t.}^{WT}\right) + C_{HS}^{waste}\left(P_{max}^{HS} - P_{s.t.}^{HS}\right)\right] \tag{6}$$

The term 'Abandoned wind, light, and water' describes a situation where the power grid produces more electricity than is needed. The unutilized potential generating capacity of renewable energy sources that could theoretically produce more energy but due to natural conditions or technological constraints produce less than their maximum potential can also be considered 'waste'. As a result, the excess electricity generated by these sources is not effectively utilized. In response to this challenge, numerous countries and regions have instituted penalty charges for the abandonment of wind, solar, and hydroelectric energy [34]. Such a policy aims to incentivize power generation entities to refine their renewable energy forecasting and planning practices, thereby diminishing the propensity for energy abandonment, and concurrently bolstering the power grid's reliability and economic efficiency.

In Equation (6), C'_{waste} is defined as the penalty cost of the microgrid. The variable D denotes the annual total number of days. S represents the peak number of days characterized by the occurrence of events leading to the abandonment of solar, wind, and hydroelectric resources. The function $P(s)$ quantifies the likelihood of such abandonment on the s-th day for wind, solar, and hydroelectric sources. Furthermore, the coefficients C_{PV}^{waste}, C_{WT}^{waste}, and C_{HS}^{waste} serve as penalization factors for the abandonment of solar, wind, and hydroelectric power, respectively. The terms P_{max}^{PV}, P_{max}^{WT}, and P_{max}^{HS} denote the maximal power outputs achievable by photovoltaic systems, wind turbines, and hydro stations, respectively. The actual power outputs from photovoltaic systems, wind turbines, and hydroelectric stations at a given time t are represented by $P_{s.t.}^{PV}$, $P_{s.t.}^{WT}$, and $P_{s.t.}^{HS}$, respectively. Lastly, T signifies the maximal quantity of hours per day during which electrical power is wasted.

The total cost of construction and operation of rural microgrids, taking into account the three types of costs of rural microgrid construction, is as follows:

$$\begin{aligned} MinC_{MG} &= C_{CONST} + C_{OMT} + C_{waste} \\ &= (C_{PV}N_{PV} + C_{WT}N_{WT} + C_{HS}N_{HS} + C_{ES}N_{ES} + C_{GCI})\frac{i(1+i)^n}{(1+i)^n - 1} \\ &+ (C_{PV}^{OMT}N_{PV} + C_{WT}^{OMT}N_{WT} + C_{HS}^{OMT}N_{HS} + C_{ES}^{OMT}N_{ES} + C_{GCI}^{OMT})\frac{i(1+i)^n}{(1+i)^n - 1} \\ &+ \left\{ \sum_{s=1}^{S} DP(s) \sum_{t=1}^{T} \begin{bmatrix} C_{PV}^{waste}(P_{max}^{PV} - P_{s.t.}^{PV}) \\ +C_{WT}^{waste}(P_{max}^{WT} - P_{s.t.}^{WT}) \\ +C_{HS}^{waste}(P_{max}^{HS} - P_{s.t.}^{HS}) \end{bmatrix} \right\} \frac{i(1+i)^n}{(1+i)^n - 1} \end{aligned} \quad (7)$$

C_{MG} represents the comprehensive economic cost.

Microgrid systems must follow specific constraint conditions during operation. These constraints are established based on practical demands and scenarios, defining the acceptable range for setting decision variables as follows.

Constraints on the number of distributed power source installations:

$$0 \leq N_{PV} \leq N_{PV}^{max} \quad (8)$$

$$0 \leq N_{WT} \leq N_{WT}^{max} \quad (9)$$

$$1 \leq N_{HS} \leq N_{HS}^{max} \quad (10)$$

The variables N_{PV}^{max}, N_{WT}^{max}, and N_{HS}^{max} denote the upper limits on the number of photovoltaic, wind turbine, and hydroelectric devices, respectively, that can be installed, taking into account site-specific and miscellaneous constraints. These variables are integers, representing the count of units. In light of the plentiful water resources available in the Yudaokou region, the power grid company has formulated plans to erect a hydropower station, aiming to harness the full potential of hydropower generation. Consequently, the construction of at least one hydropower station is mandated.

The power constraints are as follows:

$$P_{DG} \geq P_{load}(1 + \mu) \quad (11)$$

$$P_{DG} = P_{PV}N_{PV} + P_{WT}N_{WT} + P_{HS}N_{HS} \quad (12)$$

The symbol P_{DG} denotes the aggregate output power generated by the distributed power sources. P_{load} presents power consumption. The generation margin μ within the microgrid is introduced due to the need to ensure that the microgrid system can operate stably and cope with possible load fluctuations or emergencies. Furthermore, the variables P_{PV}, P_{WT}, and P_{HS} correspond to the output powers of an individual photovoltaic unit, a wind turbine, and a hydropower unit, respectively.

3.2. Maximum User Satisfaction Model

Rural consumers prioritize electrical stability and affordability, acknowledging that rural microgrids often suffer from inferior power quality compared to their urban counterparts. Consistent with the prevailing research on customer satisfaction, this study proposes the assessment of satisfaction through the dimensions of reliability U_R and the cost-effectiveness U_E of electricity consumption [35]. Consequently, the objective function to quantify customer satisfaction is delineated as follows:

$$MaxU = \alpha U_R + \beta U_E \tag{13}$$

$$\alpha + \beta = 1 \tag{14}$$

The parameters α and β are assigned to quantify the importance of electricity reliability and cost-effectiveness, respectively. In recognition of the escalating demand for an uninterrupted and stable electricity supply in rural regions crucial for residential and agricultural development, α is apportioned a value of 0.6, whereas β is allocated a value of 0.4.

(1) Reliability in the context of microgrid systems signifies the system's ability to provide a stable and uninterrupted power supply. This aspect is particularly pivotal in rural locales, where the consistency of electricity directly influences the community's quality of life and operational normalcy. A dependable power supply underpins the smooth operation of essential infrastructure, thereby enhancing the living conditions of residents, especially in education and healthcare. The measure of reliability is typically gauged by the duration of power outages [36], given that the extent of these disruptions bears a significant impact on the daily lives and productivity of the rural populace. Extended power interruptions can severely hamper community life, impacting vital sectors like agriculture and healthcare. The formula to quantify reliability is detailed as follows:

$$U_R = \left(1 - \frac{T_{PO}}{T_{year}}\right) \times 100\% \tag{15}$$

The variable T_{PO} represents the annual duration of power outages experienced within the rural microgrid, a metric intrinsically linked to the quantity of distributed power sources integrated during the microgrid's construction. Concurrently, T_{year} denotes the period constituting one calendar year.

(2) Cost-effectiveness encapsulates the optimal utilization of electrical resources to satisfy residents' electricity needs in an economical manner. Given the prevalent concern about electricity pricing in rural settings, the ability to deliver cost-efficient electrical services is paramount to enhancing the satisfaction levels for residential electricity consumption. The cost-effectiveness metric is quantifiable through the ratio of the diminished electricity bill post-microgrid implementation to the preceding electricity bill [37]. The formula for calculating this indicator is specified as follows:

$$U_E = \frac{P_m - P_g}{P_m} \times 100\% \tag{16}$$

The variable P_m denotes the electricity tariff charged to residents prior to the establishment of the rural microgrid, whereas P_g represents the rate post-establishment; both metrics are expressed in USD per kilowatt-hour.

Current standards mandate that the reliability of a power supply in rural areas should not dip below the national benchmark, identified as $U_{R,min}$. As a result, customer satisfaction concerning rural microgrids is subject to the specified constraint.

$$U_R \geq U_{R,min} \tag{17}$$

The two-tier planning model described in this investigation includes a crucial data exchange process between its hierarchical levels. The upper-tier enterprises formulate and disseminate the construction, operational, and maintenance blueprints for the rural microgrid. These actions invariably influence critical parameters, including electricity reliability for sub-tier users. As a result, there are consequential impacts on customer satisfaction. After receiving feedback on customer satisfaction, these enterprises will recalibrate the microgrid's optimization scheme based on the input from the sub-tier users, with the objective of realizing a global optimum.

4. Solution of a Two-Tier Planning Model for Rural Microgrid

The development of a comprehensive two-tier planning model for grid-connected rural microgrids is presented in this study. Initially, the planning problem, inherently two-tiered, is reformulated into a single-tier problem utilizing the KKT conditions. Subsequently, the particle swarm optimization algorithm is employed to effectively solve the reformulated model.

4.1. Decoupling of Two-Tier Planning Models

A two-tier model addressing both enterprise costs and user satisfaction is developed. Initially, the user satisfaction objectives and constraints are transformed into a system of equations and inequalities through the construction of a Lagrangian function for the sub-tier problem. Subsequently, the derived Karush–Kuhn–Tucker (KKT) conditions are incorporated as additional constraints within the overarching enterprise cost framework, thereby converting the two-tier problem into a unified single-tier optimization challenge that integrates both the upper-tier directives and the sub-tier KKT conditions.

The KKT conditions embed the sub-tier optimization problem as a constraint of the upper-tier problem, so that the whole optimization problem can be treated uniformly at one level, thus transforming the two-tier optimization problem into a single-tier optimization problem. Subsequently, the sub-tier of this study is modeled as a KKT condition that includes a single inequality constraint, expressed in the following general form:

$$\min f(X) \tag{18}$$

$$s.t.g(X) \leq 0 \tag{19}$$

Then, define the Lagrangian function as follows:

$$L(X, \lambda) = f(X) + \lambda g(X) \tag{20}$$

The KKT condition containing only one inequality constraint is as follows:

$$\nabla_X L = 0 \tag{21}$$

$$\lambda g(X) = 0 \tag{22}$$

$$\lambda \geq 0 \tag{23}$$

$$g(X) \leq 0 \tag{24}$$

The sub-tier model of this study can be summarized as equations (13) and (17). Upon establishing definite values for the variables N_{PV}, N_{WT}, N_{HS} within the upper-tier model, the corresponding Lagrangian function for the sub-tier model can be articulated as follows:

$$L(N, \lambda) = -\alpha U_R - \beta U_E + \lambda U \tag{25}$$

$$U = U_{R,\ min} - U_R \tag{26}$$

In Formula (25), λ is the Lagrangian operators with inequality constraints.

Based on the KKT conditions of the sub-tier model, the following is deduced:

$$\alpha + \lambda = 0 \tag{27}$$

$$\lambda(U_{R,\ min} - U_R) = 0 \tag{28}$$

$$\lambda \geq 0 \tag{29}$$

The transformation of the two-tier programming model into a unified single-tier programming framework is achieved by applying the KKT conditions. This reconstructed single-tier planning model has Equation (7) as the objective, and (8) to (12) in the original upper constraints and (27) to (29) in the original lower constraints are made into the constraints of the single-tier planning model.

4.2. Solution Algorithm

This study uses the particle swarm optimization (PSO) algorithm to solve the planning problem, which is recognized as the most effective algorithm to date [38,39]. The algorithm has high applicability and is often applied to solve problems such as the optimal scheduling of microgrids. Initially, the number of particle swarms is set to 50 and the maximum number of iterations is 100, with each particle having different position and velocity attributes. It then evaluates the fitness of each particle against the objective function, with the aim of minimizing the comprehensive cost to the enterprise. Following this, both the individual and group optimal solutions are updated, with subsequent adjustments made to the velocity and position of each particle in alignment with these solutions. The pursuit of the group optimal solution is conducted through relentless iteration and meticulous convergence checks. Adjustments to the velocity and position of the particles are continuously made in response to the evolving individual and group optimal solutions, culminating in the attainment of the group optimal solution via persistent iteration and convergence verification.

Upon converting the two-tier planning problem into a single-tier model, this study employs the particle swarm optimization algorithm to address the solution. The algorithm enhances its capability to escape local optima through adjustments in the inertia weight, achieving a balance between global and local searches [38]. Furthermore, its capacity to memorize optimal solutions notably improves its performance in addressing the two-tier planning challenges [39]. Initially, the algorithm randomly initializes a population of particles, each characterized by distinct spatial coordinates x_i and velocity attributes v_i. x_i represents the decision variable, specifically the number of devices deployed in a rural microgrid, whereas v_i denotes the velocity of each particle within the decision space. Subsequently, the particle swarm optimization algorithm computes the fitness value $f(x_i)$ for each particle based on the objective function, which aims to minimize the total enterprise cost $f(x)$, and the respective positions x_i of each particle. The algorithm then updates both the individual and collective optimal solutions, refining the personal best position $pbest_i$ and the global best position $gbest_i$ based on the fitness values $f(x_i)$ of the particles. Further adjustments to each particle's velocity and position are governed by the inertia weight ω, along with the individual and social learning coefficients c_1 and c_2, as detailed in Equations (30) and (31). r_1 and r_2 are random numbers with values between zero and one, ensuring the randomness of the speed updates and helping to avoid getting stuck in local optima. The updated particle velocity and position are v_i^{t+1} and x_i^{t+1}, respectively.

$$v_i^{t+1} = \omega v_i^t + c_1 r_1 (pbest_i - x_i^t) + c_2 r_2 (gbest_i - x_i^t) \tag{30}$$

$$x_i^{t+1} = x_i^t + v_i^{t+1} \tag{31}$$

Larger values for C1 enhance the local search but may cause the algorithm to get stuck in local optima. Increasing C2 strengthens the global search, helping to avoid local optima, but it might lead to an excessively fast convergence. The parameter w controls the global search capability and adjusts the search precision. To achieve better search accuracy, the learning coefficients c1 and c2 were set to 2 and the inertia weight was set to 0.8 [1]. If the maximum number of iterations is reached or the global optimal solution stabilizes, exhibiting negligible changes, the algorithm terminates and outputs the results. Otherwise, the algorithm persists in computing the fitness values $f(x_i)$ for each particle, continuing iterations until it can output both the optimal design solution for the microgrid, represented by $gbest$, and the minimal total enterprise cost, denoted by

$f(gbest)$. The flowchart depicting the particle swarm optimization algorithm is illustrated in Figure 2 below.

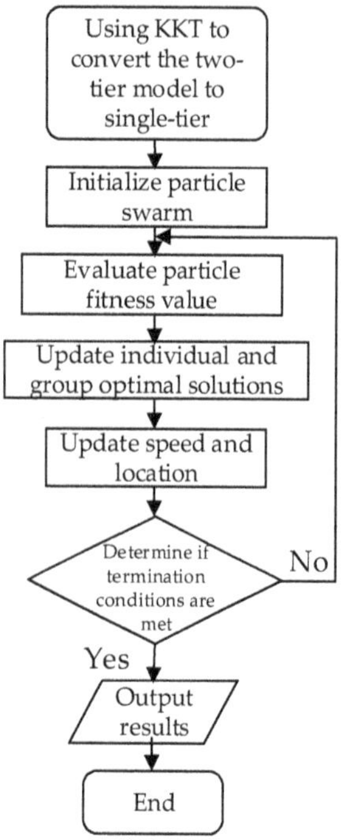

Figure 2. Solution flowchart.

Optimal solutions in particle swarm optimization algorithms are achieved through rigorous computation and meticulous convergence verification. When compared to the existing ant colony algorithm, the particle swarm algorithm exhibits superior computational efficiency [40]; relative to the simulated annealing algorithm, the particle swarm algorithm demonstrates faster convergence rates [41]; in comparison to mixed integer programming, the particle swarm algorithm is more adaptable to handling nonlinear and nonconvex challenges [42]. Consequently, the exceptional performance of PSO on the continuous optimization challenges affords it significant advantages in addressing the microgrid planning issues.

5. Case Study

5.1. Input Data

Yudaokou epitomizes the plateau countryside, situated at the confluence of the northern Hebei mountains and the Mongolian plateau. It is endowed with an abundance of renewable energy resources, including wind and solar energy. Despite its wealth of resources, the area contends with a frail distribution network, an extensive power supply radius, and the challenges inherent to rural microgrids, including a substandard voltage and three-phase imbalance. These issues make it an exemplary case study. The geographical location of Yudaokou is shown in Figure 3. In this study, wind and solar resource data, along with load data from Yudaokou, serve as the inputs for a comprehensive simulation and analysis, with the resultant data map depicted in Figure 4. The average daily local load is 3670 kW and the variance is 138,094.3. Detailed information for each distributed power device within the system is catalogued in Table 2, while the penalty costs associated with the rural microgrid are uniformly set at 0.0828 USDs/kW·h.

Figure 3. Geographical location of Yudaokou.

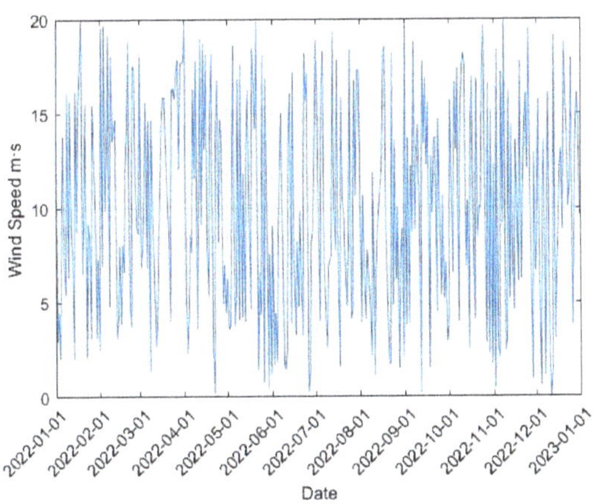

(**a**) Wind speed curve

Figure 4. *Cont.*

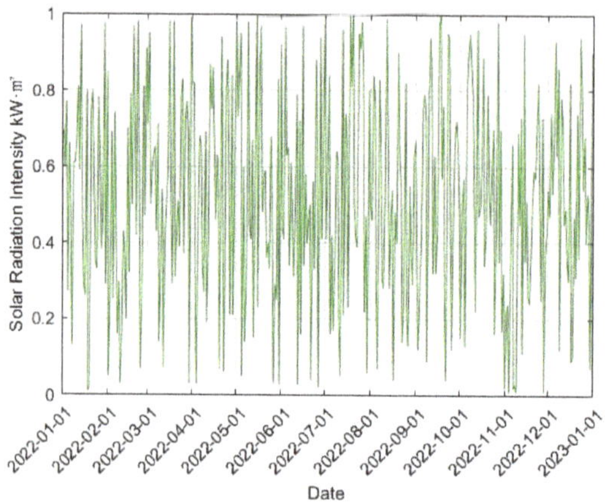

(**b**) Solar radiation intensity curve

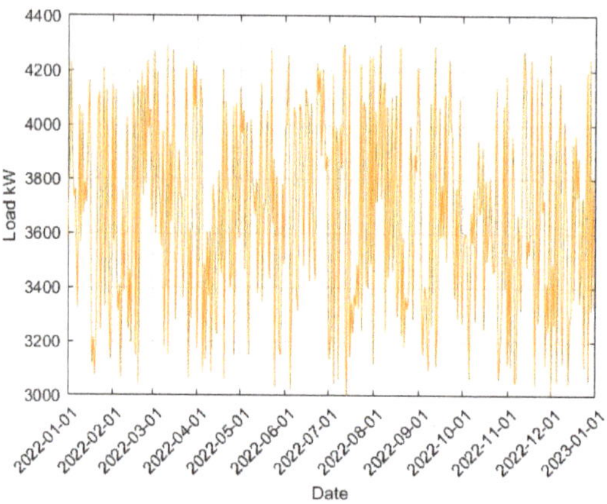

(**c**) Load curve

Figure 4. Wind speed, solar radiation intensity, and load data curves.

Table 2. Distributed power supply equipment information.

Equipment	Construction Costs (USD/Group)	Operation and Maintenance Costs (USD/kw·h)
Photovoltaic	27,600	1.4×10^{-3}
Fan	41,400	4.1×10^{-3}
Small hydropower	414,000	3.59×10^{-2}
Energy storage	13,800	1.4×10^{-3}
Grid connected inverter	13,800	0

The reference to 'USD/group' in the table refers to the construction cost of each complete unit of equipment, rather than the cost of the individual components or parts of the equipment.

5.2. Optimization Results

Different objectives are considered in this study by constructing three scenarios including the cost-only [12] and user satisfaction-only [15] schemes commonly seen in current research.

Scheme 1: This cost-only scheme takes enterprise profits as the main starting point, and takes the lowest comprehensive cost of construction, operation, and maintenance of the rural microgrid enterprises as the planning objective, and reduces the construction and operation cost of the microgrids by reducing the number of equipment units, so as to control enterprise expenditures. At the same time, this scheme will also incorporate user satisfaction into the constraints to ensure that it can meet the most basic power requirements of users.

Scheme 2: This user satisfaction-only scheme takes the user as the main part, and takes maximizing user satisfaction as the main goal of rural microgrid construction. By increasing the amount of equipment to improve the reliability of the user's power consumption, it improves the user's satisfaction. At the same time, this scheme incorporates the construction, operation, and maintenance costs of the microgrid enterprises into the constraints to ensure that they are not beyond the affordability of the enterprises.

Scheme 3: This scheme considers the cost of enterprise construction, operation, and maintenance of the microgrids, as well as user satisfaction, ensuring that neither the construction and operation costs are too high nor that user satisfaction with electricity services is too low. This is achieved through the planning of rural microgrids using the two-tier planning model proposed in this paper.

The data from Yudaokou and the specified equipment parameters yield varied configuration outcomes, as delineated in Table 3. Observation reveals that Scheme 1 uses 15 sets of photovoltaic panels and 12 sets of wind turbines, marking it as the configuration with the fewest devices. While this scheme stands out for its cost-effectiveness, securing the lowest construction, operation, and maintenance costs, it unfortunately leads to diminished customer satisfaction. Such shortcomings could adversely affect rural activities, including livestock farming and electric heating, thereby hampering the cultivation of positive relations between companies and their users. The underlying cause of the diminished customer satisfaction likely stems from an insufficient number of photovoltaic panels and wind turbines to meet the peak demands during operation, thereby detracting from the users' electricity consumption experience.

Table 3. Optimization results of rural microgrids under different schemes.

Scheme	Photovoltaics/Group	Fan/Group	Small Hydropower/Group	Energy Storage/Group	Construction Cost (USD)	Operation Cost (USD)	Total Cost (USD)	User Satisfaction
1	15	12	1	11	5,187,822	4,236,198	9,424,020	0.83
2	19	18	1	15	6,343,729	4,741,811	11,085,540	0.99
3	17	12	1	15	5,793,297	4,306,923	10,100,220	0.90

Scheme 2 is characterized by the deployment of 19 PV sets and 18 wind turbines. The augmentation in the number of photovoltaic panels and wind turbines enhances the system's power supply capacity and reliability, thereby significantly elevating customer satisfaction. Although high customer satisfaction is assured, the utilization of additional and more expensive equipment incurs elevated construction, operation, and maintenance costs for the microgrid, potentially imposing a financial burden on the company. Consequently, opting for this solution presents a significant challenge for companies.

The rural microgrid construction plan delineated in this study, Scheme 3, thoughtfully balances business costs and customer satisfaction by using 17 PV sets and 12 wind turbines. Since the increase in customer satisfaction is smaller when the basic needs of the customer are met by additional equipment, a higher increase in customer satisfaction can be obtained by increasing the amount of equipment by a smaller number of units only. This design endeavors to achieve a harmonious equilibrium between cost efficiency and customer satisfaction, positioning it as a strategic compromise between Scheme 1 and Scheme 2. Most rural microgrids, in practice, are developed using schemes that prioritize minimizing the total cost to the enterprise [10,11]. However, the method proposed in this study considers both the enterprise costs and user satisfaction. Compared to the cost minimization strategy, two sets of photovoltaic and four sets of energy storage devices were added, the costs of construction increased by USD 605,475, resulting in an 8.4% increase in user satisfaction. The total cost increased from USD 9,424,020 to USD 10,100,220, an increase of 7.1%. On average, an increase of USD 96,600 can increase user satisfaction with electricity services by 0.01. Additionally, the utility value, defined as the ratio of user satisfaction to total cost, is significantly higher in the proposed scheme. This analysis suggests that, compared to the conventional rural microgrid construction schemes commonly implemented, the proposed model offers considerable improvements in balancing cost efficiencies and user satisfaction, potentially revolutionizing rural electrification strategies. While Scheme 3 may not reach the pinnacle of optimization in either domain, it offers a viable compromise that ensures a considerable degree of customer satisfaction. Despite not attaining optimal results in either aspect, Scheme 3 introduces a pragmatic compromise, facilitating enhanced customer satisfaction at a reduced investment cost for the enterprise. This approach bears significant implications for fostering positive enterprise–user relations and proves more apt for practical implementation. The convergence curve of the particle swarm algorithm is shown in Figure 5, and the calculated optimal value of the firm's cost is USD 10,100,220.

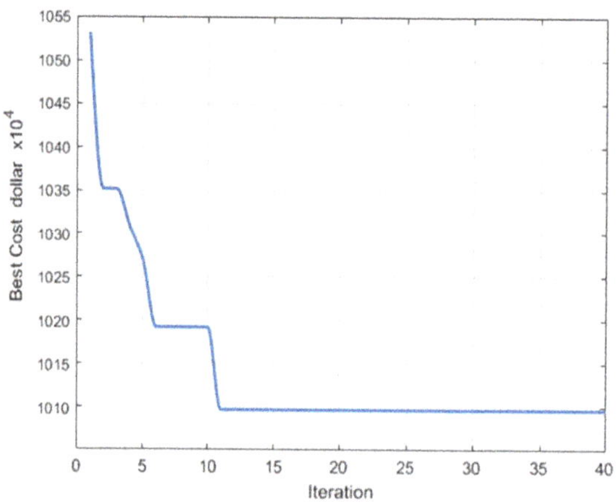

Figure 5. Iterative convergence curves for particle swarm optimization algorithms.

5.3. Parametric Analysis

(1) Anticipated construction costs

Projected construction expenses constitute a crucial component of the overall costs associated with rural microgrids, exerting a direct influence on both the feasibility and the detailed implementation strategies of such construction endeavors. The anticipated construction costs significantly dictate the volume of the equipment procured, and the scale of the microgrid, among other factors. Operating within a constrained budget may necessitate adjustments in the system's size or performance capabilities, thereby influencing the microgrid's actual efficacy. An accurately projected construction cost can optimize economic returns for the business while concurrently enhancing customer satisfaction with electricity consumption. Should the anticipated construction cost undergo alterations, the corresponding adjustments in microgrid construction schemes are illustrated in Table 4. An analysis of the three construction scenarios presented in Table 4 reveals that an increase in the anticipated construction costs correlates with simultaneous rises in both the total costs of rural microgrids and customer satisfaction. However, an analysis of the data in Table 4 indicates that the expected construction costs, total construction costs, and user satisfaction do not escalate in equal proportions, nor do they follow a linear progression. Further scrutiny of the construction scenarios in Scenario 2 and Scenario 3 reveals that even minor modifications to the expected construction costs can result in significant enhancements in user satisfaction. This implies that companies may avoid increasing the initial investment, which could adversely affect the financial sustainability of the project, without necessarily enhancing the customer's experience.

Table 4. Optimization configuration results under different anticipated construction costs.

Scheme	Anticipated Construction Cost (USD)	Photovoltaics/ Group	Fan/ Group	Small Hydropower/ Group	Energy Storage/ Group	Operation Cost (USD)	Total Cost (USD	User Satisfaction
1	4,444,738	12	14	1	11	4,178,882	8,623,620	0.80
2	5,614,406	16	15	1	13	4,150,474	9,764,880	0.89
3	5,187,822	15	12	1	11	4,236,198	9,424,020	0.83

The configuration of microgrids exhibits pronounced disparities across varying levels of the anticipated construction costs. Within the constrained budget scenarios, companies might gravitate towards more cost-effective yet lower-performing equipment. Such decisions could lead to a failure to meet user demands during peak periods, consequently affecting customer satisfaction adversely. Conversely, a more generous budget facilitates the incorporation of more efficient albeit costlier devices, thereby enhancing the system's overall efficiency and customer satisfaction, albeit at the expense of a higher total cost. Furthermore, these findings suggest that the relationship between customer satisfaction and escalating costs is not invariably linear. Beyond a specific cost threshold, further financial inputs may yield only marginal enhancements in satisfaction. This intimates the presence of an optimal cost nexus, beyond which the returns on investment progressively diminish.

(2) Customer satisfaction

The construction process for rural microgrids must also prioritize user satisfaction, given its significant impact on the requisite quantity of microgrid equipment. A paramount objective of rural microgrids is the provision of stable and dependable electrical power. Elevating investment in equipment can bolster the power supply's reliability through enhanced system redundancy and adaptability, among other strategies, culminating in heightened user satisfaction. Table 5 delineates the construction scenarios for the microgrids across different levels of user satisfaction. It is manifest that both the total construction costs and the quantity of equipment units within the rural microgrids escalate in correlation with increasing user satisfaction. However, an examination of the data in Table 5 on user satisfaction and total construction costs reveals that higher construction costs yield diminishing returns in terms of increased satisfaction with electricity services. This observation corroborates the existence of a rural microgrid construction strategy that can deliver a more satisfactory electrical service experience at a moderate total construction cost.

Table 5. Optimization configuration results of rural microgrids under different user satisfaction levels.

Scheme	User Satisfaction	Photovoltaics/ Group	Fan/ Group	Small Hydropower/ Group	Energy Storage /Group	Construction Cost (USD)	Operation Cost (USD)	Total Cost (USD)
1	0.70	10	12	1	11	3,811,742	4,059,778	7,871,520
2	0.90	17	12	1	15	6,343,729	4,741,811	10,100,220
3	0.80	12	14	1	11	4,444,738	4,178,882	8,623,620

The configuration schemes for equipment within rural microgrids demonstrate notable variations across differing anticipated levels of user satisfaction. Diminished user satisfaction precipitates a reduction in both the number of equipment units and the overall enterprise cost. However, this trade-off, balancing lower user satisfaction against reduced enterprise costs, may aggravate tensions between users and enterprises, undermining efforts to forge and nurture positive cooperative relationships.

A combination table is included in Table 6 to facilitate a comparative analysis and more intuitively observe variations in microgrid construction schemes under different parameter settings. From this analysis, it can be observed that the anticipated construction costs represent a pivotal factor for enterprises engaged in the development of rural microgrids. This cost directly influences the quantity of equipment to be deployed. The optimal configuration scheme endeavors to maximize customer satisfaction while remaining within the enterprise's financial constraints. Enterprises have the capability to enhance the electricity experiences of users by tailoring the rural microgrids' configuration scheme to the anticipated levels of user satisfaction. Consequently, variables, including the anticipated construction costs and customer satisfaction, significantly impact the rural microgrids' optimal configuration, necessitating enterprises to weigh both cost-effectiveness and user experience in their planning and decision-making processes to ascertain the most appropriate configuration under specific conditions.

Table 6. Optimization configuration results of rural microgrids under different objectives.

	Scheme	User Satisfaction	Photovoltaics/ Group	Fan/ Group	Small Hydropower/ Unit	Energy Storage /Group	Total Cost (USD)
Construction solutions in different schemes	1	0.70	10	12	1	11	7,871,520
	2	0.90	17	12	1	15	10,100,220
	3	0.80	12	14	1	11	8,623,620
Construction solutions under different anticipated construction costs	1	0.80	12	14	1	11	8,623,620
	2	0.89	16	15	1	13	9,764,880
	3	0.83	15	12	1	11	9,424,020
Construction solutions under different user satisfaction	1	0.70	10	12	1	11	7,871,520
	2	0.90	17	12	1	15	10,100,220
	3	0.80	12	14	1	11	8,623,620

6. Conclusions

A two-tier planning model is proposed to address the insufficient consideration of users' electricity experiences in rural microgrid construction. This model focuses on both comprehensive costs and user satisfaction. The proposed scheme minimizes enterprise costs while maximizing user satisfaction, effectively resolving the conflict between these two factors in microgrid construction. The model takes the minimum enterprise comprehensive cost as the upper objective function, considers the microgrid construction, operation, maintenance, and power abandonment costs, and reasonably plans the microgrid scale, equipment configuration, and operation and maintenance strategies; using the user's satisfaction with electricity services as the lower objective function, considers reliability and the economy, improves the user's quality of life and electricity experience, and puts forward the configuration scheme of the rural microgrid through the case study. The findings indicate that enhancements in construction costs frequently correlate with improvements in customer satisfaction with electricity services, consistent with prior scholarly work. However, these variables do not change proportionately or follow a linear relationship. In contrast to the cost-only and user satisfaction-only schemes, the scheme proposed in this study, which balances the costs and satisfaction, increased both the construction and operation costs by adding two photovoltaic groups and four energy storage groups compared to the original scheme, which increased the total cost by 7.1%, but customer satisfaction with electricity services increased by 8.4%. The final construction cost was USD 5,793,297 and the operation cost was USD 4,306,923 for a total cost of USD 10,100,220, demonstrating its high utility value. This approach effectively resolves the tension between enterprise costs and customer satisfaction, achieving a better balance of the objectives for both enterprises and users. Furthermore, this study examines the impacts of expected construction costs and user satisfaction on the optimal allocation outcomes of rural microgrids, offering crucial insights for future microgrid developments. Currently, this study used the case of Yudaokou for a simulation analysis. Although the area has typical wind and solar resources, it cannot represent all rural microgrids. The differences in resources and electricity demands in different geographical regions may lead to a decrease in the applicability of these results. Therefore, the promotion and application of these research results in other regions or countries may be limited, and this research focuses solely on general rural microgrid construction scenarios. Future efforts will aim to design and implement rural microgrids tailored to the unique requirements of AC/DC hybrid systems.

Author Contributions: Writing—original draft, M.L.; Writing—review & editing, Y.F. and Z.L.; Funding acquisition, Y.Y. All authors have read and agreed to the published version of the manuscript.

Funding: This research was funded by the Key Research Project of State Grid Jibei Electric Power Company Limited (SGTYHT/21-JS-223); Science and Technology Project Contract Number: SGIBC-DOOSWIS2310456.

Data Availability Statement: The original contributions presented in the study are included in the article, further inquiries can be directed to the corresponding author.

Conflicts of Interest: Author Yunli Yue was employed by State Grid Jibei Electric Power Company Limited. The remaining authors declare that the research was conducted in the absence of any commercial or financial relationships that could be construed as a potential conflict of interest.

References

1. Kamal, M.M.; Ashraf, I.; Fernandez, E. Optimal sizing of standalone rural microgrid for sustainable electrification with renewable energy resources. *Sustain. Cities Soc.* **2023**, *88*, 104298. [CrossRef]
2. Li, S.; Zhang, L.; Su, L.; Nie, Q. Exploring the coupling coordination relationship between economic environment and renewable energy development in rural areas: A case of China. *Sci. Total Environ.* **2023**, *880*, 163229. [CrossRef] [PubMed]
3. Cao, M.; Yu, J. Sales channel classification for renewable energy stations under peak shaving resource shortage. *Int. J. Electr. Power Energy Syst.* **2024**, *160*, 110115. [CrossRef]
4. Zhang, X.; Guo, K.; Wang, L.; Cong, Y.; Wang, Q. Analysis of the Influence of Distributed Generation on Distribution Network Voltage. *J. Phys. Conf. Ser.* **2023**, *2418*, 012034. [CrossRef]
5. Min, C. Investigating the Effect of Uncertainty Characteristics of Renewable Energy Resources on Power System Flexibility. *Appl. Sci.* **2021**, *11*, 5381. [CrossRef]
6. Wang, J.; Chen, L.; Tan, Z.; Du, E.; Liu, N.; Ma, J.; Sun, M.; Li, C.; Song, J.; Lu, X.; et al. Inherited spatial uncertainty of renewable power in China. *Nat. Commun.* **2023**, *1*, 5379. [CrossRef]
7. Semshchikov, E.; Negnevitsky, M.; Hamilton, J.; Wang, X. Cost Efficient Strategy for High Renewable Energy Penalty in Isolated Power Systems. *IEEE Trans. Power Syst.* **2020**, *5*, 3719–3728. [CrossRef]
8. Vaka, S.S.K.R.; Matam, S.K. Optimal sizing of hybrid renewable energy systems for reliability enhancement and cost minimization using multi-objective technology in microgrids. *Energy Storage* **2022**, *5*, e419. [CrossRef]
9. Huang, Y.X.; Li, G.F. Resilient Distribution Networks by Microgrid Formation Using Deep Reinforcement Learning. *IEEE Trans. Smart Grid* **2022**, *13*, 4918–4930. [CrossRef]
10. Wongdet, P.; Boonraksa, T.; Boonraksa, P.; Pinthurat, W.; Marungsri, B.; Hredzak, B. Optimal Capacity and Cost Analysis of Battery Energy Storage System in Standalone Microgrid Consulting Battery Lifetime. *Batteries* **2023**, *9*, 76. [CrossRef]
11. Boonraksa, T.; Pinthurat, W.; Wongdet, P.; Boonraksa, P.; Marungsri, B.; Hredzak, B. Optimal Capacity and Cost Analysis of Hybrid Energy Storage System in Standalone DC Microgrid. *IEEE Access* **2023**, *11*, 65496–65506. [CrossRef]
12. Abdelghany, M.B.; Al-Durra, A. A Coordinated Optimal Operation of a Grid-Connected Wind-Solar Microgrid Incorporating Hybrid Energy Storage Management Systems. *IEEE Trans. Sustain. Energy* **2024**, *15*, 39–51. [CrossRef]
13. Abid, M.S.; Apon, H.J.; Hossain, S.; Ahmed, A.; Ahshan, R.; Lipu, M.S.H. A novel multi-objective optimization based multi-agent deep reinforcement learning approach for microgrid resources planning. *Appl. Energy* **2024**, *353*, 122029. [CrossRef]
14. Li, B.; Zhao, R.; Lu, J.; Xin, K.; Huang, J.; Lin, G.; Chen, J.; Pang, X. Energy management method for microgrids based on improved Stackelberg game real-time pricing model. *Energy Rep.* **2023**, *10*, 1247–1257. [CrossRef]
15. Torkan, R.; Ilinca, A.; Ghorbanzadeh, M. A genetic algorithm optimization approach for smart energy management of microgrid. *Renew. Energy* **2022**, *197*, 852–863. [CrossRef]
16. Wang, T.H.; Hua, H.C. A bi-level dispatch optimization of multi-microgrid considering green electricity consumption willingness under renewable portfolio standard policy. *Appl. Energy* **2024**, *356*, 122428. [CrossRef]
17. Jiménez-Vargas, I.; Rey, J.M. Sizing of hybrid microgrids considering life cycle assessment. *Renew. Energy* **2023**, *202*, 554–565. [CrossRef]
18. Pramila, V.; Kannadasan, R. Smart grid management: Integrating hybrid intelligent algorithms for microgrid energy optimization. *Energy Rep.* **2024**, *12*, 2997–3019. [CrossRef]

19. Khodabakhsh, R.; Sirouspour, S. Optimal Control of Energy Storage in a Microgrid by Minimizing Conditional Value-at-Risk. *IEEE Trans. Sustain. Energy* **2016**, *7*, 1264–1273. [CrossRef]
20. Song, Y.; Sahoo, S.; Yang, Y.; Blaabjerg, F. Probabilistic Risk Evaluation of Microgrids Considering Stability and Reliability. *IEEE Trans. Power Electron.* **2023**, *38*, 10302–10312. [CrossRef]
21. Zhao, T.Y.; Pan, X.W.; Yao, S.H. Strategic Bidding of Hybrid AC/DC Microgrid Embedded Energy Hubs: A Two-Stage Chance Constrained Stochastic Programming Approach. *IEEE Trans. Sustain. Energy* **2020**, *11*, 116–125. [CrossRef]
22. Muduli, U.R.; El Moursi, M.S. Impedance Modeling with Stability Boundaries for Constant Power Load During Line Failure. *IEEE Trans. Ind. Appl.* **2024**, *60*, 1484–1496. [CrossRef]
23. Arai, J.; Taguchi, Y. Coordinated control between a grid forming inverter and grid following inverters suppling power in a standalone microgrid. *Glob. Energy Interconnect.* **2022**, *3*, 259–265. [CrossRef]
24. Singh, V.K.; Verma, A.; Bhatti, T.S. Bhatti. Integration and Control of Renewable Energy-Based Rural Microgrids. *IETE J. Res.* **2022**, *6*, 4492–4502. [CrossRef]
25. Yang, S.; Fang, J.; Zhang, Z.; Lv, S.; Lin, H.; Ju, L. Two-stage coordinated optimal dispatching model and benefit allocation strategy for rural new energy microgrid. *Energy* **2024**, *292*, 130274. [CrossRef]
26. Herwandi, H.; Kamajaya, L.; Fitri, F. Designing and Analyzing a Hybrid Photovoltaic-Biomass Microgrid for Rural Communities. *Int. J. Renew. Energy Res.* **2023**, *3*, 1070–1081.
27. Kamal, M.M.; Asharaf, I.; Fernandez, E. Optimal energy scheduling of a standalone rural microgrid for reliable power generation using renewable energy resources. *Energy Sources Part A Recovery Util. Environ. Eff.* **2023**, *1*, 485–504. [CrossRef]
28. Yang, C.; Meng, T.; Ma, H.; Qi, S.; Jia, Z. Research on Optimal Operation of Low Carbon Rural Microgrid Integrated with Optical Storage and Charging. *J. Phys. Conf. Ser.* **2023**, *2527*, 012007. [CrossRef]
29. Yadav, P.; Davies, P.J.; Sarkodie, S.A. The prospects of decentralised solar energy home systems in rural communities: User experience, determinants, and impact of free solar power on the energy poverty cycle. *Energy Strategy Rev.* **2019**, *26*, 100424. [CrossRef]
30. Mirsaeidi, S.; Dong, X.Z.; Shi, S.X. AC and DC Microgrids: A Review on Protection Issues and Approaches. *J. Electr. Eng. Technol.* **2017**, *12*, 2089–2098.
31. Ribó-Pérez, D.; Bastida-Molina, P.; Gómez-Navarro, T. Hybrid assessment for a hybrid microgrid: A novel methodology to critically analyse generation technologies for hybrid microgrids. *Renew. Energy* **2020**, *157*, 874–887. [CrossRef]
32. Ansari, S.; Chandel, A.; Tariq, M. A comprehensive review on power converters control and control strategies of AC/DC microgrid. *IEEE Access* **2020**, *9*, 17998–18015. [CrossRef]
33. Wang, Q.; Zhang, W.; Li, J.; Ma, Z.; Chen, J. Benefits or harms? The effect of online review manipulation on sales. *Electron. Commer. Res. Appl.* **2023**, *57*, 101224. [CrossRef]
34. Liu, D.N.; Wang, L.X.; Wang, W.Y. Strategy of Large-Scale Electric Vehicles Absorbing Renewable Energy Abandoned Electricity Based on Master-Slave Game. *IEEE Access* **2021**, *9*, 92473–92482. [CrossRef]
35. Gusain, C.; Nangia, U.; Tripathi, M.M. Optimal sizing of standalone hybrid renewable energy system based on reliability indicator: A case study. *Energy Convers. Manag.* **2024**, *310*, 118490. [CrossRef]
36. Watts, C.; McCarthy, C.; Levite, B. The Need for Consumer-Centric Reliability Metrics. *IEEE Power Energy Mag.* **2022**, *20*, 117–124. [CrossRef]
37. Rigo-Mariani, R.; Sareni, B. Fast power flow scheduling and sensitivity analysis for sizing a microgrid with storage. *Math. Comput. Simul.* **2016**, *131*, 114–127. [CrossRef]
38. Hizarici, H.; Demirel, O.; Turkay, B.E. Distribution network reconfiguration using time-varying acceleration coefficient assisted binary particle swarm optimization. *Eng. Sci. Technol. Int. J.-JESTECH* **2022**, *35*, 101230. [CrossRef]
39. Suman, G.K.; Guerrero, J.M.; Roy, O.P. Optimisation of solar/wind/bio-generator/diesel/battery based microgrids for rural areas: A PSO-GWO approach. *Sustain. Cities Soc.* **2021**, *67*, 102723. [CrossRef]
40. Valdez, F.; Melin, P. A survey on nature-inspired optimization algorithms with fuzzy logic for dynamic parameter adaptation. *Expert Syst. Appl.* **2014**, *41*, 6459–6466. [CrossRef]
41. Gad, A.G. Particle Swarm Optimization Algorithm and Its Applications: A Systematic Review. *Arch. Comput. Methods Eng.* **2023**, *30*, 3471. [CrossRef]
42. Jain, M.; Saihjpal, V.; Singh, N. An Overview of Variants and Advancements of PSO Algorithm. *Appl. Sci.* **2022**, *12*, 8392. [CrossRef]

mathematics

Article

A Double-Layer Coupled Network Model of Network Density Effects on Multi-Stage Innovation Efficiency Dynamics: Agent-Based Modeling Methods

Jing Han, Wenjing Zhang *, Jiutian Wang and Songmei Li

International Business School, Shaanxi Normal University, Xi'an 710119, China; hanjing@snnu.edu.cn (J.H.); jiutian@snnu.edu.cn (J.W.); lisongmei@snnu.edu.cn (S.L.)
* Correspondence: zhangwenjing@snnu.edu.cn; Tel.: +86-17829823010

Abstract: This paper proposes a double-layer coupled network model to analyze the multi-stage innovation activities of online, and the model consists of two layers: the online layer, which represents the virtual interactions among innovators, and the offline layer, which represents the physical interactions among innovators. The model assumes that the innovation activities are influenced by both the online and offline network structures, as well as the coupling effect between them. And it simulates the entire innovation process including knowledge diffusion and knowledge recombination. The model also incorporates the concept of network density, which measures the degree of network connectivity and cohesion (network structure). Observing the network density influence on innovation efficiency during the innovation process is realized through setting the selection mechanism and the knowledge recombination mechanism. The coupling relationship between the two layers of network density on the three stages of innovation is further discussed under the theoretical framework of the innovation value chain. Simulation and experimental results suggest that when the offline network density is constant, a higher online network density is not always better. When the online network density is low, the sparse structure of the online network reduces innovation efficiency. When the online network density is high, the structural redundancy caused by the tight network structure prevents innovation efficiency from improving. The results of the study help enterprises to adjust and optimize the internal cooperation network structure at different stages of innovation in order to maximize its effectiveness and improve the innovation efficiency of enterprises.

Keywords: online social media; double-layer coupled network; network density; multi-stage innovation

MSC: 91D30; 68V30

1. Introduction

With the development of information technology, Online Social Media (OSM) has enabled knowledge flow activities to a large extent, and organizations are witnessing yet another revolution in their paradigm of knowledge flow [1]. More and more organizations are adopting social and office software for online communication and work. Employees in enterprises often share knowledge in an online manner through enterprise social media, WeChat groups and other social networking platforms. Compared with offline face-to-face communication, employees can communicate online across time, space and organizational hierarchical barriers, more conveniently and with timely interaction [2]. Through online communication, employees can share knowledge, information, and ideas with many colleagues at the same time to conduct innovation activities [3–5] and form an online cooperation network [6], However, some scholars have pointed out that for knowledge that is more difficult to share, such as ideas and know-how, employees rely solely on online communication, which is less efficient in terms of dissemination; additionally, in person (offline) face-to-face direct communication is still needed to improve the performance of knowledge dissemination [7]. Nowadays, online and offline social networks are the two main channels for members of an organization to exchange knowledge, and the dissemination and innovation of knowledge in an organization is increasingly characterized by the "interaction between online and offline" [8]. Furthermore, the innovation process is evolving in switching and interacting between the two network platforms.

The online cooperative network, established through OSM, is coupled with the offline cooperative network, which implies that the two still interact with each other despite their independent structures. In particular, when one network forms a tight connection, the tightness of the two networks will inevitably affect the tightness of the other. The close-knit network of relationships formed among an organization's employees is the social capital that employees possess, and it is this particular social capital that supports organizational innovation, change capacity, and knowledge integration in cooperation networks [9]. Additionally, the tightness of the organization can laterally reflect the local network characteristics [10]. Meanwhile, it has been shown that network characteristics impose a significant impact on organizational innovation performance [11]. Therefore, with online and offline cooperative networks coupled, it is necessary to explore the innovation efficiency of organizations by using the tightness of cooperative networks (hereafter referred to as network density), which both reflects the network characteristics and has an impact on innovation performance. Furthermore, the need for network density at different stages of innovation is dynamic, due to the differences in the main needs at different stages of innovation. The impact of organizational cooperation network density on innovation must not neglect the multi-stage differences in innovation and the multi-dimensional characteristics of the network [12,13].

In this study, we introduce the coupling network method, then build a definite model under the selection mechanism of knowledge flow and recombination. Through simulation experiments, the effects of online network density, offline network density, and the density relationship between double-layer networks on innovation efficiency were explored, where the innovation efficiency was measured by the number of knowledge owners and the frequency of exchanges. The simulation results provide numerical support for the integration of enterprise online cooperative network and offline cooperative network as two knowledge communication channels for organizations, thereby revealing the effect of OSM on innovation. The key contributions of this study are summarized as follows.

First, this study clarifies the realistic background of online cooperative networks embedded in offline cooperative networks in the OSM context. According to the behavior of members in the organization through OSM communication, an online–offline double-layer coupling network model is constructed to simulate innovation behavior in the organization.

Second, differing from previous research models that only focus on the influence of offline cooperative networks on innovation, our study analyzes the relationship between online cooperative networks and offline cooperative networks and reveals their interaction. By constructing a knowledge vector, our study extends the dimension of the knowledge state based on the original research.

Third, by comparing the innovation efficiency of the online–offline double-layer coupling network with different structural combinations, we explain the differences and causes of innovation efficiency under different structural combinations. Based on the innovation value chain theory, the promotion of innovation by online and offline cooperative networks and their different functions at different stages are further explored from the multi-stage perspective of innovation, and the relationship between the double-layer networks is elaborated.

Based on social network theory and knowledge dissemination theory, this study constructs an online–offline double-layer coupled network model by combining the structure and characteristics of the internal cooperation network of the organization, and proposes a selection mechanism and a knowledge restructuring mechanism to study the mechanism by which the double-layer cooperation network of the organization has an impact on the innovation efficiency. These provide theoretical basis for the relevant subjects to optimize the organizational structure and improve the implementation measures of innovation efficiency, expand the application of multi-layer network theory in innovation research, enrich the research method of technological innovation, and further deepen the influence of cooperative network structure on innovation efficiency.

The remainder of the paper is organized as follows. Section 2 provides a comparative discussion of prior studies that are highly relevant to our study and presents the research hypotheses of this paper. Section 3 introduces the appropriate notation and formulas to accurately describe the decision model. Section 4 formulates the innovation process model and the algorithm employed to derive the simulation results. Section 5 analyzes the results of the numerical experiments and derives management insights. Section 6 summarizes the conclusions and further recommendations of this study.

2. Materials and Methods

A social network is a collection of social members based on their relationships, which can be formed spontaneously or naturally. The role of social networks is a necessary element of research innovation, providing social members with different ways and means to integrate and apply knowledge, thus promoting knowledge innovation. Social networks, through their unique network structure, can effectively facilitate cooperation work between groups [14]. In a social network, each individual can connect with any other individual, forming a complex network structure. This network structure allows information to spread quickly through the network, reducing the negative impact of most users hitching a ride and not wanting to reciprocate [15], thus facilitating inter-group collaboration [16]. Online social networks are where members of a social network create and exchange content through online social media, and since online social networks can be realized with the help of convenient carriers, such as smartphones and computers, they can transmit information to any member of the online social network, and this is a very important aspect of social networking, such as for members in the online social network, which greatly reduces the cost of information transfer. Face-to-face interactions in offline social networks help to build and strengthen trust [17], build stronger teamwork and deeper personal relationships [18], thus promoting better cooperation, integration and synergy among unaffiliated groups [15]. A study by Schötteler et al. suggests that online social networks facilitate communication, collaboration, and knowledge sharing among employees in an organization [19]. A study by Pee et al. suggests that individual employees utilize online social networks to cross traditional hierarchical boundaries or organizational departmental boundaries for intra-team knowledge sharing, collaboration, or cross-organizational communication and collaboration with extra team members to obtain more heterogeneous information [20]. Leonardi's study found that employees can establish a good communication and collaboration relationship with other members of the organization through online social networks, and at the same time, in the context of the widespread use of digital concepts in the enterprise, online social networks provide an opportunity for employees to express their views. Since the members of online social networks are all employees within the organization, the information posted can resonate with members and enhance the sense of belonging [21]. Pillet and Carillo found that employees' use of online social media positively contributes to the organizational effectiveness of the organization, based on the data collected from a large international IT services company that was one of the first in the world to undergo a digital transformation. Online social media positively contributes to the formation of member connectivity in an organization's social network, and employees' communication habits are positively influenced by comparative advantage and perceived ease of use, while comparative advantage positively affects the ability to share knowledge [22]. By exploring the impact of social networks on the perceptions of speedy relationships and institutional mechanisms, Chong et al.'s study found that speedy relationships built on interactivity and presence in a social network strengthened member trust, which further increases members' willingness to share [17]. Pollet et al. investigated the relationship between social networks, network size, and emotional closeness in a sample of 117 individuals between the ages of 18 and 63, and the experiment showed that individuals were emotionally closer to members of offline social networks [18].

2.1. *Online–Offline Cooperation Network Coupling*

2.1.1. Online Social Media-Related Research

OSM is an Internet application based on Web 2.0 concepts and technologies. OSM allows users to create and exchange content. This public social media allows information to be delivered to any member using OSM with the help of more convenient carriers, such as smartphones, etc. It greatly reduces the cost of information dissemination, and hence, is rapidly gaining wide acceptance in the work scenario [23]. According to research, the use of OSM facilitates communication, collaboration, knowledge sharing, and knowledge diffusion among employees in enterprises [24].

The original OSM was for the public, that is, anyone could use it, for example, Facebook, Twitter, etc. Employees can communicate with employees within the organization through OSM. Some enterprises develop or customize OSM software for enterprise users according to their own needs to support internal communication and collaboration [23]. As for the definition of enterprise online social media, researchers generally agree with the definition proposed by Leonardi: enterprise online social media is an integrated platform that integrates many social media functions based on the Internet [25]. Organizations hope to increase discussion among employees through enterprise online social media, promote knowledge flow, stimulate employee innovation vitality, and add value to the organization. A large number of studies have focused on the positive effects of using OSM [26]. However, some studies exploring the relationship between OSM and innovation performance have found that OSM does not always promote employees' innovation performance and may have some negative impact on it. According to the study [27], rules and standardization can be powerful tools for promoting OSM within an organization, but overly strict policies limit employees' autonomous exploratory behaviors, which may lead to the stagnation of their innovative behaviors. Therefore, while encouraging the use of OSM to promote innovation, excessive and inappropriate use of OSM should be prevented, and the combination and interaction between OSM and offline cooperation networks should be considered.

2.1.2. Offline Cooperation Networks Related Research

In recent years, scholars have extensively studied the concept of innovation from the perspective of cooperative networks, where knowledge diffusion as a network-level phenomenon is a necessary condition for innovation. Different aspects of knowledge transmission within an organization have been studied, including the influence of both extrinsic and intrinsic motivational drivers, where anticipated reciprocal relationships [11] and interpersonal trust [28] contribute to developing favorable attitudes of members regarding knowledge sharing behaviors. Social relationships are determinants of organizational members' attitudes toward knowledge seeking and knowledge sharing [11,29], and scholars have developed a generic model by incorporating the degree of forgetting in the knowledge dissemination process in complex networks; their simulation results indicate that different network structures have different degrees of influence on knowledge dissemination and diffusion [30]. Researchers focused on the topology of cooperative networks. Simulation experiments with different network characteristics are conducted around offline cooperation networks, and the experimental numerical results show that scale-free networks are the most effective network structure for knowledge growth and diffusion [31]. The connectivity of the content network between researchers was demonstrated to be conducive to creative diffusion through a network-linking approach [32]. From a network relational perspective, it is argued that weak relational connectivity provides access paths to non-redundant knowledge on a non-redundant network structure, which allows for stronger divergent thinking and thus facilitates the creation of ideas [33]. On this basis, scholars further explore the relationship among network location, social capital, knowledge transfer, and innovation ability [34], and considered the knowledge flow through offline cooperative network channels [35], but the perspective of the single-layer network has certain limitations, multi-level and multi-dimensional discussion of knowledge flow in different channels is ignored, and there is a lack of discussion on the relationship between online and offline cooperation networks.

2.1.3. Online–Offline Cooperation Network Coupling: Implications for Organizational Knowledge Communication

As OSM promotes employee communication within organizations, it also creates new contacts among employees, which changes the original social network structure of organizations to a certain extent. One scholar's research focuses on how social media affects the structure within organizations [36]. His research shows that the use of OSM creates a complex organizational structure that is different from offline cooperative networks, and, at the same time, the use of OSM increases the competitiveness of enterprises. The change in organizational cooperation network structure brought by OSM is of practical significance, because the understanding of cooperative network structure can help enterprises understand the influence of social media degree on organizational performance, and it is the interaction of social and technical factors, which determines users' participation in OSM. Online cooperative networks can provide a wider range of communication options [37] and long-term cooperative relationships [9].

Different from stable member relationships in offline cooperative networks, members in online cooperative networks are more flexible. The flexible structure enables employees to transfer the main channels of communication from offline to online, forming a scene of interactive coexistence of online and offline cooperation networks. Therefore, this paper proposes that there is a coupling between online and offline cooperation networks and that this coupling affects knowledge exchange within an organization. The relationship between the two may be diverse and complex. The online network can either supplement the offline cooperative network or replace the offline cooperative network under certain conditions. At the same time, some innovative activities are naturally better suited to online cooperation networks. Therefore, the coupling problem of double-layer networks is very novel.

2.2. *The Impact of Network Density on Innovation Efficiency*

2.2.1. Network Density Reflects Network Structural Characteristics

Previous studies have focused on "hubs" in organizations, that is, key employees with a lot of connections. Employees in such a central location are surrounded by enormous potential for communication. However, the connection in the real organization is not only the social links of users, but also highly related to the actual communication activities of users, that is, the exchange of information. Previous research has highlighted the importance of user communication activities: "in the absence of communication activities, regardless of the structure, the structural resources in the organization will remain dormant and provide no benefits" [38]. This means that the network resources occupied by employees are dormant when they do not communicate, so the centrality of employees does not affect the knowledge exchange within the organization in real-time.

Current research also focuses on the network of users based on actual interaction. In the network related to OSM, researchers point out that social capital within an organization is constantly changing, not only through fixed social connections, but also through real-time communication, which is often referred to as the dynamic network. Some of the characteristics of organizational structure change dynamically, so it is difficult to accurately capture the dynamic organizational structure data, and the impact of periodic organizational structure change on innovation becomes difficult to describe. However, since the overall structure within the organization will have a certain influence on the local structure, we can still reflect the local characteristics of nodes in the organization on the side through the tightness of the organization. Some studies have shown that in more close-knit organizations, other employees are more likely to connect with employees with high centrality, and it is easier to generate new center members [39]. Since it is easier to produce "central" employees in a tight structure, and employees in a tight network may have a higher centrality, the study on the degree of tightness of an organization may also reflect the centrality of nodes in an organization. The sparse organization tends to have more structural holes and is less prone to structural redundancy. Therefore, the measurement of the loose organizational structure reflects the non-redundant structure in the organization. Exploring the influence of organizational tightness on innovation efficiency and considering the possibility of other structures in an organization does not ignore the network structure concerned in previous studies.

2.2.2. The Impact of Network Density on Innovation Efficiency: The Double Edged Sword of Social Capital

Research has shown that a closely connected cooperative network is an essential social capital for employees [9]. The special social capital of employees supports innovation in cooperation teams [40]. The amount of social capital owned by individuals in an organization is closely related to the degree of connection among members of the organization. When the degree of familiarity between employees is low, the connection between members is loose and the communication between employees is correspondingly less. It is difficult for organizations to achieve network sanctions through mutual constraints such as trust, which increases the opportunism risk brought by information asymmetry and leads to employees' reluctance to share their knowledge and information, further reducing the efficiency of innovation [41]. With the increasingly frequent interaction among employees, members can communicate with mutual friends to reduce the risks brought by information asymmetry and reduce opportunistic behaviors within the organization, thus improving employees' willingness to transfer complex silent knowledge related to core technologies. At the same time, close member relations provide more diversified transmission paths for knowledge transmission within the organization, expand the channels of knowledge transmission, and further promote the flow of knowledge within the organization [42,43].

To sum up, the degree of organizational closeness has an important impact on innovation performance, and the degree of closeness among organization members also reflects the communication cost within the organization. To maintain social relations, employees need to pay a certain amount of energy cost, and organizations with close members need to pay more relationship costs than those with loose members. Previous studies have proved that knowledge transmission is more efficient in tighter organizations than in loose organizational structures. However, some studies have pointed out that the higher the investment, the higher the return; if an organizational structure is too tight, it may hinder knowledge transmission. When the organization's social network is too dense, further improving the connections among organization members will increase the cost of repeated management, enhance the difficulty of information screening, accelerate the knowledge convergence among nodes, and bring about the risk of relationship locking and behavioral consistency pressure, which will hinder the knowledge diffusion and knowledge innovation of cooperation research and development network. In the sparse enterprise social network, increasing the network density can effectively promote the diffusion and knowledge innovation of network tacit knowledge, help members to obtain rich and high-quality information, and carry out in-depth understanding and development of complex knowledge in the network to improve the lack of existing knowledge and technology.

2.2.3. Research Hypotheses on the Impact of Network Density on Innovation Efficiency

This study chooses the tightness of organizational structure as the main organizational structure variable for analysis and measures the tightness of connections among organizational members through enterprise social network density to explore the influence of organizational structure cost on innovation efficiency [44]. When the level of familiarity between employees in an organization is low, there is less communication between employees, which is manifested in low network density in cooperative networks. Less connection between members in the organization makes it difficult for mutual constraints, such as trust, to work. A loose organizational structure attenuates the effect of network sanction in the organization: employees are difficult to trust each other, and Shadow Spur is reluctant to share the knowledge and information they possess, reducing the willingness of employees to transfer complex knowledge involving core technology, thus impeding the exchange and integration of critical knowledge in the organization. With the increasingly frequent interaction among employees, members reduce the risk of information asymmetry by communicating with mutual friends, thus curbing opportunistic behaviors such as "free riding" within the organization. It provides a good information exchange environment for the organization, thus improving the employees' willingness to transfer complex tacit knowledge related to core technologies [45]. The closeness of the connection between members of an organization also reflects the communication cost within the organization. To maintain social relations, employees need to pay a certain amount of energy costs. Organizations with close members need to pay more relationship costs than those with loose members.

The online cooperative network is different from the offline cooperative network due to the use of OSM. Both online and offline cooperative networks will have an impact on the communication of members, thus affecting the innovation efficiency of the organization. Although the variation in the degree of tightness in the two networks may be the same, the cost of the isomorphic two networks is different. For the online cooperative network with the same structure and the offline cooperative network, the cost of constructing the online cooperative network is much lower than that of the offline cooperative network with the same structure because online communication is more convenient.

Based on the above demonstration, this study proposes hypotheses about the impact of double-layer coupled networks on innovation efficiency:

Hypothesis 1 (H1). *When the density of the online cooperation network is constant, the time required for innovation shows a U-shaped change with the increase of offline cooperation network density.*

Hypothesis 2 (H2). *When the density of the offline cooperation network is constant, the time required for innovation shows a U-shaped change with the increase of online cooperation network density.*

2.3. Comparison of Research Methods

The process of innovation evolution is complex and subject to many uncertainties, and there are two main existing approaches to portraying the process of innovation evolution, one being an extreme, thick description of an in-depth case study analysis of a firm's actual situation. Bernstein and Singh, based on a multi-case study design of nine biotechnology firms and one peak industry organization from Australia, proposed the intentional stage process model as the backbone of the conceptual model and incorporated the dual mechanisms of market pull and technology push into the model [46], which reveals the complex causal processes involved in the innovation process, but cannot be easily generalized.

The other is a thin description of the results of sample survey-type studies, which are more generalized, but are generally abstract studies regarding the mechanisms, processes, events, or choices by which different types of variables interrelate and influence outcomes. Most of the articles on sample survey type of research use two methods, one of which is the traditional method using statistical models such as regression modeling or structural equation modeling. Roper et al. conducted a questionnaire survey of a large group of manufacturing firms in Ireland and Northern Ireland, and analyzed the recursive process of knowledge acquisition, knowledge transformation, and knowledge utilization to form an innovation value chain [47]. Chen and Guan introduced structural equation modeling to study the non-sustainability and interdependence of causal effects during the innovation production process, and investigated the operation mechanism of the innovation production process based on systemic thinking [48]. Another mathematical approach includes differential equations as well as equilibrium and limiting behavior analyses. Guidolin and Manfredi proposed a system of ordinary differential equations with a one-way stage and a decision-making stage to describe the interactions between subjects in the diffusion of innovations [49]. Liu and Liu constructed an evolutionary game model of the knowledge transfer behavior of team members who have reciprocal preferences in the team's innovation activities, behavior in an evolutionary game model, and simulated the evolutionary equilibrium strategies of the model under different parameter changes, analyzing equilibrium and limit behaviors from the perspective of behavioral economics, which extends the mutual cooperation of knowledge teams [50]. However, these approaches do not formalize the overall characteristics of how individual employee behaviors and decisions bring about innovations during the innovation process, which occurs through the interactions between individual employees; this formalization is particularly important.

Whereas the Agent-Based Modeling approach (hereafter referred to as ABM) is the middle ground between thick description and thin description [51]. ABM reflects the performance of the system as a whole by explicitly defining the microscopic features in a complex system and utilizing a large number of interactions between microscopic subjects on the basis of macroscopic features. Through ABM, the dynamic process of knowledge exchange between individuals can be well modeled, and the information implied in the dynamic interactions of individuals can be further explored, and the interactions between subjects are not affected by external human operations, and are only related to the initial setup of the system [52]. Therefore, the use of the ABM methodology can be more realistically and intuitively modeled, and the overall changes of the system can be fully reflected, which can lead to a more effective study of the innovation process. In conclusion, the modeling by ABM in this study can effectively simulate the innovation process in the organization and better characterize the behavioral characteristics of knowledge interaction among members, thus exploring the internal mechanism of knowledge flow within the organization.

3. Methods

Innovation is accompanied by a combination of knowledge. As the innovation process is affected by many factors, the success of innovation is also affected by many uncertainties, for example, subject diversity (including subject knowledge diversity, subject network location diversity, diversity of communication methods), subject intelligence initiative, and technical complexity [53]. The ABM can well simulate the dynamic process of inter-individual knowledge exchange, and further explore the information implied in the dynamic interaction of individuals, and the interaction between subjects is not affected by external human operation, only related to the initial setting of the system, so the use of ABM can provide a more realistic and intuitive modeling and fully reflect the overall changes in the system, so as to more effectively study the innovation process [54].

3.1. Double-Layer Coupled Network

Employees of the enterprise have the opportunity to use corporate OSM for both online communication and face-to-face offline communication, so all employees can appear in any network; here, we define the double-layer coupled network model $G = \{G_o, G_f\}$, where $G_o = \{V_o, E_o\}$ represents the online social network layer formed by employees using enterprise social software, and $G_f = \{V_f, E_f\}$ represents the offline cooperation network formed by face-to-face communication among employees, where V_f in the offline cooperative network is the set formed by all nodes, and E_f represents the set formed by all connected edges in the network. Additionally, V_o represents all nodes in the online cooperative network, and E_o represents all connected edges in the online cooperative network. Some studies consider the situation where offline individuals do not participate in online social networks due to factors such as not being able to access the Internet in time and set up a network model for the situation where the nodes in the online and offline networks are not identical, namely, $V_o \neq V_f$. However, failure to participate does not imply never participating in online innovation activities, so our proposed model will make adjustments to the mechanism of knowledge exchange in the node. Therefore, the nodes of the double-layer network in the double-layer coupled network model in this paper are consistent. This suggests that the set $V_o = \left\{V_{o(1)}, V_{o(2)}, \ldots, V_{o(N_o)}\right\}$ composed of all nodes in the online social network is equal to the set $V_f = \left\{V_{f(1)}, V_{f(2)}, \ldots, V_{f(N_o)}\right\}$ of the replica in the offline cooperative network, which represents the total number of nodes in the two networks in the initial instance, respectively, whereas not all nodes participate in the communication during the simulation. $E_o = \left\{e_{(V_{c(i)}, V_{c(j)})}, V_{o(i)}, V_{o(j)} \in V_o\right\}$ represents a collection of connections in an online cooperation network. Employees (subjects) are represented by nodes in the network, and each employee participates in online and offline innovation activities of the enterprise through online cooperation networks and offline cooperation networks. Therefore, we can regard the complex system in which the subject participates in innovation as a set of double-layer coupled networks. The framework diagram of a double-layer coupled network is shown in Figure 1. As we all know, Google is a company known for Its innovation, and its products and services cover a wide range of fields such as search engine, cloud computing, and advertising technology. Within Google, there is an online collaboration platform called "Google Docs", which allows employees to edit and comment on the same document in real time, no matter where they are. Google also encourages face-to-face communication and collaboration. Their office environments are designed to be very open to facilitate interaction between employees. They even have a tradition known as "TGIF", where every Friday all Google employees get together for face-to-face interaction and discussion. At this time, the company's employees have the opportunity to use "Google Docs" online collaboration platform for online communication as well as face-to-face offline communication, so all employees can be present in any network to participate in innovative activities. This coupling of online and offline social networks creates a powerful double-layered cooperative network within Google, which greatly improves their innovation efficiency. Online platforms allow employees to collaborate anytime, anywhere, while face-to-face interactions help build stronger teamwork and deeper personal relationships. The coupling of online–offline networks allows Google to generate and implement innovative ideas in a short period of time, thus maintaining its leadership position in the global technology industry [55]. The nodes of the online and offline collaboration network layers are identical because all employees in the company participate in the online collaboration platform "Google Docs", as well as in offline face-to-face communication, and the nodes represent the company's employees. The inner edges of the layers represent the connections between employees through online or offline communication. The inter-layer edges are connected only by each employee and his/her copy in the other network layer. In a double-layer sub-network, weights and directions are not even considered, so both online and offline cooperative networks are incapacitated and un-directed. Since the number of face-to-face communication per unit time of each employee at work is the same, it is assumed that the offline cooperation network is regular. However, the number of employees communicating online is greatly influenced by their work content. For example, some employees may need to communicate with colleagues frequently concerning work-related content, while others may rarely need to communicate with other colleagues. Therefore, it is assumed that the online cooperation network of employees is random. In the experiment, the number of nodes in both networks was $N = 100$. To further reveal the coupling relationship between the two networks, the number of connected edges in the network will be adjusted according to the network density.

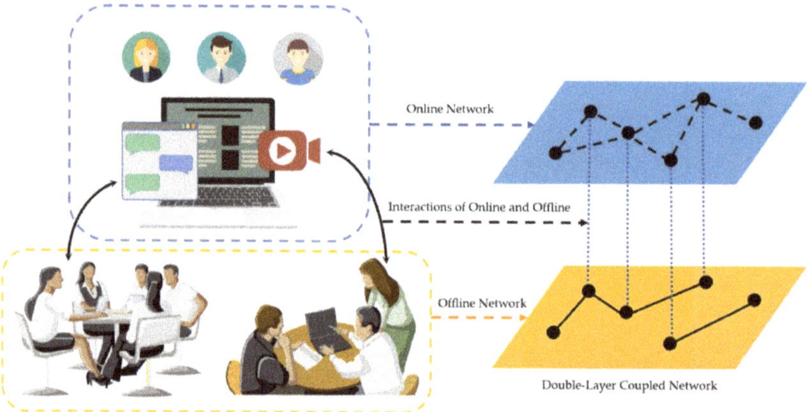

Figure 1. Overall model design and framework of the multi-layer network model. The model contains two sub-networks, online and offline, which correspond to two communication modes, respectively.

3.2. Selection and Recombination Mechanisms

Based on the idea that innovation is a process of searching, recombining, and selecting knowledge of existing literature, we therefore construct an innovation model consisting of two parts, namely (1) the selection mechanism, and (2) the recombination of knowledge. Before providing the details of the model settings, we present a simple description of these two parts of the model. The expressions of relevant parameters used in this research model are shown in Table 1.

Table 1. Related parameters used in this experiment.

Parameters	Definition
N_1	The number of an online network subjects
N_2	The number of an offline network subjects
L_1	The number of edges in online network
L_2	The number of edges in offline network
d_{on}	The density of online networks, which is expressed as $d_{on} = \frac{2L_1}{N_1(N_1-1)}$
d_{off}	The density of offline networks, which is expressed as $d_{off} = \frac{2L_2}{N_2(N_2-1)}$
λ	Vector expression of knowledge, $\lambda_i = (k_1, k_2, \ldots, k_m)$
k	The value of a knowledge component in a knowledge vector
m	The number of knowledge components in the knowledge vector
p	Probability of communication between subjects
q	The probability that the subject chooses online channels for communication
$1-q$	The probability that the subject chooses offline channels for communication
α	The probability of acquiring knowledge after communication
θ	The coefficient of innovation achievement

N_1 is the number of subjects in the online network, and N_2 is the number of subjects in the offline network. Technological innovation is often difficult to be accomplished independently by one researcher, and often requires multiple subjects to collaborate with each other to accomplish it. The communication methods of the subjects are also diversified. In the digital age, the subjects can use online social media communication, then belong to the subjects in the online network. At the same time, they can also use face-to-face communication, which belongs to the subjects in the current network.

L_1 represents the number of connected edges actually measured in the online network. L_2 represents the number of connected edges actually measured in the offline network. Reflects the number of interactions between subjects in the network, the more interactions occur between subjects, the more edges are connected in the network.

d is the network density, which is the ratio between the actual number of edges and the possible number of edges in the network, where "possible number of edges" refers to the maximum number of edges that the network may have. d_{on} is the online network density, and d_{off} is the offline network density, and the value range is [0, 1]. The larger the value of, the more closely the nodes are connected in the network.

λ is a knowledge vector that describes the knowledge level of the organization members. The expression $\lambda_i = (k_1, k_2, \ldots, k_m)$ denotes that each subject i is assigned an m-dimensional knowledge vector at the initial stage of the model, where the knowledge vector is λ Each component in k_m ($k_m \succcurlyeq 0$) denotes the degree of the m-th knowledge in the knowledge vector possessed by subject i. k on denotes the value of the knowledge component in the knowledge vector when $k_m = 0$ indicates that subject i does not currently possess the m-th kind of knowledge.

m is the number of knowledge components in the knowledge vector, and reflects the richness of knowledge in the organization and the breadth of knowledge elements included in the innovation. When the number of categories owned by the subject is small, the type of knowledge in the organization is relatively homogeneous; when the number of knowledge categories owned by the subject is too large, not only does it not correspond to the reality of innovation activities, but also greatly increases the amount of calculations in simulation experiments. Therefore, the number of categories owned by the subject m should not only reflect the richness of knowledge in innovation, but also take into account the difficulty of innovation.

p denotes the probability of communication between subjects, in reality it is not necessary that all employees communicate online or offline at the same time, so this study sets the communication probability. The communication probability allows a portion of employees not to communicate in a time step, ensuring that the model is more in line with the reality that members of an organization need to have a certain amount of time to digest what they have learned. Also the communication probability allows the model to better simulate innovation activities at multiple organizational scales.

q is the probability that the subject chooses the online channel for communication, then $1 - q$ is the probability that the subject chooses the offline channel for communication. In order to prevent employee communication preferences from affecting the interaction between the organization's online and offline cooperation networks, this study does not set the online communication preferences and offline communication preferences of employee communication species, so the probability of employees using online communication and offline communication is equal.

α for the probability of acquiring knowledge after communication, in the stochastic network model, the probability of each subject acquiring knowledge depends on the state of its neighbors. When the more neighbors a subject has, or the more subjects in its neighbors who have already acquired knowledge, then the probability of this subject acquiring knowledge will be larger. So, the size of the probability of acquiring knowledge after exchange is related to the number of subjects in the network, the connected edges, and the probability of exchange between subjects.

θ is the innovation outcome coefficient, which indicates the degree to which the innovation has been completed, and when the innovation outcome coefficient is 1, it means that the innovation has been produced.

3.2.1. Selection Mechanism

In the process of innovation, the subject will constantly acquire new knowledge to improve their knowledge stock before realizing innovation. The major way to acquire knowledge between subjects is communication, and every subject can only communicate with its neighbor in the network, so the structure of the network will influence the manner and results of the subjects significantly. Since the subject's energy is not infinite, it is difficult for the subject to participate in offline and online innovation activities simultaneously. In this study, we assume that the probability of subjects participating in innovation activities via the online network is q, and the probability of subjects participating in innovation activities via the offline network is $1-q$. Each of the subjects possesses different knowledge, and learns from each other in communications, making knowledge recombine.

3.2.2. Recombination of Knowledge

As pointed out by Frederik [45], not all new ideas are feasible, so there needs to be a mechanism of recombination to filter the results that satisfy the environmental requirements. The model assumes that the implementation of an innovation requires m different types of knowledge. Initially, all knowledge is distributed among different innovation subjects in the network. During the process of knowledge transmission and recombination, the innovation subject will constantly acquire new knowledge to improve their knowledge combination. Innovation occurs when a subject's knowledge mix is consistent with the knowledge mix required for innovation.

To model the above discussion, each node i is given an m-dimensional knowledge vector $\lambda_i = (k_1, k_2, \ldots, k_m)$, each component of λ, $k_m \succcurlyeq 0$ represents the knowledge level of the m-type knowledge possessed by the innovation subject i, when $k_m = 0$, it means node i does not possess m-type knowledge at present. The level of knowledge possessed by nodes in online and offline networks is synchronous in real-time, that is, when nodes acquire knowledge of a certain dimension in online networks, they also acquire such knowledge in offline networks immediately.

At the initial state, knowledge elements are randomly assigned to nodes in the network. m nodes are randomly selected from N nodes ($m < N$), and the m nodes are set as follows: select a dimension from the m-dimension vector of each node, then set the knowledge content of this dimension as k and that of other dimensions as 0, make all m vectors linearly independent, and the knowledge vectors of other $N-m$ nodes as 0 vectors. The specific explanation of the above settings is that at the beginning of the experiment, all kinds of knowledge shall meet the technical opportunities that are distributed among different subjects of the network, and m subjects have only one of the m kinds of different knowledge. When $m > N$, the knowledge m-dimension required for innovation is greater than the total number of network nodes N, and each knowledge vector is linearly independent, which will lead to the lack of necessary knowledge elements in the network, which may cause failure in the innovation. Therefore, the initial number of nodes with knowledge elements m must satisfy $m < N$. At time T, each node preferentially selects an online or offline communication mode, and then selects one of its adjacent idle nodes in the online (offline) social network in turn for communication. In this model, there are mainly two ways to communicate and acquire knowledge between nodes; the examples are presented as follows.

$$\lambda_i = (1,0,1,0) + \lambda_j = (1,0,1,1) \rightarrow \lambda'_i = (1,0,1,1) + \lambda'_j = (1,0,1,1) \quad (1)$$

Equation (1) represents the situation where the corresponding knowledge vector $\lambda_i = (1,0,1,0)$ of node i without knowledge of one dimension acquires knowledge elements of this dimension after communicating with node $j(\lambda_j = (1,0,1,1))$, thus possessing the knowledge of that dimension [56].

$$\lambda_i = (1,0,1,0) + \lambda_j = (1,0,3,0) \rightarrow \lambda'_i = (1,0,2,0) + \lambda'_j = (1,0,3,0) \quad (2)$$

Equation (2) denotes that node $i(\lambda_i = (1,0,1,0))$ has a deeper understanding of its knowledge after communicating with node $j(\lambda_j = (1,0,3,0))$, which is more professional than node i; the value of this dimension in the knowledge vector corresponding to node i has also been improved [57].

3.2.3. Suspension Conditions

Since the energy of each subject energy is not infinite, it is assumed that nodes can only discuss one topic (one knowledge dimension) each time they communicate on the premise of non-generality. At each moment T, each node can communicate no more than once. When no nodes in the network can communicate with each other, time T ends. In the above process, knowledge flows through the network in the process of communication between subjects, which enables subjects to increase their existing knowledge level while acquiring new knowledge needed for innovation through the network. This is the process of knowledge recombination. Assume the knowledge element required for innovation is m-dimensional vector $A = (k_1, k_2, \ldots, k_m)$, the nodes in the network continuously communicate and learn from each other; when the knowledge vector of a node i in the network becomes $\lambda_i = (k_1, k_2, \ldots, k_m) = A$, innovation is generated. This is because the knowledge vector of this node is consistent with the requirement of generating this innovation.

3.2.4. Model Simulation

Due to a certain degree of randomness of a single experiment, in order to network the error generated by the randomness, 10 simulations of the innovation process under each group parameter are carried out, and the average value of the 10 simulation results is finally taken as the final data. The simulation process is as follows (Algorithm 1).

Step 1: Set the network model parameters and the initial knowledge vectors for each node;

Step 2: Each node first chooses whether or not to communicate (communicate or not), and if it chooses to communicate then it again chooses the method of this communication (online or offline);

Step 3: Communicate with a random neighbor node but satisfy the knowledge diffusion condition with the probability of α. Knowledge diffusion occurs and records the node where knowledge diffusion occurs. When the condition is not satisfied, the knowledge vectors of both parties do not change.

Step 4: Go to Step 2 until the first innovation appears in the network and record the total number of hours to complete the innovation.

Step 5: Change the network parameters and repeat the experiment.

Algorithm 1 STVMD based on STFT (Note: Set different initialization according to different situations).

```
Initialization: {λ1, λ2, ... λm}, α, Gon = {N1, L1}, Goff = {N2, L2}
results ← { }
repeat
    G ← Choose(Gon, G)
    for n ∈ G do
        if n ∉ results & Random( ) >= α then
            m ← Random(n.neighbor)
            communicate(n, m, G, λn, λm)
            Update λn, λm ← Max(λn, λm)
            results.append(n, m)
        end if
        Update Gon
        Update Goff
    end for
until Sum(λGon) = N1
```

3.3. *Variable-Network Density*

The tightness of organizational structure can be obtained by measuring network density. The density of a network refers to "the ratio between the actual number of edges in the network and the possible number of edges", whereas "the possible number of edges" refers to the maximum number of edges that can be had in the network. The maximum number of edges that can exist in a network is equal to $N(N-1)/2$ [58]. Therefore, the density calculation formula can be expressed as:

$$D = \frac{L}{N(N-1)/2} \tag{3}$$

where L represents the number of connected edges measured in the network, and N is the number of nodes in the network. The value range of network density D is $[0, 1]$. The larger the network value is, the closer the relationship between nodes is. When the density is 1, it means that all nodes in the network are closely connected. When the density value is 0, it indicates that there is no connection between any two nodes in the network.

Density Relations for Double-Layer Coupled Networks

In multi-layer networks, the attributes of nodes are multidimensional and multi-layered, and there is a hierarchical relationship between the layers of the network and relationships, so describing the structural attributes through a single-layer network may neglect the relationships between different layers. Therefore, this study introduces the concept of a double-layer coupled network density relationship to explore the overall network structure relationship between online and offline cooperative networks in order to better understand the relationship between online–offline double-layer coupling networks. This study starts from the network density calculation formula, and describes the relationship between the two layers of the coupled network through the ratio of their densities:

$$V = \frac{D_{on}}{D_{off}} = \frac{N_{off}(N_{off}-1)}{N_{on}(N_{on}-1)} \times \frac{L_{on}}{L_{off}} \tag{4}$$

When the value of V is 0, it indicates that the online cooperative network does not exist, and then the model is the offline single-layer network. When the V value is greater than 0 but less than 1, it indicates that the online network exists, but the density of the online network is less than the density of the offline cooperative network. At this time, the structural resources in the offline cooperative network are richer, and the path of knowledge flow between members is richer than that in the online cooperative network. When the value of V is greater than 1, it means that the density of the online cooperation network is greater than the density of offline cooperation network; at this time, the structure of online cooperation network is more compact than the offline cooperation network. According to the above discussion, at this time, the knowledge flow paths in the online cooperative network are richer and more likely to produce more efficient paths than the offline cooperative network.

This study measures the time step to finish innovation and the frequency of communication during innovation. Innovation time is used to describe the total simulation time step required by the organization to finish innovation, and the time step can be used to reflect the innovation efficiency of our model. The communication frequency in the innovation process is used to describe each communication in the simulation model, and the communication frequency can be used to measure the total cost of innovation. Both variables can be obtained directly from the simulation model.

3.4. *Robustness Test*

In this experiment, the initially assigned knowledge vector and innovation vector have equal rank, the innovation could finish if communication reasonably occurs. When the network is too sparse, the presence of isolated regions in the network makes the completion of innovations difficult or outright avoidable. To prevent this from occurring in the model, this study uses the backtracking search algorithms in distributed constraint satisfaction problems to calculate the maximum time of the innovation process [59].

3.4.1. Constraint Satisfaction Problem

The constraint satisfaction problem is the problem of finding assignments for all variables that satisfy their constraint relationships with each other over a certain range of values, consisting of the variables, the value domains of the variables, and the constraints between the variables, which are the density ratios of a double-layer network.

Definition 1. *(Constraint Satisfaction Problem) The constraint satisfaction problem can be formalized as a constraint network, defined by the set of double-layer network density ratios, the set of value domains for each double-layer network density ratio, and the set of constraint relationships between the double-layer network density ratios, denoted as the triad* (V, D, C), *where:*

V is the set of double-layer network density ratios $\{v_i, \ldots, v_n\}$;

D is the set of value domains of all double-layer network density ratios, and $D = \{D_1, \ldots, D_n\}$, D_i *are finite domains of all possible values of the double-layer network density ratio* v_i;

C is the set of constraint relations between the density ratios of the double-layer network $C = \{C_1, \ldots, C_m\}$, *where each constraint contains a subset of* V, $\{v_i, \ldots, v_n\}$ *and a constraint relation* $R \subseteq D_i \times \ldots \times D_j$.

The constraint satisfaction method is an efficient problem solving method that finds an assignment for each double-layer network density ratio in its value domain such that all constraints are satisfied.

Definition 2. *(Solution of Constraint Satisfaction Problem) A solution of a constraint satisfaction problem is a set of assignments to all the double-layer network density ratios in the problem that do not violate any constraints. That is, a set of assignments to all double-layer network density ratios* $S(v_i, \ldots, v_n) = \{d_1 \in D_1, \ldots, d_n \in D_n\}$, $\forall C_r \in C$ *have* $S(v_{ri}, \ldots, v_{rj}) = \{d_{ri}, \ldots, d_{rj}\} \in R_r$.

3.4.2. Distributed Constraint Satisfaction Problem

The distributed constraint satisfaction problem is a constraint satisfaction problem in which both the density ratio and constraints of a double-layer network are distributed among different autonomous subjects (employees). Based on the definition of constraint satisfaction problem, the distributed constraint satisfaction problem can be defined as follows:

Definition 3. *(Distributed Constraint Satisfaction Problem) n subjects denoted as* $N_1, N_2, \ldots, N_n$, *m double-layer network density ratios as* $v_1, v_2 \ldots, v_m$, *m double-layer network density ratios in the value domain of* $D_1, D_2 \ldots, D_m$, *the constraints between the double-layer network density ratios are still denoted by C; each subject has one or more double-layer network density ratios, and each double-layer network density ratio* v_j *belongs to a* N_i *denoted as belongs* (v_j, N_i); *constraints between the double-layer network density ratios are distributed either within the subjects or between the subjects when* N_l *knows the constraint relation* C_k, *denoted as* $Known(C_k, N_l)$.

Constraints distributed within subjects are called local constraints, while inter-subject constraints are called global constraints; local constraints can be handled by the computation of the subjects, whereas global constraints require not only the computation of the subjects, but also inter-subjects communication to handle them, thus requiring the following communication model assumptions:

Assumption 1. *Inter-subject communication is accomplished by passing messages to other subjects when and only when one subject knows the address of the other.*

Assumption 2. *The delay in transmitting messages is random but finite, and the order in which messages are received between any pair of subjects is the same as the order in which they are sent.*

Assumption 3. *Each subject knows only part of the information about the whole innovation.*

Subjects in distributed constraint satisfaction are computational entities that comply with cooperation mechanisms to perform decision-making behavior.

Each subject is responsible for a number of double-layer network density ratios and determines their values, since there are also intrinsic inter-subject constraints that must be satisfied by the assignment. The formal definition of the solution to the distributed constraint satisfaction problem is:

Definition 4. *(Solution of Distributed Constraint Satisfaction Problem) A solution to a distributed constraint satisfaction problem is found if and only if the following conditions are satisfied:* $\forall N_i$, $\forall v_j$ *there exists a relation belongs* (v_j, N_i), *and* $\forall C_k$, $\forall N_l$ *Known*(C_k, N_l) *are both* C_k *satisfied when the assignment of* v_j *to* $d_j \in D_j$. *That is, at this point the assignment of all variables in the problem satisfies all inter-subjective and intro-subjective constraints.*

3.4.3. Backtracking Search Algorithms

The two basic ideas of the backtracking search method are introducing a minimum conflict heuristic in order to reduce the risk of unfavorable assignments, and creating a dynamically changeable priority order of the subjects so that unfavorable assignments can be corrected without exhaustive search.

Because the knowledge vectors of the subjects endowed at the initial stage of the model ground are linearly independent, the problem of studying the avoidance of the presence of isolated regions in the network, which makes it difficult to complete the innovation, can be understood as the problem of solving a chi-square linear equation, and since the matrix formed by the knowledge vectors of the subjects and the innovation vectors are equal-ranked, there is a solution to the model, i.e., the innovation can be achieved in the organization.

The probability of two nodes communicating and acquiring knowledge is p. For a knowledge vector with m-dimensions, the probability that all dimensions participate in the communication (considering the longest innovation time) is $p^{\frac{m(m-1)}{2}}$. The components of each knowledge vector have k values, so there are k^m possible values in m-dimensions. Therefore, the expected value of the node knowledge vector value that forms after communication is $k^m p^{\frac{m(m-1)}{2}}$. In the whole system, the probability of failing to reach innovation after i check is $p^{i-1}(1-p)$. Therefore, for I checks, the communication frequency of each node can be expressed in Equation (5):

$$\sum_{i=1}^{m-1} ip^{i-1}(1-p) + (I-1)p^{m-1} = \frac{1 - mp^{m-1} + (m-1)p^m}{1-p} \tag{5}$$

The expected communication frequency is equal to the number of nodes multiplied by the frequency of communication performed by the nodes; the total communication frequency required for the innovation process is the sum of the expected communication frequency from 1 to I for the backtracking search process:

$$\sum_{i=1}^{m} \frac{1 - mp^{m-1} + (m-1)p^m}{1-p} k^m p^{\frac{m(m-1)}{2}} \tag{6}$$

The dimension of the knowledge vector designed in this experiment is $m = 10$ (The number of knowledge categories (m) held by the subject reflects the richness of knowledge in the organization and the breadth of knowledge elements included in the innovation. When m is small, there is just a single category in the organization; when m is large, it not only corresponds to the reality of innovative activities, but also greatly increases the computational volume of the simulation experiment. Therefore, in order to ensure that this experiment can reflect the diversity of knowledge in innovation, set m = 10), and the total number of nodes in the network $N = 100$ (A study states that the number of employees in an organization should not exceed 150 and when the number is exceeded, the organization will face disintegration [60]. Therefore, the number of network members in this experiment is less than 150 people, and, at the same time, the network structure is needed to be measured in the subsequent calculations, so N = 100 is set to reduce the amount of calculations in the subsequent analysis). The maximum communication frequency calculated by backtracking search, according to Equation (6), is 4922. When the communication frequency in the experiment is larger than this value, it indicates that there is an isolated area in the network, which is an invalid experimental result.

4. Results

To verify the influence of the online cooperative network structure on the innovation duration under the condition of ensuring the stability of the experiment, in Experiment 1, keep the offline cooperation network density unchanged, and adjust the online cooperation network density for the simulation experiment; In Experiment 2, the density of online cooperation network was kept unchanged, and the density of offline cooperation network was adjusted for the simulation experiment to meet the requirement of changing the double-layer coupled network density in two ways. The values of the coupling density of the double-layer network were 0.3, 0.6, 0.9, 1.2, 1.5, 1.8, 2.1, 2.4, 2.7, and 3.0 in ten cases. Ten experiments were conducted under each density ratio, and the average value of the ten experiments was taken as the analysis data. Similarly, when the influence of offline cooperation network structure on innovation is verified, the structure of the cooperation network on the control line only changes the structure of the offline cooperation network. Ten experiments are conducted to obtain the experimental results.

According to the simulation results, the effect of network density on innovation time is verified by stepwise regression. In the regression results, the correlation coefficients between the quadratic term of the density ratio R of the double-layer coupled network and the innovation time were 379.9 and 387.1, respectively, in Experiment 1 and Experiment 2, and were verified at the significance level of 1%, indicating that there was a positive U-shaped relationship between the density ratio of the double-layer coupled network and the innovation time. Therefore, the two hypotheses (H1, H2) proposed in this study have been verified (Table 2).

Table 2. A stepwise regression model of network density on innovation times.

Variable	E1	E2
	$\ln y_1$	$\ln y_2$
R	−27.31 *** (−8.12)	−27.83 *** (−7.72)
R^2	379.9 *** (6.96)	387.1 *** (6.62)
cons	4.682 *** (102.01)	4.628 *** (94.11)
N	110	110

Note: *** indicates significant at the 1% significance level.

According to the results of the simulation experiment, the influence parameters on the change of innovation efficiency caused by the change of online and offline cooperative networks in Experiment 1 and Experiment 2 are similar. Although the effect of online and offline cooperative network structure on innovation time is very close according to the results of stepwise regression analysis, the cost of communication through the online cooperative network is lower than that through offline communication, and members who need to pay a huge cost to communicate offline may be easily realized through the online cooperative network. At the same time, the convenience of communication through online cooperative networks also reduces the sunk costs of communication to some extent. Employees cannot obtain useful information in every communication each time. Compared with face-to-face communication, OSM communication, to some extent, hedges the risk that communication cannot bring useful knowledge.

The following results are obtained after simulating the innovation process of online–offline networks under different density combination conditions. The total time to finish innovation is the most intuitive indicator to reflect the speed of innovation. Due to the difference in network structure, the frequency of subject communication in a time-step network is also different, so the total time step of innovation is also different under different network structures. The simulation process will be used to explain the influence of network structure in the innovation process. This study analyzes the characteristics of OSM participation in the innovation process, as shown in Figure 2. In the generation phase, the number of knowledge owners in the organization is still very low, and it is difficult for knowledge to be widely spread within the organization, so the communication in online and offline networks is at a low level. The dense online network provides more opportunities for employees to communicate; communication in the online network is more active during this phase. The frequency of communication in both online and offline networks increases synchronously over time. In the elaboration phase, the communication between online and offline networks presents an obvious complementary relationship. The use of OSM makes up for deficiencies in offline communication, and the communication between online and offline networks changes alternately with time. When offline communication is sufficient, online communication will not occupy the time of offline communication. At the same time, when online communication is insufficient, online communication replenishes the vacancy of communication. The apparent interaction between the two communication modes fully demonstrates that the use of OSM complements and promotes the original communication channels of an organization. In the championing phase, the frequency of offline communication is higher than that of online communication, because offline networks can provide more stable connections and necessary support for innovation. In this phase, online communication is not ineffective, but provides a good guarantee and auxiliary role for offline communication. In the last time step of the experiment, innovation has been completed and the terminating condition is satisfied, so communication between nodes no longer occurs.

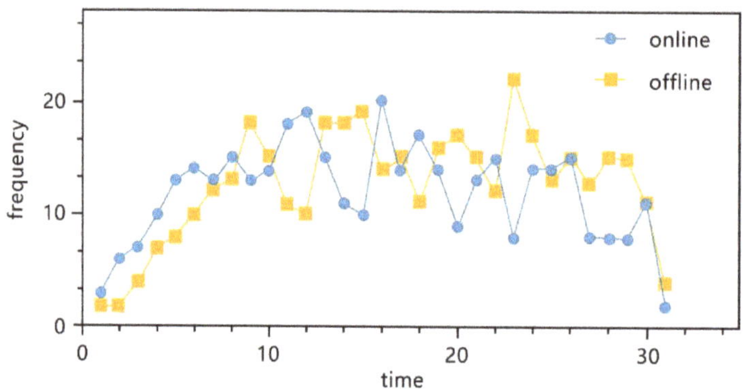

Figure 2. Data graph of communication frequency in online and offline networks during the innovation process.

The process of innovation demands constant interaction among subjects. When the online network has a low density, its structure becomes sparse, and subjects with knowledge often cannot be contacted through the online network, which further results in a longer time for innovation. As its density increases, the online network forms a closer coupling relationship with the offline network, under which circumstance the subject can not only contact an adjacent subject through the offline network, but also the distant one in reality through the online network, which greatly accelerates the propagation speed of knowledge within the organization. Therefore, we further analyze the impact of density coupling on innovation in double-layer networks. Figure 3 shows the data obtained after several tests, which reflects the variation trend of the total time steps of innovation caused by changes in network structure. In Figure 3, the horizontal axis represents the ratio of online network density to offline network density, the vertical axis represents the time step achieved by innovation. It can be observed from Figure 3 that when the density ratio of the online–offline double-layer coupling network is less than 1.5, the time step of innovation consumption decreases sharply with the increase of online network density. When the density value is greater than 1.5, the innovation consumption time slowly rises with the increase of online network density.

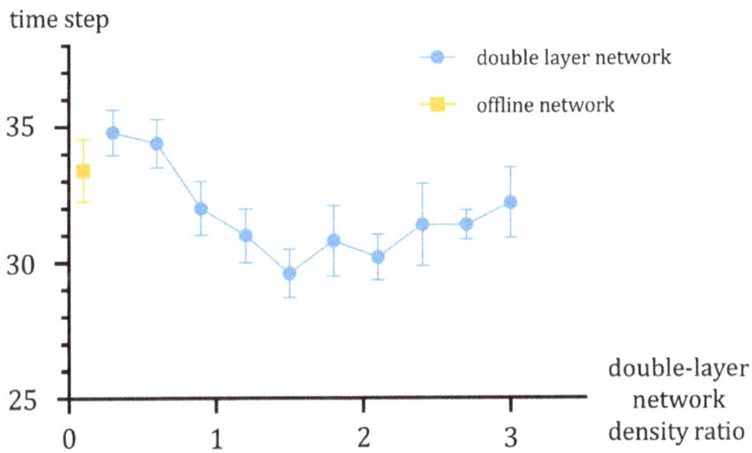

Figure 3. The effect of coupling relation of the density of double-layer network on innovation efficiency. The first group of data is obtained in an offline single-layer network as the control group.

In this experiment, the density ratio between the online network and offline network is 1.5, to which the total time consumed for innovation is the shortest. As the online network further increases, its structure also becomes closer, which increase online network structure and the increase of invalid communication. This is also the reason why the innovation time step gradually increases when the density ratio of the online network to the offline network is greater than 1.5. Although, a redundancy in the network may induce continuous transmission of important knowledge elements in a cohesive subgroup, however, they cannot reach the outside of the subgroup. This generates sufficient information benefits while further reducing the efficiency of knowledge transmission in the network.

In this experiment, the minimum total time consumed by innovation is a 1.5 density ratio of online network to offline network. In organizations, due to the different scales of different organizations, the actual optimal density ratio may fluctuate under the influence of the formed cooperative network scale. It is not feasible for organizations to adjust the density of online or offline cooperation networks, but it can still strengthen innovative behaviors at different stages through a series of activities. For example, in the generation phase, organizations can increase the frequency of online meetings within the organization, or organize external personnel's lectures and other activities within the organization. New activities can strengthen the original connection and form a new connection within the organization. In the elaboration phase, offline knowledge exchange activities should be advocated. Since both online and offline play an important role in this phase, employees are likely to enter a dilemma of choice. Organizations should provide certain guidance to employees' activities to avoid employees from investing too much energy online or offline, affecting their innovative behaviors. In the championing phase, offline activities should be encouraged. One-to-one communication between leaders and members cannot only grasp the needs of employees in the innovation process timely, but also provide help for their innovation through their influence.

Nevertheless, the role of online–offline coupling networks may not be sufficiently described merely by the time step of innovation completion. This study also acquired each communication in the innovation process and made statistics on the total communication frequency when the innovation was completed, in which the result is shown in Figure 4. The number of conversations to be finished reflects the total cost of innovation, in which the number of communication in the online network reflects the cost of communication in itself. Similarly, the number of communication in offline networks demonstrates the cost of innovation. Based on the information presented in Figure 4, the following fact can be derived: as the density ratio of online network to offline network increases, innovation activities depend more heavily on online communication.

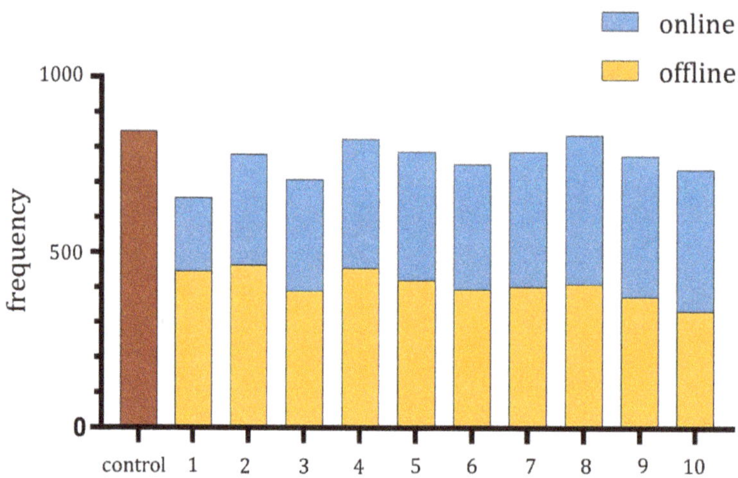

Figure 4. The effect of coupling relationship of double-layer network density on average communication frequency in the innovation process. The first group of data is obtained in an offline single-layer network as the control group.

In the process of knowledge diffusion, subjects cannot communicate with unknown ones. Therefore, the increase in online network density suggests that when the number of subjects in the network is definite, the number of connected edges in the network increases accordingly, thereby increasing the number of adjacent subjects in the network. As online network density increases, the amount of communication through online networks increases during the process of innovation. Combined with the data obtained from the experiment, the trend of total communication frequency when innovation is generated is relatively stable. Therefore, we can understand that as the density ratio of online networks and offline networks continues to increase, more offline communication activities are transferred to online networks.

5. Discussion

Through the analysis of the results of the simulation experiment, this study verifies the impact of online cooperation networks on innovation time. However, as the innovation process is complex and phased, does online cooperation always play a role in promoting it? This study analyzes the innovation process based on the multi-stage innovation theory and hopes to provide suggestions for organizations to explore the use of OSM decisions. Therefore, we follow Perry Smith's idea [53], defining three phases from the beginning to the achievement of innovation as the generation phase, elaboration phase, and championing phase.

In the generation phase, creators generate many different ideas and then self-select one. Importantly, the selected idea is merely a vague idea or core concept to be elaborated upon in future phases. In this phase, it is not the mastery of knowledge that matters, but rather the accumulation of new knowledge. To clearly show the phenomenon that employees communicate through different networks, all the communication within a period is formed as edges, as shown in Figure 5. The edges in the figure are the actual communication between nodes. Communication times are the number of all communications that occur between agents. While individuals are in conversation, they cannot be working on other tasks; communication times in the system reflects the opportunity cost of people's time. An online network structure will provide more chances for subjects to communicate with others. New knowledge enhances the cognitive flexibility of the subject, which enables uncommon associations between conceptually distant ideas.

(a) (b)

Figure 5. Communication on networks that takes place during a certain period time. (**a**) When t = 1, the total number of communication times in the system (hereinafter we use "the value" to represent the total number of communication times in the system) is 6; (**b**) When t = 4, the value is 34.

In the elaboration phase, creators systematically evaluate a novel idea's potential and then further clarify and develop the idea. Differing from the previous phase, developing the idea needs to enhance the knowledge of different fields. Because of the specialized nature of some of the knowledge, detailed conversations with experts in the field are often required. Meanwhile, creators refine the idea by checking for inconsistencies and making improvements in this phase. On the one hand, creators can communicate with experts face-to-face through offline networks and learn the required knowledge. On the other hand, they can revise their ideas by listening to their opinions widely through online networks. Therefore, in this phase, communication in both networks soared, which is shown in Figure 6.

In the championing phase, given that highly novel ideas have a high risk of rejection, creators aim at obtaining approval to push the idea forward and, consequently, also obtain money, time, or political cover. Strong ties are characterized by norms of reciprocity that facilitate the exchange of favors and mutual support, and individuals through strong ties are motivated to help and support each other's initiatives. Moreover, by contributing strong ties with subjects who own high influence, creators could increase their legitimacy stock and help creators reduce perceived uncertainty by drawing on others' behavioral cues. Offline networks are easier to build strong connections, so it is not difficult to reveal the fact from Figure 7 that communication in offline networks is more significant in this phase.

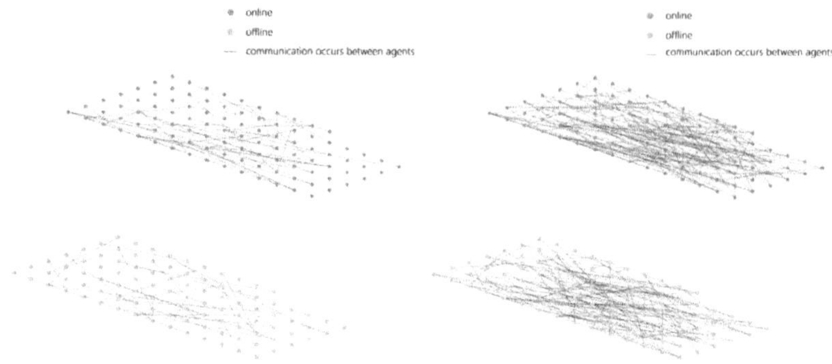

(a) (b)

Figure 6. Communication on networks that takes place during a certain period time. (**a**) When t = 5, the value is 57; (**b**) When t = 20, the value is 497.

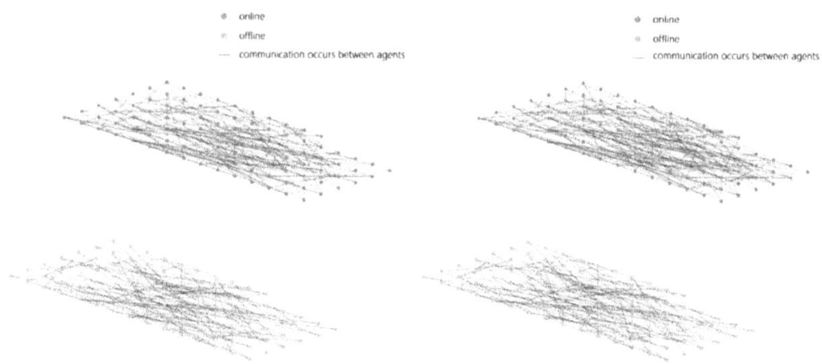

(a) (b)

Figure 7. Communication on networks that takes place during a certain period time. (**a**) When t = 21, the value is 512; (**b**) When t = 28, the value is 746, the innovation has been achieved.

6. Conclusions

In this paper, we establish an innovative simulation analysis model on a double-layer coupled network. An online cooperative network differs from offline ones and is characterized by a more flexible structure. By introducing the structure of the online cooperative network, we investigate the impact of the double-layer network relationship on innovation from the perspective of a multi-layer network. Furthermore, we set the selection mechanism to simulate the process of internal knowledge diffusion in the process of innovation. Different from previous studies which merely focused on a specific stage in the innovation process, our proposed recombination mechanism makes the innovation process in the model more complete. Our proposal lays the theoretical foundation in the scope of innovation research from the social network perspective and further extends the meaning of the multi-layer network coupling theory. It is of practical significance to guide enterprises to adjust the structure of their online cooperation network and optimize the internal cooperation relationship.

The online–offline double-layer coupling network with different coupling relations is simulated, and the conclusions are defined as follows.

At the beginning of the innovation process, the generation phase, employees need to contact new knowledge to expand their knowledge reserve and change their cognitive structure. Organizations could shorten the time cost of this stage by increasing the communication between employees by using OSM, such as online meetings. Online meetings offer many advantages such as flexibility, convenience, time, and cost savings, as well as increasing opportunities for communication.

Different from the previous stage, when an idea is initially determined, extensive knowledge is no longer important, and more precise and profound knowledge becomes necessary. Face-to-face communication will be very helpful; while OSM solves the circumstances of absence, online communication has the same effect on knowledge enhancement.

The championing phase aimed at obtaining approval to push the idea forward. OSM is no longer beneficial for obtaining relevant support. Instead, offline communication might obtain influence and legitimacy. Influence is fundamental to protecting ideas from encroachment and criticism, removing obstacles to their acceptance, and persuading relevant decision-makers to provide their approval and resources for implementation. In this phase, organizations should promote offline communication instead of using OSM.

OSM is not always effective, but tighter networks do facilitate innovation. It is worth noting that the closeness of online cooperative networks is not always better; the redundancy of tight networks might reduce the efficiency of innovation. Under the network scale simulated in this study, the optimal double-layer network density coupling relationship does not represent all networks, because this coupling relationship may change with the scale of networks.

This study proves the promoting effect of online cooperative networks on innovation and explores the mechanism of the relationship between online cooperative network and offline cooperative network density on innovation. The conclusions of this study facilitate a better understanding of the coupling relationship in double-layer networks. The model adopted in this study simulates the internal cooperative relationship of contemporary enterprises well, and the online cooperative network extended by this model may have further application in social structures.

Despite the above findings, our future interest will be focusing on collecting real signed social network data to verify the effectiveness of several main conclusions obtained in this study and other vital network structure indexes. The proposed model may also be adaptive to other dynamic problems, involving, but not limited to, knowledge diffusion in asymmetrical networks, and innovation in the case of inconsistent efficiency of knowledge transmission.

Author Contributions: Conceptualization, J.H., W.Z., J.W. and S.L.; methodology, J.W.; formal analysis, J.H.; data curation, W.Z.; writing—original draft preparation, W.Z.; writing—review and editing, W.Z., J.W. and S.L.; visualization, J.W.; supervision, J.H.; funding acquisition, J.H. All authors have read and agreed to the published version of the manuscript.

Funding: This research was funded by National Natural Science Foundation of China, grant number 72074139.

Data Availability Statement: The data presented in this study are available on request from the corresponding author. The data are not publicly available due to privacy.

Acknowledgments: The authors would like to thank the anonymous referees as well as the editors.

Conflicts of Interest: The authors declare no conflict of interest. The funders had no role in the design of the study; in the collection, analyses, or interpretation of data; in the writing of the manuscript; or in the decision to publish the results.

References

1. Ramon Saura, J.; Palacios-Marques, D.; Ribeiro-Soriano, D. Exploring the Boundaries of Open Innovation: Evidence from Social Media Mining. *Technovation* **2023**, *119*, 102447. [CrossRef]
2. Fulk, J.; Yuan, Y.C. Location, Motivation, and Social Capitalization via Enterprise Social Networking. *J. Comput.-Mediat. Commun.* **2013**, *19*, 20–37. [CrossRef]
3. Cheng, C.C.J.; Shiu, E.C. How to Enhance SMEs Customer Involvement Using Social Media: The Role of Social CRM. *Int. Small Bus. J.-Res. Entrep.* **2019**, *37*, 22–42. [CrossRef]

4. De Zubielqui, G.C.; Jones, J. How and When Social Media Affects Innovation in Start-Ups. A Moderated Mediation Model. *Ind. Mark. Manag.* **2020**, *85*, 209–220. [CrossRef]
5. Wang, G.; Zhang, W.; Zeng, R. WeChat Use Intensity and Social Support: The Moderating Effect of Motivators for WeChat Use. *Comput. Hum. Behav.* **2019**, *91*, 244–251. [CrossRef]
6. Ali-Hassan, H.; Nevo, D.; Wade, M. Linking Dimensions of Social Media Use to Job Performance: The Role of Social Capital. *J. Strateg. Inf. Syst.* **2015**, *24*, 65–89. [CrossRef]
7. Karakayali, N.; Kilic, A. More Network Conscious Than Ever? Challenges, Strategies, and Analytic Labor of Users in the Facebook Environment: More Network Conscious Than Ever. *J. Comput.-Mediat. Commun.* **2013**, *18*, 61–79. [CrossRef]
8. Wang, W.; Liang, Q.; Mahto, R.; Deng, W.; Zhang, S.X. Entrepreneurial Entry: The Role of Social Media. *Technol. Forecast. Soc. Chang.* **2020**, *161*, 120337. [CrossRef]
9. Coleman, J.S. Social Capital in the Creation of Human Capital. *Am. J. Sociol.* **1988**, *94*, S95–S120. [CrossRef]
10. Hua, L.; Yang, Z.; Shao, J. Impact of Network Density on the Efficiency of Innovation Networks: An Agent-Based Simulation Study. *PLoS ONE* **2022**, *17*, e0270087. [CrossRef]
11. Havakhor, T.; Soror, A.A.; Sabherwal, R. Diffusion of Knowledge in Social Media Networks: Effects of Reputation Mechanisms and Distribution of Knowledge Roles. *Inf. Syst. J.* **2018**, *28*, 104–141. [CrossRef]
12. Perry-Smith, J.E.; Mannucci, P.V. From Creativity to Innovation: The Social Network Drivers of the Four Phases of the Idea Journey. *Acad. Manag. Rev.* **2017**, *42*, 53–79. [CrossRef]
13. Chan, T.H.; Liu, H.; Keck, S.; Tang, W. When Do Teams Generate Valuable Inventions? The Moderating Role of Invention Integrality on the Effects of Expertise Similarity, Network Cohesion, and Gender Diversity. *Prod. Oper. Manag.* **2023**, *32*, 1760–1777. [CrossRef]
14. Almaatouq, A.; Noriega-Campero, A.; Alotaibi, A.; Krafft, P.M.; Moussaid, M.; Pentland, A. Adaptive Social Networks Promote the Wisdom of Crowds. *Proc. Natl. Acad. Sci. USA* **2020**, *117*, 11379–11386. [CrossRef] [PubMed]
15. Mustafa, S.; Zhang, W.; Naveed, M.M. How to Mend the Dormant User in Q&A Communities? A Social Cognitive Theory-Based Study of Consistent Geeks of StackOverflow. *Behav. Inf. Technol.* **2023**, 1–20. [CrossRef]
16. Dong, Y.; Zha, Q.; Zhang, H.; Kou, G.; Fujita, H.; Chiclana, F.; Herrera-Viedma, E. Consensus Reaching in Social Network Group Decision Making: Research Paradigms and Challenges. *Knowl.-Based Syst.* **2018**, *162*, 3–13. [CrossRef]
17. Chong, A.Y.L.; Lacka, E.; Boying, L.; Chan, H.K. The Role of Social Media in Enhancing Guanxi and Perceived Effectiveness of E-Commerce Institutional Mechanisms in Online Marketplace. *Inf. Manag.* **2018**, *55*, 621–632. [CrossRef]
18. Pollet, T.V.; Roberts, S.G.B.; Dunbar, R.I.M. Use of Social Network Sites and Instant Messaging Does Not Lead to Increased Offline Social Network Size, or to Emotionally Closer Relationships with Offline Network Members. *Cyberpsychol. Behav. Soc. Netw.* **2011**, *14*, 253–258. [CrossRef]
19. Schötteler, S.; Laumer, S.; Schuhbauer, H. Consequences of Enterprise Social Media Network Positions for Employees: A Literature Review and Research Agenda. *Bus. Inf. Syst. Eng.* **2023**, *65*, 425–440. [CrossRef]
20. Pee, L.G. Affordances for Sharing Domain-Specific and Complex Knowledge on Enterprise Social Media. *Int. J. Inf. Manag.* **2018**, *43*, 25–37. [CrossRef]
21. Leonardi, P.M. Social Media, Knowledge Sharing, and Innovation: Toward a Theory of Communication Visibility. *Inf. Syst. Res.* **2014**, *25*, 796–816. [CrossRef]
22. Pillet, J.-C.; Carillo, K.D.A. Email-Free Collaboration: An Exploratory Study on the Formation of New Work Habits among Knowledge Workers. *Int. J. Inf. Manag.* **2016**, *36*, 113–125. [CrossRef]
23. Martín-Rojas, R.; Garrido-Moreno, A.; García-Morales, V.J. Social Media Use, Corporate Entrepreneurship and Organizational Resilience: A Recipe for SMEs Success in a Post-Covid Scenario. *Technol. Forecast. Soc. Chang.* **2023**, *190*, 122421. [CrossRef]
24. McAfee, A.P. Enterprise 2.0: The Dawn of Emergent Collaboration. *IEEE Eng. Manag. Rev.* **2006**, *34*, 38. [CrossRef]
25. Leonardi, P.M.; Huysman, M.; Steinfield, C. Enterprise Social Media: Definition, History, and Prospects for the Study of Social Technologies in Organizations. *J. Comput.-Mediat. Commun.* **2013**, *19*, 1–19. [CrossRef]
26. Moqbel, M.; Kock, N. Unveiling the Dark Side of Social Networking Sites: Personal and Work-Related Consequences of Social Networking Site Addiction. *Inf. Manag.* **2018**, *55*, 109–119. [CrossRef]
27. Bretschneider, S.; Parker, M. Organization Formalization, Sector and Social Media: Does Increased Standardization of Policy Broaden and Deepen Social Media Use in Organizations? *Gov. Inf. Q.* **2016**, *33*, 614–628. [CrossRef]
28. Hsu, M.-H.; Chang, C.-M. Examining Interpersonal Trust as a Facilitator and Uncertainty as an Inhibitor of Intra-Organisational Knowledge Sharing: Interpersonal Trust and Uncertainty. *Inf. Syst. J.* **2014**, *24*, 119–142. [CrossRef]
29. Aalbers, R.H.L.; Dolfsma, W.; Leenders, R.T.A.J. Vertical and Horizontal Cross-Ties: Benefits of Cross-Hierarchy and Cross-Unit Ties for Innovative Projects: Vertical and Horizontal Cross-Ties. *J. Prod. Innov. Manag.* **2016**, *33*, 141–153. [CrossRef]
30. Cao, B.; Han, S.; Jin, Z. Modeling of Knowledge Transmission by Considering the Level of Forgetfulness in Complex Networks. *Phys. A* **2016**, *451*, 277–287. [CrossRef]
31. Qiao, T.; Shan, W.; Zhang, M.; Liu, C. How to Facilitate Knowledge Diffusion in Complex Networks: The Roles of Network Structure, Knowledge Role Distribution and Selection Rule. *Int. J. Inf. Manag.* **2019**, *47*, 152–167. [CrossRef]
32. Deichmann, D.; Moser, C.; Birkholz, J.M.; Nerghes, A.; Groenewegen, P.; Wang, S. Ideas with Impact: How Connectivity Shapes Idea Diffusion. *Res. Policy* **2020**, *49*, 103881. [CrossRef]

33. Goclowska, M.A.; Ritter, S.M.; Elliot, A.J.; Baas, M. Novelty Seeking Is Linked to Openness and Extraversion, and Can Lead to Greater Creative Performance. *J. Pers.* **2019**, *87*, 252–266. [CrossRef]
34. Mueller, J.; Melwani, S.; Loewenstein, J.; Deal, J.J. Reframing the Decision-Makers' Dilemma: Towards a Social Context Model of Creative Idea Recognition. *Acad. Manag. J.* **2018**, *61*, 94–110. [CrossRef]
35. Ter Wal, A.L.J.; Alexy, O.; Block, J.; Sandner, P.G. The Best of Both Worlds: The Benefits of Open-Specialized and Closed-Diverse Syndication Networks for New Ventures' Success. *Adm. Sci. Q.* **2016**, *61*, 393–432. [CrossRef]
36. Kwayu, S.; Lal, B.; Abubakre, M. Enhancing Organisational Competitiveness Via Social Media—A Strategy as Practice Perspective. *Inf. Syst. Front.* **2018**, *20*, 439–456. [CrossRef]
37. Phan, T.Q.; Airoldi, E.M. A Natural Experiment of Social Network Formation and Dynamics. *Proc. Natl. Acad. Sci. USA* **2015**, *112*, 6595–6600. [CrossRef] [PubMed]
38. Lavie, D.; Rosenkopf, L. Balancing Exploration and Exploitation in Alliance Formation. *Acad. Manag. J.* **2006**, *49*, 797–818. [CrossRef]
39. Burt, R.S. Structural Holes and Good Ideas. *Am. J. Sociol.* **2004**, *110*, 349–399. [CrossRef]
40. Scaringella, L.; Miles, R.E.; Yann, T. Customers Involvement and Firm Absorptive Capacity in Radical Innovation: The Case of Technological Spin-Offs. *Technol. Forecast. Soc. Chang.* **2017**, *120*, 144–162. [CrossRef]
41. Argyres, N.; Rios, L.A.; Silverman, B.S. Organizational Change and the Dynamics of Innovation: Formal R&D Structure and Intrafirm Inventor Networks. *Strateg. Manag. J.* **2020**, *41*, 2015–2049. [CrossRef]
42. Gunasekaran, A.; Papadopoulos, T.; Dubey, R.; Wamba, S.F.; Childe, S.J.; Hazen, B.; Akter, S. Big Data and Predictive Analytics for Supply Chain and Organizational Performance. *J. Bus. Res.* **2017**, *70*, 308–317. [CrossRef]
43. Butler, B.S. Membership Size, Communication Activity, and Sustainability: A Resource-Based Model of Online Social Structures. *Inf. Syst. Res.* **2001**, *12*, 346–362. [CrossRef]
44. Cennamo, C.; Ozalp, H.; Kretschmer, T. Platform Architecture and Quality Trade-Offs of Multihoming Complements. *Inf. Syst. Res.* **2018**, *29*, 461–478. [CrossRef]
45. Von Briel, F.; Schneider, C.; Lowry, P.B. Absorbing Knowledge from and with External Partners: The Role of Social Integration Mechanisms: Absorbing Knowledge from and with External Partners. *Decis. Sci.* **2019**, *50*, 7–45. [CrossRef]
46. Bernstein, B.; Singh, P.J. An Integrated Innovation Process Model Based on Practices of Australian Biotechnology Firms. *Technovation* **2006**, *26*, 561–572. [CrossRef]
47. Roper, S.; Du, J.; Love, J.H. Modelling the Innovation Value Chain. *Res. Policy* **2008**, *37*, 961–977. [CrossRef]
48. Chen, K.; Guan, J. Mapping the Innovation Production Process from Accumulative Advantage to Economic Outcomes: A Path Modeling Approach. *Technovation* **2011**, *31*, 336–346. [CrossRef]
49. Guidolin, M.; Manfredi, P. Innovation Diffusion Processes: Concepts, Models, and Predictions. *Annu. Rev. Stat. Appl.* **2023**, *10*, 451–473. [CrossRef]
50. Liu, C.; Liu, X. Research on Knowledge Transfer Behaviour in Cooperative Innovation and Simulation. *Econ. Res.-Ekon. Istraživanja* **2019**, *32*, 1219–1236. [CrossRef]
51. McKelvey, B. Toward a Complexity Science of Entrepreneurship. *J. Bus. Ventur.* **2004**, *19*, 313–341. [CrossRef]
52. Held, F.P.; Wilkinson, I.F.; Marks, R.E.; Young, L. Agent-Based Modelling, a New Kind of Research. *Australas. Mark. J.* **2014**, *22*, 4–14. [CrossRef]
53. Wang, Z.; Zhang, M.; Sun, H.; Zhu, G. Effects of Standardization and Innovation on Mass Customization: An Empirical Investigation. *Technovation* **2016**, *48–49*, 79–86. [CrossRef]
54. Dou, R.; Zong, C.; Nan, G. Multi-Stage Interactive Genetic Algorithm for Collaborative Product Customization. *Knowl.-Based Syst.* **2016**, *92*, 43–54. [CrossRef]
55. Opara, V.; Spangsdorf, S.; Ryan, M.K. Reflecting on the Use of Google Docs for Online Interviews: Innovation in Qualitative Data Collection. *Qual. Res.* **2023**, *23*, 561–578. [CrossRef]
56. March, J.G. Exploration and Exploitation in Organizational Learning. *Organ. Sci.* **1991**, *2*, 71–87. [CrossRef]
57. Levinthal, D.A.; March, J.G. The Myopia of Learning. *Strat. Mgmt. J.* **1993**, *14*, 95–112. [CrossRef]
58. Shiau, W.-L.; Dwivedi, Y.K.; Yang, H.S. Co-Citation and Cluster Analyses of Extant Literature on Social Networks. *Int. J. Inf. Manag.* **2017**, *37*, 390–399. [CrossRef]
59. Wang, Q.-H. Research and Development of Distributed Constraint Satisfaction Problems. *J. Softw.* **2006**, *17*, 2029. [CrossRef]
60. Chakravarty, S.; Dogan, K.; Tomlinson, N. A Hedonic Study of Network Effects in the Market for Word Processing Software. *Decis. Support Syst.* **2006**, *41*, 747–763. [CrossRef]

mathematics

MDPI

Article

Multiplex Social Network Analysis to Understand the Social Engagement of Patients in Online Health Communities

Yingjie Lu *, Xinwei Wang, Lin Su and Han Zhao

School of Economics and Management, Beijing University of Chemical Technology, Beijing 100029, China
* Correspondence: luyingjie982@163.com

Abstract: Social network analysis has been widely used in various fields including online health communities. However, it is still a challenge to understand how patients' individual characteristics and online behaviors impact the formation of online health social networks. Furthermore, patients discuss various health topics and form multiplex social networks covering different aspects of their illnesses, including symptoms, treatment experiences, resource sharing, emotional expression, and new friendships. Further research is needed to investigate whether the factors influencing the formation of these topic-based networks are different and explore potential interconnections between various types of social relationships in these networks. To address these issues, this study applied exponential random graph models to characterize multiplex health social networks and conducted empirical research in a Chinese online mental health community. An integrated social network and five separate health-related topic-specific networks were constructed, each with 773 users as network nodes. The empirical findings revealed that patients' demographic attributes (e.g., age, gender) and online behavioral features (e.g., emotional expression, online influence, participation duration) have significant impacts on the formation of online health social networks, and these patient characteristics have significantly different effects on various types of social relationships within multiplex networks. Additionally, significant cross-network effects, including entrainment and exchange effects, were found among multiple health topic-specific networks, indicating strong interdependencies between them. This research provides theoretical contributions to social network analysis and practical insights for the development of online healthcare social networks.

Keywords: multiplex social network analysis; online health communities; exponential random graph models

MSC: 91D30

1. Introduction

With the rapid development of social media, an increasing number of patients are turning to the Internet to seek social support [1]. Many patients may find that their family and friends are unable to provide the necessary support due to various reasons such as distance, lack of knowledge about the specific health condition, or emotional limitations [2]. In such cases, online health communities (OHCs) can fill the gap by connecting individuals with others who have firsthand experience with similar health issues [3]. OHCs offer several potential benefits for those seeking support. Firstly, these platforms significantly enhance the accessibility of support resources, overcoming barriers like geographic distance or limited availability of in-person support groups [4,5], which is particularly valuable for those with limited mobility, residing in remote areas, or encountering social stigma when seeking health-related assistance. Secondly, OHCs offer an opportunity to connect with others facing similar challenges [6]. This sense of shared experience and mutual understanding can be particularly comforting for those who may feel isolated or misunderstood within their immediate social circles [7,8]. Thirdly, in addition to emotional support, OHCs serve as platforms for the exchange of health information and coping strategies [9]. Patients can access information about diverse treatment options, self-care techniques, and valuable resources that may not be easily found elsewhere, thereby enhancing their self-management abilities [10]. Finally, online platforms provide a level of anonymity that may be particularly appealing to individuals who prefer not to disclose personal health information to their immediate social circle [11]. This anonymity allows patients to openly share their concerns, ask questions, and seek advice without revealing their identities.

Engaging in OHCs enables patients to establish support networks where they can connect with others facing similar health conditions, share experiences, provide emotional support, exchange information, and foster a sense of belonging, potentially enhancing their own health management [8,9]. Given the diverse backgrounds and health conditions of users in these online health networks, it is essential to understand which patient characteristics, such as age, gender, and online behaviors, play a key role in the formation of social relationships. Investigating these attributes can provide valuable insights into the underlying patterns and determinants that shape social connections in OHCs.

Moreover, patients in OHCs engage in diverse discussions on health topics [12], forming multiplex social networks that encompass various aspects of their illnesses. Many of them utilize online platforms to exchange information and experiences related to disease diagnosis [13], symptoms [14], and treatment approaches [15]. Additionally, some patients are dedicated to sharing valuable disease management resources [16], such as links to helpful websites, self-help materials, books, articles, and recommendations for therapists and support services. These OHCs not only provide informational support but also offer emotional support and compassion, particularly for those with chronic illnesses, severe conditions, and mental health disorders [17,18]. Furthermore, they facilitate the development of new friendships that can help to alleviate feelings of loneliness [19,20]. These interactions go beyond discussions about illnesses, encompassing various aspects of their lives, such as personal interests and hobbies [21], contributing to the development of meaningful friendships that offer a sense of belonging and support in individuals' lives. Therefore, it is essential to explore the differences in online social behaviors among patients across various topic-based networks within multiplex social networks. This can provide valuable insights into how individuals interact in specific contexts, such as discussing symptoms, sharing treatment experiences, exchanging resources, expressing emotions, and developing new friendships. Understanding this diversity and complexity of social interactions can optimize online platforms and develop tailored interventions that enhance social support and engagement within each topic-specific network.

Finally, we tried to investigate whether there exist some cross-network effects when patients participate in different health topic discussions and establish multiple social networks. This can provide valuable insights into the interconnectedness and interdependence of these diverse network relationships [22]. For instance, we wondered whether active participation in a symptom discussion network may lead to increased involvement in treatment-related interactions, suggesting that those frequently discussing symptoms are more likely to seek or offer treatment-related information and support. Another interesting aspect to consider is whether emotional support is influenced by engagement in a resource sharing network, which will help us to determine whether individuals actively involved in resource sharing also experience increased emotional support within the community. Additionally, it is worthwhile to explore how emotional support networks and friendship networks interact with other information support networks. This examination will provide insights into whether emotional support is influenced by the availability of information resources, or whether building friendships is facilitated by engagement in specific information support networks. Exploring these potential cross-network effects can reveal how interactions within one network may spill over or impact individuals' experiences and behaviors in other networks. However, the previous literature has primarily focused on single networks in isolation, without thoroughly exploring potential relationships or dependencies among networks [23]. Therefore, our examination of cross-network effects can fill this gap and offer a more comprehensive understanding of potential correlations and interdependencies within multiple social networks. Ultimately, this research can provide valuable insights into how participation in diverse health topic discussions influences the formation of relationships across these networks.

In summary, this study tried to address the following research questions using social network analysis:

RQ1: Which patient characteristics are more likely to contribute to the formation of social relationships with peers in OHCs?

RQ2: How do individual characteristics of patients play distinct roles in the formation of multiplex social networks established for discussing various health topics in OHCs?

RQ3: Do cross-network effects exist in the formation of multiplex health social networks, indicating potential correlations or interdependencies between various types of social relationships?

Over the years, many theoretical frameworks and analytical methods for studying social networks have been developed and implemented across various fields. Among these, exponential random graph models (ERGMs) [24] have emerged as a prominent and widely acknowledged approach to examining social networks, providing valuable insights into various social phenomena. ERGMs are tie-based models that aim to explain the mechanisms behind the formation of social network ties [25]. These models can incorporate different types of network configurations and assess their influence on network formation. For instance, ERGMs can consider binary, categorical, and continuous attributes of individuals involved in the network to determine whether these attributes are associated with the formation of network ties. Furthermore, ERGMs can be extended to analyze multiplex social networks, which involve multiple types of relationships or networks among the same set of actors [26,27]. This allows researchers to investigate the cross-network effects within multiplex social networks and explore how ties in one network may influence or be influenced by ties in another network. Therefore, this study employed ERGMs to conduct an analysis of multiplex social support networks in OHCs. The findings provide valuable insights into the social engagement of patients within these communities and can serve as a valuable reference for researchers and practitioners. This knowledge can help them to develop effective strategies and interventions aimed at enhancing social engagement, promoting positive social interactions, and optimizing community resources for the benefit of patients.

2. Literature Review

2.1. Social Network Theory

The ERGMs employed in this study were built upon a set of theoretical principles from social network theory, which suggest that social connections within a network not only spontaneously organize themselves, indicating there are interconnections between relationships, but also are affected by the characteristics of individuals and external factors [28]. Therefore, beyond examining the structural effects within the network itself (endogenous), we placed emphasis on the effects of actor attributes (exogenous) and investigate their significant roles in the formation of social connections within OHCs.

2.1.1. Network Structural Effects

Network structural effects in social network theory refer to the patterns and phenomena where certain relationships within a network give rise to the formation of other relationships [29]. These effects focus on the inherent interdependence and patterns of connectivity among nodes or individuals in a social network. Several key network structural effects include popularity (in-degree effects), indicating some individuals receive more connections; activity (out-degree effects), showing that some individuals initiate connections more frequently; and reciprocity, reflecting mutual connections between two individuals within a social network. In this study, we were concerned with the reciprocal effects within social support networks in OHCs. OHCs serve as knowledge-sharing platforms, promoting a mutual exchange of information that benefits both the contributors and receivers and facilitating shared knowledge for all participants [30]. Patients with similar health concerns or conditions often create a sense of empathy and understanding among members. When they receive support from others, they often feel a sense of community and mutual care, which encourages them to give back to those who have helped or supported them. Therefore, we proposed the following:

Hypothesis 1: *Patients in OHCs are likely to engage in reciprocal support behaviors.*

2.1.2. Actor Attribute Effects

Actor attribute effects in social network analysis refer to certain effects that are influenced by the characteristics of the actors involved in the network, consisting of three basic types: sender, receiver, and homophily/heterophily [29]. The sender and receiver effects only focus on one actor's attributes in a social relationship, while the homophily and heterophily effects consider the attributes of both actors involved in the dyad. The sender effect investigates how the sender's attributes affect the likelihood of initiating a social tie to another actor, and the receiver effect explores how the receiver's attributes influence the likelihood of accepting a social tie from another actor. The homophily effect (applicable to binary and categorical attributes) focuses on the tendency of actors with the same characteristics or attributes to be more likely to form social ties with each other, exploring how similarity between individuals' attributes promotes the formation of ties between them. The heterophily effect (applicable to continuous attributes), in contrast to the homophily effect, focuses on the tendency of actors with different attributes or characteristics to form social ties with each other, exploring how dissimilarity between individuals' attributes affects the formation of ties between them.

In previous studies on user behavior in OHCs, it was often believed that patients' individual attributes, such as gender and age, had a significant impact on their willingness to participate and long-term engagement in OHCs [31]. In addition, patients' online behaviors in OHCs also showed significant differences. Therefore, this study aimed to explore the impact of certain patient demographic characteristics including gender and age and their online behavior characteristics including online emotional expression, online influence, and the duration of online engagement on the development of social relationships in OHCs.

(1) Gender. Gender can play a significant role in interpersonal communication within online social networks, including OHCs [32]. Studies have shown that female patients exhibit a greater tendency to actively engage in OHCs to seek and provide social support compared to male patients [33]. This disparity may be attributed to the fact that females generally utilize healthcare services more often than males, leading to increased participation in OHCs to seek and provide support [34]. Therefore, female patients are more likely to initiate social connections within the context of social network relationships in OHCs. Additionally, traditional gender roles and societal expectations may encourage women to express their emotions and seek support from others, while men may feel societal pressure to appear self-reliant and avoid openly showing vulnerability or seeking help [35]. Thus, female patients in OHCs are more likely to seek and accept social ties initiated by others. Moreover, patients may tend to establish social support connections with others of the same gender in OHCs. This may be due to a perceived sense of understanding or shared experiences related to gender-specific health issues or simply because they find it more comfortable to interact with others of the same gender. Therefore, we proposed the following:

Hypothesis 2a: *Female patients are more likely to initiate social connections in OHCs by providing social support compared to male patients in OHCs.*

Hypothesis 2b: *Female patients are more likely to receive social ties initiated by others compared to male patients because they are more inclined to seek social support in OHCs.*

Hypothesis 2c: *Patients of the same gender are more likely to form social relationships with each other in OHCs.*

(2) Age. Older patients generally have more life experience and are more empathetic, with a stronger sense of community. The accumulated knowledge and wisdom may make them more willing and capable of offering support to others facing similar health challenges. Therefore, older patients are more likely to initiate social connections by actively providing social support to other members within the OHCs. However, compared to younger patients, older individuals may experience a greater number of health issues or chronic conditions, which can make them appear more vulnerable. Thus, older patients are more likely to receive social ties initiated by others, as they are more inclined to seek social support and other members may perceive them as more receptive to accepting social support [36,37]. Moreover, it is believed that patients of similar ages often share common health concerns and experiences related to specific stages of life or age-related health issues. This shared background can create a sense of understanding and empathy among members, making it easier for them to form social support relationships. Therefore, we proposed the following:

Hypothesis 3a: *Older patients are more likely to initiate social connections in OHCs by providing social support compared to younger patients in OHCs.*

Hypothesis 3b: *Older patients are more likely to receive social ties initiated by others compared to younger patients because they are more inclined to seek social support in OHCs.*

Hypothesis 3c: *Patients of similar ages are more likely to form social relationships with each other in OHCs.*

(3) Emotional expression. When people feel positive emotions, such as happiness, empathy, or compassion, they tend to be more prosocial and altruistic, seeking opportunities to assist others. In the context of OHCs, patients who are optimistic about their own health or treatment outcomes may be more likely to share their experiences, offer support, and give advice to others facing similar health issues [38]. Therefore, they are more likely to initiate social connections with other members within the OHCs. Conversely, individuals who express negative emotions, such as sadness, fear, or frustration, might receive more social ties initiated by other community members who might empathize or have undergone comparable challenges because their negative emotional expressions positively influence the likelihood of accepting social ties from others providing social support. [39]. Additionally, patients who express similar emotional valence online may have an increased the likelihood of forming social support connections within OHCs. This is because individuals who express emotions similarly feel more comfortable and connected to each other. When they share similar emotions, they often have common experiences, challenges, and feelings related to their health conditions, fostering companionship and mutual understanding [40]. Consequently, this similarity makes it easier for them to establish social support relationships with one another within OHCs. Therefore, we proposed the following:

Hypothesis 4a: *Patients who tend to express positive emotions are more likely to initiate social connections in OHCs by providing social support in OHCs.*

Hypothesis 4b: *Patients who tend to express negative emotions are more likely to receive social ties initiated by others because they are more inclined to seek social support in OHCs.*

Hypothesis 4c: *Patients who express similar emotional valence online are more likely to form social relationships with each other in OHCs.*

(4) Online influence. Patients with significant online influence may be seen as trustworthy and knowledgeable in OHCs [41]. As a result, they may feel a sense of responsibility to offer support, share their experiences, and provide guidance to others seeking help or information [42], making them more likely to initiate social connections with other members within the OHCs. On the other hand, because they are more visible, their posts or requests for support are more likely to be seen by others, increasing the likelihood of receiving social connections from other members who are willing to offer them help [43,44]. Moreover, it can be inferred that patients with greater disparities in online influence are more likely to provide social support to each other. This is because influential patients tend to show empathy and altruism towards less influential individuals, thereby providing them with social support. Consequently, this reciprocal dynamic fosters a higher likelihood of influential users receiving support in return from those with lower online influence. Therefore, we proposed the following:

Hypothesis 5a: *Patients with higher online influence are more likely to initiate social connections in OHCs by providing social support in OHCs.*

Hypothesis 5b: *Patients with higher online influence are more likely to receive social ties initiated by others because they are more inclined to seek social support in OHCs.*

Hypothesis 5c: *Patients with different levels of online influence are more likely to form social relationships with each other in OHCs.*

(5) Online duration. Experienced patients who have been active in OHCs for a longer time may have accumulated valuable knowledge about managing their health conditions and coping with difficulties [45]. This knowledge enhances their capacity to provide meaningful support, as they possess a deeper comprehension of community norms and the needs of fellow members. Consequently, they develop a stronger sense of community belonging, motivating them to offer valuable social support to others [46]. Therefore, they are more likely to initiate social connections with other members within the OHCs. In contrast, individuals who are relatively new to OHCs are more likely to receive social ties initiated by other members, as they tend to be more proactive in seeking support. The existing members are generally more willing to provide support to newcomers, creating a welcoming atmosphere that encourages their continued engagement in the community [47]. Additionally, it can be inferred that individuals with different durations of online engagement in OHCs tend to form social support connections, because newcomers are more likely to receive strong support from experienced members, and in turn, those experienced members willingly offer guidance and assistance to newcomers. Therefore, we proposed the following:

Hypothesis 6a: *Experienced patients are more likely to initiate social connections in OHCs by providing social support in OHCs.*

Hypothesis 6b: *Newcomers are more likely to receive social ties initiated by others because they are more inclined to seek social support in OHCs.*

Hypothesis 6c: *Patients with different durations of online engagement in OHCs are more likely to form social relationships with each other in OHCs.*

2.2. Multiplex Social Network

Multiplex social networks refer to networks where individuals are connected to each other through multiple types of relationships simultaneously, rather than being limited to a single type of connection [48]. These connections can be based on various factors such as family ties, friendships, professional collaborations, common interests, or geographical proximity [49]. In the study of multiplex social networks, focusing only on one type of relational tie can overlook important information about the overall structure and dynamics of the social network, resulting in an incomplete understanding of the complexity of social connections [29]. Conversely, considering multiple types of relationships simultaneously allows researchers to gain a more comprehensive and detailed understanding of the structure and dynamics of the social network. Many studies emphasize the importance of considering the interdependencies between different types of relationships [50], as in numerous cases these relationships are not independent but interconnected and influence each other [51]. Some scholars further propose that in multiplex social networks, various forms of interdependence exist among different types of relationships, including co-occurrence where different types of relational ties can occur between the same two individuals simultaneously, and reciprocal causality where one type of tie can act as an antecedent to another type of tie [52].

In our study, we aimed to investigate cross-network effects in OHCs where patients participate in discussions on different health topics and form multiplex health topic-specific networks. This study focused on two types of cross-network effects: entrainment effects, which refer to a tendency for different types of relational ties in two topic-specific networks to align, and exchange effects, which indicate a likelihood of different types of relational ties in two topic-specific networks to be exchanged. Understanding these effects can provide valuable insights into the interrelation and mutual dependence of various network relationships, including symptom discussions, treatment-related interactions, resource sharing, emotional support, and building friendships among patients in these networks.

It is often observed that when patients actively participate in discussions related to their health, they often develop multiple social connections across various social topic-specific networks. For instance, if two patients connect within a social network discussing the symptoms of a disease, it is highly likely that they will also connect within a network focused on treatments for that disease. Another notable finding, as indicated by certain studies, is that patients tend to combine emotional and informational support when interacting with others in OHCs [53]. This indicates that the social support networks formed for sharing health-related information may align with the networks formed for emotional support. Furthermore, the exchange of emotional support between patients has been found to contribute to the formation of friendships within these OHCs, or individuals seeking friendship within these communities are more likely to engage in emotional support exchanges, which strengthens the alignment between emotional support and friendship networks [54]. Based on these observations, we have reason to believe that multiple types of social relationships in the multiplex health topic-specific network exhibit a consistency effect. Therefore, we proposed the following:

Hypothesis 7: *There are entrainment effects across multiple health topic-specific networks within OHCs, revealing that patients who provide social support to a fellow patient in one topic-specific network are more likely to provide social support to the same patient in another topic-specific network.*

Another research question of interest is the potential exchange of relationships across multiple health topic-specific networks. It has been proved that patients who provide a certain type of social support in one topic-based network tend to receive reciprocal social support in another topic-based network. For example, if someone frequently offers valuable insights or resources concerning disease diagnosis or health management, other patients who benefit from this knowledge might provide support in return by sharing their own experiences related to the diagnosis and treatment of the same disease [55]. Similarly, when patients seek support regarding symptoms and treatment options for a particular illness, they often respond with emotional encouragement towards those assisting them [56]. Furthermore, when patients try to establish friendships through online social networks, they are more likely to actively connect with those who have provided them with informational and emotional support [57]. Based on the above, we have reason to believe that there is an exchange effect between different types of relationships within the multiplex social network formed by users engaged in OHCs. Therefore, we proposed the following:

Hypothesis 8: *There are exchange effects across multiple health topic-specific networks within OHCs, revealing that patients who provide social support to a fellow patient in one topic-specific network are more likely to receive social support from the same patient in another topic-specific network.*

3. Methods

3.1. Research Context and Data Collection

This study selected an OHC in China that is targeted toward patients with psychological disorders as the research subject. The chosen OHC serves as a convenient and efficient platform for individuals affected by psychological disorders to exchange information and emotions. Currently, this community has attracted over ten thousand registered members, with the majority of users suffering from mental and psychological disorders such as depression and bipolar disorder. Members can share their experiences, emotions, and coping strategies, which helps to alleviate feelings of isolation and foster understanding among peers. Such mutual support communities can provide a sense of belonging and may offer valuable insights and advice.

We utilized web crawling to collect publicly accessible personal information including gender and age, as well as posting details such as post content and timestamps, from user profiles on the website. After filtering out users with incomplete age and gender information, we identified 773 users who indicated in their condition descriptions that they had been clinically diagnosed with mental disorders following medical assessments at hospitals. These users collectively contributed a total of 297,052 posts, encompassing both initial discussion topics and subsequent replies. We constructed an integrated social network by analyzing the reply interactions among these participants, treating the 773 users as network nodes, and translating the reply interactions between users into directed edges. In this directed network, each edge originates from the initiator of a post and terminates at its recipient.

Subsequently, we constructed multiple social networks based on the diverse health-related topics discussed by users in the OHC. To achieve this, we employed a latent Dirichlet allocation (LDA) [58] topic model to identify distinct health-related topics from user-generated posts. The procedure can be summarized as follows: (1) All user-generated posts were subjected to preprocessing using the jieba Chinese text segmentation package in Python. This involved segmenting the text into words, removing stop words, and replacing synonyms. (2) The open-source gensim package in Python was employed to train an LDA topic model. The optimal number of latent topics was determined using the perplexity metric [58]. It was observed that as the number of topics increased, the perplexity metric tended to decrease overall. However, an excessive number of topics can lead to overfitting. It is noted that after surpassing 70 topics, the rate of decrease in perplexity started to diminish gradually. As a result, this study established 70 as the optimal number of topics. (3) Following the extraction of 70 latent topics through the LDA topic model, these topics were subsequently grouped into six major thematic categories. These categories included discussions on disease symptoms, treatments, medical resource sharing, emotional exchanges, social interactions, and friendships, as well as off-topic comments. (4) Apart from off-topic discussions, we constructed five separate social topic-specific networks for the remaining major categories, which were named *Symptom* network, *Treatment* network, *Resource* network, *Emotion* network, and *Friendship* network. Within each of these topic-specific networks, the same 773 users were considered as nodes, but the edges in the network were formed only by interactions related to that specific topic. This resulted in multiple social networks with the same node set across the five networks but featuring diverse types of relationships between the nodes.

The *Symptom* network allows patients to discuss symptoms of diseases and share personal experiences. The *Treatment* network focuses on exchanging information about medications and treatment plans. The *Resource* network allows users to share valuable information about disease diagnosis, treatment resources, and materials on self-health management. The *Emotion* network provides a platform for users to express their feelings related to their struggles with the disease and provide mutual encouragement among peers facing similar conditions. The *Friendship* network primarily focuses on providing a platform for community members to actively seek long-term companionship and support from fellow patients. It also facilitates the arrangement of offline support group meetings and the coordination of various social gatherings within the community.

In the visualization of the overall network and five topic-specific networks presented in Figure 1, we observed a consistent "core–periphery" distribution in all networks. Nodes located in the core positions connected with many other nodes, while those at the periphery formed connections with only a select few nodes, and some even remained isolated. In particular, the *Symptom* network and *Emotion* network demonstrated denser interconnectivity, forming a cohesive structure around core nodes with fewer isolated nodes at the periphery. Conversely, the *Treatment* network, *Friendship* network, and *Resource* network exhibited a comparatively looser structure, characterized by a higher presence of isolated nodes or node pairs at the periphery of the network.

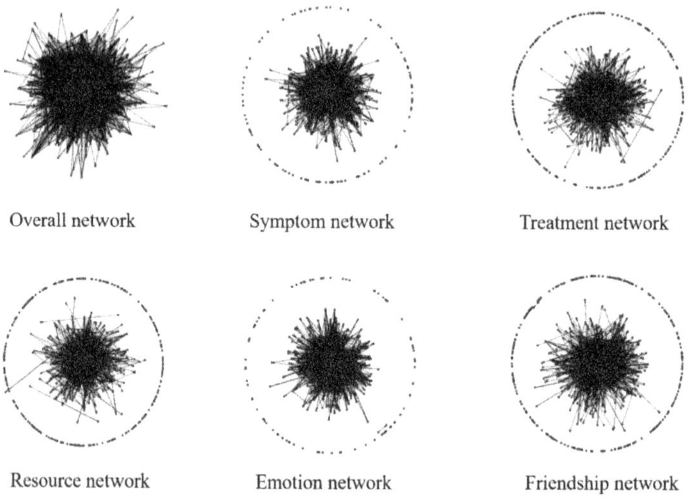

Figure 1. Illustration of the overall network and five topic-specific networks.

The statistical analysis of the number of arcs and density for the overall network and five topic-specific networks, as presented in Table 1, showed consistently low density across all networks. This suggests that social relationships in OHCs are loosely connected, aligning with the characteristics of most empirically observed online social networks. Within the five topic-specific networks, the *Emotion* network exhibited the highest count of arcs and network density, followed by the *Symptom* network. The *Treatment* network, *Resource* network, and *Friendship* network had fewer arcs and comparatively lower network densities.

Some key variables related to patient characteristics were measured to examine the actor attribute effects in our network. The variable *Gender* was measured as a dummy variable with 1 for males and 0 for females. The variable *Age* was measured as a continuous variable. We used the variable *Sentiment* to represent the user's emotional expression while engaging in the OHC. This variable was calculated using the sentiment scores from their posts. The Baidu AI Open Platform's sentiment analysis API was employed to compute the sentiment score for each post. By summing up these sentiment scores across all the posts made by the user, we derived an ultimate overall sentiment score reflecting the user's emotional valence in the OHC. We used the variable *Influence* to represent the online influence of users, which was measured using the H-index [59]. Users' posts were ranked by the number of replies received. If a user's h-th highest replied post has at least h replies, and the (h + 1)-th post has fewer than (h + 1) replies, the user's influence is rated as h. We used the variable *Duration* to represent users' engagement duration in the OHC, which was measured using cumulative online time since registration.

Table 1. Statistics of No. of arcs and density for all networks.

Network	No. of Arcs	Density
Overall	12,276	0.0206
Symptom	4483	0.0075
Treatment	2261	0.0038
Resource	2686	0.0045
Emotion	6402	0.0107
Friendship	2306	0.0039

3.2. Exponential Random Graph Models

The exponential random graph models (ERGMs) are advanced statistical models used in the analysis of social networks [25]. Unlike traditional regression methods, the ERGMs do not assume independence among network ties, making them better suited for network data analysis. The ERGMs can incorporate various patterns of ties, also known as "network configurations", and estimate how these configurations impact the formation of network ties [25]. Additionally, the ERGMs can handle multiple types of actor attributes (binary, categorical, continuous) and dyad-specific covariates, and determine whether these attributes influence the creation of network ties. Moreover, the ERGMs can be applied to diverse types of networks with different types of nodes and relationships and can even model two separate networks simultaneously. This makes the ERGMs particularly suitable for studying complex social networks.

We used the notation and terminology described by Robins et al. (2007) [25]. For each pair i and j of a set N of n actors, X_{ij} is a network variable that represents a tie between actor i and actor j ($X_{ij} = 1$ if there is a tie from actor i to actor j, and 0 otherwise). These ties are represented in an $n \times n$ adjacency matrix (n is the number of actors in the network), which is denoted as X. We specify x_{ij} as the observed value of X_{ij}, and x denotes a matrix of observed ties of the network. A general form of the ERGMs can be expressed as follows:

$$Pr(X = x) = \frac{1}{\kappa} \exp \sum_A \theta_A z_A(x) \quad (1)$$

where:

- $Pr(X = x)$ represents the probability of the network variable X taking the observed value x;
- A defines the network configurations that are patterns of social network ties assumed to represent underlying social processes or mechanisms of network tie formation;
- $\sum_A$ is the summation over all different configuration types in the model;
- $z_A(x)$ is the network statistic corresponding to the network configuration of type A;
- θ_A is the parameter corresponding to the configuration of type A;
- κ is a normalizing constant to ensure that the sum of probabilities in Equation (1) over all possible x equals 1; that is,

$$\kappa = \sum_{x \epsilon X} \exp \sum_A \theta_A z_A(x) \quad (2)$$

The ERGMs were subsequently expanded to analyze multivariate social network [60], where a set of M networks was defined on a set of n nodes, x was a set of tie variables (x_{ijm}, mϵM), and the networks can be represented by an "n by n by M" adjacency array. In the directed networks, $x_{ijm} = 1$ if there is a tie sent from node i to node j in network m; otherwise, $x_{ijm} = 0$. The graph statistics $z_k(x)$ were defined both within and across ties from different types of networks. Thus, they were more complex than the graph statistics for single networks and had the following general form:

$$z_k(x) = \sum_{A \epsilon A_k} \prod_{(i,j,m) \epsilon A} x_{ijm} \tag{3}$$

where A_k is the collection of isomorphic configurations A of tie variables.

In this study, we focused on the basic specifications of a multiplex social network model applied to networks that incorporate two distinct types of connections within a shared set of nodes. The ERGM specifications consisted of within-network effects which defined graph configurations using ties from a single network and cross-network effects where graph configurations were defined involving ties from two networks. In this study, the within-network effects included network structural effects and actor attribute effects. Let $Y = \{Y_i\}$ be a set of variables representing the attribute value for node i, where $0 < i \leq n$, and $y = \{y_i\}$ be its realization. A general form of the ERGMs for single networks can be expressed as follows:

$$Pr(X = x|Y = y) = \frac{1}{\kappa} \exp \sum_{Q,\Lambda} \{\theta_Q Z_Q(x) + \theta_\Lambda Z_\Lambda(x, y)\} \tag{4}$$

where:

- Q is a network configuration of type Q comprising tie variables that are conditionally dependent given the rest of the network;
- Λ is a joint attribute-network configuration comprising tie variables as well as nodal attribute variables;
- $Z_Q(x)$ are sufficient statistics representing the network endogenous effects;
- θ_Q is the vector of parameters corresponding to the graph statistics without nodal attributes;
- $Z_\Lambda(x, y)$ are sufficient statistics for the interactions between the network and nodal attributes;
- θ_Λ is the vector of parameters corresponding to the graph statistics representing the interaction between network tie variables X_{ij} and nodal attributes Y_i.

Our main focus is on two types of cross-network effects for associations between two directed networks at the dyadic level: entrainment effects and exchange effects. Let us consider two directed networks, A and B, with tie variables represented as x_{ijA} and x_{ijB}. The entrainment effect ("ArcAB") represents the extent to which the two network ties align within the dyad (i.e., both ties in network A and B are directed from node i to node j), whereas the exchange effect ("Reciprocity AB") represents the extent to which the dyad exchanges ties of different types (network A from node i to node j, and network B from node j to node i). The relevant statistics can be calculated as follows:

$$z_{\mathrm{Arc}AB}(x) = \sum_{i,j} x_{ijA} x_{ijB} \tag{5}$$

$$z_{\mathrm{Reciprocity}AB}(x) = \sum_{i,j} x_{ijA} x_{jiB} \tag{6}$$

to provide a clearer understanding of the application of the ERGMs in analyzing multiplex social networks and validate our hypotheses, we offer a visual representation illustrating both within-network effects and cross-network effects incorporated into the model. The detailed specifications of the ERGMs are presented in Table 2. In our ERGM specifications, we included the reciprocity parameter as part of network structural effects, in addition to the arc parameter, to test hypothesis H1. We then incorporated three basic actor attribute effect types: sender, receiver, and homophily/heterophily. These effects were applied to each individual's demographic attributes and online behavioral features, including *Gender*, *Age*, *Sentiment*, *Influence* and *Duration*. In total, our model comprises fifteen actor-relation effects. Specifically, there are five sender parameters for the five users' individual attributes to test H2a, H3a, H4a, H5a, and H6a, and five receiver parameters for these same individual attributes to test H2b, H3b, H4b, H5b, and H6b. A homophily parameter for *Gender* is included in the model to test H2c, while four heterophily parameters for the remaining four attributes are included to test H3c, H4c, H5c and H6c. Furthermore, we applied multivariate ERGMs to analyze the multiplex social topic-specific networks, specifically incorporating entrainment and exchange effects in order to test H7 and H8.

Table 2. Summary of network configurations included in ERGMs.

Network Effect	Configuration	Statistic	Hypothesis
Network structural effects			
Arc		$\sum_{i,j} x_{ij}$	
Reciprocity		$\sum_{i,j} x_{ij}x_{ji}$	H1
Actor attribute effects			
Sender effects		$\sum_{i,j} y_i x_{ij}$	H2a, H3a, H4a, H5a, H6a
Receiver effects		$\sum_{i,j} y_j x_{ij}$	H2b, H3b, H4b, Hb, H6b
Homophily effects		$\sum_{i,j} x_{ij} y_i y_j$	H2c
Heterophily effects		$\sum_{i,j} \lvert y_i - y_j \rvert x_{ij}$	H3c, H4c, H5c, H6c
Cross-network effects			
Entrainment effects	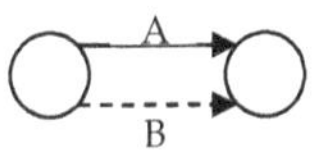	$\sum_{i,j} x_{ijA} x_{ijB}$	H7
Exchange effects	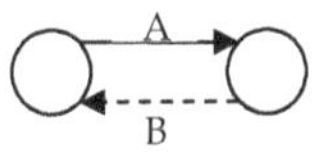	$\sum_{i,j} x_{ijA} x_{jiB}$	H8

4. Results

This research employed the Metropolis–Hastings algorithm, which is a widely used Markov Chain Monte Carlo (MCMC) method, along with maximum likelihood estimation to estimate the parameters of the applied ERGM. The procedure involves iteratively simulating the creation of random networks, comparing them with the actual networks, gradually improving the model's parameters, and repeating this process until the simulated network closely approximates the actual network and the parameters reach stability. This approach results in an estimated set of model parameters that align with the actual observations. The model evaluation is conducted through a comparison of models using the Bayesian Information Criterion (BIC) and the Akaike Information Criterion (AIC), with smaller values of BIC and AIC indicating a better fit of the model.

All models successfully converged and fitted the data well. The parameter estimation results for the overall networks were shown in Table 3. Three models with different parameters were constructed to demonstrate the significance of these effects and whether they changed with the inclusion of additional effects. Model 1 only included network structural effects, while Model 2 added users' demographic attributes to validate actor attribute effects. Model 3 extended this by incorporating users' online behavioral characteristics to further investigate actor attribute effects.

Table 3. Parameter estimates for the overall network.

Parameter	Model 1			Model 2			Model 3		
	Estimate	SE	*p*-Value	Estimate	SE	*p*-Value	Estimate	SE	*p*-Value
Network structural effects									
Arc	−4.252	0.011	<0.001	−5.529	0.031	<0.001	−6.275	0.065	<0.001
Reciprocity	3.550	0.031	<0.001	3.352	0.032	<0.001	1.717	0.045	<0.001
Actor attribute effects									
Gender-Sender				0.113	0.019	<0.001	0.245	0.023	<0.001
Gender-Receiver				−0.235	0.019	<0.001	−0.055	0.023	0.015
Gender-Homophily				0.044	0.015	0.004	0.061	0.021	0.003
Age-Sender				3.026	0.067	<0.001	1.364	0.084	<0.001
Age-Receiver				1.653	0.069	<0.001	0.476	0.084	<0.001
Age-Heterophily				−1.228	0.069	<0.001	−1.347	0.085	<0.001
Sentiment-Sender							1.139	0.068	<0.001
Sentiment-Receiver							−0.581	0.069	<0.001
Sentiment-Heterophily							−1.131	0.076	<0.001
Influence-Sender							7.133	0.171	<0.001
Influence-Receiver							12.395	0.168	<0.001
Influence-Heterophily							−7.167	0.134	<0.001
Duration-Sender							3.335	0.140	<0.001
Duration-Receiver							−0.132	0.142	0.353
Duration-Heterophily							−0.218	0.125	0.083
AIC	110,799			106,854			84,459		
BIC	110,822			106,945			84,651		

Note: SE = standard error.

As shown in Model 1, both the arc and reciprocity parameters were significant. The parameter *Arc* was significantly negative, indicating a lower network density, which aligned with previous statistical findings regarding the actual network. The parameter *Reciprocity* was significantly positive, indicating the presence of a significant reciprocity effect within the social network. Users in the OHC tended to respond after receiving social connections from others, thus forming a mutually beneficial relationship. Therefore, Hypothesis 1 was supported.

After incorporating the effects of gender and age as demographic attributes into Model 2, we observed a decrease in both the AIC and BIC values. This indicated that the incorporation of demographic attributes resulted in an improved fitness of the model. In the analysis of gender-related attribute effects, we observed significant differences in the sender and receiver effects of gender. The sender effect of *Gender* was significantly positive, indicating that males tended to provide social support to others more frequently, while the receiver effect of *Gender* was significantly negative, meaning that females were more likely to receive social support from others. Additionally, we observed a positive and significant homophily effect of *Gender*, indicating that users of the same gender were more likely to form social relationships. Therefore, Hypothesis 2a was rejected, while Hypotheses 2b and 2c were supported. In terms of age-related attribute effects, we observed that the sender and receiver effects of *Age* were significantly positive, while the heterophily effect of *Age* was significantly negative. This indicated that compared to younger users, older users were not only more willing to actively provide social support but also received more social support from others. Additionally, users with closer ages were more likely to provide social support to each other. Therefore, Hypotheses 3a, H3b, and H3c were supported.

After integrating network structural effects and all actor attribute effects in Model 3, we observed a significant decrease in both the AIC and BIC values compared to previous models. This indicated that the full model accounting for users' online behavioral characteristics provided a better fit with the actual data. This highlighted the importance of users' online behavioral characteristics in influencing the formation of social relationships in the OHC.

The results for actor attribute effects of users' online emotional expression showed that the sender effect of *Sentiment* was significantly positive, but the receiver effect of *Sentiment* was significantly negative, suggesting that users with positive emotional tendencies online were more likely to provide social support, while those who tended to express negative emotions were more likely to receive social support. Additionally, the heterophily effect of *Sentiment* was significantly negative, indicating that users preferred to provide social support to fellow patients who expressed similar emotional valence. Therefore, Hypotheses 4a, 4b, and 4c were supported.

The results for actor attribute effects of users' online influence showed that the sender and receiver effects of *Influence* were both significantly positive, indicating that users with higher online influence were more willing to provide social support to others and received social support. Additionally, a significant and negative heterophily effect of *Influence* suggested that there was a greater probability of forming social support connections among patients with similar levels of online influence. Therefore, Hypotheses 5a and 5b were supported, while Hypothesis 5c was rejected.

The results for actor attribute effects of users' online duration indicated a significant positive sender effect of *Duration*, suggesting that experienced patients who had spent longer duration participating in the OHC were more likely to provide social support to others. However, the receiver effect and heterophily effect of *Duration* were both not statistically significant, indicating that there was no empirical evidence to conclude that the likelihood of users receiving social support was influenced by the duration of their engagement in the OHC. Similarly, there was no evidence supporting a correlation between the duration of online participation in health communities and mutual social support among users. Therefore, Hypothesis 6a was supported, while Hypotheses 6b and 6c were rejected.

In order to further explore the differences in factors influencing the formation of social relationships among users within the multiplex social network emerging from discussions on different topics, we employed the ERGMs to model the five topic-specific networks that were previously established. The model specifications for each of the five topic-specific networks remained consistent with the overall model developed earlier, incorporating the same network structural effects and actor attribute effects as employed in the overall network modeling process. The results of the parameter estimation for the five topic-specific networks were presented in Table 4.

Table 4. Parameter estimates for five topic-specific networks.

Parameter	Symptom	Treatment	Resource	Emotion	Friendship
Network structural effects					
Arc	−6.752 ***	−6.853 ***	−7.827 ***	−6.873 ***	−8.592 ***
Reciprocity	1.595 ***	2.425 ***	1.381 ***	1.685 ***	1.244 ***
Actor attribute effects					
Gender-Sender	0.430 ***	0.322 ***	0.378 ***	0.148 ***	0.403 ***
Gender-Receiver	−0.030	−0.060	0.177 ***	−0.248 ***	0.130 *
Gender-Homophily	0.052	0.054	−0.022	0.099 ***	0.009
Age-Sender	1.574 ***	2.356 ***	0.933 ***	1.161 ***	1.362 ***
Age-Receiver	0.813 ***	0.968 ***	0.580 ***	0.354 **	0.101
Age-Heterophily	−1.714 ***	−1.799 ***	−1.329 ***	−1.391 ***	−1.980 ***
Sentiment-Sender	0.747 ***	0.106	0.898 ***	1.326 ***	1.567 ***
Sentiment-Receiver	−1.348 ***	−1.396 ***	−0.688 ***	−0.372 ***	0.028
Sentiment-Heterophily	−1.233 ***	−1.611 ***	−1.407 ***	−1.265 ***	−0.435 **
Influence-Sender	6.969 ***	5.028 ***	7.701 ***	7.597 ***	6.993 ***
Influence-Receiver	11.142 ***	8.865 ***	11.046 ***	12.219 ***	11.342 ***
Influence-Heterophily	−7.219 ***	−5.616 ***	−7.525 ***	−7.404 ***	−7.257 ***
Duration-Sender	1.790 ***	1.713 ***	2.341 ***	2.567 ***	1.587 ***
Duration-Receiver	−1.731 ***	−2.004 ***	0.879 ***	−0.400 *	−0.805 ***
Duration-Heterophily	1.655 ***	1.543 ***	0.610 ***	0.262	1.800 ***
AIC	40,134	24,455	23,080	49,575	21,842
BIC	40,326	24,647	23,272	49,767	22,034

Note: ***, **, *, and no * represent $p < 0.001$, $p < 0.01$, $p < 0.05$, and $p < 0.1$, respectively. Approximate Wald Test was used (Parameter estimate is greater than two times the standard error in absolute value).

In terms of network structural effects, we found significant negative arc parameters and positive reciprocity parameters across the five topic-specific networks, aligning with the overall network parameter estimates. Consequently, we focused on analyzing how individual attributes, such as user demographics and online behavior, impacted the formation of network relationships across these various topic-specific networks.

The parameter estimates shown in Table 4 regarding actor attribute effects on the five topic-specific networks revealed some distinct differences in these effects among diverse networks, despite the general consistency observed for most actor attribute effects across these networks. The significant differences were found in the following aspects: (1) Gender effects. In terms of receiver effects of gender, the *Emotion* network was the only one that showed a significant negative effect, aligning with the overall network. Conversely, in the *Resource* and *Friendship* networks, the receiver effects of gender were significantly positive, while they were not significant in the *Symptom* and *Treatment* networks. As for the homophily effects of gender, only the *Emotion* network exhibited a significant positive effect, aligning with the overall network, whereas the other four topic-specific networks did not show statistically significant gender homophily effects. (2) Age effects. In terms of the receiver effects of age, positive and significant effects were found in all topic-specific networks, aligning with the overall network, except the *Friendship* networks where the receiver effect of age did not show significance. (3) The effects of online emotional expression. We identified two areas where certain networks differed significantly from others. The first was in the *Treatment* network, where the sender effect of online emotional expression lacked statistical significance, and the second was in the *Friendship* network, where the receiver effect of online emotional expression was also not statistically significant. (4) The effects of online duration. In terms of the receiver effects of online duration, the Resource network was the only one that demonstrated a significant positive effect, whereas the remaining four networks showed significant negative effects. Additionally, positive and significant heterophily effects of online duration were found in all topic-specific networks except the *Emotion* network where the heterophily effect did not show significance.

Based on the above analysis, we can conclude that users' individual attributes, including demographic factors like gender and age, as well as online behavioral characteristics such as emotional expression and engagement duration, have significant differences in their impacts on the formation of social relationships within multiplex social networks formed through discussions on various health topics.

We conducted additional analyses to determine whether cross-network effects occur when patients discuss various health topics and establish multiple social networks. Our examination focused on two categories of cross-network effects within the multiplex social network in the OHC: entrainment effects and exchange effects. In this modeling specifications, we expanded upon the baseline Model 1, which only accounted for network structural effects, by incorporating entrainment effects and exchange effects as the specific cross-network effects of interest. The results are summarized in Table 5.

The results for entrainment effects revealed that there were significant and positive entrainment effects between any two of the five health-related topic-specific networks, indicating that multiple types of relationships within the multiplex topic-specific network tended to align with each other. When one patient started discussing a particular health topic, he or she was also likely to engage in discussions on other health topics, providing multi-dimensional social support simultaneously. Therefore, Hypothesis 7 was supported.

In addition, the results for exchange effects revealed that there were significant and positive exchange effects between any two of the five health-related topic-specific networks, meaning that individuals providing social support to fellow patients in one topic-specific network were more likely to receive reciprocal support from the same patients in other topic-specific networks. These cross-network exchange effects indicated that patients tended to reciprocate support across diverse health topics, thereby developing diverse social relationships within the OHC. These findings emphasized the interconnected and reciprocal nature of multiplex social topic-specific networks in OHCs. Thus, Hypothesis 8 was supported.

Table 5. ERGM estimates of cross-network effects for two topic-specific networks.

Cross-Network Effects	Entrainment Effect			Exchange Effect		
	Estimate	SE	t-Ratio	Estimate	SE	t-Ratio
Symptom—Treatment	4.335 *	0.064	0.026	0.787 *	0.121	0.058
Symptom—Resource	3.944 *	0.064	0.03	0.548 *	0.097	0.023
Symptom—Emotion	4.125 *	0.043	0.027	0.679 *	0.077	0.064
Symptom—Friendship	3.901 *	0.069	0.086	1.155 *	0.097	−0.062
Treatment—Resource	3.376 *	0.082	−0.039	0.750 *	0.112	−0.044
Treatment—Emotion	3.732 *	0.063	0.056	0.622 *	0.091	0.055
Treatment—Friendship	3.344 *	0.081	0.09	0.851 *	0.122	−0.025
Resource—Emotion	4.110 *	0.052	0.044	1.117 *	0.082	−0.009
Resource—Friendship	3.849 *	0.068	0.098	1.238 *	0.112	−0.004
Emotion—Friendship	3.855 *	0.066	0.062	1.305 *	0.085	0.009

Note: SE = standard error. Effects with * are significant using the Approximate Wald test (Parameter estimate is greater than two times the standard error in absolute value).

We further conducted goodness-of-fit tests to examine whether the ERGMs in this study fitted the actual network well. Specifically, we focused on four key graph features of directed networks: the distributions of out-degree, in-degree, shared partner distributions, and geodesic distances representing the pairwise shortest distances between the nodes. The results are presented in Figure 2, where four plots are employed to assess the quality of fit for the four network statistics. In each plot, the solid line represents a given network statistic from the observed network and the boxplots represent the same statistic from the 100 simulated networks including the median and interquartile range, while the gray lines indicate the 95% confidence interval of simulated network measures. As illustrated in Figure 2, the goodness of fit for the four network statistics revealed a lack of significant difference between the actual and simulated networks, indicating that the ERGMs applied in our study effectively captured the characteristics of the observed data.

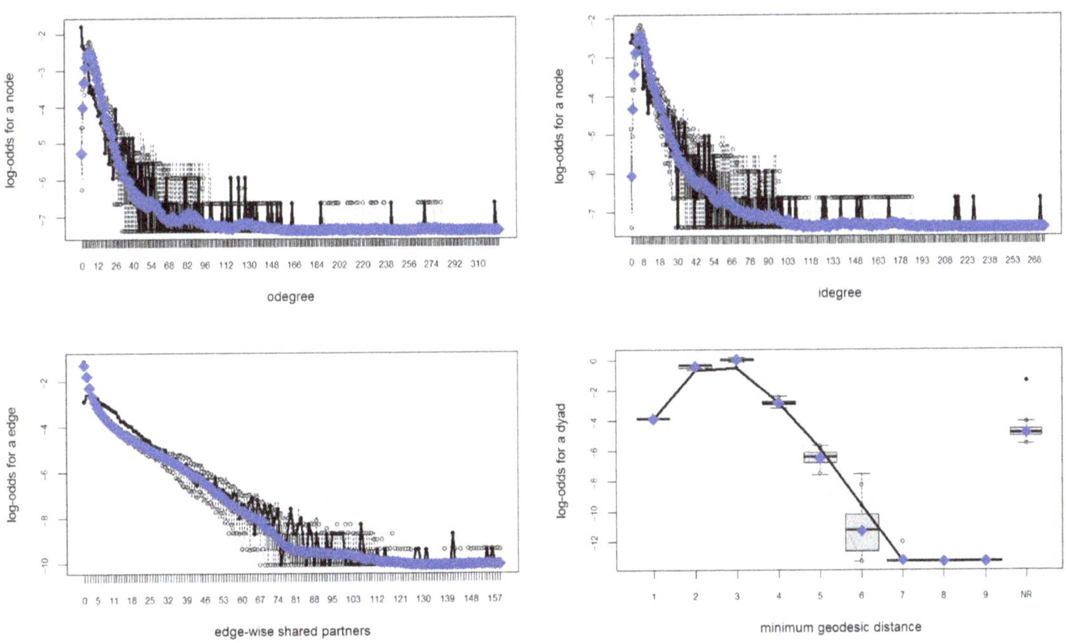

Figure 2. Goodness-of-fit plots for the ERGMs.

5. Conclusions

In recent years, social network analysis methods have been widely developed and applied in various fields, including online social networks in OHCs. However, due to the complexity of the formation of social networks, it remains challenging to fully understand how patients' individual characteristics and online behaviors impact the development of these networks in the healthcare field. In particular, users participating in OHCs often focus on different health-related topics based on their unique interests and participation purposes, resulting in multiplex social topic-specific networks. Further research is necessary to examine whether the factors that influence the formation of various types of social relationships in multiple social networks are different and explore whether there are certain interconnections between various types of social relationships in multiplex social networks.

To address these issues, this study employed an exponential random graph model to model the multiplex social networks within OHCs. Through empirical research, some valuable findings were obtained: (1) Firstly, we discovered that patients' demographic attributes, such as age and gender, along with their online behavioral features, including online influence, emotional expression, and participation duration, significantly impacted the formation of social relationships within the OHC. (2) Moreover, our further investigation revealed that these patients' characteristics had significantly different effects on the formation of various types of social relationships within the multiple social networks created by patients participating in different topic discussions in the OHC. (3) Additionally, we found that there were significant cross-network effects within the multiplex social networks in the OHC. These cross-network effects included both the entrainment effects and exchange effects, indicating strong interdependencies between the formation of these different topic-specific networks.

This research makes several theoretical contributions and have practical implications in the field of social network analysis. This study contributes to the development of social network analysis theories and provides valuable guidance for future research on the formation process of online healthcare social networks. We conducted a comprehensive investigation into the formation of multiplex topic-specific networks in OHCs, exploring the specific factors that influence the development of diverse social connections within these networks and examining the interconnectedness and interdependencies of different types of social relationships within these networks. These theoretical explorations provide valuable insights into understanding the complexities and underlying mechanisms of multiplex online social networks. Our findings have valuable implications for the designers and administrators of online healthcare platforms. They provide valuable insights into the complexity and interconnectedness of multiplex healthcare social networks, enabling a deeper understanding of patient characteristics and their role in creating multiplex topic-specific networks. These insights can help platform designers and managers to better serve users and promote the improved development of online healthcare social networks.

This study has some limitations that require further discussion. Firstly, it is important to note that the inferences drawn from the statistical analysis in this paper are limited to the specific patient population within this OHC. Given that the data were not collected through a proper random mechanism, the generalizability of our findings beyond this population is constrained. Secondly, we only focused on one specific disease forum as the source of experimental research data. Due to the significant differences in symptoms, treatments, and patient experiences across various diseases, health topics related to these diseases also vary significantly, resulting in distinctly different social networks formed around these topics. Therefore, the findings of this study may not be directly applicable to healthcare social networks related to other diseases. To conduct differential analysis and make more accurate and generalizable conclusions about the features of online healthcare social networks, further data collection from online health forums focusing on other diseases is necessary to understand how online healthcare social networks differ across different diseases. Lastly, in our examination of how user demographic attributes impact the formation of online healthcare social networks, we only considered a limited set of demographic attributes like gender and age. It is possible that other important attributes, including geographic location, health conditions, and the level of health literacy, could have a significant influence on network formation and the subsequent analysis of multiplex topic-specific networks. Further investigation and identification of these significant attributes are needed for future studies.

Author Contributions: Conceptualization, Y.L.; methodology, H.Z.; validation, X.W., L.S. and H.Z.; resources, X.W.; data curation, H.Z. and L.S.; writing—original draft preparation, X.W.; writing—review and editing, Y.L.; visualization, X.W.; supervision, Y.L.; project administration, Y.L.; funding acquisition, Y.L. All authors have read and agreed to the published version of the manuscript.

Funding: This research was funded by the National Social Science Fund of China, grant number 20BTQ080, and the Funds for First-Class Discipline Construction, grant number XK1802-5.

Data Availability Statement: The data used to support the findings of this study are available from the corresponding author upon request.

Conflicts of Interest: The authors declare no conflict of interest.

References

1. Rains, S.A.; Peterson, E.B.; Wright, K.B. Communicating Social Support in Computer-mediated Contexts: A Meta-analytic Review of Content Analyses Examining Support Messages Shared Online among Individuals Coping with Illness. *Commun. Monogr.* **2015**, *82*, 403–430. [CrossRef]
2. Leimeister, J.M.; Schweizer, K.; Leimeister, S.; Krcmar, H. Do virtual communities matter for the social support of patients? *Inf. Technol. People* **2013**, *21*, 350–374. [CrossRef]
3. Coulson, N.S.; Bullock, E.; Rodham, K. Exploring the Therapeutic Affordances of Self-Harm Online Support Communities: An Online Survey of Members. *JMIR Ment. Health* **2017**, *4*, e44. [CrossRef] [PubMed]
4. Deng, Z.; Mo, X.; Liu, S. Comparison of the middle-aged and older users' adoption of mobile health services in China. *Int. J. Med. Inform.* **2014**, *83*, 210–224. [CrossRef]
5. Dickerson, S.S. Women's Use of the Internet: What Nurses Need to Know. *J. Obstet. Gynecol. Neonatal Nurs.* **2010**, *35*, 151–156. [CrossRef]
6. Bi, Q.; Shen, L.; Evans, R.; Zhang, Z.; Dai, W. Determining the Topic Evolution and Sentiment Polarity for Albinism in a Chinese Online Health Community: Machine Learning and Social Network Analysis. *JMIR Med. Inform.* **2020**, *8*, e17813. [CrossRef]
7. Ziebland, S.; Chapple, A.; Dumelow, C.; Evans, J.; Rozmovits, L. How the internet affects patients' experience of cancer: A qualitative study. *BMJ* **2004**, *328*, 564. [CrossRef]
8. Swan, M. Emerging Patient-Driven Health Care Models: An Examination of Health Social Networks, Consumer Personalized Medicine and Quantified Self-Tracking. *Int. J. Environ. Res. Public Health* **2009**, *6*, 492–525. [CrossRef]
9. Eijk, M.V.D.; Faber, M.J.; Aarts, J.W.; Kremer, J.A.; Bloem, B.R. Using Online Health Communities to Deliver Patient-Centered Care to People With Chronic Conditions. *J. Med. Internet Res.* **2013**, *15*, e115. [CrossRef]
10. Willis, E. The making of expert patients: The role of online health communities in arthritis self-management. *J. Health Psychol.* **2013**, *19*, 1613–1625. [CrossRef]
11. Ma, D.; Zuo, M.; Liu, L. The Information Needs of Chinese Family members of Cancer Patients in the Online Health Community: What and Why? *Inf. Process. Manag.* **2021**, *58*, 102517. [CrossRef]
12. Wang, T.-H.; Zhou, X.-F.; Ni, Y.; Pan, Z.-G. Health information needs regarding diabetes mellitus in China: An internet-based analysis. *BMC Public Health* **2020**, *20*, 990. [CrossRef] [PubMed]
13. Lu, Y.; Wu, Y.; Liu, J.; Li, J.; Zhang, P. Understanding Health Care Social Media Use From Different Stakeholder Perspectives: A Content Analysis of an Online Health Community. *J. Med. Internet Res.* **2017**, *19*, e109. [CrossRef] [PubMed]
14. Little, M.; Wicks, P.; Vaughan, T.; Pentland, A. Quantifying Short-Term Dynamics of Parkinson's Disease Using Self-Reported Symptom Data From an Internet Social Network. *J. Med. Internet Res.* **2013**, *15*, e20. [CrossRef]
15. Eichhorn, K.C. Soliciting and Providing Social Support Over the Internet: An Investigation of Online Eating Disorder Support Groups. *J. Comput. Mediat. Commun.* **2008**, *14*, 67–78. [CrossRef]
16. Nath, C.; Huh, J.; Adupa, A.K.; Jonnalagadda, S.R. Website Sharing in Online Health Communities: A Descriptive Analysis. *J. Med. Internet Res.* **2016**, *18*, e11. [CrossRef]
17. Buis, L.R. Emotional and Informational Support Messages in an Online Hospice Support Community. *Comput. Inform. Nurs. CIN* **2008**, *26*, 358. [CrossRef]
18. Park, A.; Conway, M. Longitudinal Changes in Psychological States in Online Health Community Members: Understanding the Long-Term Effects of Participating in an Online Depression Community. *J. Med. Internet Res.* **2017**, *19*, e71. [CrossRef]
19. Wang, L.W.; Liu, X.; Li, J. The Establishment of Friendship Ties in the Online Health Forum Based on Exponential Random Graph Model. In Proceedings of the 2016 Pacific Asia Conference on Information Systems, Chiayi City, Taiwan, 27 June–1 July 2016.

20. Li, Y.; Yan, X. How Could Peers in Online Health Community Help Improve Health Behavior. *Int. J. Environ. Res. Public Health* **2020**, *17*, 2995. [CrossRef]
21. Wang, X.; Zhao, K.; Street, N. Analyzing and Predicting User Participations in Online Health Communities: A Social Support Perspective. *J. Med. Internet Res.* **2017**, *19*, e130. [CrossRef]
22. Stewart Loane, S.; Webster, C.M.; D'Alessandro, S. Identifying Consumer Value Co-created through Social Support within Online Health Communities. *J. Macromarketing* **2014**, *35*, 353–367. [CrossRef]
23. Dang-Pham, D.; Pittayachawan, S.; Bruno, V. Applying network analysis to investigate interpersonal influence of information security behaviours in the workplace. *Inf. Manag.* **2017**, *54*, 625–637. [CrossRef]
24. Robins, G.; Snijders, T.; Wang, P.; Handcock, M.; Pattison, P. Recent developments in exponential random graph (p*) models for social networks. *Soc. Netw.* **2007**, *29*, 192–215. [CrossRef]
25. Robins, G.; Pattison, P.; Kalish, Y.; Lusher, D. An introduction to exponential random graph (p*) models for social networks. *Soc. Netw.* **2007**, *29*, 173–191. [CrossRef]
26. Caimo, A.; Gollini, I. A multilayer exponential random graph modelling approach for weighted networks. *Comput. Stat. Data Anal.* **2020**, *142*, 106825. [CrossRef]
27. Koskinen, J.; Broccatelli, C.; Wang, P.; Robins, G. Bayesian analysis of ERG models for multilevel, multiplex, and multilayered networks with sampled or missing data. In *New Statistical Developments in Data Science*; Springer Proceedings in Mathematics & Statistics; Springer: Berlin/Heidelberg, Germany, 2019; Volume 288, pp. 105–117.
28. Todd, N.R.; Blevins, E.J.; Yi, J. A Social Network Analysis of Friendship and Spiritual Support in a Religious Congregation. *Am. J. Community Psychol.* **2019**, *65*, 107–124. [CrossRef]
29. Lusher, D.; Koskinen, J.; Robins, G. *Exponential Random Graph Models for Social Networks: Theory, Methods and Applications*; Cambridge University Press: Cambridge, UK, 2013.
30. Xu, R.; Zhang, Q. Understanding Online Health Groups for Depression: Social Network and Linguistic Perspectives. *J. Med. Internet Res.* **2016**, *18*, e63. [CrossRef]
31. Yang, H.; Du, H.S.; Wang, L.; Wu, T. The Influence of Social Support Networks on Health Conditions Via User Engagement: Gender as a Moderator. *J. Electron. Commer. Res.* **2019**, *20*, 35–54.
32. Thompson, A.E.; Anisimowicz, Y.; Miedema, B.; Hogg, W.; Wodchis, W.P.; Aubrey-Bassler, K. The influence of gender and other patient characteristics on health care-seeking behaviour: A QUALICOPC study. *BMC Fam. Pract.* **2016**, *17*, 38. [CrossRef]
33. Chai, S.; Das, S.; Rao, H.R. Factors Affecting Bloggers' Knowledge Sharing: An Investigation Across Gender. *J. Manag. Inf. Syst.* **2014**, *28*, 309–342. [CrossRef]
34. Lieberman, M.A. Gender and online cancer support groups: Issues facing male cancer patients. *J. Cancer Educ. Off. J. Am. Assoc. Cancer Educ.* **2008**, *23*, 167–171.
35. Matud, M.P. Gender differences in stress and coping styles. *Personal. Individ. Differ.* **2004**, *37*, 1401–1415. [CrossRef]
36. Mackenzie, C.S.; Gekoski, W.L.; Knox, V.J. Age, gender, and the underutilization of mental health services: The influence of help-seeking attitudes. *Aging Ment. Health* **2006**, *10*, 574–582. [CrossRef] [PubMed]
37. Li, L.; Ding, H.; Li, Z. Does Internet Use Impact the Health Status of Middle-Aged and Older Populations? Evidence from China Health and Retirement Longitudinal Study (CHARLS). *Int. J. Environ. Res. Public Health* **2022**, *19*, 3619. [CrossRef] [PubMed]
38. Setoyama, Y.; Yamazaki, Y.; Namayama, K. Benefits of Peer Support in Online Japanese Breast Cancer Communities: Differences Between Lurkers and Posters. *J. Med. Internet Res.* **2011**, *13*, e122. [CrossRef]
39. Liu, J.; Liu, Y. Exploring the User Interaction Network in an Anxiety Disorder Online Community: An Exponential Random Graph Model with Topical and Emotional Effects. *Int. J. Environ. Res. Public Health* **2022**, *19*, 6354. [CrossRef]
40. Nambisan, P. Information seeking and social support in online health communities: Impact on patients' perceived empathy. *J. Am. Med. Inform. Assoc.* **2011**, *18*, 298–304. [CrossRef]
41. Lu, Y.; Luo, S.; Liu, X. Development of Social Support Networks by Patients With Depression Through Online Health Communities: Social Network Analysis. *JMIR Med. Inform.* **2021**, *9*, e24618. [CrossRef]
42. Mustafa, S.; Zhang, W. Why Do I Share? Participants' Personality Traits and Online Participation. *Int. J. Hum.–Comput. Interact.* 2023; 1–19. [CrossRef]
43. Yan, L.; Tan, Y. Feeling Blue? Go Online: An Empirical Study of Social Support Among Patients. *Inf. Syst. Res.* **2014**, *25*, 690–709. [CrossRef]
44. Song, X.; Yan, X.; Li, Y. Modelling liking networks in an online healthcare community: An exponential random graph model analysis approach. *J. Inf. Sci.* **2014**, *41*, 89–96. [CrossRef]
45. Batenburg, A.; Das, E. Emotional Approach Coping and the Effects of Online Peer-Led Support Group Participation Among Patients With Breast Cancer: A Longitudinal Study. *J. Med. Internet Res.* **2014**, *16*, e256. [CrossRef] [PubMed]
46. Zhou, T. Understanding users' participation in online health communities: A social capital perspective. *Inf. Dev.* **2019**, *36*, 403–413. [CrossRef]
47. Kim, H.-S.; Shyam Sundar, S. Can online buddies and bandwagon cues enhance user participation in online health communities? *Comput. Hum. Behav.* **2014**, *37*, 319–333. [CrossRef]
48. Heaney, M.T. Multiplex networks and interest group influence reputation: An exponential random graph model. *Soc. Netw.* **2014**, *36*, 66–81. [CrossRef]

49. Krivitsky, P.N.; Coletti, P.; Hens, N. A Tale of Two Datasets: Representativeness and Generalisability of Inference for Samples of Networks. *J. Am. Stat. Assoc.* **2022**, 1–11. [CrossRef]
50. Bianchi, F.; Casnici, N.; Squazzoni, F. Solidarity as a byproduct of professional collaboration: Social support and trust in a coworking space. *Soc. Netw.* **2018**, *54*, 61–72. [CrossRef]
51. Krivitsky, P.N.; Koehly, L.; Marcum, C.S. Exponential-Family Random Graph Models for Multi-Layer Networks. *Psychometrika* **2020**, *85*, 630–659. [CrossRef]
52. Lusher, D.; Robins, G.; Pattison, P.E.; Lomi, A. "Trust Me": Differences in expressed and perceived trust relations in an organization. *Soc. Netw.* **2012**, *34*, 410–424. [CrossRef]
53. Liu, X.; Sun, M.; Li, J. Research on gender differences in online health communities. *Int. J. Med. Inform.* **2018**, *111*, 172–181. [CrossRef]
54. Chung, J.E. Social Networking in Online Support Groups for Health: How Online Social Networking Benefits Patients. *J. Health Commun.* **2013**, *19*, 639–659. [CrossRef]
55. Yan, Z.; Wang, T.; Chen, Y.; Zhang, H. Knowledge sharing in online health communities: A social exchange theory perspective. *Inf. Manag.* **2016**, *53*, 643–653. [CrossRef]
56. Sinha, A.; Porter, T.; Wilson, A. The Use of Online Health Forums by Patients With Chronic Cough: Qualitative Study. *J. Med. Internet Res.* **2018**, *20*, e19. [CrossRef]
57. Zhang, X.; Liu, S.; Deng, Z.; Chen, X. Knowledge sharing motivations in online health communities: A comparative study of health professionals and normal users. *Comput. Hum. Behav.* **2017**, *75*, 797–810. [CrossRef]
58. Blei, D.M.; Ng, A.Y.; Jordan, M.I. Latent Dirichlet Allocation. *J. Mach. Learn. Res.* **2003**, *3*, 993–1022.
59. Hirsch, J.E. An index to quantify an individual's scientific research output. *Proc. Natl. Acad. Sci. USA* **2005**, *102*, 16569–16572. [CrossRef] [PubMed]
60. Pattison, D.P.; Wasserman, S. Logit models and logistic regressions for social networks: II. Multivariate relations. *Br. J. Math. Stat. Psychol.* **1999**, *52*, 169–193. [CrossRef]

mathematics

MDPI

Article

Research on Short-Term Passenger Flow Prediction of LSTM Rail Transit Based on Wavelet Denoising

Qingliang Zhao, Xiaobin Feng, Liwen Zhang and Yiduo Wang *

School of Economics and Management, Beijing University of Chemical Technology, Beijing 100029, China; zhaoql@mail.buct.edu.cn (Q.Z.); 2021201301@buct.edu.cn (X.F.); 13163175122@163.com (L.Z.)
* Correspondence: wangyd@mail.buct.edu.cn

Abstract: Urban rail transit offers advantages such as high safety, energy efficiency, and environmental friendliness. With cities rapidly expanding, travelers are increasingly using rail systems, heightening demands for passenger capacity and efficiency while also pressuring these networks. Passenger flow forecasting is an essential part of transportation systems. Short-term passenger flow forecasting for rail transit can estimate future station volumes, providing valuable data to guide operations management and mitigate congestion. This paper investigates short-term forecasting for Suzhou's Shantang Street station. Shantang Street's high commercial presence and distinct weekday versus weekend ridership patterns make it an interesting test case, making it a representative subway station. Wavelet denoising and Long Short Term Memory (LSTM) were combined to predict short-term flows, comparing the results to those of standalone LSTM, Support Vector Regression (SVR), Artificial Neural Network (ANN), and Autoregressive Integrated Moving Average Model (ARIMA). This study illustrates that the algorithms adopted exhibit good performance for passenger prediction. The LSTM model with wavelet denoising proved most accurate, demonstrating applicability for short-term rail transit forecasting and practical significance. The research findings can provide fundamental recommendations for implementing appropriate passenger flow control measures at stations and offer effective references for predicting passenger flow and mitigating traffic pressure in various cities.

Keywords: rail transit short-term passenger flow prediction; LSTM; wavelet denoising analysis; SVR

MSC: 03-08; 03-11; 65J08; 68U99; 97N80; 97P40

1. Introduction

The modern development of the city constantly promotes the rapid growth of traffic demand [1]. Urban rail transit, as an important part of urban public transportation, is greatly significant for improving urban passenger flow and transportation efficiency, as well as alleviating traffic congestion. Scientific passenger flow prediction plays an extremely important role in feasibility studies for urban rail transit, layout planning of urban rail transit networks, and decision-making around urban rail transit construction scales and levels. On the one hand, it is conducive to dredging passengers, rationally arranging the flow lines of passengers in the station, and improving the quality of passenger flow organization. On the other hand, it helps the urban transportation system take timely response measures and ensure public safety [2,3].

Short-time passenger flow forecasting is a dynamic control method that mainly forecasts passenger flow in the future based on existing passenger flow data [4]. The research on the traditional forecasting model of rail transit passenger flow is quite mature. The passenger flow prediction models of rail transit mainly include time series models, regression models, and some related linear and nonlinear models. Roos [5] proposed a dynamic Bayesian network approach to forecast the short-term passenger flows of the urban rail network of Paris, which could deal with the incompleteness of the data caused by failures or a lack of collection systems. Zhao [6] used a support vector machine to predict the passenger flow of Xinzhuang subway station and concluded that the nonlinear support vector machine model can predict the working day better. Anl [7] developed a long short-term memory-based (LTSM-based) deep learning model to predict short-term transit passenger volume on transport routes in Istanbul using a dataset that included the number of people who used different transit routes at a one-hour interval between January and December 2020 and compared that with popular models such as random forest (RF), support vector machines, autoregressive integrated moving average, multilayer perceptron, and convolutional neural networks. Taking the passenger flow of Chengdu East Railway Station as an example, Tan [8] verified the higher prediction accuracy and better prediction performance of the GRNN neural network model based on parameter optimization (GA) compared with other models. Pekel [9] developed two hybrid forecasting methods, POA-ANN and IWD-ANN, to forecast passenger demand, compared the forecasting results with GA-ANN, and concluded that the new algorithm had a good effect on passenger prediction.

In order to improve prediction accuracy, many scholars have studied the application of neural networks and combined models to short-term passenger flow prediction. Alghamdi [10] proposed an end-to-end deep learning-based framework with a novel architecture to predict multi-step-ahead real-time travel demand along with uncertainty estimation. Asce [11] presented a novel nonparametric dynamic time-delay recurrent wavelet neural network model for forecasting traffic flow that exploited the concept of wavelet in the model to provide flexibility and extra adaptable translation parameters in the traffic flow forecasting model. Nagaraj [12] used a greedy layer-wise algorithm to enter the processed cluster data into the long- and short-term memory models and a recurrent neural network to solve the passenger flow prediction problem in public transport. Ermagun [13] examined spatiotemporal dependency between traffic links, proposed a two-step algorithm to search and identify the best look-back time window for upstream links, and indicated the best look-back time window depends on the travel time between two study detectors. Dong [14] used a genetic algorithm to optimize the BP model, which significantly improved the prediction accuracy of short-term passenger flow on Beijing Line 4. Mirzahossein [15] proposed a novel hybrid method based on deep learning to estimate short-term traffic volume at three adjacent intersections, combined with a time window and normal distribution of WND-LSTM for traffic flow prediction, and the MAPE obtained was 60–90% lower than that of ARIMA, LR, and other models.

The current research primarily focuses on the global prediction of passenger flow for all stations or the entire subway line. However, there is a lack of sufficient precise prediction research that takes into account the specific characteristics of individual stations. Furthermore, there are a limited number of prediction models available for comparison, and the existing models do not achieve a high level of accuracy. In general, the accuracy of passenger flow prediction is greatly influenced by the changing trends observed in previous data. Therefore, it is crucial to conduct a detailed analysis of the characteristics of subway stations and evaluate multiple prediction models to enhance the accuracy and effectiveness of the predictions [16]. The combination of wavelet denoising and the LSTM model in this study has several benefits and innovations. Wavelet denoising enhances data quality by reducing noise interference, while the LSTM model effectively handles the time-series relationships and dynamic characteristics of non-stationary data. For complex AFC data, by combining them and comparing them with other related models, the future trend of non-stationary data can be predicted more accurately, and the accuracy and stability of prediction results can be improved. In addition, this method is innovative and provides a new idea and solution for the prediction and analysis of non-stationary data related to subway passenger flow. Different suitable models are selected for different types of stations to predict. Based on the cluster analysis of subway stations, this paper carries out detailed prediction analysis for typical stations. This paper examines Shantang Street station in Suzhou, chosen for its high commercial nature and weekday/weekend passenger differences. Wavelet denoising processed the short-term flow data, which an LSTM model used to predict volumes versus standalone LSTM, SVR, ANN, and ARIMA. The wavelet-denoised LSTM model [17–19] significantly improved accuracy, indicating effectiveness for real-world rail transit forecasting.

2. Research Methods

2.1. Wavelet Denoising Analysis

2.1.1. Principle of Wavelet Denoising Analysis

Wavelet denoising analysis [20–22] has been successfully utilized in many fields. Due to the irregularity of short-term passenger flow data at stations, the prediction error for short-term rail transit passenger flow may be substantial.

The short-term passenger flow data of rail transit stations fluctuates constantly, with a certain level of noise. High-frequency signals can be denoised through threshold values, and then data can be reconstructed to achieve denoising. The traffic signal for short-term traffic volume containing noise can be formulated as follows:

$$S(x) = f(x) + \sigma e(x) \tag{1}$$

$f(x)$: data after noise removal
$e(x)$: contained noise
σ: noise intensity
$S(x)$: short-term passenger flow data of rail transit with noise signal

2.1.2. Wavelet Denoising Process

The basic process of wavelet denoising analysis is shown in Figure 1 below:

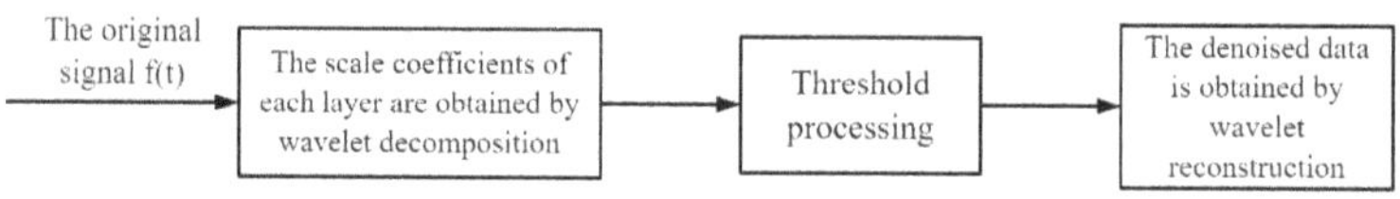

Figure 1. Flow chart of wavelet denoising.

Therefore, when utilizing wavelet denoising to analyze short-term passenger flow data for rail transit, it can be simplified into five processes: selecting the wavelet function, wavelet base order, threshold function, decomposition layer, and wavelet reconstruction.

2.2. Basic Principles of Long Term Memory Networks

2.2.1. LSTM Process

The LSTM neural network [23] has four structures: forgetting gate, input gate, output gate, and memory unit. The cell structure of the unit is controlled through the forgetting and input gates. The LSTM process is (Figure 2):

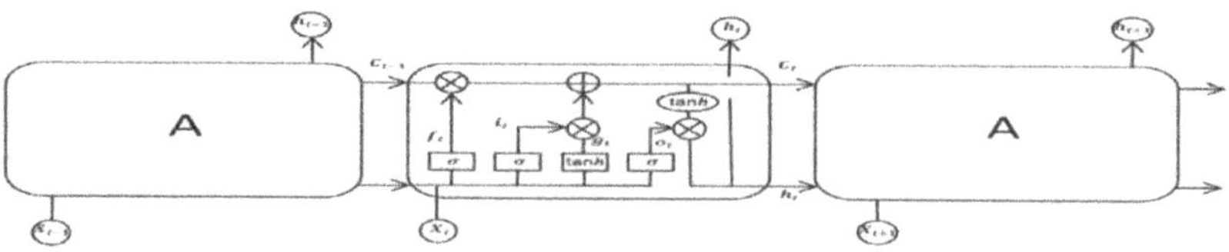

Figure 2. LSTM process structure diagram.

The arrows in the figure above represent vectors, showing input from the previous node to the node the arrows point to. LSTM controls information flow through three gate structures, consisting of sigmoid activation functions and a multiplicative structure with an output of 0 or 1. The sigmoid activation function in the gate is Equations (2) and (3), with the tanh functions being (4) and (5).

$$\sigma(z) = y = \frac{1}{1+e^{-z}} \tag{2}$$

$$\sigma'(z) = y(1-y) \tag{3}$$

$$tanh(z) = y = \frac{e^z - e^{-z}}{e^z + e^{-z}} \tag{4}$$

$$tanh'(z) = 1 - y^2 \tag{5}$$

C_{t-1}: The cell state passed in at the previous time.

x_t: The new value of information that is read at the present moment causes the module to generate a new memory.

h_{t-1}: The output value of the previously hidden neuron module.

C_t: Belongs to the current time output information, to the next time transmitted unit state.

h_t: New output at the current time.

2.2.2. Calculation of LSTM Forward Propagation

The LSTM forward propagation calculation process is from the forgetting gate to the input gate, updating the unit state, and finally to the output gate [24].

The forgetting gate determines how much information can be retained from the previous moment to the current one. After h_{t-1} and x_t are activated by activation function, f_t is obtained, representing the degree of retention of the previous hidden neuron state. The activation function is sigma, with the f_t expression being:

$$f_t = \sigma(W_f h_{t-1} + U_f x_t + b_f) \tag{6}$$

W_f: Represents the weight of the input forgetting gate of the previous hidden neuron module.

U_f: The information value of the input layer flows into the weight of the forgetting gate.

b_f: Calculate the bias parameters of the forgetting door.

The input gate determines how much information will be received and can determine the new information generated and what percentage of the new information will be used. The calculation process is as follows:

$$i_t = \sigma(W_i[h_{t-1}, x_t] + b_i) \tag{7}$$

$$\widetilde{C}_t = tanh(W_c[h_{t-1}, x_t] + b_c) \tag{8}$$

After passing through the input gate, the output of the input gate is: $i_t \times C_t$.

The updating of memory cell state means that the output f_t of the forgetting gate is multiplied by the cell state C_{t-1} at the previous time and combined with the output of the input gate to obtain a new cell state C_t. The expression of C_t is as follows:

$$C_t = f_t \times C_{t-1} + i_t \times \widetilde{C}_t \tag{9}$$

Finally, we need to go through the output door, which is composed of two parts of calculation, partly by the current information combined with short-term memory thus calculated, and o_t, another part is calculated combined with long-term memory and concluded h_t, o_t by the module of a hidden neurons on the output value of h_{t-1} combined with the current input value x_t and activated by sigma function. The calculation process is as follows:

$$o_t = \sigma(W_o[h_{t-1}, x_t] + b_o) \tag{10}$$

The final output after LSTM model is as follows:

$$h_t = o_t \circ (tanh((C_t)) \tag{11}$$

2.2.3. Reverse Calculation of LSTM

After LSTM model forward propagation, the weight set and relevant bias terms must be updated; therefore, reverse calculation can be performed by propagating the error up the layer.

2.3. Principles of Support Vector Machine Regression

The training samples of the SVR model [25–27] are D = $\{(x_1, y_1), (x_2, y_2)..., (x_n, y_n)\}$, with $y_i \in$R. The goal is to learn a model $f(x)$ with a value close to y. When model $f(x)$ exactly matches y, the final loss is 0. In the SVR model, the deviation between $f(x)$ and y is set at most to ε. When the difference between $f(x)$ and y is greater than ε, the loss is calculated; otherwise, the loss is ignored. This is equivalent to establishing a 2ε wide tolerance band centered on $f(x)$. The red horizontal line is the standard data cable. The two dashed lines in the figure represent the soft interval. The data between the soft interval is represented by a blue dot, and the data outside the soft interval is represented by a white dot. If sample data falls within the tolerance bands, the prediction is accurate, as shown (Figure 3):

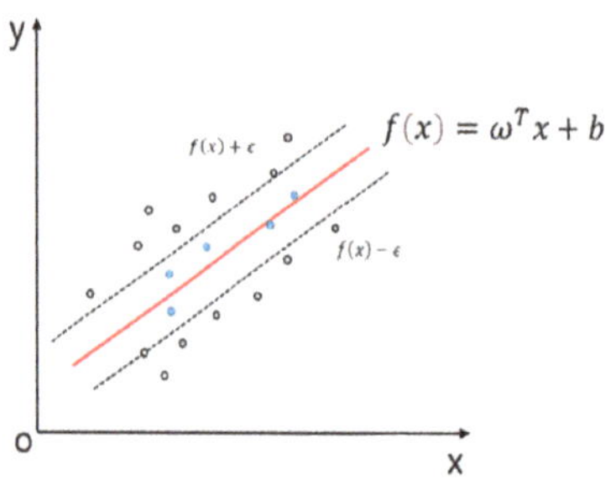

Figure 3. Support vector machine regression display.

Parameters involved in support vector machine (SVM) regression include ε and C. ε is the loss function and affects model precision and training speed. Parameter C is a penalty factor, aiming to balance the model. The smaller C means a lower model complexity and penalty. The choice of C should not be too large or small; otherwise, overfitting or underfitting may occur.

2.4. Principles of Artificial Neural Networks

An Artificial Neural Network (ANN) consists of an input layer, a hidden layer(s), and an output layer [28,29]. The state of the hidden layer remains unaffected by external factors; however, its state changes can lead to variations in the output. The back propagation algorithm is commonly utilized in ANN. It involves forward propagation, where the input layer is sequentially propagated through each layer, followed by back propagation, which adjusts the weights and related thresholds. This iterative process aims to minimize the error until the desired outcome is achieved. The calculation process is illustrated in the diagram [30] (Figure 4).

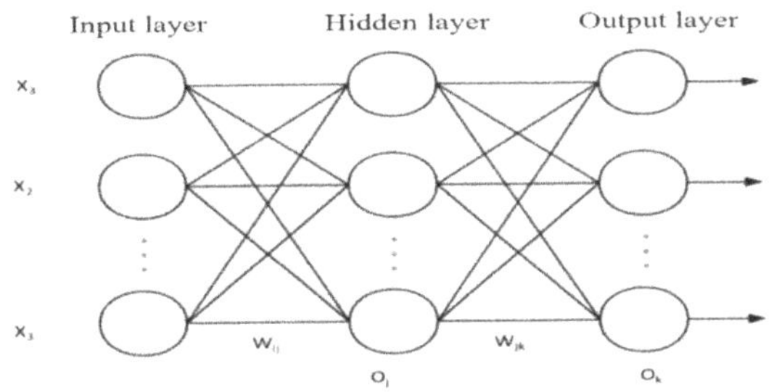

Figure 4. Flowchart of artificial neural network.

(1) Forward propagation process The output value of the input layer is denoted as O. The connection weights between the input layer and the hidden layer are represented as w_{ij}. The output value of the input layer is multiplied by the corresponding weights w_{ij}. The resulting values are then passed through an activation function, typically the sigmoid function, to obtain the output values of the hidden layer. This process is repeated for each subsequent layer until the output layer is reached [31].
(2) Backward propagation process The backward propagation process involves adjusting the parameters of the artificial neural network model to optimize its performance. The connection weights and cell thresholds are then modified accordingly to minimize the error. This adjustment is performed iteratively to refine the model's performance.
(3) Training termination conditions The training process can be terminated based on certain conditions. Once these conditions are met, the training process is concluded.

2.5. Basic Principles of Time Series Model

The ARIMA model is a statistical model used for analyzing and predicting time series data [32,33]. It is particularly effective in forecasting future values based on past observations and the autocorrelation within the series. The model consists of three main components: the autoregressive (AR) part, the differencing (I) part, and the moving average (MA) part. These components work together to capture the patterns and trends in the data, allowing for accurate predictions [34].

(1) Autoregressive Model (AR) The autoregressive model utilizes historical data to construct a predictive model for its own data. It is important to note that the autoregressive model assumes the data to be stationary. The formula for a p-order autoregressive model is as follows:

$$y_t = \mu + \sum_{m=1}^{p} r_m y_{t-m} + \varepsilon_t \quad (12)$$

y_t: The current value of the variable μ: Constant term p: Order γ_m: Autocorrelation coefficient ε_t: Residual

(2) Moving Average Model (MA) The moving average model utilizes the past values of the residual to represent the linear relationship, aiming to observe the magnitude of its fluctuations. The formula for a p-order moving average model is as follows:

$$y_t = \mu + \sum_{m=1}^{q} \theta_m \varepsilon_{t-m} + \varepsilon_t \quad (13)$$

(3) Auto-Regression and Moving Average Model (ARMA) The ARMA model combines the autoregressive (AR) model and the moving average (MA) model. It expresses the relationship between the current value and both past values and past residuals. The formula for the ARMA model is as follows:

$$y_t = \mu + \sum_{m=1}^{p} r_m y_{t-m} + \varepsilon_t + \sum_{m=1}^{q} \theta_m \varepsilon_{t-m} + \varepsilon_t \quad (14)$$

(4) Integrated (I) Before determining the parameters p and q in the ARIMA model, it is necessary to conduct a stationarity test on the data. If the data fails the test, differencing is performed. After differencing, the data should meet the stationarity condition.

3. Empirical Study

3.1. Data Preprocessing

This article examines short-term traffic predictions for the Shantang Street station of the Suzhou Rail Transit system. The AFC system data used in this article is collected from the automatic ticket machines at various stations in the rail transit system, which record the card swipes of people entering and exiting the stations. The data utilized in this study were obtained from the Suzhou Rail Transit AFC system and include transaction time, ticket ID and type, inbound and outbound station codes and names, and inbound and outbound times. The experiments in this article were conducted on a Windows 10 64-bit operating system. The hardware used includes an AMD Ryzen 7 5800H with a Radeon Graphics 3.20 GHz processor and 16 GB of memory. The programming language used is Python 3.7, and the Matplotlib 3.0.2 plotting tool was utilized for generating plots.

MySQL was used to clean the raw data. Relevant database rules were applied to extract the required information, resulting in over 14 million data points for the month of July that were used in this analysis. Given the high commercial nature and distinct weekday versus weekend ridership patterns, outbound passenger traffic from Shantang Street station was selected as the prediction target. The 1–27 July inbound passenger flow was used as the training set, while the 28–29 July (Monday and Sunday) data were held out as the test set. Based on the extracted swipe card data from Shantang Street station in MySQL, the inbound passenger flow at Shantang Street is calculated with a time interval of 1 h. Each column represents the inbound passenger flow at Shantang Street every hour throughout the day. The processed Shantang Street passenger flow data are summarized, and a portion of the hourly passenger flow data are shown in Table 1 below:

Table 1. Hourly passenger flow data for Shantang Street station (person/hour).

Time	Station	Monday	Tuesday	Wednesday	Thursday	Friday	Saturday	Sunday
5:00:00	Shantang Street	4	2	4	12	3	9	10
6:00:00	Shantang Street	220	235	203	250	237	198	133
7:00:00	Shantang Street	472	471	495	470	471	432	410
8:00:00	Shantang Street	519	491	467	543	491	601	513
9:00:00	Shantang Street	497	525	595	596	552	655	572
10:00:00	Shantang Street	461	538	537	531	516	583	656
18:00:00	Shantang Street	415	360	317	382	409	527	621
19:00:00	Shantang Street	391	396	400	425	466	640	636
20:00:00	Shantang Street	407	479	536	497	494	845	772
21:00:00	Shantang Street	306	365	371	431	463	703	551
22:00:00	Shantang Street	77	81	129	94	149	100	171

3.2. LSTM Model Construction and Prediction Analysis

The training dataset for the LSTM network consists of the inbound passenger flow data at Shantang Street for the month of July. The objective is to predict the outbound passenger flow at Shantang Street. The training set includes the inbound passenger flow data from 1–27 July, while the test set comprises the inbound passenger flow data from 28–29 July (which corresponds to Monday and Sunday). The LSTM model is trained on each subset, and the validation subset is used to evaluate the model's performance. According to the size of the passenger flow data set and the limitation of computing resources, K = 5 was determined, 5-fold cross-validation was selected, and the training set was divided into 5 subsets, of which 4 subsets were used to train the model and the remaining 1 subset was used to verify the model, and the performance index of each fold number was recorded.

Root Mean Squared Error (RMSE) was selected as the evaluation index, and the parameters were constantly evaluated and optimized. Ultimately, the output layer is set to have a dimension of 1, the hidden layer is set to 4, the number of iterations is set to 1000, and the historical time step length is set to 30. To capture traffic patterns, a historical time step of 30 was used. A batch size of 10 and dropout layers were incorporated to improve accuracy and prevent overfitting. Sigmoid activation functions were utilized for all fully connected layers during training; the prediction results are compared in the final summary figure.

Compare the forecast results with the chart, and analyze the result index values. This model configuration was trained and used to predict the test set ridership. The results were compared to the actual values using the RMSE, MAE, and MAPE metrics for both weekdays and weekends. As seen in the figure, the LSTM model predictions did not match the true values very closely, indicating poor performance that needs improvement across all accuracy metrics.

3.3. LSTM Model Construction and Prediction Analysis of Wavelet Denoising

3.3.1. Steps of Model Construction and Prediction

To address these limitations, a wavelet denoising approach was applied prior to LSTM modeling. The key steps were:

1. Perform a 3-level discrete wavelet transform on the time series data using the db6 wavelet.
2. Decompose the signal into low- and high-frequency components.
3. Apply soft thresholding denoising to the three high-frequency signals.
4. Reconstruct the denoised signal.
5. Split the data into training and test sets.
6. Train the LSTM model on denoised training data.
7. Validate model performance on denoised test data.

The visualizations below depict the original noisy data versus the smoothed denoised signal after wavelet decomposition and thresholding.

3.3.2. Predictive Analysis

Based on the aforementioned basic prediction steps, continuous validation is performed to determine the wavelet base function and conduct wavelet decomposition. First, the db6 wavelet basis function is selected to decompose the three-layer wavelet of July inbound passenger flow data of Shantang Street station with a time interval of 10 min, and the results are shown in Figure 5 below.

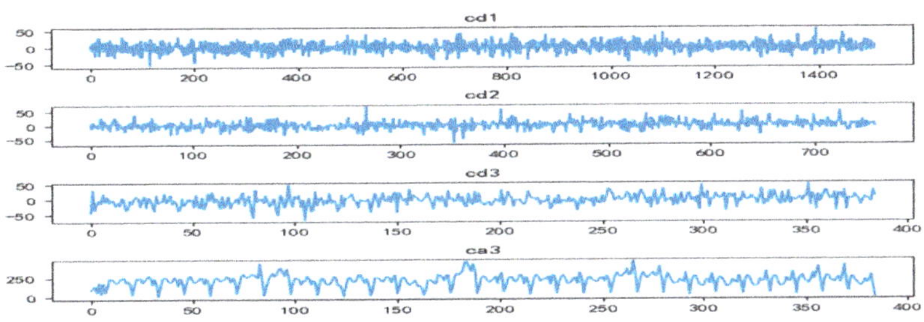

Figure 5. Data display after wavelet decomposition.

After wavelet decomposition and soft threshold denoising, the denoised data and the original data are visualized, as shown in Figure 6. It can be seen that the denoised data are smoother. The blue curve in the Figure 6 represents the original data, and the orange curve represents the data after noise removal.

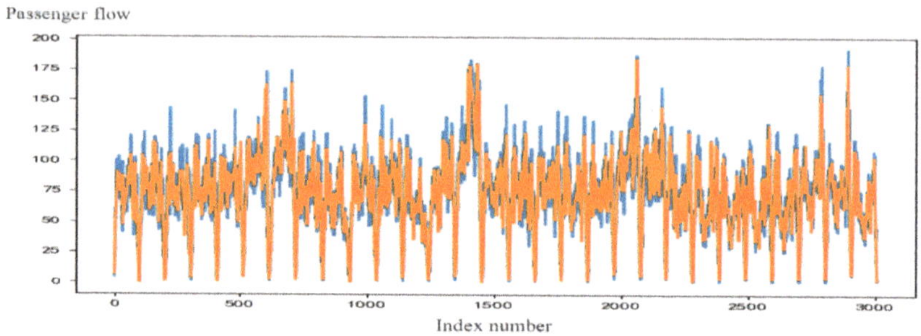

Figure 6. Comparison between denoised data and original data.

The inbound short-time passenger flow training set data of Shantang Street station after noise removal is used as the input of the LSTM network. Considering the data features and model performance after wavelet decomposition, RMSE is again selected as the evaluation metric. Cross-validation is employed to continuously assess and optimize the parameters. Ultimately, the following parameter settings are determined: the input layer has a dimension of 1, the time step length is set to 1, the output layer has a dimension of 1, the hidden layer is set to 8, the number of iterations is set to 3000, and the historical time step length is set to 30. For accurate training, the batch_size is set to 10, and the dropout layer is added. It is better to set the probability to 0.1. Based on the above settings, the training of the model is expanded, and the prediction results are compared in the final summary figure.

Compare the forecast results with the chart, and analyze the result index values. It can be seen that there is almost no difference between the prediction results of the test set data and the data after noise removal, and the prediction model effect of the processed data are more significant.

With the denoised data, the LSTM model was re-trained using the same configuration described previously. As evident in the figure, the predictions closely matched the denoised test set values, demonstrating significantly improved model performance compared to the non-denoised data. The RMSE, MAE, and MAPE were substantially lower for both weekday and weekend results, confirming the benefits of preprocessing with wavelets prior to LSTM modeling for this application. It has great significance for forecasting.

3.4. *SVR Model Construction and Prediction Analysis*

According to the existing experimental results, it can be concluded that the SVR model has good fitting ability and has a good effect on solving some complex nonlinear problems. The short-term passenger flow of rail transit has the characteristic of complexity; therefore, a support vector machine model can be used to deal with the problem of short-term passenger flow prediction.

3.4.1. Steps of SVR Model Construction and Prediction

1. Separate the data into training (1–27 July) and test sets (28–29 July).
2. Train support vector machines (SVMs) with different kernels, selecting RBF based on best fit.
3. Initialize hyperparameter values for penalty factors C and gamma.
4. Refine hyperparameters via grid search cross-validation to minimize MSE.
5. Assess the model on test data.

3.4.2. Predictive Analysis

The step of prediction is set to 1. It is proven that the first 30 data points are used to predict the next data points, and the calculated error is relatively small. Firstly, the penalty factor parameter C was set as 1, 5, 10, 30, 100, and the parameter gamma was set as 0.1, 0.12, 0.01, 0.05, 0.001, 1, 0.5, and 0.9. The rbf function was selected as the kernel function. In the prediction, RMSE is chosen as the evaluation metric to continuously assess the model's performance using cross-validation and evaluate the model's generalization ability. The parameters are continuously evaluated and optimized to select the optimal hyperparameters. Finally, C = 5 and gamma = 0.1 were determined to predict the test set data based on the parameters, and the prediction results are compared in the final summary figure.

Compare the forecast results with the chart, and analyze the result index values. By calculating the predicted results, it can be seen that the predicted results do not deviate much from the actual values; however, there is still a certain gap compared with the LSTM model of wavelet denoising. However, in general, the SVR model is relatively reasonable for the prediction of short-term passenger flow.

3.5. ANN Model Construction and Prediction Analysis

Using the sklearn library in Python, an artificial neural network model was called to implement the backpropagation algorithm. The model was evaluated using the Root Mean Squared Error (RMSE) metric. Cross-validation was performed to determine the relevant parameters, and parameter tuning was conducted to optimize the model. After experimentation, it was found that setting the number of iterations to 100 and the batch size to 1 yielded relatively ideal results. The prediction step was set to 1, the network layer had 12 neurons, and the activation function used was sigmoid. The prediction results are compared in the final summary figure.

The forecast results were evaluated using RMSE, MAE, and MAPE. Compare the forecast results with the chart, and analyze the result index values. However, upon analyzing the prediction result graph, it was observed that the artificial neural network model did not perform exceptionally well. It failed to accurately predict sudden fluctuations in passenger flow and exhibited lower prediction accuracy. The predicted values were generally higher than the actual values

3.6. ARIMA Model Construction and Prediction Analysis

3.6.1. Steps of ARIMA Model Construction and Prediction

Step 1: The Augmented Dickey-Fuller test (ADF test) can be utilized to test for stationarity [35,36]. The ADF test examines the presence of a unit root in the model, which implies that b = 1 in an autoregressive equation $y_t = by_{t-1} + c + \epsilon_t$. This phenomenon can create spurious relationships between independent and dependent variables. The ADF test assumes the existence of a unit root and evaluates the significance test statistic at three confidence levels (1%, 5%, and 10%).

White noise [37,38] is characterized by data that lacks any discernible patterns, with mean values fluctuating around zero and no clear trend. It follows a normal distribution with a mean of 0 and a variance of σ^2. If the data contains white noise after testing, it indicates that there is no useful information, and modeling would be meaningless. Conversely, if there is no white noise, it suggests that the data can be modeled.

Step 2: Determine the values of pmax and qmax. This can be achieved by examining the autocorrelation and partial autocorrelation plots of the original time series data. Table 2 can be used as a guide to determine the appropriate values for pmax and qmax in the ARIMA model.

Step 3: Determine the final values of p and q by considering the maximum likelihood function value and the minimum number of parameters. The higher the likelihood function value, the better the model is. Additionally, a model with fewer parameters has lower complexity and computational requirements. The optimal values of p and q can be determined by calculating the Bayesian Information Criterion (BIC) [39,40].

The BIC is a criterion based on Bayesian theory that provides a more accurate judgment, particularly for large sample sizes, compared to the Akaike Information Criterion (AIC) [41].

The BIC is calculated as BIC = ln(n) (number of parameters in the model) − 2ln (maximum likelihood function value of the model).

Table 2. pmax, qmax judgment table.

Model	ACF	PACF
AR	After decay approaches 0	p-order truncation (after a value greater than a rapid approach to 0)
MA	q order back truncated	After decay approaches 0
ARMA	Attenuation tends to 0 after order q	Attenuation tends to 0 after order p

Step 4: Test the model's validity using the Durbin-Watson (DW) test [42,43] and the QQ plot test [44]. The DW test assesses the autocorrelation of a dataset by calculating the DW value of the residual from the established model. A DW value close to 0 or 4 indicates the presence of autocorrelation in the residual, while a value approaching 2 suggests no autocorrelation.

3.6.2. Predictive Analysis

First of all, we need to check the short-time passenger flow data series of Shantang Street to judge whether the time series data of the inbound passenger flow of Shantang Street is stable (Figure 7).

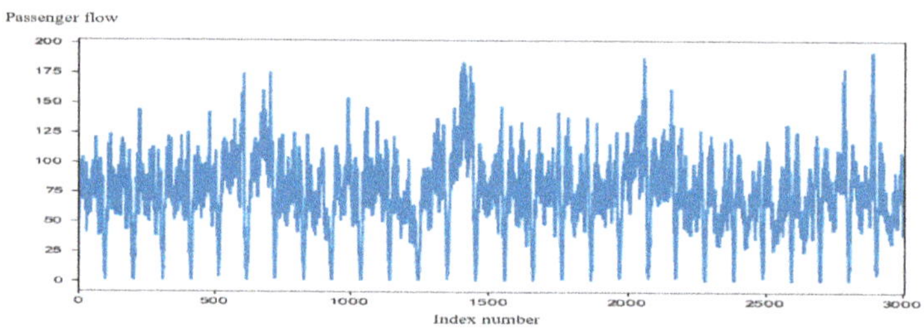

Figure 7. Time series diagram of short-term passenger flow in Shantang Street.

It can be seen from the figure above that the data are basically stable, and then the unit root and stationarity tests of the data are carried out. By calculating ADF, the test results are as follows: ($-9.19, 2.11e^{-15}, 18, 2986$, {'1%': −3.43, '5%': −2.86, '10%': −2.57}, 25241.09). All of these calculations are reserved for two decimal places. The statistical value is lower than the original hypothesis at the 1%, 5%, and 10% significance levels, indicating that the data does not have a unit root and there is no white noise present. Therefore, the data are stable and suitable for ARIMA modeling analysis. Additionally, the calculated *p*-value of $2.11e^{-15}$ is less than 0.05, further supporting the conclusion that the data does not have a unit root.

The autocorrelation and partial autocorrelation plots of the original sequence data for the Shantang Street inbound passenger flow training set were used to determine the values of p and q in the ARIMA model (Figure 8).

From the autocorrelation plot, it can be observed that the values approach 0 after the 10th order. Similarly, the partial autocorrelation plot shows that the values mostly approach 0 after the 4th order. Based on these observations, pmax = 10 and qmax = 5 were selected. The final values of p and q were determined using the Bayesian Information Criterion (BIC). The BIC calculation indicated that the smallest value was obtained when $p = 3$ and q = 3. Therefore, the ARIMA (3,0,3) model was established.

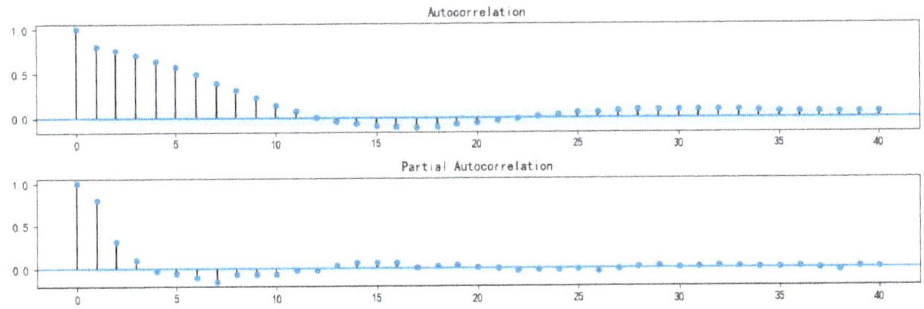

Figure 8. Autocorrelation and partial autocorrelation diagram.

The residuals of the ARIMA (3,0,3) model were tested using the Durbin-Watson (DW) test and QQ plot. The calculated DW test value was 2.008262490962122, which is close to 2. The red line is the standard data cable. The QQ plot also showed that the data points were approximately on a straight line. The blue dots in the figure are the index values of the test results. These results indicate that the model is reasonable (Figure 9).

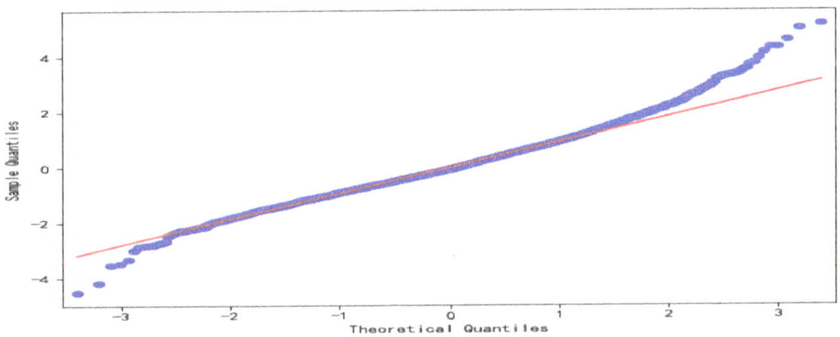

Figure 9. QQ diagramtest results.

After conducting the DW and QQ graph tests, it can be concluded that the established model is reasonable. The trained model is then utilized to predict the short-term passenger flow of Suzhou Metro on 28–29 July, and the results are compared in the final summary figure. Compare the forecast results with the chart, and analyze the result index values. Based on the calculated MAE index, it can be observed that the error in predicting short-term passenger flow on weekdays is relatively small, with an average MAPE value of around 20%. Overall, the ARIMA model demonstrates relatively good prediction performance.

3.7. Comparison of Results

By utilizing various models to forecast the short-term passenger flow of Shantang Street station, the prediction results can be visually displayed, and the corresponding prediction indices can be summarized. First, a visual representation of the predicted results is presented. Subsequently, the RMSE, MAE, and MAPE indices of the predicted results for Sunday (28 July) and Monday (29 July) are calculated based on different feature days, allowing for an analysis of the accuracy of each model's predictions. The comparison of the prediction results of different models on 28 July is shown in Figure 10. And the comparison of the prediction results of different models on 29 July is shown in Figure 11. Xiaobo_predict in the figure below is a Chinese noun for the prediction results of the LSTM model based on wavelet denoising.

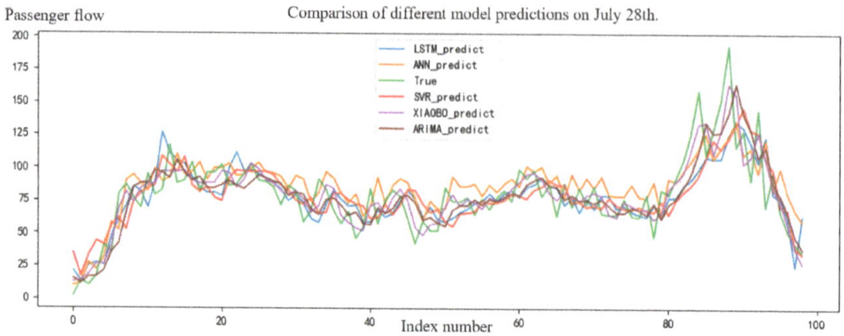

Figure 10. Comparison of prediction results of different models at Shantang Street station on 28 July.

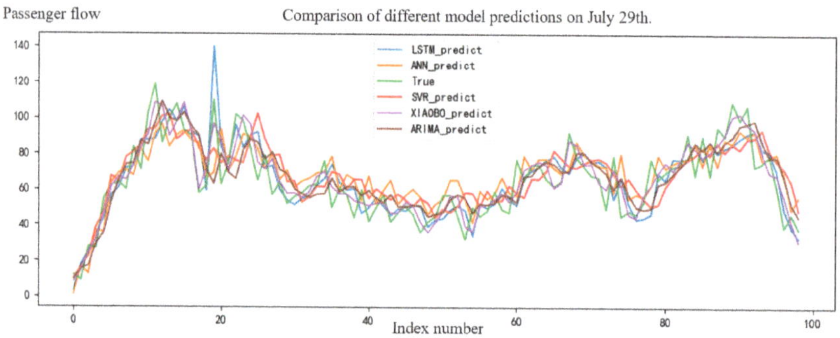

Figure 11. Comparison of prediction results of different models at Shantang Street Station on 29 July.

The forecast result chart displays the number of input indicators on the x-axis and the passenger flow, measured in terms of the number of people, on the y-axis. The green curve represents the true value, and the other curves in different colors represent the predicted value of the different models. This visual representation effectively demonstrates the model's prediction accuracy and effectiveness.

The Shantang Street station predictions reveal that the estimated volumes from all methods stayed relatively close to their true values. This suggests the selected techniques were appropriate for modeling this station's ridership. Across both weekday and weekend results, the denoised LSTM predictions aligned most tightly with the real data. The index values of prediction results of different models are shown in Table 3 below.

Upon analyzing the calculated results in the aforementioned table, it can be observed that the LSTM method, which incorporates wavelet analysis for denoising, yields lower RMSE and MAE indices compared to other methods. Furthermore, the MAPE index is also significantly reduced. Consequently, it can be concluded that this method exhibits certain advantages in terms of prediction accuracy. In the absence of wavelet denoising, the LSTM model demonstrates superior performance, followed by SVR and ARIMA, while the ANN model exhibits relatively poorer performance when predicting short-term passenger flow on weekdays. When it comes to predicting short-term passenger flow on Sundays, both the LSTM and ARIMA models outperform the ANN model. As Sundays typically experience higher station traffic compared to Mondays, it is expected that the prediction errors will be higher on Sundays compared to Mondays. Considering both predictive power and practicality, integrated wavelet denoising with LSTM emerges as the superior methodology, demonstrating its applicability to real-world forecasting.

Table 3. Index values of prediction results under different models.

Method	Index	Monday (29 July)	Sunday (28 July)
LSTM	RMSE	12.86	19.78
	MAE	10.27	15.35
	MAPE	18%	31%
The wavelet + LSTM	RMSE	8.94	12.32
	MAE	7.22	9.88
	MAPE	12%	19%
SVR	RMSE	14.15	19.25
	MAE	11.78	14.72
	MAPE	21%	38%
ANN	RMSE	15.29	20.82
	MAE	12.40	16.62
	MAPE	22%	29%
ARIMA	RMSE	14.04	17.68
	MAE	10.92	13.52
	MAPE	18%	24%

4. Conclusions

The focus of this study is to apply different short-term forecasting techniques to predict the passenger flow at Shantang Street Station of Suzhou Rail Transit. The goal was to analyze whether the proposed denoised LSTM method provided higher accuracy and effectiveness.

This paper examines Shantang Street station in Suzhou, chosen for its high commercial nature and weekday/weekend passenger differences. For short-term prediction research, wavelet denoising processed the time series data before LSTM modeling. Based on signal-to-noise ratios and rail transit passenger flow characteristics, 3-level decomposition via soft thresholding and the db6 wavelet filtered out noise. This denoised data were used to train the LSTM model and compare its forecasts against the original noisy LSTM, SVR, ANN, and ARIMA results. This study confirms the necessity of selecting appropriate methods for predicting rail transit passenger flow. The wavelet-enhanced LSTM significantly improved prediction quality, providing a new perspective for rail transit volume forecasting. Leveraging big data and scientific modeling in this manner can produce practical gains, demonstrating the value of this integrated approach.

In this paper, single-step prediction is adopted when using the model to forecast short-term passenger flow, and multi-step prediction can be carried out in future research, which may save the time of model calculation. When forecasting short-term passenger flow, only the time series data of passenger flow is used in this paper. In the next forecasting study, features such as weather and geographical location can be added so that the factors considered will be more comprehensive, which will be helpful in improving the forecasting accuracy.

Author Contributions: Conceptualization, Q.Z. and L.Z.; methodology, X.F. and Y.W.; software, X.F.; data curation, Q.Z.; writing—original draft preparation, Q.Z. and X.F.; writing—review and editing, Q.Z. and Y.W. All authors have read and agreed to the published version of the manuscript.

Funding: This research was funded by the National Natural Science Foundation of China, grant number NFC52075030.

Data Availability Statement: Not applicable.

Conflicts of Interest: The authors declare no conflict of interest.

References

1. Li, H.; Wang, Y.; Xu, X.; Qin, L.; Zhang, H. Short-term passenger flow prediction under passenger flow control using a dynamic radial basis function network. *Appl. Soft Comput.* **2019**, *83*, 105620. [CrossRef]
2. Wang, J.S.; Ou, X.W.; Chen, J.Y. Short-time passenger flow classification prediction of urban rail stations based on Combined model. *J. Railw. Sci. Eng.* **2023**, *20*, 2004–2012.
3. Lei, J.; He, M.; Shuai, C. A comparison study of short-term passenger flow forecast model of rail transit. In Proceedings of the 19th COTA International Conference of Transportation Professionals (CICTP 2019), Nanjing, China, 6–8 July 2019; pp. 1776–1787.
4. Ni, M.; He, Q.; Gao, J. Forecasting the Subway Passenger Flow under Event Occurrences with Social Media. *IEEE Trans. Intell. Transp. Syst.* **2016**, *18*, 1623–1632. [CrossRef]
5. Roos, J.; Bonnevay, S.; Gavin, G. Short-term rail passenger flow forecasting: A Dynamic Bayesian network approach. In Proceedings of the 15th IEEE International Conference on Machine Learning and Application, Anaheim, CA, USA, 18–20 December 2016.
6. Zhao, Y.T.; Yang, X.F.; Yang, K. Subway passenger flow prediction based on support vector Machine. *Urban Rapid Transit* **2014**, *27*, 35–38. (In Chinese)
7. Anl, U.; Sema, K.K. New deep learning-based passenger flow prediction model. *Transp. Res. Rec. J. Transp. Res. Board* **2023**, *2677*, 1–17.
8. Tan, Y.; Liu, H.; Pu, Y.; Wu, X.; Jiao, Y. Passenger Flow Prediction of Integrated Passenger Terminal Based on K-Means–GRNN. *J. Adv. Transp.* **2021**, *2021*, 1055910. [CrossRef]
9. Pekel, E.; Kara, S.S. Passenger flow prediction based on newly adopted algorithms. *Appl. Artif. Intell.* **2017**, *31*, 64–79.
10. Alghamdi, D.; Basulaiman, K.; Rajgopal, J. Multi-stage deep probabilistic prediction for travel demand. *Appl. Intell.* **2022**, *52*, 11214–11231. [CrossRef]
11. Jiang, X.M.; Adeli, H.; Asce, H. Dynamic wavelet neural network model for traffic flow forecasting. *J. Transp. Eng.* **2005**, *131*, 771–779. [CrossRef]
12. Nagaraj, N.; Gururaj, H.L.; Swathi, B.H.; Hu, Y.C. Passenger flow prediction in bus transportation system using deep learning. *Multimed. Tools Appl.* **2022**, *81*, 12519–12542. [CrossRef]
13. Ermagun, A.; Levinson, D. Spatiotemporal short-term traffic forecasting using the network weight matrix and systematic detrending. *Transp. Res. Part C Emerg. Technol.* **2019**, *104*, 38–52. [CrossRef]
14. Dong, S.W. Research on Short-Term Passenger Flow Prediction Method of Rail Transit Based on Improved BP Neural Network. Master's Thesis, Beijing Jiaotong University, Beijing, China, 2013. (In Chinese)
15. Mirzahossein, H.; Gholampour, I.; Sajadi, S.R.; Zamani, A.H. A hybrid deep and machine learning model for short-term traffic volume forecasting of adjacent intersections. *IET Intell. Transp. Syst.* **2022**, *16*, 1648–1663. [CrossRef]
16. Liu, Y.; Liu, Z.Y.; Ruo, J. DeepPF: A deep learning based architecture for metro passenger flow prediction. *Transp. Res. Part C Emerg. Technol.* **2019**, *101*, 18–34. [CrossRef]
17. Chi, D. Research on electricity consumption forecasting model based on wavelet transform and multi-layer LSTM model. *Energy Rep.* **2022**, *8*, 220–228. [CrossRef]
18. Chi, Y.; Cai, C.; Ren, J.; Xue, Y.; Zhang, N. Damage location diagnosis of frame structure based on wavelet denoising and convolution neural network implanted with Inception module and LSTM. *Struct. Health Monit.* **2023**, 14759217231163777. [CrossRef]
19. Peng, S.; Chen, R.; Yu, B.; Xiang, M.; Lin, X.; Liu, E. Daily natural gas load forecasting based on the combination of long short term memory, local mean decomposition, and wavelet threshold denoising algorithm. *J. Nat. Gas Sci. Eng.* **2021**, *95*, 104175. [CrossRef]
20. Goyal, B.; Dogra, A.; Agrawal, S.; Sohi, B.S.; Sharma, A. Image denoising review: From classical to state-of-the-art approaches. *Inf. Fusion* **2020**, *55*, 220–244. [CrossRef]
21. Gilles, J. Empirical wavelet transform. *IEEE Trans. Signal Process.* **2013**, *61*, 3999–4010. [CrossRef]
22. Sardy, S.; Tseng, P.; Bruce, A. Robust wavelet denoising. *IEEE Trans. Signal Process.* **2001**, *49*, 1146–1152. [CrossRef]
23. Houdt, G.V.; Mosquera, C.; Gonzalo, N. A review on the long short-term memory model. *Artif. Intell. Rev.* **2020**, *53*, 5929–5955. [CrossRef]
24. Al-Musaylh, M.S.; Deo, R.C.; Adamowski, J.F.; Li, Y. Short-term electricity demand forecasting with MARS, SVR and ARIMA models using aggregated demand data in Queensland, Australia. *Adv. Eng. Inform.* **2018**, *35*, 1–16. [CrossRef]
25. Ceperic, E.; Ceperic, V.; Baric, A. A strategy for short-term load forecasting by support vector regression Machines. *IEEE Trans. Power Syst.* **2013**, *28*, 4356–4364. [CrossRef]
26. Nguyen, H.; Vu, T.; Vo, T.P.; Thai, H.T. Efficient machine learning models for prediction of concrete strengths. *Constr. Build. Mater.* **2021**, *266*, 120950. [CrossRef]
27. Barbu, T. CNN-based temporal video segmentation using a nonlinear hyperbolic PDE-based multi-scale analysis. *Mathematics* **2023**, *11*, 245. [CrossRef]
28. Mohiddin, M.B.; Mallikarjuna, P.; Dandagala, S. Applications of Artificial Neural Network for Streamflow Forecasting—A Review. *Artif. Intell. Syst. Mach. Learn.* **2018**, *10*, 25–29.
29. Rehman, K.U.; Shatanawi, W.; Çolak, A.B. Computational Analysis on Magnetized and Non-Magnetized Boundary Layer Flow of Casson Fluid Past a Cylindrical Surface by Using Artificial Neural Networking. *Mathematics* **2023**, *11*, 326. [CrossRef]

30. Abiodun, O.I.; Jantan, A.; Omolara, A.E.; Dada, K.V.; Umar, A.M.; Linus, O.U.; Arshad, H.; Kazaure, A.A.; Gana, U.; Kiru, M.U. Comprehensive review of artificial neural network applications to pattern recognition. *IEEE Access* **2019**, *7*, 158820–158846. [CrossRef]
31. Wu, W.Y.; Dandy, G.C.; Maier, H.R. Protocol for developing ANN models and its application to the assessment of the quality of the ANN model development process in drinking water quality modelling. *Environ. Model. Softw.* **2014**, *54*, 108–127. [CrossRef]
32. Kumar, S.V.; Vanajakshi, L. Short-term traffic flow prediction using seasonal ARIMA model with limited input data. *Eur. Transp. Res. Rev.* **2015**, *7*, 21. [CrossRef]
33. Singh, S.N.; Mohapatra, A. Repeated wavelet transform based ARIMA model for very short-term wind speed forecasting. *Renew. Energy* **2019**, *136*, 758–768.
34. Jandoc, R.; Burden, A.M.; Mamdani, M.; Lévesque, L.E.; Cadarette, S.M. Interrupted time series analysis in drug utilization research is increasing: Systematic review and recommendations. *J. Clin. Epidemiol.* **2015**, *68*, 950–956. [CrossRef] [PubMed]
35. Azam, M.; Khan, A.Q.; Zafeiriou, E.; Arabatzis, G. Socio-economic determinants of energy consumption: An empirical survey for Greece. *Renew. Sustain. Energy Rev.* **2016**, *57*, 1556–1567. [CrossRef]
36. Wang, X.Q.; Su, C.W.; Tao, R.; Lobonţ, O.R. When will food price bubbles burst? A review. *Agric. Econ. (Zemědělská Ekon.)* **2018**, *64*, 566–573. [CrossRef]
37. Sakai, H.M.; Ken-Ichi, N.; Korenberg, M.J. White-noise analysis in visual neuroscience. *Vis. Neurosci.* **1988**, *1*, 287–296. [CrossRef] [PubMed]
38. Riedy, S.M.; Smith, M.G.; Rocha, S.; Basner, M. Noise as a sleep aid: A systematic review. *Sleep Med. Rev.* **2021**, *55*, 101385. [CrossRef] [PubMed]
39. Rescorla, M. Bayesian modeling of the mind: From norms to neurons. *Wiley Interdiscip. Rev. Cogn. Sci.* **2021**, *12*, e1540. [CrossRef] [PubMed]
40. Stephens, M. The Bayesian lens and Bayesian blinkers. *Philos. Trans. R. Soc. A* **2023**, *381*, 20220144. [CrossRef]
41. Symonds, M.R.E.; Moussalli, A. A brief guide to model selection, multimodel inference and model averaging in behavioural ecology using Akaike's information criterion. *Behav. Ecol. Sociobiol.* **2011**, *65*, 13–21. [CrossRef]
42. Guzmán-Santiago, J.C.; Aguirre-Calderón, O.A.; Vargas-Larreta, B. Forest volume estimation techniques with special emphasis on the tropics. *Rev. Chapingo Ser. Cienc. For. Y Del Ambiente* **2020**, *26*, 291–306. [CrossRef]
43. Tong, H. A personal journey through time series in Biometrika. *Biometrika* **2001**, *88*, 195–218. [CrossRef]
44. Li, R.Z.; Fang, K.T.; Zhu, L.X. Some QQ probability plots to test spherical and elliptical symmetry. *J. Comput. Graph. Stat.* **1997**, *6*, 435–450.

mathematics

MDPI

Article

A Multi-Stage Model for Perceived Quality Evaluation of Clothing Brands

Minhui Ren [1], Yu Fan [1,2], Jindong Chen [1,3,*] and Jian Zhang [1,2,3]

1 School of Economics and Management, Beijing Information Science and Technology University, Beijing 100192, China; 2021020714@bistu.edu.cn (M.R.); fanyu@bistu.edu.cn (Y.F.)
2 Beijing Key Laboratory of Big Data Decision Making for Green Development, Beijing Information Science and Technology University, Beijing 100192, China
3 Beijing International Science and Technology Cooperation Base for Intelligent Decision and Big Data Application, Beijing 100192, China
* Correspondence: j.chen@bistu.edu.cn

Abstract: Perceived quality is crucial for the functioning of clothing brands. However, accurate evaluation of the perceived quality of clothing brands remains a common challenge. To achieve a multidimensional evaluation of the perceived quality of clothing brands, an index system is derived based on perceived quality theory. Then, by combining a fine-grained sentiment analysis approach with stochastic dominance criteria, a multi-stage model ECRM is proposed for the perceived quality evaluation of clothing brands based on online user reviews. ECRM comprises three stages: Extraction, Classification, and Ranking. To begin with, Contrastive Attention and dependency parsing are used to extract attribute–viewpoint phrases from online reviews. Subsequently, the pre-trained models are employed to classify the indexes and sentiment levels of these phrases. Furthermore, the perceived quality indexes are ranked using stochastic dominance criteria and the PROMETHEE-II method. Empirical analysis is conducted for the clothing brands of ALDB, AND, BNL, and QPL; the results show that, based on online user reviews, ECRM enables accurate evaluation of the perceived quality of clothing brands. Based on the evaluation results, it is found that Comfort, External, Protection, and Fineness are highly valued by consumers; moreover, the four brands focus on different indexes. Specific strategies for perceived quality improvements are proposed depending on the current status of the brands.

Keywords: perceived quality; fine-grained sentiment analysis; stochastic dominance criteria; pre-trained models

MSC: 05A05

1. Introduction

Clothing consumption is entering a rational stage of the pursuit of quality and perception [1]. Clothing brands with low perceived quality can hardly meet consumers' demands. How to evaluate the perceived quality has become a multi-attribute decision making problem (MADM) for clothing brands [2]. For the last few years, residents' online consumption habits have been consolidated in the modern business context, where online shopping for clothing prevails [3]. Clothing brands need a set of systems and methods to accurately identify the directions for perceived quality improvements.

The concept of perceived quality was first proposed in the 1980s, and many theoretical studies had been conducted, such as the theoretical system analysis of perceived quality, perceived value, and perceived effort [4], the role of perceived quality in brand research [5], and the mechanism of perceived quality on consumers [6]. Questionnaire surveys have been widely used in the study of perceived quality, but they suffer from difficulties in data collection and question design. User-generated content (UGC) has changed the way consumers share their experiences [7], and the unstructured UGC data has provided more advantages for data collection.

One type of UGC data is online user reviews. With the development of the internet, e-commerce platforms have gathered numerous user online reviews, serving as significant support in the research of consumer viewpoints and inclinations [8,9]. Many studies on perceived quality have been conducted using online reviews and sentiment analysis [10–13]. However, sentence-level sentiment analysis methods focus on the sentiment polarities of the whole sentences, and the connections of attributes and sentiments are overlooked [13]. To dig deeper into consumer perspectives, fine-grained sentiment analysis methods are needed.

Fine-grained sentiment analysis tasks include Aspect Term Extraction, Opinion Term Extraction, Aspect Sentiment Classification, etc., [14–18]. In response to these tasks, some fine-grained sentiment analysis methods are proposed using word vectors and language models. Tulkens et al. put forward an unsupervised approach to extract and classify aspect terms using Contrastive Attention [19]. Tian et al. proposed a pre-trained model, Skep (Sentiment Knowledge Enhanced Pre-training), based on sentiment knowledge augmentation. Skep acquired a unified sentiment representation via a dedicated objective function during pre-training, and demonstrated exceptional proficiency for the Aspect-level Sentiment Classification task [20]. Fine-grained sentiment analysis methods have been widely used in the evaluation studies of satisfaction [21], user experience [13], and service quality [22].

After sentiment analysis, a barometer, such as mean or variance, is needed to quantify the index. However, using only two numbers to represent the evaluation results is unreliable. Therefore, it is necessary to apply a more stable quantitative approach. Based on the result of sentiment analysis, a probabilistic linguistic term set (PLTS) can be constructed [8]. PLTS describes the reviews according to certain indexes; then, the dominance relations can be obtained using stochastic dominance criteria [23]. PROMETHEE-II is a complete ranking method based on dominance relations. It introduces an advantage function to compute the priority of the indexes, and the overall evaluation is given by the net advantages [24]. The combination of stochastic dominance criteria and PROMETHEE-II has been widely used in MADM problems [23].

In summary, the study of perceived quality holds significant importance for clothing brands, but simple sentiment and quantitative analysis methods have proven inadequate. To address the limitations of previous analyses, this paper presents an index system designed for evaluating the perceived quality of clothing brands. Further, a multi-stage model ECRM is proposed, and empirical analysis is conducted. The contributions of this paper are as follows. First, the perceived quality theory is involved to construct the index system of perceived quality evaluation for clothing brands. Second, a multi-stage model ECRM is proposed with a stochastic multi-attribute mathematical model and a fine-grained sentiment analysis method. Third, considering the online user reviews, this paper provides a multidimensional quantitative basis for evaluating the perceived quality of clothing brands.

The remainder of this paper is organized as follows. In Section 2, we present and explain the index system of perceived quality evaluation for clothing brands. In Section 3, we introduce the proposed model ECRM in detail. In Section 4, we conduct empirical analysis and discuss the results. In Section 5, we summarize this article.

2. Index System of Perceived Quality Evaluation for Clothing Brands

The clothing industry plays a significant role in consumer goods, and the perceived quality of clothing brands is crucial for resident consumption. According to the manner of online transactions and the theoretical system of perceived quality, this paper sets two evaluation targets: products and services. The index system of perceived quality evaluation for clothing brands is shown in Table 1.

Table 1. Index system of perceived quality evaluation for clothing brands.

Evaluation Targets	Evaluation Indexes
Products	Comfort Durability Fineness Protection Certification Appearance External
Services	Timeliness of response Effectiveness of communication Security of information Rationality of compensation Professionalism of service

In the classical theory, perceived quality applies exclusively to products, and is determined by three factors: external attributes, internal attributes, and perceived monetary price [4]. This conceptual model provides an overall theoretical framework but is not industry-specific. As for the perceived quality of clothing products, Liu et al. derived seven factors using questionnaire surveys [25], including Comfort, Certification, External, Fineness, Mall, Appearance, and Protection. Mall is specific to offline shopping. As consumption patterns change, more and more consumers tend to buy clothes online. The share of online clothing consumption has exceeded that of offline consumption [1], so this paper has removed the Mall index.

Parasuraman et al. summarized customer perceived service quality as five aspects: Reliability, Responsiveness, Assurance, Empathy, and Tangibility [26]. Similar to the classical perceived quality theoretical system, the perceived service quality system can provide theoretical support, but the interpretation of the indexes cannot justify their application in industries. Based on the study of Parasuraman et al. [27], Zhao et al. developed an e-tailing service quality measurement scale (E-TAIL-SQ) using in-depth interviews and empirical testing methods [28]. This paper refers to the first-order indices of E-TAIL-SQ to determine the service indexes.

Therefore, according to previous studies on perceived quality, the index system of perceived quality evaluation for clothing brands has been devised, and the indexes are determined as follows.

- Comfort: The index measures the comfort of the clothing items, considering aspects such as comfort, symmetry, and precision of sizing.
- Durability: Eugene [29] considers durability as a dimension of perceived product quality. Durability in this paper means the deformation of clothing products in daily use, including resistance to shrinkage and wrinkling of clothing.
- Fineness: Eugene [29] and Dodds [30] argue that product perceived quality should include fineness and technical level, such as dimensions. Fineness in this paper includes threads, seams, fabric breakage, pilling, and other related factors.
- Protection: Reliability should be considered as a dimension that reflects factors related to consumer safety [30], such as the color fastness or the fabric type of clothing. These factors are measured as aspects of Protection.
- Certification: Certification is employed to measure the compliance of signage.
- Appearance: Appearance is employed to measure the visual characteristics of the products, such as color or design.
- External: External is utilized to measure aspects that are not directly connected to product performance or physical components, such as brand or pricing.
- Timeliness of response: This index is derived from SERVQUAL and E-TAIL-SQ, and it is utilized to evaluate the promptness of customer service responses and punctuality of delivery.

- Effectiveness of communication: Whether the customer service is efficient and amiable in communication.
- Security of information: Whether the protection of consumers' personal information is ensured.
- Rationality of compensation: This index quantifies the rationality of the services provided during the return and exchange procedures.
- Professionalism of service: Whether the logistician can complete the distribution successfully and the retailer can process the order accurately.

3. The Multi-Stage Model for Perceived Quality Evaluation

Based on fine-grained sentiment analysis, a multi-stage model ECRM for perceived quality evaluation is proposed, where the output of each stage serves as the input for the next stage. The flowchart for ECRM is shown in Figure 1. First, the attribute–viewpoint phrases are extracted by Contrastive Attention and Dependency Parsing. Then, based on the evaluation index system, the sentiment levels and indexes of reviews are classified using the phrases. Finally, according to PLTS formed by the classification results, the indexes are ranked using stochastic dominance criteria and PROMETHEE-II.

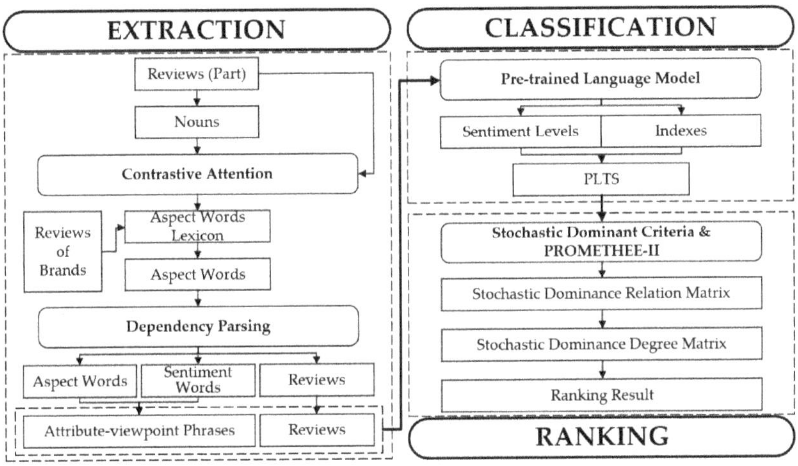

Figure 1. Flowchart for ECRM.

3.1. Extraction of Attribute–Viewpoint Phrases

In the pipeline style approaches of fine-grained sentiment analysis, the extraction of key words has always been the initial stage. In this paper, aspect words and sentiment words are extracted and combined into attribute–viewpoint phrases. The process can be described as follows.

Step 1: Obtain all the terms from the corpus by Chinese word segmentation.

Step 2: Since nouns typically provide information on attributes, select all nouns in the corpus as candidate aspect words [21].

Step 3: Select aspect words from the nouns using Contrastive Attention [21]. First, BERT is applied to obtain word embeddings [31]. Then, the Radial Basis Function (RBF) is used to compute the similarity between terms. RBF is defined as (1), where γ is a scaling factor.

$$\mathrm{RBF}(x, y, \gamma) = \exp\left(-\gamma \|x - y\|_2^2\right) \tag{1}$$

The kernel functions can be used to calculate the inner product of samples mapped to a higher dimensional space. Thus, the kernel functions can be utilized to measure the similarity between samples. RBF is one of the kernel functions. The active range of RBF can be regulated by a single parameter. RBF can normalize the distance in the vector space to (0,1]. If the embeddings of x and y are highly similar, the RBF response will be close to 1; as the distance between x and y increases, the RBF response decreases rapidly until almost 0.

Let N be the word embeddings of all the candidate aspect words, and let M be the embeddings of the corpus. Compute the attention scores between nouns and the whole corpus as (2).

$$Att = \frac{\sum_{n \in N} \mathrm{RBF}(m, n, \gamma)}{\sum_{m \in M} \sum_{n \in N} \mathrm{RBF}(m, n, \gamma)} \tag{2}$$

Att represents the possibility of each noun being an aspect word. Equation (2) means the sum of the RBF distance of each noun to the corpus divided by the sum of the RBF distance of all nouns to the corpus, and high Att means high similarity between nouns and the corpus.

Finally, retain nouns with high Contrastive Attention scores using the elbow method.

Step 4: Extract attribute–viewpoint phrases from online reviews based on dependency parsing. Dependency parsing is a commonly used method for extracting the sentiment words related to the aspect words [32]. Since the aspect words have been determined, it is feasible to extract the viewpoints of online user reviews based on dependency patterns. First, the Part-Of-Speech (POS) of words in online reviews is annotated by Jieba https://github.com/fxsjy/jieba accessed on (accessed on 13 July 2023). Subsequently, based on prior research [26,27], five rules in dependency parsing are defined and displayed in Table 2.

Table 2. Extraction rules for attribute–viewpoint phrases.

Extraction Rules	Examples of Reviews	Extraction Results
aspect + adj	The shirt is nice.	shirt nice
adj + aspect	The color is as beautiful as snow.	color beautiful
aspect + adv + adj	The delivery is very fast.	delivery very fast
adv + adj + aspect	It's the most beautiful dress I've ever had.	most beautiful dress
verb + aspect	I like that material.	like material

There are six relations in dependency parsing: subject–verb relation, verb–object relation, fronting–object relation, attribute relation, adverbial relation, complement relation, and coordinate relation. The rules defined in Table 2 can address the format of the first five relations directly. As for aspect words of coordinate relation, the sentences can be broken down into separate aspect words and then analyzed by the first five rules [32,33].

It can be seen that content words are sometimes not linked in raw reviews; however, during Chinese word segmentation, insignificant words are eliminated, and content words are retained in their original order.

3.2. Classification of Reviews

The pre-training approach has significantly enhanced the quality of the semantic representation in language models. As compared to traditional machine learning models, the pre-trained models have achieved impressive results. In this paper, the pre-trained language models are utilized to determine the indexes and sentiment levels of the attribute–viewpoint phrases. Assume that $\mathrm{CSF} = \{\mathrm{CSF}_1, \mathrm{CSF}_2, \ldots \mathrm{CSF}_{12}\}$ represents 12 indexes. $\mathrm{SET} = \{\mathrm{SET}_1, \mathrm{SET}_2, \mathrm{SET}_3\}$ represents three sentiment levels (positive, neutral, negative). Multiply CSF by SET using Cartesian multiplication to list all possible combinations of indexes and sentiment levels.

$$\mathrm{CSF} \times \mathrm{SET} = \{(\mathrm{CSF_i}, \mathrm{SET_j}) | \mathrm{CSF_i} \in \mathrm{CSF}, \mathrm{SET_j} \in \mathrm{SET}\} \tag{3}$$

Therefore, 36 index–sentiment classes have been created [34]. The inputs of models are constructed in three steps, as follows.

Step 1: Concatenate the attribute–viewpoint phrases and reviews to form sentence pairs.

Step 2: Add *[CLS]* and *[SEP]* to the sentence pairs to construct input tokens.

Step 3: Transform the input tokens into input ID according to the lexicon, and construct token type ID to indicate the segments of sentences.

Finally, the inputs of the models consist of input ID and token type ID. The classes of the sentence embedding (h_1) are determined by a fully connected layer. The losses are calculated by Softmax and Cross-Entropy function. The training process for classification based on the pre-trained models is shown in Figure 2.

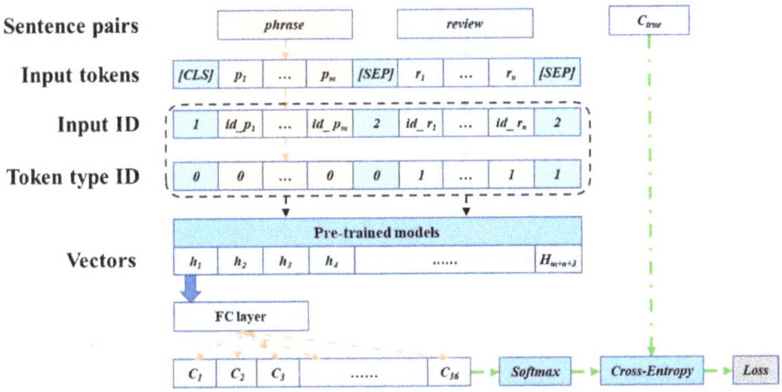

Figure 2. The training process for classification based on the pre-trained models.

In the training phase, a tuple (*phrase*, *review*) is given, and a token sequence is constructed in a form similar to "*[CLS]*, $p_1, \cdots, p_m$, *[SEP]*, $r_1, \cdots, r_n$, *[SEP]*", where $p_1, \cdots, p_m$ are words that form a *phrase*, and $r_1, \cdots, r_n$ are words that form a *review*. Moreover, *[CLS]* and *[SEP]* are special tokens in the pre-trained models. The token sequence is subsequently input into the pre-trained models, and the vector of *[CLS]* h_1 is used for classification via an FC layer.

Using the self-attention mechanism, h_1 is derived by a weighted summing-up of the embeddings of all other tokens. Therefore, h_1 aggregates the information for the entire sentence pairs, and can be used for sentence classification. There are alternative methods for acquiring the ultimate classification vector, like averaging for all the embeddings. However, those methods tend to lose important information of h_1, leading to poor classification performance.

3.3. Ranking of Perceived Quality Indexes

PLTS is constructed based on the classification results, and the sentiment levels are treated as discrete random variables. Then, stochastic dominance criteria are applied to establish the stochastic dominance relation matrix concerning each index. Based on the stochastic dominance relation matrix, the stochastic dominance degree matrix of indexes is constructed, and the overall stochastic dominance degree (comprehensive flow) of each index is obtained using the PROMETHEE-II method [35].

3.3.1. Construction of Stochastic Dominance Relation Matrix

Transform the distributions of sentiment levels concerning the indexes in PLTS into discrete percentage distributions. Afterwards, the stochastic dominance criteria are introduced to create the stochastic dominance relation matrix. The specific procedure is as follows.

For all reviews of a certain brand, the amount of reviews is counted by indexes, and the amounts of reviews with certain sentiment levels are counted separately [8,36–38], defined as:

$$Pro_k^{\varepsilon} = \frac{P_k^{\varepsilon}}{P_k}, k = 1,2,3 \cdots 12; \varepsilon = 1,2,3 \tag{4}$$

where P_k denotes the amount of phrases of the k-th index, and P_k^{ε} denotes the amount of phrases with the ε-th sentiment level of the k-th index. The cumulative distribution functions of the sentiment levels concerning CSF_k can be obtained:

$$F_k(t) = \sum\nolimits_{t \geq T^{\varepsilon}} Pro_k^{\varepsilon} \tag{5}$$

Let $E = (e_k)_{12\times 1}$ be the expectation of the cumulative distribution function, where e_k can be expressed by:

$$e_k = \sum\nolimits_{\varepsilon=1}^{3} Pro_k^{\varepsilon} T^{\varepsilon} (k = 1, 2, \cdots, 12; \varepsilon = 1, 2, 3) \tag{6}$$

T^{ε} is set to the same value as ε in this paper. On an interval $[a,b]$, if two cumulative distribution functions $F(x) \neq G(y)$ satisfy:

$$H_1(x) = F(x) - G(x) \leq 0 \tag{7}$$

then $F(x)$ dominates $G(y)$ in the first order, denoted as $F(x)$ FSD $G(y)$. Otherwise, if:

$$H_2(x) = \int_a^x H_1(y)dy \leq 0 \tag{8}$$

then $F(x)$ dominates $G(y)$ in the second order, denoted as $F(x)$ SSD $G(y)$. Otherwise, if:

$$H_3(x) = \int_a^x H_2(y)dy \leq 0 \tag{9}$$

$$E(x) > E(y) \tag{10}$$

then $F(x)$ dominates $G(y)$ in the third order, denoted as $F(x)$ TSD $G(y)$, otherwise denoted as '--'.

3.3.2. Construction of Stochastic Dominance Degree Matrix

Based on the stochastic dominance relation matrix, the stochastic dominance degree matrix SUR = [sur(CSF_k, CSF_h)] is constructed using the PROMETHEE-II method by Equation (11).

$$\text{sur}(\text{CSF}_k, \text{CSF}_h) = \begin{cases} 1, r_{kh} \in SD, e_k \geq e_h + a \\ \frac{e_k - e_h}{a}, r_{kh} \in SD, e_h \leq e_k \leq e_h + a \\ --, \text{otherwise} \end{cases} \tag{11}$$

In the equation above, SD = {FSD, SSD, TSD}, and a is the preference threshold:

$$a = \frac{2}{12 \times (12-1)} \sum_{k=1}^{12} \sum_{h=1 h \neq k}^{12} b_{kh} \tag{12}$$

$$b_{kh} = \begin{cases} e_k - e_h, e_k \geq e_h \\ 0, e_k < e_h \end{cases} \tag{13}$$

Compute leaving flow ϕ^+, entering flow ϕ^-, and the comprehensive flow ϕ for all indexes. For a certain index CSF_k:

$$\phi^+(\text{CSF}_k) = \sum_{i=1}^{12} \text{SUR}_{k,i} \tag{14}$$

$$\phi^-(\text{CSF}_k) = \sum_{i=1}^{12} \text{SUR}_{i,k} \tag{15}$$

$$\phi(\mathrm{CSF}_k) = \phi^{+}(\mathrm{CSF}_k) - \phi^{-}(\mathrm{CSF}_k) \tag{16}$$

The leaving flow $\phi^{+}(\mathrm{CSF}_k)$ represents the degree to which the index CSF_k is superior to other indexes, the entering flow $\phi^{-}(\mathrm{CSF}_k)$ represents the degree to which the index CSF_k is inferior to other indexes, and the comprehensive flow $\phi(\mathrm{CSF}_k)$ represents the degree to which the index is overall superior to all other indexes. The greater the comprehensive flow, the better the performance of the index [35].

4. Experiments and Discussions

4.1. Data Collection and Pre-Processing

For effective access to reviews, a web crawler was developed in advance. Then, following the default review display order, reviews from four brands (ALBD, AND, BNL, QPL) on JD Mall were collected in June 2023 using the web crawler; 10,000 reviews from 2020 to 2023 were collected for each brand. The annual distribution of the collected online reviews is illustrated in Figure 3.

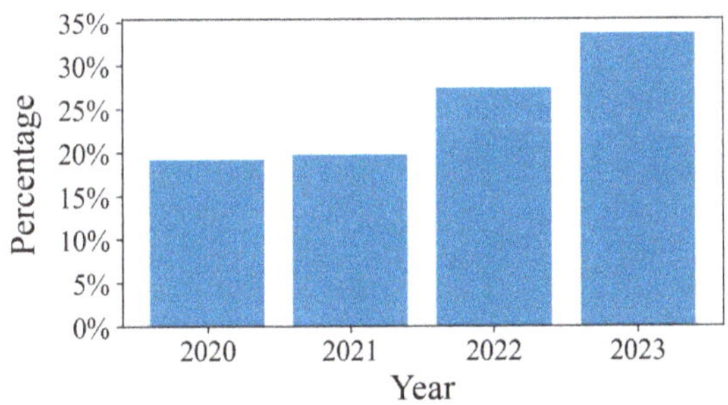

Figure 3. Annual distribution of the collected online reviews.

Considering the concentration of terms, 4000 reviews were selected randomly, and 3918 terms were obtained by Chinese word segmentation. The quantities of the 1000 most frequent terms are displayed in Figure 4.

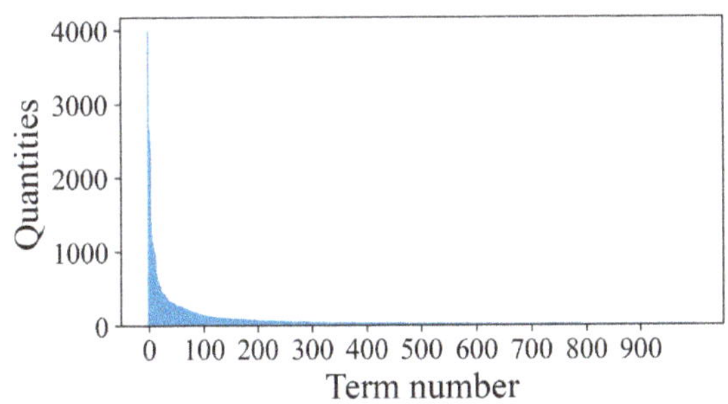

Figure 4. Quantities of the 1000 most frequent terms.

Finally, 1899 nouns and their BERT embeddings were obtained.

4.2. Extraction of Attribute-Viewpoint Phrases

Based on the BERT embeddings, the attention scores were calculated using the method introduced in Section 3.1. To determine the value of γ in Equation (1), the variances of standardized attention scores for each noun with varying γ were calculated. The formula of standardized processing is:

$$x' = \frac{x - X_{min}}{X_{max} - X_{min}} \quad (17)$$

where x is the attention score of a noun. The results of variances are shown in Figure 5a. The variance of the attention scores is the highest when γ is set to 0.003, indicating that some nouns are more likely to serve as aspect words than the others. The specific values of the attention scores for each noun are shown in Figure 5b.

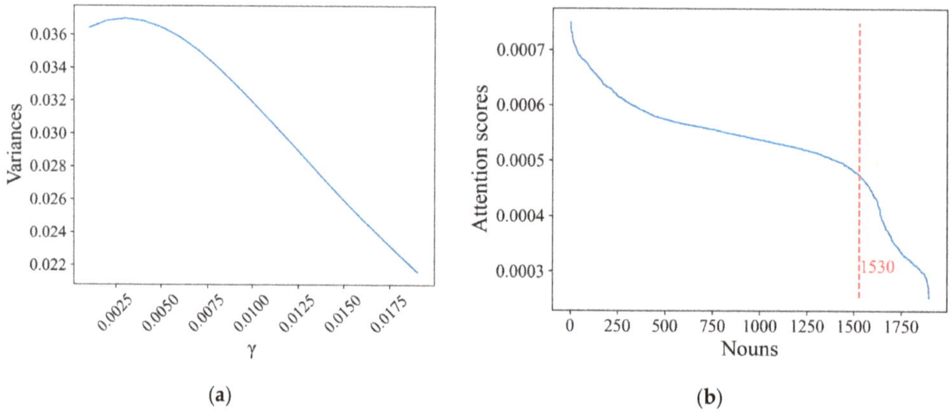

Figure 5. (**a**): Variances of standardized attention scores with varying γ; (**b**) The attention scores of each noun (γ = 0.003).

According to the principle of the elbow method, 1530 nouns were selected to construct a lexicon of aspect words. The top six words in the attention scores are shown in Table 3.

Table 3. The top six words in the attention scores.

Aspect Words	Attention Scores	Aspect Words	Attention Scores
quality	0.00074981933	necessities	0.00073796633
time	0.00073314965	health	0.00073012454
feeling	0.00071956177	service	0.00070828611

Sentiment words were extracted with regard to the aspect words based on the guidelines specified in Table 2. Then, the aspect words and corresponding sentiment words were merged to form attribute–viewpoint phrases. Examples of sentiment words extraction are shown in Table 4. The amounts of attribute–viewpoint phrases for each brand are listed in Table 5.

Table 4. Examples of sentiment words extraction.

Raw Reviews	Aspect Words	Sentiment Words
The quality is very good, the pattern is nice, and I am also very satisfied with the service. I will come again next time.	quality pattern service	very good nice very satisfied

Table 5. Amounts of attribute–viewpoint phrases for each brand.

Brands	Amounts of Attribute-Viewpoint Phrases
ALBD	20,629
AND	15,336
BNL	17,608
QPL	20,510

4.3. Classification of Reviews

4.3.1. Model Training

Attribute–viewpoint phrases and index-sentiment classes were manually annotated for model training; 1630 reviews were annotated for the training set, and 572 reviews for the test set. Three more pre-trained language models were trained and tested to select the most appropriate one for classification. Ernie 3.0: a unified framework for pre-training large-scale knowledge enhanced models, which can be easily tailored for natural language understanding and generation tasks with zero-shot learning [39]; Roberta: an improved version of BERT, in the training process of Roberta, Byte-Pair Encoding and Dynamic Mask are applied, Next Sentence Pair task is removed [40]; Macbert: a pre-trained model which improves upon Roberta in several ways, including the masking strategy that adopts *MLM* as a correction (Mac) [41].

In the training process, the hyper-parameters were established with the following values: **Epochs**: 20, representing the times the entire training dataset had been traversed. **Batch_size**: 16 or 32, representing the size of each input data provided to the model. **Lr**: 1×10^{-5} or 1×10^{-4}, representing the step size of the network weight adjustment along the gradient direction. Experiments were conducted for varying hyper-parameter configurations. The losses of the training process for each model are displayed in Figure 6.

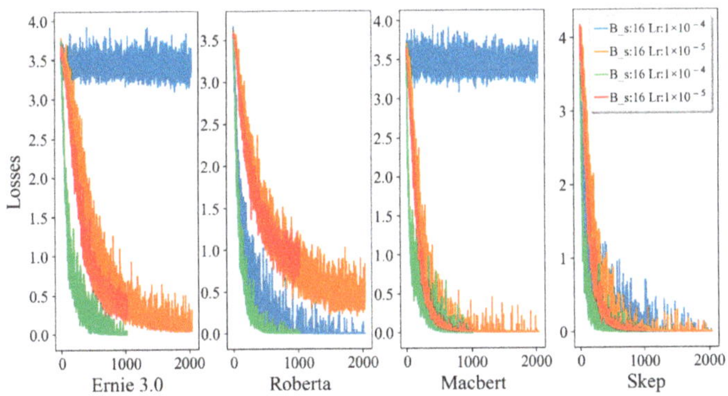

Figure 6. The losses of the training process for each model.

It can be seen that Skep exhibits better loss convergence, implying more effective fitting with the dataset in this paper. Macbert and Ernie 3.0 did not converge at a Batch_size of 16 and Lr of 1×10^{-4}. When Lr was set to 1×10^{-5}, ERNIE 3.0 and Roberta exhibited a tendency to enter local optima, and additional training was required to minimize the losses. Moreover, it was found that utilizing a Batch_size of 32 resulted in more stable losses and smaller fluctuations for each model, thus promoting the models' convergence.

Macro-P, Macro-R, and Macro-F1 were employed as metrics to evaluate the generalization effect of the models. The metrics above were computed using Equations (18)–(20).

$$\text{Macro-P} = \frac{1}{n}\sum_{i=1}^{n} P_i \tag{18}$$

$$\text{Macro-R} = \frac{1}{n}\sum_{i=1}^{n} R_i \tag{19}$$

$$\text{Macro-F1} = \frac{1}{n}\sum_{i=1}^{n} F1_i = \frac{1}{n}\sum_{i=1}^{n} \frac{2P_iR_i}{P_i + R_i} \tag{20}$$

The optimum Macro-F1 values for each model with varying hyper-parameters are presented in Table 6. Additionally, the results are compared by several traditional models based on word vectors using Tf-idf.

Table 6. Optimum Macro-F1 values for each model with varying hyper-parameters on the test set.

Model	Batch_Size	Lr	Macro-P	Macro-R	Macro-F1
Ernie-3.0	32	1×10^{-4}	0.78	0.76	0.76
Roberta	16	1×10^{-4}	0.74	0.73	0.73
Macbert	16	1×10^{-5}	0.80	0.78	0.77
Skep	32	1×10^{-5}	0.83	0.77	0.77
Text_CNN	32	1×10^{-5}	0.55	0.49	0.50
Tf-idf + SVC	-	-	0.51	0.49	0.46
Tf-idf + SGD	-	-	0.48	0.47	0.46
Tf-idf + RandomForest	-	-	0.40	0.38	0.36

According to Table 6, the traditional models exhibited unsatisfactory performance in this paper, whereas the pre-trained models demonstrated exceptional performance. Among the pre-trained models, Macbert and Skep can achieve almost the same level of effect, but, according to Figure 6, Skep exhibits better loss convergence, so the following classification task is achieved by Skep.

4.3.2. Classification Results

The reviews of the four brands were transformed and classified by Skep following the method described in Section 3.2. The results of the review classification for each brand are shown in Figure 7.

Figure 7 states that the clothing industry possesses numerous significant supplemental features, with a 20% variance in External between the four brands' highest and lowest levels. Moreover, there exist concealed hazards in safeguarding consumer information, with low Security and Certification levels for each brand.

The distribution of reviews related to each index for each brand is shown in Figure 8.

For the overall perceived quality of clothing brands, reviews primarily relate to products rather than services, indicating that the attributes of products are the main influencing factors in forming perceived quality, while services have a relatively supplementary role.

The cumulative percentage of the first six indexes attained 90%, and Comfort is the most valued index by consumers. Consequently, clothing brands should focus on Comfort, External, Protection, Fineness, Professionalism, and Appearance indexes.

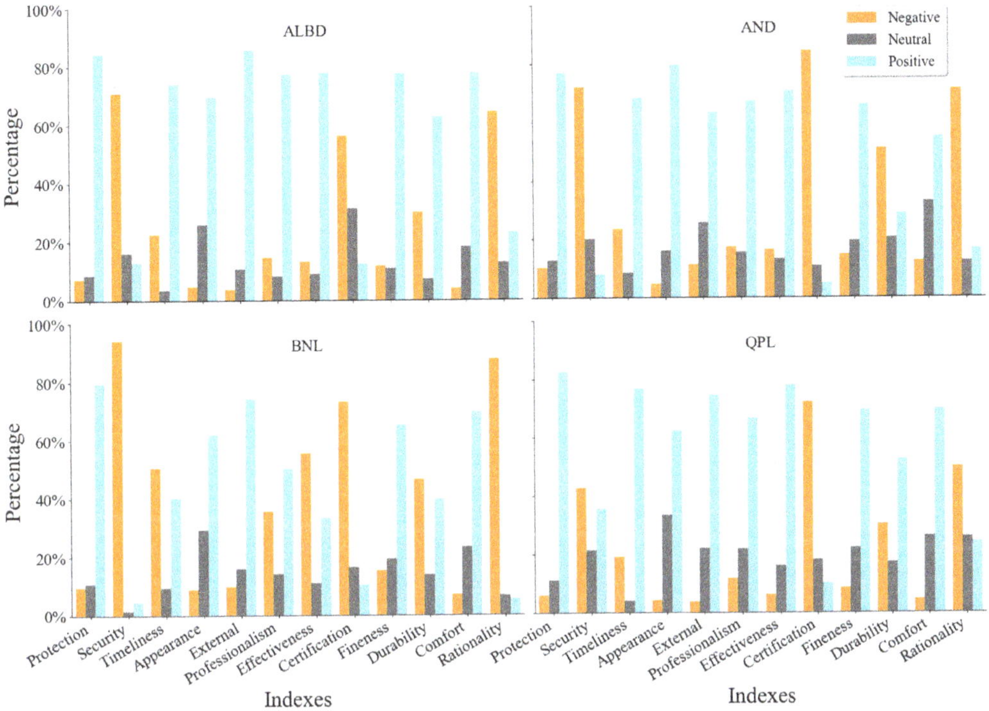

Figure 7. Results of review classification for each brand.

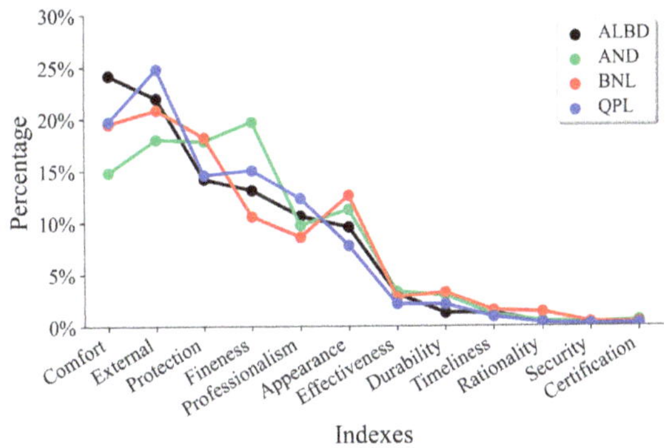

Figure 8. The distribution of reviews related to each index for each brand.

4.4. Ranking of Perceived Quality Indexes for Clothing Brands

After classification, discrete percentage distributions of sentiment levels for each index were obtained, and the PLTS were constructed. Then, stochastic dominance criteria and the PROMETHEE-II method were used to compute the comprehensive flow of the chosen brands. The result is shown in Table 7.

Table 7. Comprehensive flow of the selected brands.

Indexes	ALBD	AND	BNL	QPL
Comfort	4.6	2.9	7	4.2
Durability	−2	−5.9	−1.9	−4.2
Fineness	3.3	3.5	5.5	3.2
Protection	4.8	5.6	7.2	5.2
Certification	−8.8	−9.6	−7.5	−10.8
Appearance	3.4	6.6	6.3	3.5
External	5.9	3.7	6.8	5.2
Timeliness of response	1	2.7	−2.3	2.6
Effectiveness of communication	3.1	3.7	−3.5	4.8
Security of information	−9.6	−8.6	−9.5	−7.2
Rationality of compensation	−8.7	−8	−9	−8.6
Professionalism of service	2.8	3.3	0.9	2.2

Based on the comprehensive flow presented in Table 7, the ranking results of the four brands are shown in Figure 9.

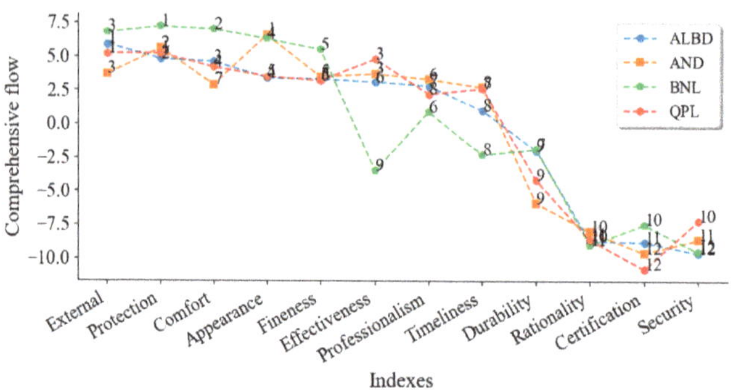

Figure 9. Ranking results of the four brands.

As demonstrated in Figure 9, the ranking results of the four brands exhibit a consistent pattern, and it can be seen that the evaluation of products is superior to that of services, indicating that clothing brands place a higher emphasis on products than services.

The differences displayed in Figure 9 for each brand highlight variations in the primary indexes of each brand. Specifically, BNL exhibits a more substantial discrepancy between its services and products compared to the other three brands, suggesting that BNL concentrates more resources on its products and spends fewer resources on its services than the other brands.

4.5. *Comprehensive Analyses and Suggestions*

External and Protection are highly ranked across indexes for all the brands and are highly valued by consumers. However, Figure 7 indicates that there are fewer variations between those brands. This phenomenon suggests that clothing consumers tend to have a positive perception of brands due to external and safety-related factors.

Comfort can show the differences between brands to some extent. According to Figure 9, Comfort ranks highly in ALBD, BNL, and QPL, but ranks only seventh in AND, indicating the differences between AND and the other brands. Additionally, Figure 7 reveals many neutral reviews of Comfort within AND, suggesting a need for improvement in product comfort to turn neutral reviews into positive ones.

The rates of Appearance also fluctuate considerably between brands, but Appearance has received limited attention from consumers. According to Figure 8, only 10% of the reviews are related to Appearance. The excellent rate of Appearance in AND could not bring a significant improvement for it, so it is suggested that AND reduce the cost of its appearance design to some extent.

According to Figure 9, BNL's Effectiveness ranks very low, at ninth place, while the effectiveness of other brands ranks higher. Unlike other brands, BNL receives more negative reviews than positive in this index; therefore, BNL needs to focus on enhancing the quality of customer service responses.

In terms of perceived service quality, communication quality (Effectiveness and Timeliness) surpasses delivery quality (Professionalism) for ALBD and AND. Regarding the correlation between Effectiveness and Timeliness, the balance between these two indexes is impacted by the commonly used auto-responder bots, which have their pros and cons. On the one hand, auto-responder bots enable brands to promptly respond to basic consumer demands, potentially enhancing efficiency. However, if the bots prove ineffective in resolving issues and manual customer service fails to respond promptly, it may result in a lackluster response. To improve the perceived service quality of consumers during the communication process, brands should establish flexible auto-responder bots that collaborate rationally with manual customer service agents to resolve issues effectively.

5. Conclusions

From the perspective of consumers, this paper has derived the evaluation index system of perceived quality for clothing brands, which provides a theoretical framework for the perceived quality evaluation of clothing brands. Based on fine-grained sentiment analysis and multi-criteria decision making methods, this paper has proposed a multi-stage model ECRM for perceived quality evaluation. In the first stage, RBF and dependency parsing are used to extract attribute–viewpoint phrases. Next, reviews are classified using pre-trained language models. Finally, indexes are then ranked using stochastic dominance criteria and PROMETHEE-II. ECRM is presented as a system composed of specific components and may serve as a reference for other industries.

Clothing is intimately connected with individuals. The results of empirical experiments show that certain common and distinct features of perceived quality exist among clothing brands. Of all the indexes, clothing brands should give priority to the comfort of clothing products and other factors closely related to people. In the environment of online shopping, consumers' demand for service quality is not particularly significant compared to product quality.

Author Contributions: Conceptualization, J.C. and J.Z.; methodology, J.C.; validation, M.R.; formal analysis, Y.F.; investigation, M.R.; resources, J.Z.; data curation, M.R.; writing—original draft preparation, M.R.; writing—review and editing, Y.F. and J.C.; visualization, M.R.; supervision, Y.F.; project administration, J.C.; funding acquisition, J.Z. All authors have read and agreed to the published version of the manuscript.

Funding: This research was funded by the National key research and development program, grant number 2019YFB1405300, the Project of Cultivation for Young Top-notch Talents of Beijing Municipal Institutions "Research on the comprehensive quality intelligent service and optimized technology for small medium and micro enterprises" (Grant No. BPHR202203233), and the National Natural Science Foundation of China "Research on the influence and governance strategy of online review manipulation with the perspective of E-commerce ecosystem" (Grant No. 72174018).

Data Availability Statement: The datasets generated during and analyzed during the current study are available from the corresponding author on reasonable request.

Conflicts of Interest: The authors declare no conflict of interest.

References

1. China Clothing Association. *2021–2022 China Clothing Industry Development Report*, 1st ed.; China Textile Publishing House: Beijing, China, 2022; pp. 19–21.
2. Chen, X.; Liang, H.; Gao, Y.; Xu, W. A method based on the disappointment almost stochastic dominance degree for the multi-attribute decision making with linguistic distributions. *Inf. Fusion* **2020**, *54*, 10–20. [CrossRef]

3. Li, L.; Yang, W.S.; Xie, Y.Q. Research on Quality Information Asymmetry in the E-commerce Market. *Manag. Rev.* **2004**, *3*, 25–30+63–64.
4. Valarie, A.Z.; Leonard, L.B.; Parasuraman, A. Consumer perceptions of price quality and value: A means end model and synthesis of evidence. *J. Mark.* **1988**, *52*, 35.
5. Chang, Y.P.; Zhu, D.H.; Zhang, J.L. Research on the Relationship between Knowledge Sharing in Virtual Communities and Consumer Brand Conversion. *J. Manag.* **2009**, *6*, 1536–1540+1554.
6. Zhu, Z.Z.; Liu, F.; Wei, H.Y. Research on the Influence Mechanism of Product Design on Consumer Word of mouth Communication—Mesomeric effect of Emotion and Perceived Quality. *J. Dalian Univ. Technol. (Soc. Sci. Ed.)* **2022**, *43*, 55–62.
7. Li, S.; Liu, F.; Zhang, Y.; Zhu, B.; Zhu, H.; Yu, Z. Text Mining of User-Generated Content (UGC) for Business Applications in E-Commerce: A Systematic Review. *Mathematics* **2022**, *10*, 3554. [CrossRef]
8. Yu, S.; Du, Z.; Lin, X.; Luo, H.; Wang, J. A Stochastic Dominance-Based Approach for Hotel Selection under Probabilistic Linguistic Environment. *Mathematics* **2020**, *8*, 1525. [CrossRef]
9. Cao, W.; Yang, X.; Yang, Y. A Large-Scale Reviews-Driven Multi-Criteria Product Ranking Approach Based on User Credibility and Division Mechanism. *Mathematics* **2023**, *11*, 2952. [CrossRef]
10. Li, Y. Research on Customer Perceived Product Quality Evaluation Based on Emotional Analysis. Master's Thesis, Hefei University of Technology, Hefei, China, 2020.
11. He, Y.K. Research on Evaluation of E-commerce Logistics Service Quality Based on Emotional Analysis. Master's Thesis, Nanjing University, Nanjing, China, 2021.
12. Zhou, M.; Li, Y. Customer Perceived Product Quality Evaluation Based on Comments on Big data. *Sci. Technol. Dev.* **2020**, *16*, 804–810.
13. Zheng, S.Y.; Wang, P.; Din, H.; Tan, G.X. A study on the user experience of museum digital services based on aspect-level sentiment analysis. *Intell. Sci.* **2022**, *40*, 171–178.
14. Lu, S.; Liu, M.; Yin, L.; Liu, X.; Zheng, W. The multi-modal fusion in visual question answering: A review of attention mechanisms. *PeerJ Comput. Sci.* **2023**, *9*, 1400. [CrossRef] [PubMed]
15. Zhang, Y.; Shao, Z.; Zhang, J.; Wu, B.; Zhou, L. The effect of image enhancement on influencer's product recommendation effectiveness: The roles of perceived influencer authenticity and post type. *JRIM* **2023**, *4*, 385–401. [CrossRef]
16. Cheng, L.; Yin, F.; Theodoridis, S.; Chatzis, S.; Chang, T.-H. Rethinking Bayesian Learning for Data Analysis: The art of prior and inference in sparsity-aware modeling. *IEEE Signal Process* **2022**, *6*, 22. [CrossRef]
17. Nie, W.; Bao, Y.; Zhao, Y.; Liu, A. Long Dialogue Emotion Detection Based on Commonsense Knowledge Graph Guidance. *IEEE Trans. Multimed.* **2023**, *8*, 1–15. [CrossRef]
18. Liu, X.; Zhou, G.; Kong, M.; Yin, Z.; Yin, L.; Zheng, W. Developing Multi-Labelled Corpus of Twitter Short Texts: A Semi-Automatic Method. *Systems* **2023**, *11*, 390. [CrossRef]
19. Zeng, X.J.; Ye, X.Q.; Liu, D. Research on User Satisfaction Analysis Based on Fine-Grained Viewpoint Mining and Kano Modeling. *Comput. Eng. Sci.* **2023**, *45*, 701–710.
20. Liu, X.X.; Chen, Z.Y. Service quality evaluation and service improvement using online reviews: A framework combining deep learning with a hierarchical service quality model. *Electron. Commer. Res. Appl.* **2022**, *54*, 101174. [CrossRef]
21. Tulkens, S.; Van, C.A. Embarrassingly Simple Unsupervised Aspect Extraction. In Proceedings of the 58th Annual Meeting of the Association for Computational Linguistics, Online, 5–10 July 2020.
22. Tian, H.; Gao, C.; Xiao, X.; Liu, H.; He, B. SKEP: Sentinel Knowledge Enhanced Pre training for Sentinel Analysis. In Proceedings of the 58th Annual Meeting of the Association for Computational Linguistics, Online, 5–10 July 2020.
23. Feng, K.; Yang, Q.; Chang, X.Y. Fresh food e-commerce customer satisfaction evaluation based on online comments and stochastic dominance criteria. *China Manag. Sci.* **2020**, *29*, 205–216.
24. Majid, B.; Kazemzadeh, R.; Albadvi, A. PROMETHEE: A comprehensive literature review on methodologies and applications. *Eur. J. Oper. Res.* **2010**, *200*, 198–215.
25. Liu, X.F.; Ji, X.F.; Wang, J. Study on Perceived Quality of Silk Clothing. *Silk* **2007**, *3*, 49–52.
26. Valarie, A.Z.; Leonard, L.B.; Parasuraman, A. Communication and Control Processes in the Delivery of Service Quality. *J. Mark.* **1988**, *3*, 35–48.
27. Parasuraman, A.; Valarie, A.Z.; Leonard, L.B. SERVQUAL: A Multiple Item Scale for Measuring Consumer Perceptions of Service Quality. *J. Retail.* **1988**, *64*, 12–40.
28. Zhao, W.H.; Xiong, X.M. Measurement and Management of Service Quality in Online Retail: Based on the Chinese Context. *Manag. Rev.* **2015**, *27*, 120–130.
29. Eugene, F.; Dianna, L.; Dharuv, G. Development of a multidimensional measure of perceived product quality. *J. Qual. Manag.* **1997**, *2*, 87–111.
30. William, B.D.; Kent, B.M.; Dharuv, G. Effects of Price, Brand, and Store Information on Buyers' Product Evaluations. *J. Mark. Res.* **1991**, *28*, 307.
31. Jacob, D.; Chang, M.W.; Lee, K. BERT: Pre-training of Deep Bidirectional Transformers for Language Understanding. In Proceedings of the Annual Conference of the North American Chapter of the Association for Computational Linguistics (NAACL-HLT), Minneapolis, MN, USA, 2–7 June 2019.

32. Zhang, J.; Lu, X.; Liu, D. Deriving customer preferences for hotels based on aspect level sentient analysis of online reviews. *Electron. Commer. Res. Appl.* **2021**, *49*, 94–101. [CrossRef]
33. Sun, B.S.; Ao, C.L.; Wang, J.X. Research on satisfaction evaluation of ecotourism based on online Text mining. *Oper. Res. Manag.* **2022**, *31*, 165–172.
34. Wan, H.; Yang, Y.F.; Du, J.F.; Liu, Y.N.; Qi, K.X.; Pan, J.Z. Target-Aspect-Sentiment Joint Detection for Aspect-Based Sentiment Analysis. In Proceedings of the AAAI Conference on Artificial Intelligence, Online, 7–12 February 2020.
35. Fan, Z.P.; Xi, Y.; Liu, Y. Supporting consumer's purchase decision: A method for ranking products based on online multi-attribute product ratings. *Soft Comput.* **2018**, *22*, 5247–5261. [CrossRef]
36. Zhang, Y.; Fan, Z.P. A stochastic multi-attribute decision-making method based on stochastic dominance. *J. Syst. Manag.* **2010**, *19*, 371–378.
37. Kazimierz, Z.; Jean, M.M. Multiattribute Analysis Based on Stochastic Dominance. *Models Exp. Risk Ration.* **1994**, *20*, 225–248.
38. Samuel, B.G.; Jeffrey, L.R. Probabilistic domain criteria for comparing unknown alternatives: A tutorial. *Omega* **2009**, *37*, 346–357.
39. Sun, Y.; Wang, S.; Feng, S. ERNIE 3.0: Large-Scale Knowledge Enhanced Pre-Training for Language Understanding and Generation. Available online: https://arxiv.org/abs/2107.02137 (accessed on 30 August 2023).
40. Liu, Y.; Ott, M.; Goyal, N. RoBERTa: A Robustly Optimized BERT Pretraining Approach. Available online: https://arxiv.org/abs/1907.11692 (accessed on 30 August 2023).
41. Cui, Y.; Che, W.; Liu, T.; Qin, B.; Wang, S.; Hu, G. Revisiting Pre-Trained Models for Chinese Natural Language Processing. In *Findings of the Association for Computational Linguistics: EMNLP*; Association for Computational Linguistics: Abu Dhabi, United Arab Emirates, 2022.

mathematics

Article

A Study on the Effects of Digital Finance on Green Low-Carbon Circular Development Based on Machine Learning Models

Xuewei Zhang [1,2], Xiaoqing Ai [3,*], Xiaoxiang Wang [3,*], Gang Zong [3] and Jinghao Zhang [1]

1 School of Economics and Management, Inner Mongolia University, Hohhot 010021, China; zhangxuewei219@126.com (X.Z.); 15147322831@163.com (J.Z.)
2 Institute of Geographic Sciences and Natural Resources Research, CAS, Beijing 100101, China
3 School of Economics and Management, Beijing University of Technology, Beijing 100124, China; 15847206038@163.com
* Correspondence: wangxiaoxiang626@163.com (X.W.); axq@bjut.edu.cn (X.A.)

Abstract: With technological transformations such as big data, blockchain, artificial intelligence, and cloud computing, digital techniques are infiltrating the field of finance. Digital finance (DF) is a resource-saving and environmentally friendly innovative financial service. It shows great green attributes and can drive the flow of financial resources towards environmentally-friendly enterprises, thereby promoting green low-carbon circular development (GLCD). However, few studies have explored the coupling mechanism between DF and GLCD. To fill this gap, this paper explores the effect of DF on GLCD, and established a mediating effect model to investigate the mechanism of DF in promoting GLCD. Additionally, this paper established a random forest model and a CatBoost model based on machine learning to examine the relative importance of DF and the factors affecting GLCD. The results show that DF has significant positive effects on GLCD, and technological innovation plays a key role in the effect of DF on GLCD; meanwhile, the effect of DF on GLCD shows nonlinear features with an increasing "marginal effect"; moreover, both DF and conventional factors have significant impacts on GLCD. Our study highlights the effect of DF on GLCD and underscores the importance of developing policies for DF and GLCD. This study provides an empirical basis and path reference for DF to achieve "carbon peak, carbon neutralization" in China.

Keywords: DF; GLCD; machine learning; double-carbon target

MSC: 91B62; 91B76

1. Introduction

Over the past decades, China has made great achievements in economic development, and has become the largest energy consumer globally. However, there is an increasingly severe contradiction between economic growth and the ecological environment [1]. Hence, the Chinese government proposed a green and low-carbon development concept aiming to achieve harmony between human beings and nature, thereby promoting coordinated development of economic growth and environmental protection. Currently, green low-carbon circular development (GLCD) has become a global trend due to its significant role in ecological civilization and the development of a beautiful China [2]. The key areas of green low-carbon industries in China are relatively underdeveloped, and future development requires great financial support. However, the conventional financial mode is constrained by structural mismatch and fails to guide a green and low-carbon transformation. With the continuous integration of Emerging technologies such as big data, blockchain, artificial intelligence, and cloud computing with traditional finance, digital finance (DF) came into being [3], which can alleviate the mismatch of financial resources [4,5]. Specifically, DF can allocate capital towards green and low-carbon projects and accelerate the research and application of advanced green and low-carbon technologies [6], thereby facilitating the ecological environment and green development [7–9]. In the context of energy saving and carbon emission reduction [10], green and low-carbon development is an inevitable requirement for China's sustainable economic development [11–14].

Previous studies have investigated the effect of DF on economic growth, industrial structure, export, household consumption, and income inequality [15–19]. Early studies focused on the impacts of financial development on environmental protection, but no conclusion is drawn [20–23]. Recently, the effect of DF on GLCD has attracted increasing attention. Most scholars believe that DF has positive impacts on GLCD. For example, Wu et al. claimed that the digitization level in DF has a positive impact on carbon emission efficiency [24]; Razzaq and Yang found that DF can facilitate green growth by supporting the digital transformation of enterprises and addressing energy deficit [25]. From the perspective of distorted element configuration, Yang conducted an empirical test regarding the role and working mechanism of DF in carbon emission reduction based on the panel data of 280 cities in China from 2011 to 2019. The results indicated that DF facilitates rational resource allocation and reduction in carbon emissions [26]. From the perspective of capital bias towards technological advances, Li analyzed the impacts of DF on low-carbon energy transformation based on the panel data of 283 cities in China, and it was found that DF can improve carbon total factor productivity and the proportion of clean energy in total energy consumption, exhibiting positive impacts on low-carbon energy transformation [27].

Some scholars have found that DF has nonlinear impacts on green growth [28]: it has negligible impacts on green growth in the early stages, but the impact continuously increases with the level of DF [29]. Nevertheless, Fang et al. (2020) pointed out that financial development stimulates economic growth in China at the cost of increased carbon emissions [30]. By using autoregressive distribution lag-bound test methods, some studies revealed the positive impacts of financial development on carbon emission [31,32].

However, there are some gaps in the literature that limit our understanding of how DF contribute to GLCD. First, although research on low-carbon circular development has attracted academic interest, few studies have considered the multidimensional nature of the GLCD. And the impact mechanism of DF on low-carbon circular development is unknown and fails to provide policy guidance for carbon emission control and environmental improvement in China. The current study aims to clarify the effect of DF on low-carbon circular development in China, then hypothesized and validated the impact mechanism of DF on GLCD. As it pertains to offering both theoretical insights and practical implications, this research contributes to the field in three critical ways. First, the GLCD indicator system is established from the perspectives of ecological civilization and green economy and measured by adopting the spatiotemporal range entropy weight method. Second, the impact mechanism of DF on GLCD is clarified, and the effect of DF on GLCD through technological innovation are clarified by using the mediating effect model. Third, the nonlinear features and regional heterogeneity of the impact of DF on GLCD are investigated to clarify the mechanism of DF affecting GLCD. To sum up, this study aims to provide references for the positive impacts of DF on GLCD by conducting empirical research from the perspectives of the ecological economy and digital economy.

The rest of this paper is as follows: Section 2 investigates the working mechanism of DF affecting GLCD, as well as the corresponding hypotheses; Section 3 proposes a GLCD indicator system and its measurement; Section 4 constructs econometrics models, mediating effect models, and threshold effect models, and introduces relevant variables and data sources; Section 5 presents an empirical test of the impacts of DF on GLCD in terms of extent, mechanism, and threshold effect; Section 6 presents an analysis of the significance of different variables by using machine learning models, heterogenic analysis by regions and basins, and robustness testing of reliability of the results, and provides some recommendations.

2. Theoretical Analysis and Hypotheses

2.1. Effects of DF on GLCD

Due to limitations in cost and technology, conventional finance cannot provide sufficient support for GLCD in China [33,34]. With advances in the Internet, big data, and artificial intelligence, DF has emerged as an integration of conventional finance and digital techniques. As a novel financial pattern, DF has broken the bottleneck of conventional finance by increasing coverage and reducing transaction costs [35]. DF can reduce the financing threshold with its inclusiveness and assists financial institutions such as banks in risk assessment of real-time transactions and behavioral characteristics of small and medium-sized enterprises by using machine learning, thereby alleviating information asymmetry issues in lending [36]. Meanwhile, the unique and superior information collection and processing capabilities of DF allow optimizing the marketization configuration of capital factors. This enhances the interaction efficiency of information data in the factor market and the matching efficiency of different subjects [37,38] and improves the utilization efficiency of capital factors, thereby providing efficient and convenient financial services to various economic entities. Moreover, DF is essentially a green development mode, and it can accurately identify green and low-carbon features of enterprises, drive the capital to environmentally-friendly enterprises [39], optimize the allocation of credit funds among environmental protection industries, and facilitate the transformation of energy-intensive industries to high profit, high value-added, and low-carbon industries [40,41], thereby promoting the development of the green low-carbon circular economy.

Hypothesis 1 (H1): *DF can improve utilization efficiency of capital factor, and promote GLCD.*

2.2. Effects of DF on GLCD through Technological Innovation

DF can alleviate the financing constraints of enterprises, and promote innovation and upgrading of the financial industry in various aspects [42]. It increases the coverage of financial services and the depth of financial services, thereby alleviating the mismatch of financial resources [43,44]. Therefore, DF can accelerate financial digitization and provide sufficient financial resources for small and micro enterprises and private enterprises with market potential [45,46]. Financing incentives can strengthen the drive of enterprises on innovations. Digital techniques such as big data and cloud computing allow searching, analysis, and decision-making of consumption information of different users, thereby providing financing support for innovation activities with a high probability of success, which helps entities to explore innovations and improves the output and transformation of technological research and development achievements [47]. In this way, a comprehensive graph of technology and financial application scenarios is developed, and the financing channels for innovations are expanded, thereby promoting urban innovations.

With positive impacts on economic growth, carbon emission, and environmental protection, technological innovation is a key driving factor of GLCD [48,49]. It allows precise labor division, collaboration, and production in the production process, which effectively reduces resource factor loss during production and transmission and enhances energy utilization efficiency. In this way, technological innovation can achieve carbon-free, carbon reduction, and decarbonization before, during, and after the production process, thus promoting intensification and circular utilization of resources. Meanwhile, the technological innovation can optimize and upgrade carbon treatment and pollution control facilities and drive the transformation of the environmental governance mode from control-based end treatment to prevention-based clean production, thereby reducing pollution and enhancing environmental resilience. Attributed to advances in technological innovation and the concept of green development, the conventional production–circulation–consumption-discard linear mode is transformed into the green "production–circulation–consumption–discard–recycle" circular mode [50]. To sum up, DF plays a key role in promoting technological innovation and optimizing resource allocation, thereby possessing indirect impacts on GLCD [51].

Hypothesis 2 (H2): *DF can indirectly facilitate GLCD through technological innovation.*

This paper puts forward two research hypotheses for DF to promote GLCD, and establishes the mechanism of DF affecting GLCD (Figure 1).

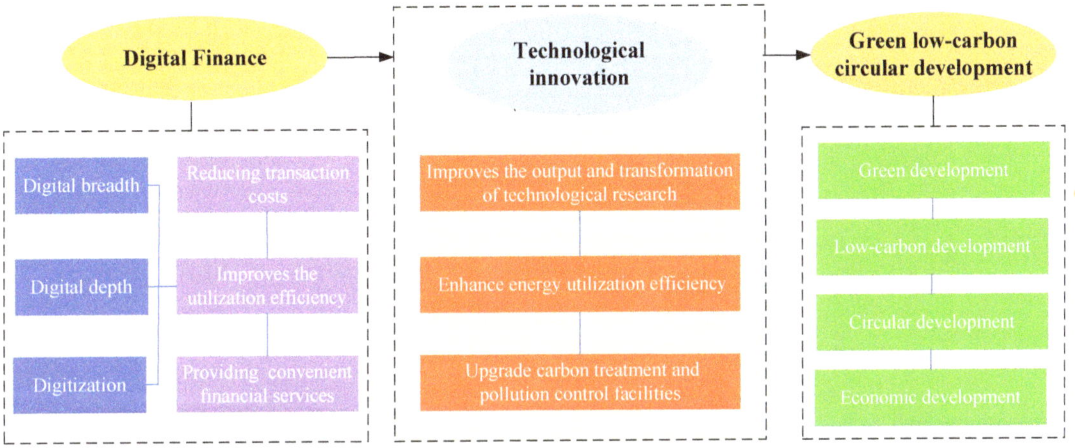

Figure 1. The mechanism of DF affecting GLCD.

3. Establishment of an Indicator System for GLCD

3.1. The Measure of GLCD

GLCD is essentially an integration of green development, low-carbon development, and circular development. Specifically, green development emphasizes rational utilization of natural resources and environmental protection, low-carbon development focuses on carbon emission reduction, and circular development aims at efficient resource utilization. Therefore, this research established a measurement system of GLCD in China (see Table 1) from four dimensions: green development, low-carbon development, circular development, and economic development, and calculates the comprehensive development level of GLCD in China by using spatiotemporal range entropy weight method.

Table 1. Comprehensive index system of GLCD.

Primary Indicator	Secondary Indicator	Tertiary Indicator	Indexes
GLCD indicator system	Green development	Natural resources	Water resource per capita (m^3/capita) The number of nature reserves Forest coverage (%)
		Ecological environment	Green coverage in urban areas (%) The local green space area Local forest area
	Low-carbon development	Carbon emission	Carbon emission/GDP (10,000 t/100 million yuan) Carbon emission/population (10,000 t/10,000 residents) Carbon emission/area
		Carbon productivity	GDP/carbon emission (100 million yuan/10,000 t) GDP of the secondary industry/carbon emission GDP of the tertiary industry/carbon emission

Table 1. *Cont.*

Primary Indicator	Secondary Indicator	Tertiary Indicator	Indexes
GLCD indicator system	Circular development	Utilization capability	The comprehensive utilization rate of industrial solid waste (%) Industrial water utilization rate (%) Recycling water utilization rate in urban areas (%)
		Processing capacity	Industrial waste gas treatment capacity (10,000 cm^3/h) Sewage treatment rate in urban areas (%) Hazard-free treatment rate of domestic waste (%)
	Economic development	Economic benefits	GDP per capita The proportion of tertiary industry in GDP (%) Total import/export volume/GDP (%)
		Social benefits	The average salary of employees (yuan) Public library collections per capita (copies) The registered unemployment rate in urban areas (%)

3.2. Method

At present, methods to determine indicator weights include subjective weighting methods, objective weighting methods, and integrated weighting methods. In this paper, the GLCD level of 31 provinces in China from 2008 to 2019 is measured by using the spatiotemporal range entropy weight method. Conventional entropy weight methods can only determine indicator weights at a specific moment, while the spatiotemporal range entropy weight method can determine indicator weights in both temporal and spatial dimensions, thereby updating indicator weights dynamically.

Assume that a multi-level evaluation system consists of n evaluation indicators of m evaluation objects in k periods. The indicator system is X_i ($i = 1, 2, \ldots, n$), and its indicator in period t is X_{ijt} ($j = 1, 2, \ldots, m$ and $t = 1, 2, \ldots, k$).

(1) Data standardization: let x_{ijt} be X'_{ijt}, a dimensionless decision matrix can be obtained: If x_i is a positive indicator,

$$x_{ijt}{}' = \left[x_i - \min(x_{ijt})\right] / \left[\max(x_{ijt}) - \min(x_{ijt})\right] \tag{1}$$

If x_i is a negative indicator,

$$x_{ijt}{}' = \left[max(x_{ijt}) - x_{ijt}\right] / \left[\max(x_{ijt}) - \min(x_{ijt})\right] \tag{2}$$

(2) Calculation of weights based on information entropy:

$$e_i = -ln(km)^{-1} \sum_j \sum_t p_{ijt} ln(p_{ijt}) \tag{3}$$

where

$$p_{ijt} = x_{ijt}{}' / \sum_j \sum_t x_{ijt}{}' \tag{4}$$

(3) The weight of X_i can be calculated by:

$$W_i = (1 - e_i) / (\sum_i 1 - e_i) \tag{5}$$

(4) Weighted summation of various indicators:

$$Z_{it} = \sum W_i \times x_{ijt} \tag{6}$$

4. Research Design

4.1. Model Establishment

4.1.1. Benchmark Regression Model

To capture and validate Hypothesis 1, this paper developed a panel benchmark model. The panel benchmark model is expressed as follows:

$$GLCD_{i,t} = \alpha + \beta_1 DF_{i,t} + \beta_2 Edu_{i,t} + \beta_3 Fdi_{i,t} + \beta_4 Gov_{i,t} + \beta_5 Pop_{i,t} + u_i + \varepsilon_{i,t} \quad (7)$$

where i denotes the city, t denotes the year, and GLCD denotes the green low-carbon circular development, which indicates the high-quality economic development level; DF is the digital finance index, which reflects the regional digital economy development level; $Edu_{i,t}$ represents the education level; $Fdi_{i,t}$ represents the direct foreign investment level; $Gov_{i,t}$ represents the government expenditure level; $Pop_{i,t}$ represents the population level; u_i represents the individual fixed effect; $\varepsilon_{i,t}$ represents the error term.

4.1.2. Mediating Effect Model

To clarify the transmission mechanism of DF affecting GLCD, a mediating effect model is constructed with technological innovation as follows:

$$TEC_{i,t} = \alpha + \beta_1 DF_{i,t} + \beta_2 Edu_{i,t} + \beta_3 Fdi_{i,t} + \beta_4 Gov_{i,t} + \beta_5 Pop_{i,t} + u_i + \varepsilon_{i,t} \quad (8)$$

$$GLCD_{i,t} = \alpha + \lambda TEC_{i,t} + \beta_1 DF_{i,t} + \beta_2 Edu_{i,t} + \beta_3 Fdi_{i,t} + \beta_4 Gov_{i,t} + \beta_5 Pop_{i,t} + u_i + \varepsilon_{i,t} \quad (9)$$

where i denotes the city, t denotes the year, and TEC is the mediating variable, representing technological innovation level; u_i represents the individual fixed effect; $\varepsilon_{i,t}$ represents the error term.

4.1.3. Threshold Effect Model

The impact of DF and technological innovation on GLCD was investigated by using a panel benchmark regression model and a mediating effect model. Due to the "online effect", the impacts of DF on GLCD may be nonlinear. In this section, the linearity/nonlinearity of such impacts is further investigated and verified by using the following threshold regression model:

$$\begin{aligned} GLCD_{i,t} \; &= \alpha + \beta_1 DF_{i,t} I(DF_{i,t} \leq \gamma_1) + \beta_2 DF_{i,t} I(\gamma_1 < DF_{i,t} \leq \gamma_2) + \\ &\beta_n DF_{i,t} I(\gamma_{n-1} < DF_{i,t} \leq \gamma_2) + \beta_n + DF_{i,t} I(DF_{i,t} > \gamma_n) + \\ &\phi X_{i,t} + \varepsilon_{i,t} \end{aligned} \quad (10)$$

To further explore the nonlinearity of the impacts of DF on green low-carbon circular development, a nonlinear effect model is developed with innovation input and innovation output as the threshold variables (TEC):

$$\begin{aligned} GLCD_{i,t} \; &= \alpha + \beta_1 DF_{i,t} I(TEC_{i,t} \leq \gamma_1) + \beta_2 DF_{i,t} I(\gamma_1 < TEC_{i,t} \leq \gamma_2) + \\ &\beta_n DF_{i,t} I(\gamma_{n-1} < TEC_{i,t} \leq \gamma_2) + \beta_n + DF_{i,t} I(TEC_{i,t} > \gamma_n) + \\ &\phi X_{i,t} + \varepsilon_{i,t} \end{aligned} \quad (11)$$

where $\gamma_1, \gamma_2, \ldots, \gamma_n$ are the thresholds to be estimated; $I(\cdot)$ is the indicator function, and its value is based on the expression in parentheses; X represents the control variable, which is the same that in Equation (1).

4.1.4. Machine Learning Model

As the impact of DF on GLCD is affected by various elements, multicollinearity and DOF degradation can be alleviated by using the nonlinear random forest model and the nonlinear CatBoost model in machine learning. The contributions of variables are calculated by establishing the random forest model and the CatBoost model, respectively, to clarify the effects of different variables on GLCD.

In random forest regression tree models, splitting nodes are selected by taking the least mean square error as the optimization criteria, and the variables are sorted according to their contributions to the reduction in the residual sum of square:

$$\min_{j,m}\left[\min\sum_{Yi\in R_1(j,m)}(Yi-\overline{Y_{R1}})^2+\min\sum_{Yi\in R_2(j,m)}(Yi-\overline{Y_{R2}})^2\right] \tag{12}$$

where $\overline{Y_{R1}}$ and $\overline{Y_{R2}}$ are the determined mean of each spurious copy of output variables; j and m refer to the splitting nodes of variables and threshold, respectively.

In the CatBoost model, more effective strategies are adopted to reduce over-fitting, and the entire dataset is used for training to effectively utilize the data information:

$$x_{i,k}=\frac{\sum_{j=1}^{p-1}\left[x_{\sigma_j,k}=x_{\sigma_p,k}\right]\times Y_j+\alpha\times p}{\sum_{j=1}^{p-1}\left[x_{\sigma_j,k}=x_{\sigma_p,k}\right]+\alpha} \tag{13}$$

where σ_j is the jth data, $x_{i,k}$ is the kth discrete feature of the ith data in the training set, a is a priori weight, and p is a priori distribution term (Table 2).

Table 2. The summary of all methods.

Method	Explanation
Benchmark regression model	To clarify the effect of DF on GLCD
The mediation effect model	To clarify the mechanism of DF affecting GLCD
Threshold regression	To Prove whether there is a nonlinear characteristic in the effect of DF on GLCD
Machine learning model	To examine the relative importance of DF and the factors affecting GLCD

4.2. Variable Selection

4.2.1. Explained Variables

In this study, a multi-dimensional evaluation system consisting of four dimensions (economic development, green development, low-carbon development, and circular development) is constructed, with the GLCD level measured by the spatio-temporal range entropy weight method as explained variable.

4.2.2. Key Explanatory Variable

In this study, the regional DF development level is investigated from three dimensions: breadth (*Bre*), depth (*Dep*), and digitization (*Dig*), with the total index of digital inclusive finance (*DF*) of China as the proxy variable of regional DF development level.

4.2.3. Mediating Variables

In this study, regional technological innovation is evaluated based on the proportion of science and technology expenditure in financial expenditure (*Sci*) and the number of patent applications per capita (*Pat*). This is consistent with the investigation of the influences of DF on GLCD through technological innovation.

4.2.4. Control Variables

To clarify the effect of DF on GLCD, the control variables affecting GLCD should also be set: (1) education level (*Edu*), which is evaluated based on the proportion of education expenditure in GDP; (2) direct foreign investment (*Fdi*), which is evaluated based on the proportion of direct foreign investment in GDP; (3) population (*Pop*), which is evaluated based on the permanent residents in this region; (4) government expenditure (*Gov*), which is evaluated based on the proportion of government expenditure in GDP.

4.3. Data Sources and Descriptive Statistics

In this study, the effect of DF on GLCD is investigated in terms of 31 provinces in China. The variables come from the Statistical Yearbook of China, the Energy Statistical Yearbook of China, and the Environment Statistical Yearbook of China from 2012 to 2020. The digital inclusive finance index comes from the Digital Inclusive Finance Indicator System and Index Compilation released by the Institute of Internet Finance, Peking University. The technological innovation data are collected from the website of the World Intellectual Property Organization (WIPO); missing data are determined by the interpolation method. The descriptive statistical results of the main variables are listed in Table 3.

Table 3. Descriptive statistics for all variables.

Variables	Symbol	Calculation Method
Green low-carbon circular development	GLC	Spatio-temporal range entropy weight method
Digital finance	DF	The digital finance level
	Bre	Breadth
	Dep	Depth
	Dig	Digitization
technological innovation	Sci	The proportion of science and technology expenditure in financial expenditure (%)
	Pat	The number of patent applications per capita (/10,000 residents)
education level	Edu	The proportion of education expenditure in GDP (%)
direct foreign investment	Fdi	The proportion of direct foreign investment in GDP (%)
population	Pop	Permanent population (10,000 residents)
government expenditure	gov	The proportion of financial expenditure in GDP (%)

5. Empirical Analysis

5.1. Benchmark Analysis

Table 4 presents the benchmark regression results. Model 1 corresponds to the estimated result with considering control variables. The results show that DF significantly promoted an improvement of GLCD. Promoting digital finance was conductive to developing green low-carbon circular development. The regression results (Table 4, Model 1) showed that for every 1% increase in DF, GLCD increased by 0.014%, The cause of this phenomenon is that "Data + Algorithm + Computing Power" can break temporal and spatial limitations to achieve rapid flow of various resource elements, thereby realizing effective docking and precise matching. It may continuously induce revolutions in the industry and facilitate the green transformation of energy-intensive industries. Model 2–Model 4 denote the dimension-reduction regression results of the effect of breadth (Bre), depth (Dep), digitization (Dig) on GLCD. The regression results (Table 4, Model 2–Model 4) showed that for every 1% increase in Bre, Dep, and Dig, GLCD increased by 0.011%, 0.011%, and 0.013%, respectively. This can be attributed to the fact that digital techniques such as artificial intelligence, big data, cloud computing, and blockchain significantly enhance labor productivity and decision-making efficiency, improving the efficiency of environmental management, ultimately leading to a reduction in energy consumption, thereby promoting GLCD. This proves the validity of Hypothesis H1.

Furthermore, the analysis of the control variables yields insightful results. The coefficient of Edu exhibits a significant positive relationship, indicating that higher levels of education level contribute to a promotion in GLCD. In contrast, the coefficient of Fdi demonstrates a negative association, confirming that foreign direct investment growth leads to a decrease in GLCD. The expansion of the foreign direct investment stimulates production and daily activities, resulting in higher energy demands and pollution emissions, inhibiting GLCD levels. However, the coefficient of Pop and Gov fail to pass the significance test, indicating that the effect of population and government expenditure on GLCD has not been effectively demonstrated. Despite the recent intensification of government expenditure on green development in China, their actual projects need improvement.

Table 4. The benchmark regression results.

Variables	Baseline Regression	Dimension-Reduction Regression		
	Model 1	Model 2	Model 3	Model 4
DF	0.014 ***			
	(0.002)			
Bre		0.011 ***		
		(0.001)		
Dep			0.011 ***	
			(0.002)	
Dig				0.013 ***
				(0.002)
Edu	0.203 *	0.188	0.178	0.210 *
	(0.116)	(0.116)	(0.119)	(0.114)
Fdi	−0.037 ***	−0.035 ***	−0.040 ***	−0.037 ***
	(0.010)	(0.010)	(0.010)	(0.010)
Pop	0.068	0.086	0.142 *	0.091
	(0.077)	(0.076)	(0.078)	(0.070)
Gov	−0.002	0.007	0.027	0.004
	(0.060)	(0.059)	(0.061)	(0.057)
cons	−0.265	−0.390	−0.849	−0.453
	(0.622)	(0.615)	(0.628)	(0.565)
N	279	279	279	279
R^2	0.223	0.219	0.181	0.256

Statistical significance at: * $p < 0.01$, *** $p < 0.01$. The t-values are in parentheses. The Hausman test is conducted to assess the appropriateness of random or fixed effects models. Rejecting Ho indicates that the fixed effect is valid.

5.2. Mechanism Analysis

The benchmark regression results illustrate that DF contributed toward improving GLCD. However, we have yet to determine whether the interaction mechanism between DF and GLCD conforms to the above theoretical analysis. Therefore, we further tested whether DF promotes GLCD improvement through certain mechanisms, such as technological innovation effects.

Table 5 shows the regression results of the mechanism test. Model 1 and Model 3 demonstrate that the mechanism test of science and technology expenditure in financial expenditure (Sci) and the number of patent applications per capita (Pat). Model 2 and Model 4 demonstrate the results of the mediating effects with the mediating variables. The coefficient of DF is statistically positive (passing the significance test at the 1% level) when Sci and Pat are explanatory variables, demonstrating that DF has a mediating influence on promoting GLCD. Therefore, the transmission mechanism that DF affects GLCD through technological invention transformation is valid.

Table 5. Analysis of mediating effects.

Variables	Sci	GLCD	Pat	GLCD
	Model 1	Model 2	Model 3	Model 4
Sci		0.959 ***		
		(0.271)		
Pat				0.001 ***
				(0.000)
DF	0.001 ***	0.012 ***	1.235 ***	0.012 ***
	(0.000)	(0.002)	(0.380)	(0.002)
Edu	−0.006	0.209 *	−31.020 *	0.249 **
	(0.027)	(0.113)	(17.240)	(0.114)
Fdi	0.002	−0.040 ***	8.615 ***	−0.050 ***
	(0.002)	(0.010)	(1.547)	(0.010)
Pop	0.050 ***	0.021	28.010 **	0.027
	(0.018)	(0.076)	(11.500)	(0.076)
Gov	−0.055 ***	0.050	−13.690	0.017
	(0.014)	(0.061)	(8.920)	(0.059)
cons	−0.379 ***	0.098	−221.700 **	0.0626
	(0.144)	(0.616)	(92.300)	(0.615)
N	279	279	279	279
R^2	0.193	0.262	0.413	0.261

Statistical significance at: * $p < 0.01$,** $p < 0.05$, *** $p < 0.01$. The t-values are in parentheses.

5.3. Threshold Regression

We used the benchmark regression model and mediation effect model to verify the effect of DF on GLCD through technological innovation in previous sections. In this section we use the threshold effect model to test the existence and number of panel thresholds (see Table 6). It was found that only the single threshold passed the significance test at 5% in terms of DF, with a threshold value of 5.38. This suggested that there was a single threshold for the impact of the DF on GLCD. In terms of Sci, the single threshold passed the test at the significance level of 5% with a value of 0.033, while the significance test was not passed for the double threshold. In terms of Pat, the significance test was not passed for the single and double thresholds. This showed that there was no threshold based on the increase in patents. To further investigate the threshold effect of DF on GLCD, the single threshold models were estimated based on the threshold value test, with the results reported in Table 7.

Table 6. Verification of threshold effects.

Threshold Variables	Threshold Numbers	Threshold Value	Critical Value			
			F	1%	5%	10%
DF	Single threshold	5.380 **	28.65	31.684	21.882	18.675
	Double threshold	4.610	8.62	22.975	16.118	13.459
Sci	Single threshold	0.033 **	28.32	31.849	25.960	22.517
	Double threshold	0.056	4.65	25.842	22.133	18.155
Pat	Single threshold	1.138	14.48	40.778	28.654	24.545

Statistical significance at: ** $p < 0.05$, The t-values are in parentheses.

Table 7. The results of threshold regression.

Variables	DF		Sci	
	Coef	T	Coef	T
DF_1 ($DF \leq 5.38$)	0.010 ***	2.39		
DF_2 ($DF > 5.38$)	0.013 ***	3.66		
DF_1 ($Sci \leq 0.033$)			0.013 ***	5.33
DF_2 ($Sci > 0.033$)			0.019 ***	7.24
Control variables	Yes	Yes	Yes	Yes
R^2	0.308		0.306	
N	279		279	
F	15.39 ***		15.23 ***	

Statistical significance at: *** $p < 0.01$. The t-values are in parentheses.

Table 7 summarizes the regression results of threshold models. As indicated by the table, the impacts of DF on GLCD are positively nonlinear. In the first case, DF is employed as the threshold variable for threshold estimation. If the DF development level is lower than the threshold (5.38), the estimation coefficient of DF on GLCD is 0.010; if the DF development level is higher than the threshold (5.38), the estimation coefficient of DF on GLCD is 0.013. The results indicate that the positive impacts of DF on GLCD depend on the DF system, and such impacts are more significant in the late stage. In the second case, the innovation input is taken as a threshold variable for threshold estimation. If Sci is lower than the threshold (0.033), the positive impacts of DF on GLCD are low; if the SCi is higher than the threshold (0.033), the positive impacts of DF on GLCD are greatly enhanced. When the innovation level varies, the impacts of DF on GLCD change with the innovation input; as the innovation input increases, the impacts of DF on GLCD exhibit significant positive nonlinear features with increasing "marginal effect".

6. Discussion

6.1. Interpretation of Findings

The promotion of DF significantly improved GLCD during the study period. Technological innovation effect promoted GLCD, which supports Hypothesis 1 (i.e., DF can promote GLCD). Therefore, exploring the impact of DF on GLCD is an important measure and path choice to achieve "carbon peak, carbon neutralization". At the same time, it should be noted that the current theoretical research on the impact of DF on GLCD is still in its infancy, and its mechanism research has only obtained some preliminary results. The green optimization effect of DF will be the key content of theoretical research to achieve GLCD in the future. In addition, in view of the heterogeneity of different regions in China, in-depth exploration of the regional suitability and applicability of DF affecting GLCD will be the core proposition that must be tackled when green theory is applied to practice. Pilot policies can make important contributions to GLCD in digital inclusive financial reform pilot zone and digital financial service platform. The establishment of the national digital inclusive financial reform pilot zone has accumulated experience in the exploration of financial support for the development of economic civilization and ecological civilization. The digital inclusive financial reform pilot zone has achieved positive results, and through accelerating the innovation of digital financial inclusion and other pilot means, guides funds to invest in green fields. More importantly, the mode of financial production and service must also be changed from high carbon to low carbon or even zero carbon.

6.2. Machine Learning Model of Nonlinear Effects

The importance of explanatory variables, mediating variables, and control variables that affect GLCD can be identified using the random forest model and the CatBoost model, and these variables are sorted according to their impacts on GLCD. According to Figures 2 and 3, GLCD has a significantly positive correlation with DF, with a contribution rate of 2.2% and 9.8%, respectively, indicating that GLCD can benefit from DF. Meanwhile, the other six characteristic variables have significantly positive impacts on GLCD, which is consistent with the expectation. Herein, the proportion of technology expenditure and population exhibit significantly higher contribution rates than other economic factors, which indicates that technology and talent are determining factors in economic development. Technology is the primary factor of production, and talent is the primary resource, and they can promote GLCD.

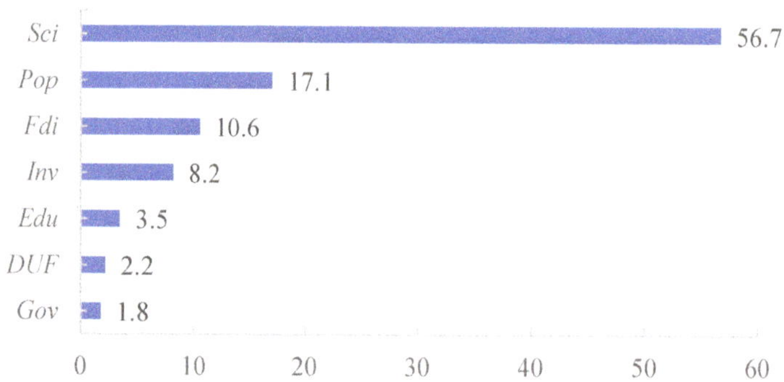

Figure 2. The significance of different variables (by the random forest model).

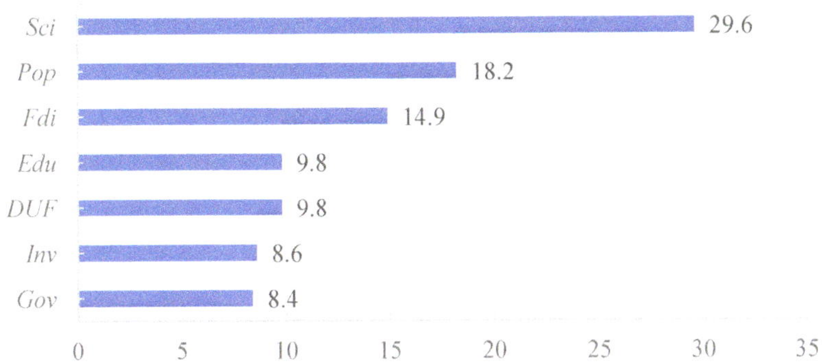

Figure 3. The significance of different variables (by the CatBoost model).

6.3. Heterogeneity Analysis

The impacts of DF on GLCD and the transmission mechanism, as well as the threshold effect, have been discussed in previous sections. However, regional differences, which lead to varying impacts of DF on GLCD, are not considered. Table 8 shows the impacts of DF on GLCD in different regions and basins. First, 31 provinces are divided into eastern, central, and western China, as shown in Model 1–Model 3, respectively. Both "Development of the Yangtze River Economic Belt" and "Ecological Conservation and High-Quality Development of the Yellow River Basin" have become key national strategies and benchmarks for the governance of large rivers in China. To clarify such differences from the perspective of national strategy, the Yangtze River Economic Belt and the Yellow River Basin are taken for regression analysis, where the former includes Shanghai, Jiangsu, Zhejiang, Anhui, Jiangxi, Hubei, Hunan, Chongqing, Sichuan, Yunnan, and Guizhou, and the latter includes Qinghai, Sichuan, Gansu, Ningxia, Inner Mongolia, Shaanxi, Shanxi, Henan, and Shandong, as shown in Model 4 and Model 5.

Table 8. The heterogeneity regression results.

Variables	East	Middle	West	Yangtze River Belt	Yellow River Basin
	Model 1	**Model 2**	**Model 3**	**Model 4**	**Model 5**
DUF	0.007	0.017 ***	0.021 ***	0.023 ***	0.017 ***
	(0.005)	(0.004)	(0.003)	(0.005)	(0.005)
Edu	0.121	0.114	0.236	−0.202	0.306
	(0.224)	(0.185)	(0.180)	(0.218)	(0.222)
Fdi	−0.027 **	0.040	−0.082 ***	−0.065 **	−0.085 **
	(0.013)	(0.050)	(0.028)	(0.029)	(0.038)
Pop	0.162	0.272	−0.210 *	−0.109	−0.227
	(0.133)	(0.198)	(0.110)	(0.222)	(0.311)
Gov	−0.156	−0.369 ***	0.276 ***	0.049	0.056
	(0.144)	(0.118)	(0.075)	(0.142)	(0.123)
cons	−0.915	−1.970	1.695 **	1.275	2.010
	1.093	(1.663)	(0.821)	(1.889)	(2.488)
N	99	90	90	99	81
R^2	0.124	0.401	0.476	0.348	0.263

Statistical significance at: * $p < 0.01$, ** $p < 0.05$, *** $p < 0.01$. The t-values are in parentheses.

According to the sub-region heterogeneity regression results obtained by Model 1–Model 3 shown in Table 8, the impact of DF on GLCD are maximized in western China. This can be attributed to the fact that central and western China have abundant resources and energy-intensive industries. DF can relieve this situation by significantly promoting digitalization and low-carbon transformation of traditional industries in western China. Specifically, energy digitalization will accelerate the growth of energy conservation and environmentally-friendly industries, and continuously facilitate the low-carbon development of all industries.

According to the sub-region heterogeneity regression results obtained by Model 4 and Model 5, the impacts of DF on GLCD are significantly positive in both the Yangtze River Economic Belt and the Yellow River Basin. This is because DF can enhance the green technological innovation capability, optimize industrial structure and spatial layout in the region, and improve the utilization efficiency of energy and resources, thereby facilitating GLCD.

6.4. Robustness Testing

To demonstrate the reliability of the empirical results obtained, robustness testing is conducted in three aspects: (1) Beijing, Shanghai, Tianjin, and Chongqing are excluded due to their unique economic development level and economic policies. As indicated by Model 1 in Table 9, the regression coefficient of DF on GLCD remains significantly positive (verified by a 1% significance level test), which is consistent with the results of baseline regression analysis. (2) Instrumental variable method: to mitigate endogeneity, estimation is conducted by using the two-stage least squares (2SLS) method with Internet popularity as the instrumental variable. As indicated by Model 2 in Table 9, the Internet popularity coefficient is significantly positive, which agrees with the conclusions of previous studies. (3) Change variation method: robustness testing is carried out by introducing the lagging phase of GLCD into the model and using mixed OLS and dynamic panel system GMM models, as indicated by Model 3 and Model 4 in Table 9. Model 3 refers to the mixed OLS regression, and the coefficient is significantly positive. As illustrated in Model 4, the regression coefficient of the previous phase of GLCD level on the current phase of GLCD level is significantly positive. That is, the process of GLCD evolves dynamically, and the regression coefficient of DF on GLCD levels remains significantly positive, indicating the high stability of the regression results.

Table 9. Robustness testing.

Variables	Model 1	Model 2	Model 3	Model 4
L.GLC				0.955 ***
				(0.037)
DUF	0.015 ***	0.046 ***	0.014 ***	0.022 *
	(0.002)	(0.013)	(0.002)	(0.013)
Edu	0.221 *	0.847 ***	0.328 **	−0.056
	(0.125)	(0.198)	(0.158)	(0.520)
Fdi	−0.049 ***	0.116 ***	−0.008	0.002
	(0.012)	(0.015)	(0.018)	(0.004)
Pop	0.065	0.030 **	0.009	0.005
	(0.089)	(0.009)	(0.020)	(0.003)
Gov	−0.000	0.175	0.012	0.026
	(0.065)	(0.031)	(0.095)	(0.010)
cons	−0.264	−0.337 **	0.179	−0.143
	(0.723)	(0.069)	(0.179)	(0.075)
AR(2)				0.559
Hansen				0.459
R^2	0.237	0.309	0.197	

Statistical significance at: * $p < 0.01$, ** $p < 0.05$, *** $p < 0.01$. The t-values are in parentheses.

7. Conclusions

Combined with theoretical analysis, this study evaluated the effect of DF on GLCD, analyzed the mechanism of action, and examined the heterogeneity effects between the two. The conclusions are summarized below.

According to the benchmark analysis results, DF significantly promoted GLCD. A series of robustness and endogeneity analyses also supported this conclusion. Specifically, the technological innovation effect contributed to the promotion mechanism of DF. DF has an increasing "marginal effect" on GLCD with its nonlinear characteristics. Moreover, a machine learning model is used to identify the importance of explanatory variables, mediating variables, and control variables that affect GLCD. We found that technological innovation contributes most to the impact of GLCD. Additionally, the promotion effect in China's central and western regions was greater than that in the eastern region. This can be attributed to the fact that central and western regions have abundant resources and energy-intensive industries, and energy digitalization will accelerate the growth of energy conservation and environmentally-friendly industries, and continuously facilitate green low-carbon development of all industries.

The research outcome of this paper provides consolidation of the evidence on the positive effects of DF on GLCD by the empirical research from the perspectives of the ecological economy and digital economy. With this study, we propose the following suggestions to make use of DF to facilitate GLCD.

Firstly, we suggest accelerating green transformation in key industries and fields to promote clean production and develop environmentally-friendly industries. This would further help to achieve low-carbon, safe, and efficient energy utilization of treatment sludge of domestic waste and sewage. For this reason, we should enhance the recycling of urban recycled water, and integrate the concept of green development into industry and daily life, to reduce carbon emission.

Secondly, we suggest that DF infrastructure should be constructed to facilitate the digital transformation of various industries, and the empowering channels of DF shall be expanded. Additionally, we should stimulate the innovation capability of DF and improve digital productivity, as well as strengthen the positive impacts of DF on GLCD.

Thirdly, based on regional differences in development levels, we suggest encouraging cooperation between regions, strengthening cooperation and mutual assistance, and market integration of different regions and basins with different resource endowments, and to improve the infrastructure of DF, in order to further unleash the spillover dividends of DF for green development.

Last but the least, technical cooperation and transactions can be achieved with the assistance of user-friendly and efficient digital platforms, which would help to promote the synergistic development of developed and underdeveloped regions and exploit the positive impact of DF on GLCD.

Author Contributions: Conceptualization, X.Z. and X.A.; Data curation, X.Z.; Funding acquisition, G.Z.; Methodology, X.Z.; Resources, X.Z. and X.A.; Software, X.Z.; Supervision, X.W.; Writing—original draft, X.Z.; Writing—review and editing, X.A., X.W. and J.Z. All authors have read and agreed to the published version of the manuscript.

Funding: This research was supported by the Innovative Research Group Project of the National Natural Science Foundation of China (NSFC) (Grant no.42121001), the National Natural Science Foundation of China (NSFC) (Grant Nos.72364027 and 72164030), the Natural Science Foundation of Inner Mongolia (Grant No.2023QN07008), and the Inner Mongolia Foundation of Philosophy and Social Sciences (Grant No.2022NDB134). All authors approved the version of the manuscript to be published.

Data Availability Statement: Data is available upon request to any of the authors.

Conflicts of Interest: The authors declare no conflict of interest.

References

1. Khan, M.K.; Rehan, M. The relationship between energy consumption, economic growth and carbon dioxide emissions in Pakistan. *Financ. Innov.* **2020**, *6*, 1. [CrossRef]
2. Fang, C.L.; Wang, Z.B.; Liu, H.M. Exploration on The Theoretical Basis and Evalution Plan of Beautiful China Construction. *Acta Geogr. Sin.* **2019**, *74*, 619–632.
3. Awan, U.; Sroufe, R.; Shahbaz, M. Industry 4.0 and the circular economy: A literature review and recommendations for future research. *Bus. Strat. Environ.* **2021**, *30*, 2038–2060. [CrossRef]

4. Moll, B. Productivity Losses from Financial Frictions: Can Self-Financing Undo Capital Misallocation? *Am. Econ. Rev.* **2014**, *104*, 3186–3221. [CrossRef]
5. Klapper, L.; Miller, M.; Hess, J. *Leveraging Digital Financial Solutions to Promote Formal Business Participation*; World Bank Group: Washington, DC, USA, 2019.
6. Shahbaz, M.; Shahzad, S.J.H.; Ahmad, N.; Alam, S. Financial development and environmental quality: The way forward. *Ener. Poli.* **2016**, *98*, 353–364. [CrossRef]
7. Feng, Y. Research on the Impact Evaluation of Digital Finance on the Synergy between Economic Development and Ecological Environment. *J. Environ. Public Health.* **2022**, 1714609. [CrossRef]
8. Feng, S.; Chong, Y.; Yu, H.; Ye, X.; Li, G. Digital financial development and ecological footprint: Evidence from green-biased technology innovation and environmental inclusion. *J. Clean. Prod.* **2022**, *380*, 135069. [CrossRef]
9. Liu, Y.; Xiong, R.C.; Lv, S.G.; Gao, D. The Impact of Digital Finance on Green Total Factor Energy Efficiency: Evidence at China's City Level. *Energies* **2022**, *15*, 5455. [CrossRef]
10. Mi, Z.; Zhang, Y.; Guan, D.; Shan, Y.; Liu, Z.; Cong, R.; Yuan, X.-C.; Wei, Y.-M. Consumption-based emission accounting for Chinese cities. *Appl. Energy* **2016**, *184*, 1073–1081. [CrossRef]
11. Li, J.; Wu, Y.; Xiao, J.J. The impact of digital finance on household consumption: Evidence from China. *Econ. Model.* **2020**, *86*, 317–326. [CrossRef]
12. Awan, U.; Kraslawski, A.; Huiskonen, J. Progress from blue to the green world: Multilevel governance for pollution prevention planning and sustainability. In *Handbook of Environmental Materials Management*; Springer: Berlin/Heidelberg, Germany, 2019; pp. 1–22.
13. Mi, Z.; Meng, J.; Guan, D.; Shan, Y.; Song, M.; Wei, Y.-M.; Liu, Z.; Hubacek, K. Chinese CO_2 emission flows have reversed since the global financial crisis. *Nat. Commun.* **2017**, *8*, 1712. [CrossRef] [PubMed]
14. Mi, Z.; Wei, Y.M.; Wang, B.; Meng, J.; Liu, Z.; Shan, Y.; Liu, J.; Guan, D. Socioeconomic impact assessment of China's CO_2 emissions peak prior to 2030. *J. Clean. Prod.* **2017**, *142*, 2227–2236. [CrossRef]
15. Miled, K.B.H.; Rejeb, J.E.B. Microfinance and poverty reduction: A review and synthesis of empirical evidence. *Procedia Soc. Behav. Sci.* **2015**, *195*, 705–712. [CrossRef]
16. Mushtaq, R.; Bruneau, C. Microfinance, financial inclusion and ICT: Implications for poverty and in equality. *Technol. Soc.* **2019**, *59*, 101–154. [CrossRef]
17. Ren, Y.M.; Gao, J.Y. Does the development of digital finance promote firm exports? Evidence from Chinese enterprises. *Fin. Res. Lett.* **2023**, *53*, 103514. [CrossRef]
18. Xie, S.; Jin, C.; Song, T.; Feng, C. Research on the long tail mechanism of Digital finance alleviating the relative poverty of rural households. *PLoS ONE* **2023**, *18*, e0284988. [CrossRef]
19. Syed, A.A.; Ahmed, F.; Kamal, M.A.; Trinidad Segovia, J.E. Assessing the role of Digital finance on shadow economy and financial instability: An empirical analysis of selected south asian countries. *Mathematics* **2021**, *9*, 3018. [CrossRef]
20. Jalil, A.; Feridun, M. The impact of growth, energy and financial development on the environment in China: A cointegration analysis. *Energy Econ.* **2011**, *33*, 284–291. [CrossRef]
21. Shahbaz, M.; Khan, S.; Tahir, M.I. The dynamic links between energy consumption, economic growth, financial development and trade in China: Fresh evidence from multivariate framework analysis. *Energy Econ.* **2013**, *40*, 8–21. [CrossRef]
22. Fang, Z.; Gao, X.; Sun, C. Do financial development, urbanization and trade affect environmental quality? Evidence from China. *J. Clean. Prod.* **2020**, *256*, 120892. [CrossRef]
23. Umar, M.; Ji, X.; Kirikkaleli, D.; Xu, Q. COP21 Roadmap: Do innovation, financial development, and transportation infrastructure matter for environmental sustainability in China? *J. Environ. Manag.* **2020**, *271*, 111026. [CrossRef] [PubMed]
24. Wu, J.; Zhao, R.Z.; Sun, J. What role does digital finance play in low-carbon development? Evidence from five major urban agglomerations in China. *J. Environ. Manag.* **2023**, *341*, 118060. [CrossRef] [PubMed]
25. Razzaq, A.; Yang, X.D. DF and green growth in China: Appraising inclusive digital finance using web crawler technology and big data. *Technol. Forecast. Soc. Chang.* **2023**, *188*, 122262. [CrossRef]
26. Yang, G.; Ding, Z.; Wu, M.; Gao, M.; Yue, Z.; Wang, H. Can digital fnance reduce carbon emission intensity? A perspective based on factor allocation distortions: Evidence from Chinese cities. *Environ. Sci. Pollut. Res.* **2023**, *30*, 38832–38852. [CrossRef]
27. Li, G.; Wu, H.; Jiang, J.; Zong, Q. Digital finance and the low-carbon energy transition (LCET) from the perspective of capital-biased technical progress. *Energy Econ.* **2023**, *120*, 106623. [CrossRef]
28. Wen, H.; Yue, J.; Li, J.; Xiu, X.; Zhong, S. Can Digital finance reduce industrial pollution? New evidence from 260 cities in China. *PLoS ONE* **2022**, *17*, e0266564. [CrossRef]
29. Zhong, K.Y. Does the digital finance revolution validate the environmental Kuznets Curve? Empirical findings from China. *PLoS ONE* **2022**, *17*, e0257498. [CrossRef]
30. Wang, T.Y.; Umar, M.; Li, M.G.; Shan, S. Green finance and clean taxes are the ways to curb carbon emissions: An OECD experience. *Energ. Econ.* **2023**, *124*, 106842. [CrossRef]
31. Liu, H.; Li, J.; Long, H.; Li, Z.; Le, C. Promoting energy and environmental efficiency within a positive feedback loop: Insights from global value chain. *Ener. Poli.* **2018**, *121*, 175–184. [CrossRef]
32. Shen, Y.; Su, Z.-W.; Malik, M.Y.; Umar, M.; Khan, Z.; Khan, M. Does green investment, financial development and natural resources rent limit carbon emissions? A provincial panel analysis of China. *Sci. Total. Environ.* **2021**, *755*, 142538. [CrossRef]

33. Wei, Z.; Yuguo, J.; Jiaping, W. Greenization of venture capital and green innovation of Chinese entity industry. *Ecol. Indic.* **2015**, *51*, 31–41. [CrossRef]
34. Ji, Q.; Zhang, D. How much does financial development contribute to renewable energy growth and upgrading of energy structure in China? *Ener. Poli.* **2019**, *128*, 114–124. [CrossRef]
35. Chen, H.; Zhang, X.; Wu, R.; Cai, T. Revisiting the environmental Kuznets curve for city-level CO_2 emissions: Based on corrected NPP-VIIRS nighttime light data in China. *J. Clean. Prod.* **2020**, *268*, 121575. [CrossRef]
36. Lu, Z.; Wu, J.; Li, H.; Nguyen, D.K. Local bank, digital financial inclusion and SME financing constraints: Empirical evidence from China. *Emerg. Mark. Finance Trade* **2021**, *58*, 1712–1725. [CrossRef]
37. Niebel, T. ICT and economic growth–Comparing developing, emerging and developed countries. *World Dev.* **2018**, *104*, 197–211. [CrossRef]
38. Karakara, A.A.W.; Osabuohien, E. ICT adoption, competition and innovation of informal firms in West Africa: A comparative study of Ghana and Nigeria. *J. Enterp. Commu.* **2020**, *14*, 397–414. [CrossRef]
39. Demertzis, M.; Merler, S.; Wolff, G.B. Capital markets union and the fintech opportunity. *J. Financ. Regul.* **2018**, *4*, 157–165. [CrossRef]
40. Li, J.; Li, B. Digital inclusive fnance and urban innovation: Evidence from China. *Rev. Dev. Econ.* **2021**, *26*, 1010–1034. [CrossRef]
41. Liu, X.S.; Lv, L.L. The effect of China's low carbon city pilot policy on corporate financialization. *Financ. Res. Lett.* **2023**, *54*, 103787. [CrossRef]
42. Luo, S. Digital finance development and the digital transformation of enterprises: Based on the perspective of financing constraint and innovation drive. *J. Math.* **2022**, *3*, 1607020. [CrossRef]
43. Ryals, L.; Payne, A. Customer relationship management in financial services: Towards information-enabled relationship marketing. *J. Strat. Mark.* **2001**, *9*, 3–27. [CrossRef]
44. Serrano-Cinca, C.; Guti'errez-Nieto, B. Microfinance, the long tail and mission drift. *Int. Bus. Rev.* **2014**, *23*, 181–194. [CrossRef]
45. Gomber, P.; Koch, J.A.; Siering, M. Digital finance and FinTech: Current research and future research directions. *J. Bus. Econ. Stat.* **2017**, *87*, 537–580. [CrossRef]
46. Li, Y.; Ji, Q.; Zhang, D. Technological catching up and innovation policies in China: What is behind this largely successful story? *Technol. Forecast. Soc. Chan.* **2020**, *153*, 119918. [CrossRef]
47. Wu, Y.; Huang, S. The effects of digital finance and financial constraint on financial performance: Firm-level evidence from China's new energy enterprises. *Energy Econ.* **2022**, *112*, 106158. [CrossRef]
48. Anser, M.K.; Khan, M.A.; Awan, U.; Batool, R.; Zaman, K.; Imran, M.; Sasmoko; Indrianti, Y.; Khan, A.; Abu Bakar, Z. The Role of Technological Innovation in a Dynamic Model of the Environmental Supply Chain Curve: Evidence from a Panel of 102 Countries. *Processes* **2020**, *8*, 1033. [CrossRef]
49. Sun, C. Digital finance, technology innovation and marine ecological efficiency. *J. Coastal Res.* **2020**, *108*, 109–112. [CrossRef]
50. Wang, H.R.; Cui, H.R.; Zhao, Q.Z. Effect of Green Technology Innovation on Green Total Factor Productivity in China: Evidence from Spatial Durbin Model Analysis. *J. Clean. Prod.* **2021**, *288*, 125624. [CrossRef]
51. Sun, H.; Kporsu, A.K.; Taghizadeh-Hesary, F.; Edziah, B.K. Estimating environmental efficiency and convergence: 1980 to 2016. *Energy* **2020**, *208*, 118224. [CrossRef]

mathematics

MDPI

Article

Enhancing Sensor-Based Mobile User Authentication in a Complex Environment by Deep Learning

Zhengqiu Weng [1,2], Shuying Wu [3,*], Qiang Wang [4] and Tiantian Zhu [2]

[1] School of Data Science and Artificial Intelligence, Wenzhou University of Technology, Wenzhou 325035, China; derisweng@163.com
[2] College of Computer Science & Technology, Zhejiang University of Technology, Hangzhou 310023, China
[3] School of Artificial Intelligence, Wenzhou Polytechnic, Wenzhou 325035, China
[4] School of Economics and Management, Wenzhou University of Technology, Wenzhou 325035, China
* Correspondence: wushuying@wzpt.edu.cn

Abstract: With the advent of smart mobile devices, end users get used to transmitting and storing their individual privacy in them, which, however, has aroused prominent security concerns inevitably. In recent years, numerous researchers have primarily proposed to utilize motion sensors to explore implicit authentication techniques. Nonetheless, for them, there are some significant challenges in real-world scenarios. For example, depending on the expert knowledge, the authentication accuracy is relatively low due to some difficulties in extracting user micro features, and noisy labels in the training phrase. To this end, this paper presents a real-time sensor-based mobile user authentication approach, ST-SVD, a semi-supervised Teacher–Student (TS) tri-training algorithm, and a system with client–server (C-S) architecture. (1) With S-transform and singular value decomposition (ST-SVD), we enhance user micro features by transforming time-series signals into 2D time-frequency images. (2) We employ a Teacher–Student Tri-Training algorithm to reduce label noise within the training sets. (3) To obtain a set of robust parameters for user authentication, we input the well-labeled samples into a CNN (convolutional neural network) model, which validates our proposed system. Experimental results on large-scale datasets show that our approach achieves authentication accuracy of 96.32%, higher than the existing state-of-the-art methods.

Keywords: mobile user authentication; deep learning; large-scale data analysis; implicit authentication; user micro feature

MSC: 68T07; 68T09

1. Introduction

With the advancement of mobile communication technology and hardware updates, mobile intelligent terminal devices have become increasing popular and are widely used in people's daily lives. The mobile application market has an anticipated annual consumer spending of USD 233 billion on the Apple App Store and Google Play store in 2022–2026 [1]. According to Grand View Research, the global mobile application market is expected to grow at a compound annual growth rate (CAGR) of 13.4% from 2022 to 2030 [2]. As more and more users transmit and even store their private data in mobile devices, it becomes very important to avoid information leakage in the network attack and defense. Especially in the instance where users are part of organizations such as enterprises, governments, and national infrastructure, the information leakage caused by advanced persistent threat attacks, conducted mainly by accessing the mobile devices to collect valuable confidential information, would be a catastrophe. Therefore, in order to safeguard their privacy and security, it is urgent to design suitable and robust user authentication models based on both the application scenarios and the features of mobile devices.

The current authentication methods for mobile users can be broadly categorized into two types: knowledge-based and biometric-based. Knowledge-based authentication methods [3] require users to explicitly input information such as passwords or patterns. Although these methods are widely used due to their low cost, they have to face challenges from the perspective of usability and security [4,5]. For example, (1) they are prone to various attacks such as brute force, shoulder surfing, smudge, inference, and social engineering attacks, and (2) inputting the same password repeatedly in small dialog boxes would have impact on the user physical experience. In contrast, biometric-based authentication methods [6] can mitigate the above issues to some extent. However, frequently using the facial or fingerprint recognition may also, especially in some ungoverned scenarios, bring psychological discomfort. Therefore, both usability and security should be the priority for the authentication systems. Recently, there has been extensive research on user dynamic authentication methods based on motion sensors. These methods identify users' information with machine learning or deep learning methods to discern unique behavioral patterns through their gait/gestures, because no privacy-related permissions are required in motion sensors. Then, researchers collect a series of non-privacy motion sensor data, such as accelerometer, gravity sensor, and gyroscope sensor data (through the system-level interface any application can obtain the data). However, in real-world and complex environments, it is hard to distinguish user micro features. The major challenges are as follows:

(1) In mobile user authentication, the majority of sensory signal transformation methods rely on expert knowledge [7,8]. They lack the in-depth data mining of motion sensor signals, and they are unable to effectively learn the complex nonlinear relationships between invariant features.
(2) Label noise is widely present in the training phase, e.g., device owners lend their phones to others. Most research has paid more attention to signal denoising, but less to reducing label noise [9,10]. If a classifier is trained with incorrect labels, continuous errors can accumulate. Even if labeled samples are obtained from the target person, the classifier may still fail to authenticate the device owner.
(3) The quality of handmade features is crucial for the performance of most classifiers. However, when dealing with complex mixed motion sensor signals, relying solely on statistical features can lead to critical information loss [7,11–13]. Additionally, the feature extraction process is typically fixed by the determined algorithm, whereas iterative optimization can be used to update the parameters of the classification model. This can hinder the improvement of algorithms for sensor-based mobile user authentication.

To address the aforementioned challenges, this paper proposes an efficient sensor-based mobile authentication method under a complex environment. Our system implicitly collects motion sensor data in the interaction between users and their mobile phones and utilizes S-transform (ST) [14] and singular value decomposition (SVD) to enhance their micro features. One-dimensional time-series signals are then sent to a server for label refactoring through a Teacher–Student (TS) tri-training semi-supervised algorithm. The resulting data are then used to train a CNN (convolutional neural network) model for feature extraction and classification, which is returned to the mobile terminal (client side) for real-time authentication. Experimental results on large-scale real-world data demonstrate that our method achieves higher accuracy, compared with existing state-of-the-art methods [7,9–12]. The main contributions of our work include the following aspects:

(1) A 2D image encoding method, ST-SVD, is proposed for 1D time-series signals by using a multi-resolution analysis. This method combines S-transform (ST) and singular value decomposition (SVD) to obtain an optimal S-matrix to enhance the time-frequency characteristics of sensory signals. Then, it allows CNN to learn high-level features. Moreover, this method takes into account the spatio-temporal properties of sensory signals.

(2) A semi-supervised Teacher–Student (TS) tri-training algorithm is proposed to address label noise in real-world motion sensor datasets. This algorithm effectively eliminates the negative impact of noisy labels and provides high-quality training data for the model.

(3) Integrating the aforementioned methods, we design a system with a client–server (C-S) architecture. Experimental results on large-scale real-world datasets demonstrate that the proposed system achieves a high authentication accuracy, outperforming existing state-of-the-art methods.

The remainder of this paper is organized as follows. Section 2 presents related work. Section 3 illustrates the system design in detail. Section 4 shows the overall evaluation of our system. Section 5 concludes our work.

2. Related Work

Authentication methods for mobile device users. Mobile device user authentication methods are essential for protecting user data. Currently, they can primarily be classified into three types: knowledge-based methods [5], static feature-based methods [6], and dynamic behavior-based methods [7]. Knowledge-based methods require users to explicitly enter a digital password or gesture pattern to unlock the mobile device or log into an application. These methods can only verify whether a user knows the credential but cannot determine whether the user is the device owner. Furthermore, they pose certain risks, such as poor human–computer interaction experience and privacy leakage. Previous studies have shown that they can easily be broken by brute force attacks [15], smudge attacks [16], shoulder surfing attacks [17], and sensor inference [18]. In contrast, static biometric authentication methods are based on fingerprints and faces, which can achieve relatively high recognition accuracy [19–21]. However, except concerns about the user experience and privacy leakage mentioned in Section 1, recent research has shown that misusing fingerprint APIs on Android can make applications vulnerable to various attacks [19], and face recognition methods based on deep learning algorithms have been proven to be circumvented by sophisticated attackers [20,21]. Dynamic behavior-based authentication methods access data from built-in sensors in mobile devices, including environmental locations, keystroke behaviors, finger movements, etc., and they work through the combination of feature engineering and model training. These methods may call privacy-related permissions to obtain user privacy data.

Static/dynamic feature authentication methods are based on credential technology and privacy risks. Given their inherent drawbacks, numerous researchers [8,11–13,22–27] proposed dynamic user authentication based on motion sensors, which has the following limitations: First, most user authentication based on motion sensors requires a user to use their phone at a fixed location or perform specific actions (in a lab environment), which is unrealistic and results in a large number of noisy labels in complex environments (non-lab environments). Second, the credibility of the data collected in complex environments is often questionable, for example, unreliable labels are generated if the phone is used by others except the owner. To achieve both good user experience and high authentication accuracy simultaneously, this paper proposes an effective sensor-based mobile user authentication method in complex environments.

Data denoising method for sensor-based mobile user authentication. Currently, most dynamic authentication methods utilize motion sensors [8–13,22–27]. They do not consider the impact of hardware noise. Then, it is very difficult for them to handle unlabeled data (noise data) in real environments. Finally, overfitting occurs and authentication accuracy decreases. In order to address the noise, some researchers [8] proposed noise elimination algorithms to obtain an effective dataset in the data preprocessing stage, but these algorithms cannot precisely distinguish the mislabeled and training samples. To overcome it, researchers used semi-supervised methods, combining noisy data with a set of clean labels [7]. Zhu et al. [7–9] observed that flat data cannot reflect the discrepancies of different user patterns in its collection. Removing it will omit analyzing its usability.

Additionally, when collecting users' data, researchers find the data are often mislabeled, such as unreliable labels we mentioned above. This paper simultaneously considers the noise and mislabeled data during the training process, fitting the training requirements to the greatest extent to provide high-quality data.

Mobile user authentication model based on motion sensors. The existing research methods using motion sensors [8–13,22–27] continuously collect sensor data and establish corresponding models to verify users' ID. Lu et al. [25] used unsupervised learning algorithms to process unlabeled data, but this method resulted in high latency. Additionally, unsupervised clustering algorithms with parameter adjustment have high overhead, and the parameter's generalization needs to be verified. Zhu et al. [7] designed a semi-supervised online learning algorithm. It has a high level of accuracy and low latency in processing unlabeled data under relatively complex environments, but the classification they used (binary class SVM) is not applicable to time series data due to ignoring the context of user behaviors. Furthermore, most existing studies [8–13,22–27] assume the input data are sufficient, which is not considered in real complex environments. In contrast, this paper proposes the transformation of 1D signals into 2D images. Meanwhile considering the spatio-temporal characteristics of sensory signals, we extract spatio-temporal features using CNN to achieve high mobile user authentication accuracy.

3. Methodology

3.1. Overview Framework

The method proposed in this paper is shown in Figure 1, consisting of the four following steps:

1. Collecting mobile user authentication data. The sensor data are collected through human–computer interaction between users and mobile devices.
2. Executing 2D optimal S-matrix coding with singular value decomposition (SVD) and S-transform (ST). In this approach, the 1D time-series signals are transformed into 2D matrix features with ST first. Then, SVD is applied to the S-matrix to enhance user micro features.
3. Filtering mislabeled data and using Teacher–Student (TS) tri-training to correct mislabeled data during training. This step can further improve the quality of the training dataset.
4. Using a Convolutional Neural Network (CNN) model to extract features from 2D optimal S-matrix images. The trained CNN model is used to authenticate whether the user is the device owner.

3.2. Sensory Signal Collecting

With the advancement in hardware technology, chips such as the Graphics Processing Unit (GPU) and Tensor Processing Unit (TPU) are being increasingly integrated into mobile devices to meet the ever-growing computational needs. Likewise, a plethora of sensors, e.g., accelerometer, gyroscope, gravity, light, and heart rate sensor, are being embedded into smart devices as privacy-neutral sensors. Specific tasks can be achieved through these sensors perceiving user behavior-related data.

Mobile devices are often equipped with various sensors of different functions to collect user behavioral features, thus eliminating cumbersome explicit operations. The more the sensor data are used for authentication, the less the attackers who can bypass the corresponding authentication system are able to do so. However, this also increases the probability that the authentication system rejects authorized device users. Therefore, we have to make the following selection criteria: (1) The sensor needs to be universal, that is, the sensor is popular and can be embedded in various mobile devices. (2) The sensor needs to be privacy-neutral, that is, the collected information does not contain personal identity-related content. For example, cameras, microphones, and GPS can, respectively, obtain users' facial features, sound, and visited locations. All these details are what users do not want to disclose to others. Under these criteria, touch sensors will not be considered because they not only collect users' fingerprints but also record their touch behaviors on the device. (3) The sensors need to be environment-neutral. For example, in noisy environments, the microphone is not effective, and in strong light, the usability of cameras is affected.

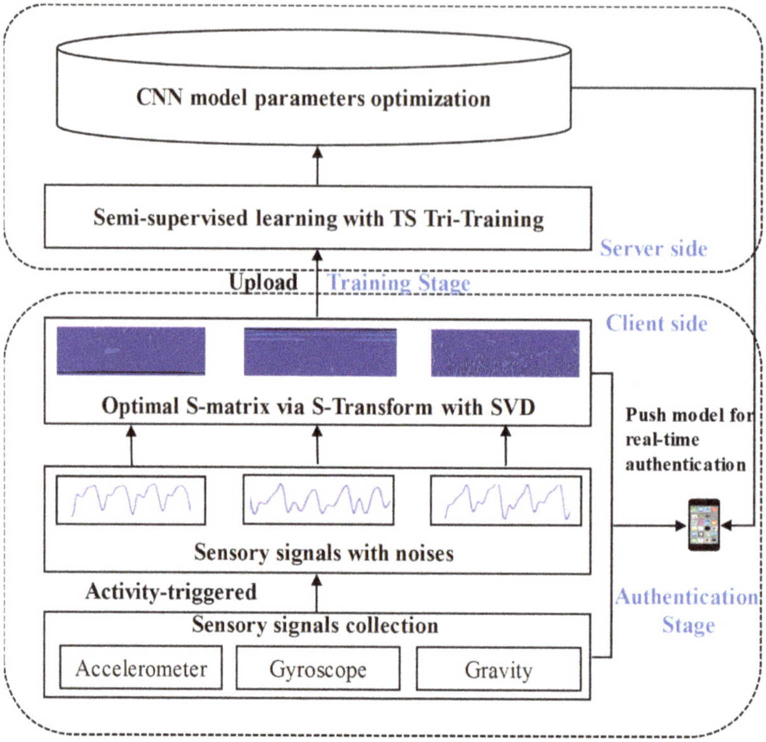

Figure 1. Sensor-based mobile user authentication process.

To effectively balance the relation among security (i.e., the system's underlying API interface can be safely used on non-rooted smartphones), privacy (i.e., the data collection does not require any privacy-related permission), and usability (i.e., any third-party application can be called to achieve device-level protection), we collect the raw data with accelerometer sensors, gyroscope sensors, and gravity sensors and conduct a large number of experimental comparisons to eventually achieve user privacy-neutral trustworthy authentication. Although the gravity sensor is a software-based sensor that utilizes accelerometer and gyroscope sensor data for processing, it can record the absolute position of the user when they use the mobile device, which is regarded as an important feature of user authentication.

We implicitly collect the above three types of motion sensor data when users use their mobile phone. Firstly, when a user opens a mobile phone application (representing a user behavior feature), we collect the smartphone's accelerometer, gyroscope, and gravity sensor X, Y, and Z axes' values as raw time sequence signal data. Inspired by [8], the following two scenarios can trigger the data collection: (1) the screen of the smartphone is lit up and (2) the foreground application of the smartphone is switched. This can greatly improve the security of mobile devices because the authentication starts no matter when users operate their mobile devices or open a particular application. In the real world, when the application starts, the ideal duration of data collection is generally 2–4 s, and its frequency is 50 Hz. Setting the collection duration t (2 s $\leq$ t $\leq$ 4 s) in advance, we obtain effective user behaviors. If the time when users use their phone is less than t (in second), that is, the screen is turned off in the collection, the collection is terminated. In this paper, we set t to 3 s.

3.3. Sensory Signal with 2D Coding Conversion

Numerous advanced techniques [11–19] for signal processing, including time-frequency diagrams and histograms, have been developed to transform 1D time-series signals into 2D matrix features. S-transform (ST) is used to create a time-frequency representation of signals. ST outperforms the Short-time Fourier Transform (STFT) since the window in ST is adaptively wider in the time domain at lower frequencies and narrower at higher frequencies, and it provides excellent frequency localization at low frequencies and good time localization at higher frequencies. Inspired by [14,28], ST is introduced as a means of 2D signal encoding. This enables deep learning models to extract complex time-frequency features and achieve a high accuracy classification for different users.

Using a localized Gaussian window, both movable and scalable, we implement ST from the time domain to two-dimensional frequency translation domains and then to Fourier frequency domains. Then, we obtain the amplitude-frequency-time spectrum and phase-frequency-time spectrum, which are useful for defining local spectral characteristics of a sensory signal. The phase information incorporation in ST makes it an excellent candidate for sensor-based mobile user authentication. The continuous ST is defined in Equation (1), where the function h(t) is a continuous wavelet transform (CWT) with a specific mother wavelet multiplied by the phase factor. The mother wavelet is a waveform primarily used as a basis for the CWT. It provides the oscillatory properties necessary to analyze signals with varying frequency content at different time scales. Here, we use Morlet wavelet as the mother wavelet.

$$S(\tau, f) = \int_{-\infty}^{+\infty} h(t)\frac{|f|}{\sqrt{2\pi}}e^{-\frac{(\tau-t)^2 f^2}{2}}e^{-i2\pi ft}\,dt \tag{1}$$

Since the signal is obtained in discrete time series with a sampling interval T, let f correspond to n/NT and τ correspond to jT, the discrete ST can be represented as in Equation (2).

$$\begin{aligned} S[jT, \tfrac{n}{NT}] &= \sum_{m=0}^{M-1} H[\tfrac{m+n}{NT}]e^{-\frac{2\pi^2 m^2}{n^2}}e^{\frac{i2\pi mj}{N}}, n \neq 0 \\ S[jT, 0] &= \sum_{m=0}^{M-1} H[\tfrac{m}{NT}], n = 0 \end{aligned} \tag{2}$$

Here, n ranges from 0 to $N-1$, where N represents the sampling number. The range of j is from 0 to 1. ST and produces a complex matrix known as the S-matrix, with rows representing time and columns representing frequency. Put it another way, each column represents a local spectrum at a specific time. Frequency-time contours are then visually obtained from the S-matrix. It is important to note that the original elements of the S-matrix are complex exponentials. To visually represent frequency-time amplitude, we have to calculate and process the magnitude of each S-matrix element.

Due to the non-stationary and non-Gaussian characteristics of sensory signals, the SVD algorithm is utilized to denoise signals and enhance user micro features. An $m \times m$ matrix A can be formulated as: $A = U\sum V^T$, where $U = [u_1, u_2, \ldots, u_m]$, and $V = [v_1, v_2, \ldots, v_m]$ are orthogonal matrices. The column vectors of matrices U and V refer to the orthonormal eigenvectors of matrices AA^{T} and $A^{\mathrm{T}}A$, respectively. The diagonal matrix $\sum$ arranges the singular values in descending order, which is designated as $\sum = [diag(\sigma_1, \sigma_2, \ldots, \sigma_l), 0]$, where $l = \min(m, n)$ and $\sigma_1 \geq \sigma_2 \geq, \ldots, \geq \sigma_l$.

From the aforementioned analysis, it is evident that how to select a suitable SV order is imperative for SVD-based denoising. Therefore, to attain SVD adaptive decomposition, this paper adopts the maximum SV mean method to determine a reasonable SV order. The SV mean is defined by Equation (3) below:

$$Z_i = \frac{\alpha_{i-1} - \alpha_{i+1}}{2} \tag{3}$$

where Z_i is the i-th SV mean. $k = \arg(maxZ_i)$ is the best SV order. α_i represents the i-th SV in the sorted descending sequence of singular values obtained from the SVD algorithm for a given signal. The maximum SV mean can originate from the uncorrelation of the fault component α_{i-1} and noise disturbance component α_{i+1} in the signal. Thus, the maximum mean value can be regarded as a demarcation point between the fault component and noise disturbance component. Ultimately, the S-matrix A is reconstructed and represented as B if we only preserve the first k SVs.

3.4. Label Correction with TS Tri-Training

In previous research, training data labels are often assumed to be perfectly tagged without any noise. However, in reality, a vast majority of labeled samples are imperfect due to various factors in the training phase. Moreover, manual labeling incurs significant time and labor costs. To address this, we use an automatic and general algorithm named Teacher–Student (TS) tri-training to mitigate label noise. TS tri-training ensures classifier differentiation by training differential data subsets extracted from the original dataset. As a result, the algorithm can recognize and correct noisy labeled samples.

TS tri-training involves the following steps: First, the original dataset I (a 10-day dataset, as will be described in Section 4) is partitioned into three sub-sets; a labeled dataset L, which may contain mislabeled data, an unlabeled dataset U, and a verification dataset V. Then, we assume that when a user starts using the mobile phone in the initial period, we regard the user as the owner. Accordingly, the data in the first two days belongs to L, while the data in the next six days—which may have been mislabeled—is placed in U. Finally, the data in the last two days, representing the user's own test data, are put in V.

Through Bootstrap Sampling on dataset L, we obtain three labeled training subsets Lc, Ll, and Ln, of which each is 1/3 of the total L. Then, three classifiers, Cd, Cl, and Cn, stem from the above three subsets, respectively. Pseudo-labeled samples in the form of "minority obeying majority" [29] are then generated by using these classifiers. Specifically, if Cd and Cl predict an unlabeled sample s is positive with a probability greater than the confidence coefficient τt, and Cn predicts it is negative with a probability less than τs, then Cd and Cl are regarded as teachers, and Cn as a student. Finally, as a pseudo-labeled positive sample, s is provided to Cn for learning. If the two teacher classifiers make the same prediction for the same unlabeled sample, this sample is considered as one with a higher label confidence and then added to the labeled training set of the third classifier after being labeled. The "minority obeying majority" [29] aims to eliminate classification errors. Though noise exists within the labeling process, it can be offset to some extent given the large number of samples utilized in this study. The intersection of Lc, Ll, and Ln is then taken as the final labeled training dataset L$'$. We choose binary classification because it can better distinguish whether the device is used by its owner. According to the tri-training based image classification methods [30], classifiers of Decision Tree, Support Vector Machine, and K-Nearest Neighbors require a certain proportion of counterexamples. Strategic sampling [8] is adopted to extract the most representative counterexample data samples from the massive data of other people. We set τt = 0.8 and τs = 0.2 through fine-tuning.

3.5. Convolutional Neural Networks Construction

In order to achieve sensor-based mobile user authentication, we use a Convolutional Neural Network (CNN) structure that comprises an input layer, two convolutional layers (CL1, CL2), followed by max pooling layers (MP1, MP2), two fully connected layers (FCL), and an output layer as a classifier. A detailed account is presented in Table 1.

Table 1. Structure of CNN model.

Layer	Input Shape	Structure	Output Shape
Input	9×150	-	$9 \times 100 \times 150$
CL1	$9 \times 100 \times 150$	$20@(2 \times 3)$	$20@(24 \times 148)$
MP1	$20@(24 \times 148)$	2×4	$20@(12 \times 37)$
CL2	$50@(12 \times 37)$	$50@(3 \times 8)$	$50@(10 \times 30)$
MP2	$50@(10 \times 30)$	2×6	$50@(5 \times 5)$
FC	750×1	256×1	256×1
Output	256×1	2×1	2×1

Input Layer. We collect nine time signals (i.e., X, Y, and Z axes' values from accelerometer, gyroscope, and gravity sensor as raw time sequence signal data) as the input (9×150). Then, an ST/SVD matrix is created (totally $9 \times 100 \times 150$). As mentioned in Section 3.3, the optimal S-matrix is obtained and used as an input for the CNN model. The input layer, unlike traditional RGB images, is solely connected with a matrix derived from 2D encoding features. Moreover, it should be noted that the original elements of the S-matrix are complex exponential. Thus, computing the magnitude of each element is necessary for further processing the visualization of frequency-time amplitude.

Convolutional Layers. Two-dimensional convolutional operations are carried out across these layers, where local features are transformed into global ones. Their main purpose is to achieve weight sharing, and then improve the efficiency and feasibility of the model. In this paper, the stride is set to 1. The sizes of the convolutional kernels in the Convolutional Layer1 (CL1) and the Convolutional Layer2 (CL2) are 2×3 and 3×8, respectively. The number of kernels in CL1 is 20, while in CL2, it is 50. The activation function is ReLU.

Max-Pooling Layers. Max-pooling layers down-sample vital and invariant information. These layers aim to reduce training time and avoid overfitting. The sizes of the Max-Pooling Layer 1 (MP1) and the Max-Pooling Layer 2 (MP2) are 2×4 and 2×6, respectively.

Fully Connected Layers. These layers aim to flatten the learned features into a single vector. The size of the Fully Connected Layer (FCL) is 256×1.

Output Layer. The output layer serves as a classification vector via a softmax function (loss function), and the optimizer is Adam.

4. Experimental Evaluations

This section mainly focuses on testing the performance and accuracy of the mobile user authentication method based on feature enhancement and semi-supervised learning. In the experimental environment, we use a server based on Ubuntu 20.04, equipped with an Intel(R) Intel Xeon E5 CPU and 128 GB memory.

4.1. Dataset

The dataset consists of two parts. The first part (dataset I) is from a well-known domestic Internet company, with 1513 volunteers aged from 20 to 60. With the users' permission, the dynamic data are collected as authentication data when they use their phones in complex environments. The data are from different users in an unsupervised manner and contain a large number of potential noisy labels. In the two scenarios triggering the data collection in Section 3.2, the built-in acceleration sensor, the gyroscope sensor, and the gravity sensor of the mobile devices capture relevant sensor signals at a rate of 50 Hz. The collection lasts for 10 days, and we obtain a total of 283,006,659 pieces of valid datum, with an average of 187,050 pieces per user. Dataset I is randomly divided into three groups. For each volunteer, 60% data are used for training, 20% are for validation, and 20% are for testing (to ensure the generalizability of the experimental results, all tests are cross-validated 10 times). The second part (dataset II) comes from 20 volunteers in our laboratory, aged between 20 and 60 in a supervised environment. The collection lasts for

10 days, and a total of 600,000 pieces of valid datum are collected. Dataset II is mainly used to test the label denoising algorithm.

During the label correction, classifiers such as Decision Tree, Support Vector Machine, and *K*-Nearest Neighbors are utilized to partition the labeled dataset into training and test sets at a ratio of 4:1 in the model training. The ratio of positive to negative samples is kept at 1:5, which is the same with that in the testing.

In the hybrid CNN-based training phase, the labeled dataset L′ is divided into the training and test sets, at a ratio of 4:1 as well. As in the label correction, the ratio of positive to negative samples is maintained at 1:5 as well.

For all datasets, data collection occurs at a frequency of 50 Hz, and each data collection lasts for 3 s. We use the International Mobile Equipment Identity (IMEI) to identify each user's ID and distinguish them on the server side.

4.2. Evaluation Metrics

We employ the following four metrics to evaluate the efficacy and accuracy of the model: True Positive (TP), which denotes the number of owners who have been identified correctly as the owners; False Positive (FP), which signifies the number of non-owners who have been misidentified as the owners; True Negative (TN), which indicates the number of non-owners who have been identified correctly as the non-owners; and False Negative (FN), which represents the number of owners who have been misidentified as the non-owners. In terms of classification accuracy, the following indicators are listed:

The authentication rate of the owner (sensitivity) is:

$$TPR = \frac{TP}{TP + FN} \tag{4}$$

The authentication rate of non-owner (specificity) is:

$$TNR = \frac{TN}{FP + TN} \tag{5}$$

The total accuracy is:

$$Accuracy = \frac{TP + TN}{TP + FP + TN + FN} \tag{6}$$

4.3. Performance of ST-SVD on Sensory Signals

To assess the efficiency of ST-SVD, we compared traditional ST and generalized ST [31]. We analyzed sensory signals from acceleration sensors of two different users (randomly selected from our dataset) to illustrate the superiority of ST-SVD. Figures 2 and 3 compare the original sensory signals, the matrix obtained from adopting generalized ST, the matrix obtained from adopting traditional ST, and the matrix obtained from adopting ST-SVD (our proposed method). Time-frequency diagrams obtained from generalized ST are poor in extracting features, whereas traditional ST is sensitive to background noise. ST-SVD depicts clearer user patterns excellently, revealing the sensitivity of sensor-based mobile user authentication. ST-SVD accurately captures users' subtle behavioral differences (i.e., user micro features).

From Figures 2 and 3, it can be concluded that ST-SVD exhibits energy concentration superior to traditional S-transform and Generalized S-transform (the X-axis represents the second t(s)). Additionally, ST-SVD obtains a more distinct essential characteristic, location, in user usage patterns. ST extracts multi-resolution features of sensory signals, and SVD plays a significant role in S-matrix reconstruction, which enhances user micro features in time-frequency diagrams.

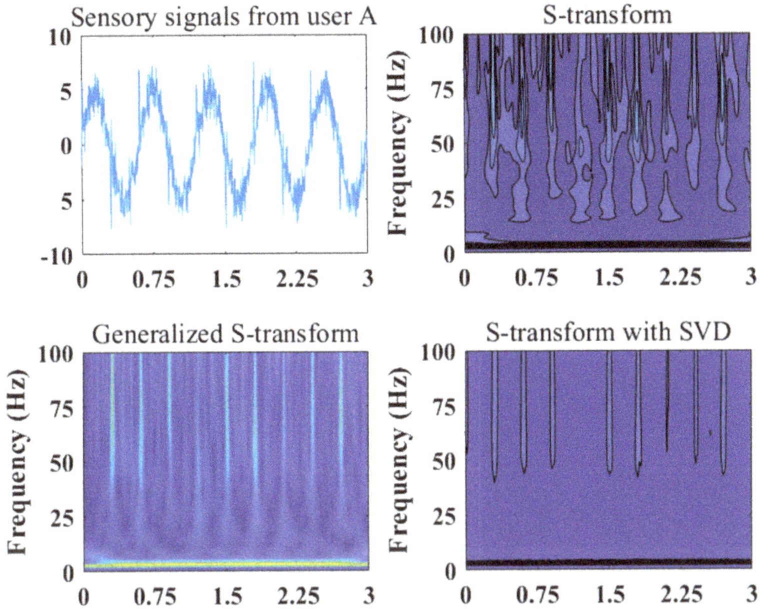

Figure 2. Comparison of different signal analysis results on User A.

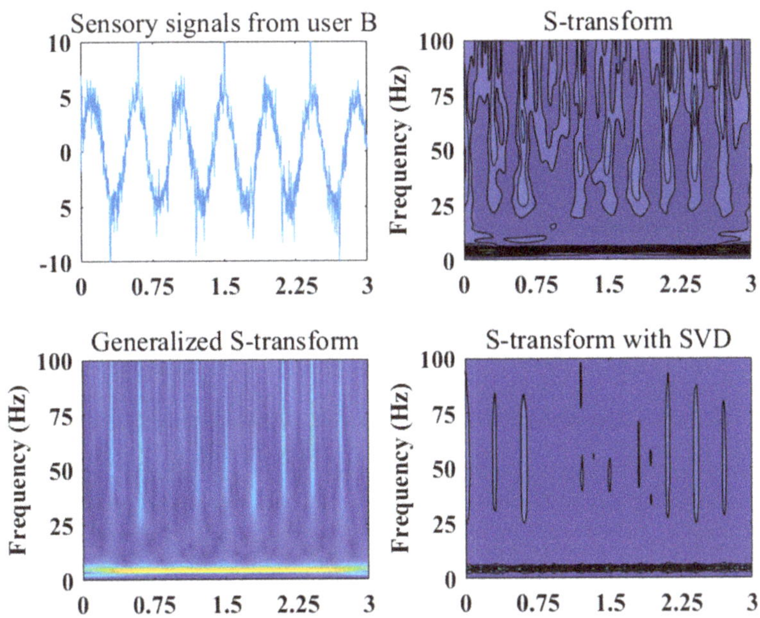

Figure 3. Comparison of different signal analysis results on User B.

4.4. Overall Accuracy on Large-Scale Dataset

Figure 4 displays the classifying performance of training, validation, and test data on dataset I with overall accuracy. It shows that all of them have a consistent and increasing convergence trend with the increase of epochs (the X-axis represents the epoch).

Notably, the accuracy of the test dataset reaches 96.32% on the 36th epoch. As mentioned, Convolutional Neural Networks (CNNs) are inspired by biological feedforward Artificial Neural Networks (ANNs) and closely resemble the mammalian visual cortex. This enables classifiers to achieve high-precision diagnoses through learning specific patterns. The average training latency for 1513 users is approximately 4825 s.

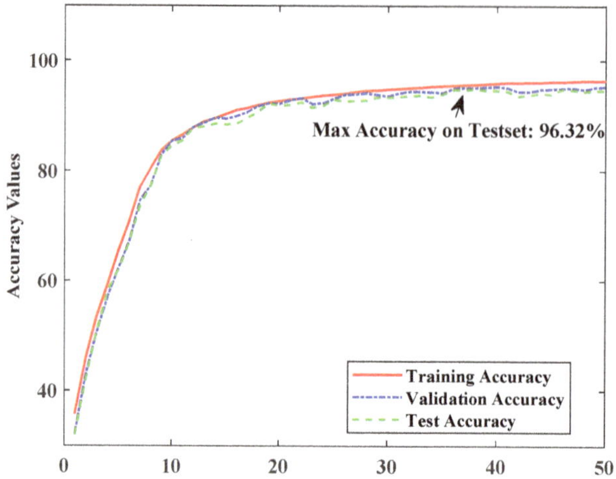

Figure 4. Comparison of different signal analysis results on dataset I.

Comparing TPR, TNR, accuracy of the method with and that without tri-training, Table 2 presents the average classification results of 10 cross-validations on 1513 users. "With TS tri-training" means the noisy labels have been removed, and vice versa.

Table 2. Average classification results with tri-training and without tri-training.

Method/Index	TPR	TNR	Accuracy	F1-Score
With TS tri-training	74.56%	98.13%	96.32%	0.9514
Without TS tri-training	72.22%	92.68%	92.89%	0.9159

As shown in Table 2, we can see that with TS tri-training, the average TPR, TNR, and accuracy increase from 72.22%, 92.68%, and 92.89% to 74.56%, 98.13%, and 96.32%, respectively, that is, eliminating noisy labels can significantly improve the final authentication. In practice, it is common that the number of positive samples (interactions from the authorized device owner) is much larger than the number of negative samples. This is because the authorized device owner primarily interacts with the device. However, a significant number of negative samples can accurately depict the usage pattern of the non-owners. This can prevent brute-force attacks from bypassing the authentication. To this end, in the training stage, the ratio of the number of samples by the owner to that by the non-owner is 1:5 to record the non-owners' behavior [7,9]. In Table 2 we find that the trained classifier can accurately represent mobile phone usage patterns of non-owners (TNR) but may miss some of the owners' usage patterns (TPR). As TN is often more critical than TP, this paper proposes to increase TN when we configure the authentication parameters. In practice, we can adjust the classification threshold for different purposes. For example, we can set a high threshold for a high security application to prevent owners' mobile devices from malicious use.

In addition, this paper employs large-scale datasets to evaluate the proposed classification method. Table 3 shows the accuracy comparison of our proposed method and other state-of-the-art methods [7,9–12,26,27]. We find our ST-SVD+CNN achieves higher accuracy. It is noteworthy that the binary-class SVM we use for training is similar to CNN+SVM (binary-class) [10]. However, our ST-SVD+CNN and CNN+SVM (binary-class) [10] outperform SVM (binary-class) [7] in feature extraction, because the latter manually extracts signs. Additionally, combining ST-SVD with CNN leads to better results compared with only using CNN, as shown in [10]. This is because transforming time-series signals into 2D time-frequency images through ST-SVD is more appropriate for CNN-based feature extraction.

Table 3. Comparison of our work and other related work.

Classifier	TPR	TNR	Accuracy	F1-Score
ST-SVD+CNN (Ours)	**74.56%**	**98.13%**	**96.32%**	**0.9514**
LSTM [9]	74.35%	97.60%	95.58%	0.9420
CNN+SVM(binary-class) [10]	74.26%	97.31%	95.01%	0.9375
SVM(binary-class) [7]	73.59%	96.42%	94.67%	0.9304
HMM [12]	71.74%	91.98%	90.54%	0.8896
Random forest [27]	72.38%	93.95%	92.36%	0.9132
DTW [26]	66.18%	89.60%	86.49%	0.8472
SVM(one-class) [11]	66.25%	89.64%	86.51%	0.8490

4.5. Performance on Noisy Labels Elimination

To validate the effectiveness of the proposed TS tri-training algorithm, we conducted experiments on dataset II with different noisy ratios. Specifically, we added noise to dataset II, which is a clean labeled dataset. The dataset contains 600,000 data samples, with a 4:1 split for training and testing. The ratio of the noisy labeled training set is set to 5%, 15%, 25%, 35%, and 45%, which means there are 24,000, 72,000, 120,000, 168,000, and 216,000 noisy labeled samples used for training, respectively.

We applied TS tri-training to reduce the number of noisy labels. Table 4 presents the performance of eliminating noisy labels. The experimental results show that the original training noisy ratio of 5%, 15%, 25%, 35%, and 45% is reduced to 0.35%, 0.68%, 1.82%, 4.53%, and 18.22%, respectively. It indicates that after TS tri-training, the remaining number of noisy labels in the training set is 1682, 3264, 7836, 21,744, and 87,456, respectively, and the accuracy reaches to above 94% at the noisy label ratio of 5%, 15%, 25%, and 35%, respectively, but not at the ratio of 45%. The reason is that the dataset at the noisy ratio of 45% is almost equivalent to a randomly labeled one, and it is unsuitable for training. Nevertheless, even under such difficult scenario, TS tri-training still shows an improvement.

Table 4. The overall accuracy before/after noisy labels elimination.

			Before TS Tri-Training		
# of Training Set	480,000	480,000	480,000	480,000	480,000
Noisy Label Ratios	5%	15%	25%	35%	45%
False Labels in Training Set	24,000	72,000	120,000	168,000	216,000
			After TS tri-training		
# of Training Set	480,000	480,000	480,000	480,000	480,000
Noisy Label Ratios	0.35%	0.68%	1.82%	4.53%	18.22%
False Labels in Training Set	1682	3264	7836	21,744	87,456
			User Authentication Result(Before TS tri-training)		
Accuracy	93.85%	84.25%	76.37%	68.30%	53.09%
			User Authentication Result (After TS tri-training)		
Accuracy	96.28%	96.12%	95.25%	94.03%	81.42%

4.6. Evaluation of Computational Cost

The experiment was conducted on a server equipped with an Intel Xeon E5 CPU, GeForce RTX 3090 Ti, and 128 G memory running Ubuntu 20.04. The average training latency for our CNN model was 30.54 s per training procedure with GPU acceleration. For TS tri-training semi-supervised learning, the average latency of each training procedure was 99.28 s. It should be noted that once the model is trained, it can be deployed to the client side for real-time verification. Therefore, clients are more concerned about their cost.

On the client side, Android is equipped with TensorFlow to perform authentication. To monitor the battery consumption, CPU usage, and memory usage, we employed the well-known Android performance testing tool, Emmagee [31]. Table 5 summarizes the obtained results.

Table 5. The overhead on three different devices.

Phone Model	Battery Consumption (mAh)	Data Collection		Authentication	
		CPU (%)	Memory (MB)	CPU (%)	Memory (MB)
Samsung S20	105.22/4000	1.20	11.05	6.38	69.38
Vivo Xplay 6	110.50/4080	1.22	11.12	6.21	65.26
M18	119.25/3400	1.25	11.09	6.46	72.64

To evaluate battery consumption, we asked a participant to use the client app for three hours, which includes the time for both data collection and offline authentication. Our application required less than 0.4% of battery in one hour. During offline authentication, CPU and memory usage on three different smartphones were slightly higher than those in data collection and ST-SVD. This is because in the real-time authentication, additional model tasks inevitably occur.

We also evaluated the latency of offline authentication when performing data collection, ST-SVD, and decision procedures 100 times on Samsung S20. The results are presented in Table 6, which shows that the entire process can be completed within 3230.60 ms. The latency introduced by steps other than data collection is negligible. Overall, the overhead on the client side fully met the requirement of real-world scenarios.

Table 6. Client Authentication Time on Samsung S20.

Procedure	Average Time (ms)
Data collection	3003.12
ST-SVD	199.58
Authentication	27.90
Overall	3230.60

4.7. Anti-Attack Capability Assessment

The security of sensor-based gait authentication has consistently been a concern of both the industry and academic communities. Previous studies [8,10] investigated its resilience to attacks, particularly mimicry attacks where an attacker observes a user's usage manner and imitates their authentic gestures and actions.

To launch a mimicry attack, we selected 20 individuals from dataset II and selected one individual as the victim in turns. First, we trained a classifier for the authorized device owner by fingerprinting their usage manner (each victim had 9240 samples for the model training). We then asked the remaining 19 individuals to imitate the victim's pattern one-by-one (100 times for each person, with each participant generating 30 samples per run). These samples were checked against the classifier, and we calculated the percentage of samples correctly labeled as other users. Our method was able to thwart imitation attacks with a probability of over 99.20%, even higher than the TNR (98.13% in Table 2) on the large dataset. This may be attributed to the fact that our ST-SVD and CNN models represented the contextual content (e.g., the owner users' inherent usage patterns) of time series data. In this way it is difficult to bypass via imitation. Similar results have been reported in [7,9].

5. Conclusions

In this paper, we proposed a real-time authentication method for mobile users in complex environments, i.e., ST-SVD. To extract subtle user features, deal with label noise, and improve the authentication accuracy in real world, we combined S-transform and singular value decomposition to transform time-series signals into 2D time-frequency images, utilized T-S tri-training to reduce label noise in the training phrase, and inputted the well-labeled samples into a CNN model to obtain a set of robust parameters for user authentication finally. Moreover, we validated the effectiveness and the high tolerance for label noise of our system through large-scale real-world data. It can meet the requirements of generality, efficiency, and usability jointly in mobile user authentication. Our future work will consider reducing the size of the dataset and improving the generalization of authentication.

Author Contributions: Conceptualization, Z.W. and S.W.; methodology, T.Z.; software, Q.W.; validation, Z.W., S.W. and T.Z.; investigation, Z.W.; resources, Z.W.; data curation, Q.W.; writing—original draft preparation, Z.W.; writing—review and editing, Z.W. and S.W.; visualization, Q.W.; supervision, S.W.; project administration, Z.W.; funding acquisition, S.W. All authors have read and agreed to the published version of the manuscript.

Funding: This research was funded by Wenzhou Key Scientific and Technological Projects (No. ZG2020031) and supported by Key Research and Development Projects in Zhejiang Province (No. 2021C01117).

Conflicts of Interest: The authors declare no conflict of interest.

References

1. Store Intelligence Data Digest Report. 2022. Available online: https://sensortower.com/resources (accessed on 6 July 2023).
2. Mobile Application Market Size, Share & Trends Report. 2030. Available online: https://www.grandviewresearch.com/industry-analysis/mobile-application-market (accessed on 6 July 2023).
3. Alhakami, H.; Alhrbi, S. Knowledge based Authentication Techniques and Challenges. *Int. J. Adv. Comput. Sci. Appl.* **2020**, *11*, 1–6. [CrossRef]
4. Dee, T.; Richardson, I.; Tyagi, A. Continuous nonintrusive mobile device soft keyboard biometric authentication. *Cryptography* **2022**, *6*, 14. [CrossRef]
5. Bošnjak, L.; Brumen, B. Examining security and usability aspects of knowledge-based authentication methods. In Proceedings of the 2019 42nd International Convention on Information and Communication Technology, Electronics and Microelectronics, Opatija, Croatia, 20–24 May 2019.
6. Ray-Dowling, A.; Hou, D.; Schuckers, S. Stationary mobile behavioral biometrics: A survey. *Comput. Secur.* **2023**, *128*, 103184. [CrossRef]
7. Zhu, T.; Qu, Z.; Xu, H.; Zhang, J.; Shao, Z.; Chen, Y.; Yang, J. RiskCog: Unobtrusive real-time user authentication on mobile devices in the wild. *IEEE Trans. Mob. Comput.* **2019**, *19*, 466–483. [CrossRef]
8. Ren, Y.; Chen, Y.; Chuah, M.C.; Yang, J. User verification leveraging gait recognition for smartphone enabled mobile healthcare systems. *IEEE Trans. Mob. Comput.* **2015**, *14*, 1961–1974. [CrossRef]
9. Zhu, T.; Weng, Z.; Song, Q.; Chen, Y.; Liu, Q.; Chen, Y.; Chen, T. Espialcog: General, efficient and robust mobile user implicit authentication in noisy environment. *IEEE Trans. Mob. Comput.* **2020**, *21*, 555–572. [CrossRef]
10. Zhu, T.; Weng, Z.; Chen, G.; Fu, L. A hybrid deep learning system for real-world mobile user authentication using motion sensors. *Sensors* **2020**, *20*, 3876. [CrossRef] [PubMed]
11. Sitová, Z.; Šeděnka, J.; Yang, Q.; Peng, G.; Zhou, G.; Gasti, P.; Balagani, K.S. HMOG: New behavioral biometric features for continuous authentication of smartphone users. *IEEE Trans. Info. Forensics Secur.* **2015**, *11*, 877–892. [CrossRef]
12. Shen, C.; Li, Y.; Chen, Y.; Guan, X.; Maxion, R.A. Performance analysis of multi-motion sensor behavior for active smartphone authentication. *IEEE Trans. Info. Forensics Secur.* **2017**, *13*, 48–62. [CrossRef]
13. Lee, W.H.; Lee, R.B. Multi-sensor authentication to improve smartphone security. In Proceedings of the International Conference on Information Systems Security and Privacy (ICISSP), Angers, France, 9–11 February 2015; pp. 1–11.
14. Stockwell, R.G.; Mansinha, L.; Lowe, R.P. Localization of the complex spectrum: The S transform. *IEEE Trans. Sig. Proc.* **1996**, *44*, 998–1001. [CrossRef]

15. Zoebisch, F.; Vielhauer, C. A test tool to support brute-force online and offline signature forgery tests on mobile devices. In Proceedings of the 2003 International Conference on Multimedia and Expo(ICME), Baltimore, MD, USA, 6–9 July 2003; p. III-225.
16. Aviv, A.J.; Gibson, K.; Mossop, E.; Blaze, M.; Smith, J.M. Smudge attacks on smartphone touch screens. In Proceedings of the 4th USENIX Conference on Offensive Technologies, Berkeley, CA, USA, 23–25 June 2010; pp. 1–7.
17. Zakaria, N.H.; Griffiths, D.; Brostoff, S.; Yan, J. Shoulder surfing defence for recall-based graphical passwords. In Proceedings of the Seventh Symposium on Usable Privacy and Security, Washington, DC, USA, 20–22 July 2011; pp. 1–12.
18. Xu, Z.; Bai, K.; Zhu, S. Taplogger: Inferring user inputs on smartphone touchscreens using on-board motion sensors. In Proceedings of the Fifth ACM Conference on Security and Privacy in Wireless and Mobile Networks, New York, NY, USA, 16–18 April 2012; pp. 113–124.
19. Bianchi, A.; Fratantonio, Y.; Machiry, A.; Kruegel, C.; Vigna, G.; Chung, S.P.H.; Lee, W. Broken fingers: On the usage of the fingerprint API in android. In Proceedings of the NDSS, San Diego, CA, USA, 18–21 February 2018; pp. 1–15.
20. Sharif, M.; Bhagavatula, S.; Bauer, L.; Reiter, M.K. Accessorize to a crime: Real and stealthy attacks on state-of-the-art face recognition. In Proceedings of the 2016 ACM Sigsac Conference on Computer and Communications Security, Vienna, Austria, 24–28 October 2016; pp. 1–12.
21. Goswami, G.; Ratha, N.; Agarwal, A.; Singh, R.; Vatsa, M. Unravelling robustness of deep learning based face recognition against adversarial attacks. In Proceedings of the AAAI Conference on Artificial Intelligence, New Orleans, LA, USA, 2–7 February 2018; pp. 1–8.
22. Kwapisz, J.R.; Weiss, G.M.; Moore, S.A. Cell phone-based biometric identification. In Proceedings of the 2010 Fourth IEEE International Conference on Biometrics: Theory, Applications and Systems, Washington, DC, USA, 27–29 September 2010; pp. 1–7.
23. Ho, C.C.; Eswaran, C.; Ng, K.W.; Leow, J.Y. An unobtrusive android person verification using accelerometer based gait. In Proceedings of the 10th International Conference on Advances in Mobile Computing & Multimedia, Bali, Indonesia, 28–30 November 2012; pp. 271–274.
24. Zhu, J.; Wu, P.; Wang, X.; Zhang, J. Sensec: Mobile security through passive sensing. In Proceedings of the 2013 International Conference on Computing, Networking and Communications, San Diego, CA, USA, 28–31 January 2013; pp. 1128–1133.
25. Lu, H.; Huang, J.; Saha, T.; Nachman, L. Unobtrusive gait verification for mobile phones. In Proceedings of the 2014 ACM International Symposium on Wearable Computers, Seattle, WA, USA, 13–17 September 2014; pp. 91–98.
26. Lee, W.H.; Liu, X.; Shen, Y.; Jin, H.; Lee, R.B. Secure pick up: Implicit authentication when you start using the smartphone. In Proceedings of the 22nd ACM on Symposium on Access Control Models and Technologies, Indianapolis, IN, USA, 21–23 June 2017; 2017; pp. 67–78.
27. Buriro, A.B.; Crispo, B.; Zhauniarovich, Y. Please hold on: Unobtrusive user authentication using smartphone's built-in sensors. In Proceedings of the 2017 IEEE International Conference on Identity, Security and Behavior Analysis, New Delhi, India, 22–24 February 2017; pp. 1–8.
28. Amirou, A.; Amirou, Y.; Ould-Abdeslam, D. S-Transform with a Compact Support Kernel and Classification Models Based Power Quality Recognition. *J. Electr. Eng. Technol.* **2022**, *17*, 2061–2070. [CrossRef]
29. Zhou, Z.H.; Li, M. Tri-training: Exploiting unlabeled data using three classifiers. *IEEE Trans. Knowl. Data Eng.* **2005**, *17*, 1529–1541. [CrossRef]
30. Wang, S.; Guo, Y.; Hua, W.; Liu, X.; Song, G.; Hou, B.; Jiao, L. Semi-supervised PolSAR image classification based on improved tri-training with a minimum spanning tree. *IEEE Trans. Geosci. Remote Sens.* **2020**, *58*, 8583–8597. [CrossRef]
31. Emmagee. 2018. Available online: https://github.com/NetEase/Emmagee (accessed on 6 July 2023).

MDPI AG
Grosspeteranlage 5
4052 Basel
Switzerland
Tel.: +41 61 683 77 34

Mathematics Editorial Office
E-mail: mathematics@mdpi.com
www.mdpi.com/journal/mathematics

www.ingramcontent.com/pod-product-compliance
Lightning Source LLC
Chambersburg PA
CBHW040749250926
51850CB00007BB/1450

* 9 7 8 3 7 2 5 8 5 9 7 9 5 *